EMANUEL RINGELBLUM AND REUVEN BEN-SHEM'S WAR WRITINGS

Emanuel Ringelblum and Reuven Ben-Shem's War Writings

PERCEPTIONS OF SPACE IN THE WARSAW GHETTO

DR. VICTORIA NIZAN

VALLENTINE MITCHELL

LONDON · CHICAGO

First published in 2025 by Vallentine Mitchell

Catalyst House,
720 Centennial Court,
Centennial Park, Elstree WD6 3SY, UK

814 N. Franklin Street,
Chicago, Illinois,
IL 60610 USA

www.vmbooks.com

Copyright © 2025 Victoria Nizan

British Library Cataloguing in Publication Data:
An entry can be found on request

ISBN 978 1 80371 071 6 (Hardback)
ISBN 978 1 80371 072 3 (Ebook)

Library of Congress Cataloging in Publication Data:
An entry can be found on request

All rights reserved. No part of this publication may be reproduced in any form or by any means, electronic, mechanical, photocopying, reading or otherwise, without the prior permission of Vallentine Mitchell & Co. Ltd.

To Gadi and Iyar
without whom this book could not have been possible.

Contents

Acknowledgements	ix
A Note on Translations and Names	x

Introduction – A Jewified Space?	1
Briefing about Sources	4
Characterization of the Diaries	5
Methodological and Theoretical Considerations	8
Chapter Overview	12

PART I: HISTORY AS A JEWISH IDENTITY – THE BIRTH OF A FRENZY

I:	**History Defines Jewishness**	**19**
	Simon Dubnow: A Concept Architect	19
	Simon Dubnow: History as a Tool and Politics as an End	19
	Emanuel Ringelblum: A Brief Account of His Life	24
	Ringelblum: A Researcher, Social Worker and Political Activist	26
	Reuven Ben-Shem: A Brief Account of His Life	31
	Ben-Shem's Activism	36
	Relationships: Emanuel Ringelblum and Reuven Ben-Shem	41

PART II: LITERATURE OF THE HOLOCAUST

II:	**Holocaust Diary Writing and Space**	**51**
	Implementation of Lebensraum in Nazi Occupied Territories	51
	Documentation: A Jewish Response	53
	Holocaust Literature	53
	Diaries of the Holocaust as Personal Narratives	55
	Interviews, Testimonies, Memoires	59
III:	**Between Historical and Personal Motivation**	**65**
	Why Write?	65
	Diaries and Testimonies as Historical Sources	79

PART III: THE PRIVATE AND PUBLIC SPHERE

IV: **Lebensraum – The Spatial and Demographic Formation of the Warsaw Ghetto** — 97

Marking Jewish Identity: The Armband Decree — 97
A Jewish Sphere: The Warsaw Ghetto — 98
The Sealed Ghetto — 103
Expelled and Displaced: Refugees — 106
After Deportations: Changes in Ghetto Topography — 109
Workshops (Shops): Ghetto Factories — 110

V: **Between the Private and Public Sphere: Documentation** — 113

Ringelblum: Writing is Political but Also Personal — 113
Politics – Ringelblum: On London Radio — 119
Reuven Ben-Shem – Writing is Personal but Also Political — 123

VI: **Between the Private and Public Sphere: Armbands** — 135

The Body as Space — 135
Briefing About Armbands in Both Diaries — 136
All Jews Are Equal — 139
Visual Shock — 143
Feelings – About Jews and Converts — 151

VII: **The Private Sphere** — 160

Aspects of Privacy: Within the House – An Uneasy Space — 160
The Production of Space: On Intimacy and Self-Restraint — 168
The Outside Goes Inside — 174

VIII: **The Public Sphere** — 179

Ghetto Public Spaces: The Visual and the Truth — 179
Point of View: Propaganda – Das Ghetto, 'Documenting' Jews — 183
The Jewish Point of View — 189
The Inside Goes Outside — 195
Collapse of Human Perception: The Shops — 200
Redefining Human Concepts — 202
Jewish Compounds: Work Area and Housing — 205

Conclusions — 213

Endnotes — 221
List of Illustrations — 292
Bibliography — 295

Acknowledgements

This book is based on a dissertation which could not have been written without the encouragement, support and help of many people to whom I am grateful. I would begin by thanking Prof. Dr. Marcela Sălăgean, my advisor at Babeş-Bolyai University, Cluj. Over the years I have met scholars who kindly agreed to discuss my research. Special thanks to Prof. Guy Miron from The Open University, who was also my teacher at the Schechter Institutes. Your inspiration and belief in my capability have been irreplaceable. I would also like to thank Dr. Bella Gutterman from Yad-Vashem, with whom it has been a real pleasure to embark on a further journey of discovering Ben-Shem's diary. I heartily thank Ann Marie Novak for our profound discussions and her support since the beginning of my research. Finally, this would not have been possible without the encouragement from the advisors at Atid LeKidum, Dr. Yehudit Od-Cohen and the directors Avishay Tal and especially, Danny Shenker, for his genuine interest.

I am truly indebted to the Ben-Shem family, Nekamia Ben-Shem Feldschuh (Kami), Reuven Ben-Shem and Ruth Halbersztadt's son. Shelly, Nekamia's wife, and Sharon Ben-Shem Da Silva, their daughter and Reuven Ben-Shem's granddaughter. I am also grateful to Reuven Ben-Shem's daughter, Yoa (Joezra) Rina Ben-Shem Feldschuh Mariuma, whose great sensitivity truly moved me. A special thank you to Sharon for her outstanding efforts organizing her grandfather's writings, letters, newspaper articles, etc., as well as bringing to my attention her grandmother's manuscript *The Days of My Three Lives.*

Last but not least, I would like to thank my dear family, my son Iyar and my dear husband Gadi who have made this journey possible.

This work is dedicated to the memory of the diarists and their families: the Ringelblums, Emanuel, Yehudit (Józia) his wife and Uri, their son, the Ben-Shems, Reuven, Pnina (Perła) his first wife, and Josima, their daughter as well as Ruth Halberstadt, Ben-Shem's second wife. All of you have had a strong presence in my life over the past years and you have become my role models.

A Note on Translations and Names

This research is based on the printed versions of Emanuel Ringelblum's diary in both Yiddish, the original language, and Hebrew. As the Yiddish books are not complete, I chose to specify/rely on the Hebrew pages in the footnotes.

Unless otherwise noted, what is quoted was translated by me relying on both the versions in Yiddish and Hebrew unless a quote appeared only in the Hebrew edition.

All of Ben-Shem's texts were originally written in Hebrew, and all translations are mine.

In some quotations, I provided the original language along with the translation and my intention was to enable authentic words to convey their full meanings to those who understand the languages. Equally, in the translations, I tried to stay as close as possible to the original wording, structure, and punctuation because in most cases, these also represented a state of mind, which I tried not to lose in translation. Any changes or clarifications were put in brackets and likewise, I used the ellipsis to indicate that parts in a text were not quoted. Quotations from the diaries that have undeciphered words or parts would be indicated with a hyphen (-).

I retained original spellings of names of cities and people in Polish except for familiar places such as Warsaw, Auschwitz, and conversely, people such as Ringelblum and Reuven Ben-Shem. For other languages, I followed the English spelling version.

I decided to use the name Ben-Shem rather than Feldschuh, because many references use his pen name in Hebrew or English. Additionally, his name poses a problem as it appears under different forms in various sources including the first as well as the last name. Ben-Shem's first name, Reuven, also has other versions: Reuven, Ruben, Rubin and so on. The same ambiguity is relevant to Ringelblum, although his name has fewer variations. Here I used 'Emanuel' and if any source spelt the name differently, I used the source's spelling. The same is true for other references in this book.

To refer to refugee shelters, or refugee centers, I adopted "points," the wording used by Dr. Lea Prais in her book *Displaced Persons at Home:*

Refugees in the Fabric of Jewish Life in Warsaw, September 1939 – July 1942. "Point/s" is a translation of *punkt/n* from Yiddish, originating in ghetto jargon to refer to public facilities like synagogues, where the displaced and refugees were housed inside the ghetto.

Introduction - A Jewified Space?

On December 17, 1940, a month after the Warsaw Ghetto was sealed, Ringelblum wrote in his daily diary:

> ... at about 3:30 in the afternoon, a taxi stopped next to a tailor's shop on 22 Smocza Street, and a Greek with Jewish companions emerged out of the car. They emptied the small shop completely and once they finished, went on their way. With rare calm, the same Greek from the Gestapo suddenly pulled out his revolver and shot into a crowd of Jews who happened to be there. All of them were merchants who worked on the other side of the street. As a result, an 11-year-old child fell dead, and a woman from Dzielna Street lay badly wounded.[1]

Ben-Shem's diary entry from around the same period, December 1940, also addressed the issue of random and capricious violence. His descriptions began by depicting a typological trend of shooting point-blank into crowds or into houses for no apparent reason. He wrote that a gendarme, considered by Jews as a 'good man', (because he tolerated smuggling), had that habit of deliberately shooting into people's houses for fun. When he was asked to explain his deeds, he said that '... he really liked the scream of the man before his death.'[2]

Unlike Ringelblum, Ben-Shem added commentary to his portrayal of the phenomenon, and this particular case was followed by a frustrated, angry, and sarcastic series of cries that go from calling the shootings '... a private sport that each German ... the son of the nation of scholars and poets, who reads a lot but who aspires to create that scream of the dying and has found here the opportunity to complete his education...'[3] to asking in astonishment, infuriated questions such as '... is it possible, can you imagine this, that a healthy man, who dominates everything, who is master of his senses, who has but one sparkle of humanity in him, would pick up his rifle and shoot for the sake of sports and kill people?!'[4]

Despite the differences between the purposes of documentation, Ringelblum's historical account and Ben-Shem's personal diary, both narratives addressed the gap between the bewildering conduct of German occupation forces and their own epistemological knowledge of the world. In other words, the issue of impetuous shooting in these texts exposed both occurrences themselves, as well as a gap in understanding what was before one's eyes, or what was expected and what was experienced in the confined space of the ghetto.

According to Hannah Arendt, 'For those engaged in the quest for meaning and understanding, what was frightening in the rise of totalitarianism was not its novelty, but that it has brought to light the ruin of our categories of thought and standards of judgment.'[5] Indeed, as far as the Jews were concerned, the Warsaw Ghetto was a no man's land. It seemed that anyone could abuse Jews as they pleased, while those attacked remained defenseless, not allowed to retaliate, nor protected by the law in any way.

Furthermore, the example of the shootings into people's houses or a crowd suggested that German occupation forces were encouraged to express impersonal violence, if not with words, with deeds – no one prevented it or judged them. This irrationality drew both sides concerned, guards and soldiers on the one hand, and their prisoners on the other, into opposing ends of conceptuality. Furthermore, not only did this unpredictable behavior on the part of guards in the ghetto violate the limits of human knowledge, but the capricious nature of their behavior made it difficult for Jews to grasp it as a pattern.[6] Thus, because violence and abuse were not rational, it appears that the war against Jews rested on a gap in what was inconceivable ontologically.

How was this gap bridged? It seems that Ringelblum, in that early stage, adopted a paradigmatic Jewish response – writing – which relied on previously acquired knowledge of Jewish history. When he chose to refer to Germans by using the word 'Greeks', or '*Yevanim*' in the original (Yiddish), he placed the event in an explicitly culturally Jewish space, thus connecting past to present. Looking back, Ringelblum's choice seems even prophetic, as by denoting the Germans, not only as the historical archetypical enemies of Judaism, 'Greeks', but also emphasizing unbridgeable cultural differences between the two nations.[7] For a Jew, the term '*Yevanim*' bears a past significance and connects to the present by suggesting the total cultural divide between Jews and Germans. At the same time, it implied the gravity of the situation in the present while insinuating about the future – that just like Jews and Judaism survived the Greeks, it was expected to happen again. Thus, by using the word '*Yevanim*' to describe Germans, Ringelblum apparently generalized the phenomenon,

Introduction - A Jewified Space?

making it closer to theorizing what had been developing in the ghetto. His manner of rendering the space Jewish, or 'Jewifying' the space, was not only in writing about it, but how he referred to the Germans, '*Yevanim*'.

When Ben-Shem described the shooting gendarme, calling him '... son of the nation of scholars and poets'[8], he too addressed the fissure between Jews and Germans, a gap expressed at the shooter's explanation for his actions. It appears that Ben-Shem's texts suggest that he was less preoccupied with the breach between Jews and Germans. Rather it was with the new German whose two opposing sides seem to have melted down into one inexplicable entity, '...scholars and poets...' but also senseless murderers. According to Ben-Shem, Germans in the ghetto seemed to have traversed the threshold between civilized and uncivilized, thus redefining the values of good and evil. Moreover, Ben-Shem insinuated that the reason Jews failed to comprehend Germans' behavior pattern, that is, shooting as a format by which '... to complete ... education...'[9] lay in radical changes to German values.

Ringelblum tried to stick to facts, but it is the language he used that gives his narrative an additional layer extending beyond the historical. The Jewish space created by the use of '*Yevanim*', renders his text into dialogue not only with historians but also with the Jewish people. In contrast, Ben-Shem wrote down his insights about the Germans plainly and clearly. His text evoked stupefaction and bewilderment at their conduct, and he could not explain the radical changes in their behavior. In this, Ben-Shem's diary represents a shift in analysis as in addition to documenting what was happening to Jews, Ben-Shem turned the Germans into an object of observation and inquiry.

While Ben-Shem seemed to be trying to understand the motives for Germans' radical change, Ringelblum's bewilderment at their conduct was expressed by creating a distinct separation by establishing a contextualized Jewish space using the word '*Yevanim*', a cultural Jewish space characterizing the enemy as well as its end. Labelling Germans as 'Greeks' represented a deviation from norms Ringelblum imposed on himself, that is, presenting an objective image. '*Yevanim*' represents an aberration that should not be overlooked for the opportunities such peculiarities may offer to understanding the text.[10]

Such examples show how important it is to conduct structural observations in the analysis of both diaries, *Emmanuel Ringelblum: Diary and Notes from the Warsaw Ghetto, September 1939 – December 1942* and *Reuven Ben-Shem's (Feldschuh), Testimonies, Diaries and Memoirs Collection*. The manner in which the writers chose to represent occurrences adds another dimension to the thematic contents. Evidently, writing reveals the 'what', but it is the 'how' that may expose attitudes through which meaning is created. As Amos Goldberg put it,'...the historical analysis of the Holocaust and the Jews should focus on texts, broadly conceived, and they should be studied as cultural expressions of the conditions of those who experienced the Holocaust.'[11] Indeed, how the writers represented sporadic shootings portrayed not only the action itself but also Ben-Shem and Ringelblum's mindsets.

Likewise, language choices create a parallel space, that of the page itself, where these occurrences are described vis-a-vis the actual space where things occurred. For Ringelblum, the ghetto was a 'Jewified' space because Jews were forced to live there. What happened in that confined space was part of Jewish history as well as the reason he documented it. Confinement, robbery and shooting at innocent people were forms of calamities that characterized the attitude toward Jews, while writing about them reclaimed the Jewish realm.

Ben-Shem's text became Jewish by contrasting Jews to Germans while highlighting irrational German behavior in the ghetto. It is the alienation of their conduct, deriving from the disintegration of rational spaces into irrational, that became a scale by which to measure what was Jewish.[12] In this context, shooting into people's houses symbolically signified that the same disintegration of limits and values was physical as well as mental. Writing about these created a space of debate, an attempt to understand, perhaps a successful venture, yet one which enabled maintaining a certain logic and reason in chaos with its own reasoning.

Briefing about Sources

The texts researched for the purposes of this book were Emanuel Ringelblum's daily diary which he started at the end of September 1939, and whose last entry seems to have been written around January 1943. In addition, short passages from *Last Writings*, which refer to the operation of the *Oneg Shabbat* archive in the ghetto are discussed, relying on both the Hebrew and Yiddish versions, because the latest printed Yiddish version does not include everything. The second document was written by Reuven Ben-Shem as a type of a diary that was probably mostly written in hiding and discussed events of the war. Sections used for the narrative analysis were deciphered by the author himself in later years, when he lived in Israel, and perhaps others. The deciphered document includes the period between November 1940 and April 4, 1943.

The Yad-Vashem archive contains the following materials:

Manuscript I: the original scanned version of the handwritten diary includes 330 photographed pages (most photos contain two pages), size similar to A4.[13] These are the three notebooks that constitute Ben-Shem's handwritten writings.

Three other scanned files which contain a handwritten version of the deciphered diary on letter notebooks, size A5, which may have been written by Mrs. Lilly Goldenberg, a family friend who also probably typed the final version of the deciphered diary.

Manuscript II: 439 photographs of handwritten pages from November 1940 until July 20, 1942.

Manuscript III: 46 photographed handwritten pages, from 20.7.1942 until sometime in August 1942.

Manuscript IV: 248 photographed handwritten pages, from November 1942 until April 4, 1943.[14]

Deciphered Diary: 700 photographed machine-typed pages, size similar to A4, and containing documentation from November 1940 until April 4, 1943.

Characterization of the Diaries

The narratives are different: Ringelblum's diary was primarily intended to be a historical diary, a sort of a field notebook, to be used for further historical research after the war.[15] Ben-Shem's document is a personal diary, and according to Ben-Shem himself, most of it was written while he and his family were hiding in the village of Pustelnik, near Warsaw.[16]

Nonetheless, both authors showed a great deal of awareness of the responsibility of the written word and a high degree of commitment to the role their writings might play for posterity. Both diaries manifest the borders of epistemology: how one knows, and how one can be sure that what one knows is authentic. It appears that the ontological body they formed, that is, the descriptions, the manner of analysis, and the relationships they attributed to occurrences, seem to have shattered previous familiar knowledge and reasoning thinking patterns, as they knew them while still documenting what was happening. Both seem to have understood, as events were happening, that the big picture and its significance may have escaped them and that they may have misinterpreted these scenes.

It seems that the essence of what was recorded was the process of losing the ability to understand. This book exposes that from life in the ghetto and how it was experienced, it was impossible to predict German intentions, not for the present, let alone the future. The speed with which events took place confused the notion of past and present. In many respects, the past became the present because the present was stretched over a longer period than usual, thus ceasing to fulfil its purpose. The present did not lead to a future – the future was death. Following the change in the subjective structure of time, both writers seem to have experienced a colossal collapse of reasoning patterns.

Initially, the very idea of recording events was completely natural for Ringelblum. After all, he had introduced this method of studying history, by recording events from the perspective of the common people, long before the war. Furthermore, his personal experience with displacement of Jews introduced by the Nazis in Zbąszyń had certainly convinced him that the war between Poland and Germany had to be documented as it was happening. Ringelblum estimated that such records would be invaluable sources of reference once the war ended and the time to research it came.[17]

Ringelblum's historical approach and methodology were strongly influenced not only by Simon Dubnow's methodology but also Communist doctrine, which argued that history was the result of material conditions, that in turn, influenced society's production. However, as time went by, the purpose of his writing changed from gathering information for future research to collecting evidence against the Nazis and disseminating the information to the outside world. This was mingled with a growing recognition that for the Germans, the economic value of Jews was insignificant.[18]

During the war, it became clear that Jewish history, whether one studied it or not, could not be a source of reference for the present. Despite the calamities the Jews experienced, Nazi annihilation, could not have been predicted by researching history.

It is more complex to define the reasons Ben-Shem kept a personal account documenting the events he underwent. Ben-Shem was preoccupied with history but unlike Ringelblum, not with its research. However, Ben-Shem made use of Jewish history as a political tactic mainly for educational purposes, for youth hoping to establish a Jewish state. In this respect, though Ben-Shem was less interested in historical academic research, he regarded Jewish history as raw material for political achievements.

In an interview with Ben-Shem's son, Nekamia, the latter stated that he had no knowledge of his father writing a diary prior to the war.[19] Indeed, it seems Ben-Shem started writing the diary some time near the beginning of the war but the notebooks we have were mostly written when he was in

Introduction - A Jewified Space?

hiding, from February 1943 until at least July 1944, when he left his hiding place for Lublin that by then had been liberated. According to Nekamia, his father had grown highly attached to his notes, managed to keep them with him and even bring them to Mandatory Palestine in 1945.

Interestingly, in many respects, studying Ben-Shem's and Ringelblum's diaries can be regarded as a manifestation of how Ringelblum envisaged what historical research was all about. According to Ringelblum, information from diaries, such as Ben-Shem's, was essential in order to understand experiences from within. Indeed, the *Oneg Shabbat*[20] team valued this type of document, as diaries allowed a peek into writers' states of mind thus representing the human experience.

Nevertheless, and despite the political chasm between the two, Ringelblum being a Communist while Ben-Shem, a high middle-class intellectual affiliated with the right, one thing stands out: Jewish history defined their personal identity, and both derived moral as well as political inspiration from it. Furthermore, despite the evident difference between the diaries, both deal directly with history, and more specifically, with the collapse of traditional concepts about history as a result of what happened in the Warsaw Ghetto. Indeed, it appears that history-wise, there is a compatibility between these diaries if only because the historical events during the Second World War were so extreme.

If Ringelblum's writings were extensively researched, Ben-Shem's notes have resurfaced only relatively recently. In fact, I first learned about the existence of these documents from a short review of the diary in an article by Amir Haskel, which led me to look it up at Yad-Vashem.[21] When I started the research, in September 2016, it was generally agreed among researchers that Ben-Shem's diary had been written while he was in the ghetto.[22] However, as the research progressed, information in the documents suggested that the issue of when the diary was written had to be examined anew.[23]

Ben-Shem's writings are unusual as they were written in Hebrew, a language not in use for daily purposes although familiar to most Jews, particularly men, who had received Jewish education. Ben-Shem wrote in exquisite Hebrew, occasionally adding words, expressions and sometimes longer passages in Yiddish, Polish, Latin and German, all languages in which he was proficient. The deciphered part consists of seven hundred typed pages, most of which are legible. Conclusive proof that at least one notebook was written in hiding exists on the first page of one of the original handwritten notebooks (there seem to have been three). On that page, he clearly stated to having begun writing in March 1943 adding a Will, giving instructions what to do with the manuscripts in case of his death and it being found by others.[24]

Ben-Shem and Ringelblum's writings and their attitude to documentation and history provide information about how they viewed their responsibility of the task that they had undertaken – to look at historical events and try to learn something from them, derive some insight, knowledge, tactics how to cope with the situation in the ghetto.

Methodological and Theoretical Considerations

In this book, I searched for evidence in the writings of Emanuel Ringelblum's daily historical diary and Reuven Ben-Shem's personal war accounts, that they had understood Nazi manipulation of space during the Second World War, as paradigmatic historical and political steps leading to annihilation. In view of the stages of shrinking ghetto space, it is important to understand whether Jews were able to intellectually and/or emotionally deduce the final point of this manipulation of space – its total extermination.

Indeed, at the heart of this discussion lies the question whether documentation was the diarists' response to declining space, an attempt to create a historical and political counter-paradigm. I will be asking what kind of space is presented and whether writing about it was actually claiming back the physical space. Equally, it is important to understand whether writing was a predicted outcome to space being squeezed and what the relationship was between physically narrowing spaces and writing about them.

Additionally, I sought to comprehend how Jews met challenges of reducing the physical space and to what extent the two writers showed conceptualization of the historical events taking place. Was documentation, by writing historical observations and diaries, their response to declining space designed to create a historical and political counter-paradigm? Was writing effectively claiming space as well as creating it through what was meant to be erased?

By examining the events related to space, I suggest a different way of studying and researching the Holocaust. This historically unprecedented event must be observed through the lens of those who experienced it. Employing their point of view, how they grasped what was happening, may expose gaps in perceptions that made these occurrences inconceivable, and therefore, unpredictable. This may explain how the lack of historical or other precedents impacted the way the concept of the Final Solution was understood as it developed during the Second World War.

Introduction - A Jewified Space?

Main Theme: Space

Issues/concepts	Destruction of the individual.	Destruction of communities - society, family, man.	Blurring boundaries: private & public dead and living personal & communal.	Converting human traits to one's work capacity.	Denial of the right to exist.	Documentation and bureaucracy as control.
Germans	Marking Jews visually.	Massive scale displacements.	Redefining the nature of dwellings, streets, "points", cemetery.	Workshops (shops) and the Umschlagplatz.	Deportations to death centers.	Extensive documentation – photographic as well as bureaucratic.
Ringelblum	Documenting difficulties encountered, particularly before the ghetto was sealed.	Documenting information acquired from refugees & displaced.	Documenting beggars, food snatching, starving children, smuggling, movement, violence, cemetery.	Circumstances downsized documentation and writing style changed mostly to thematic concise texts.	Ringelblum wrote little about deportations but what he did write, indicated great distress.	Documentation as a Jewish space - stressing the Jewish point of view while continuously documenting despite circumstances.
Ben-Shem	Hardly related to it before the ghetto was closed.	At the beginning of the war, a refugee himself. Later discussed life in "points" and refugees he knew personally.	Like Ringelblum but also related to private households and smells.	Provided a detailed account of life at Schilling's while he was hiding.	Ben-Shem reported stories he heard from individuals who escaped raids, the Umschlagplatz and Treblinka.	Ben-Shem's writings incorporated his opinions and observations. Documentation became central in hiding. In safety, he repeatedly edited his notes probably until his death in 1980.

The analysis of the diaries entailed applying qualitative methodology to texts whose initial purposes were different. The departure point for both texts assumed that despite their differences, they encompassed similar themes in communal and personal domains. The analysis comprised of reading and mapping both texts for recurrent topics, events and information. The next stage involved organizing the information meaningfully paying attention to language reflecting intentions and ethics, for example, not only in the choice of vocabulary but also in themes brought up for discussion. Through classification, reflection and interpretation, the issues were finalized in relation to the research aims and questions.[25]

To achieve insights, I adopted an interdisciplinary research approach, involving asking historical questions while using text analysis methods, namely close reading and narrative analysis. These methodologies, which originated in probing literary texts, are dominated by literary theory reflecting the approach that stories or narratives mirror human experiences in the manner they were conceived. In addition, how a story is presented in writing reflects not only what a narrator chooses to expose but what story he tells himself.[26]

Applying these approaches to diary analysis involved thematic mapping – checking for contents – what is mentioned, debated, etc., but also what is not recorded and what was avoided. Using close reading was expected to reveal contents through which it was possible to explore what each writer chose to put on paper and how it was presented. I looked at the narratives as manifestations of reflections mirroring crisis: guilt, responsibility, explanation, unpredictability, and intelligibility. This included relating to contexts and vocabulary preferences, which in thematic analysis, are not broken down and researched per se.[27]

Equally, I used structural analysis to address how a story is told. It focuses on narrative devices but also on language representations thus exploring their capacity to embody an event as well as to symbolize an agent.[28] As a critical model, the structural approach produces an additional tier that contributes to forming a more reliable picture of what is described. These methodological approaches allowed addressing the question of gaps in comprehension as well as verifying patterns and modes of drawing conclusions from events.

Henri Lefebvre's *The Production of Space* was used as a backbone, a fundamental model enabling a discussion of aspects of space in the Warsaw Ghetto as they were reflected in the diaries. According to Lefebvre, the production of space rests on three interdependent factors: First, spatial practice, which describes the physical; where and what kinds of social activity take place, such as daily chores of buying foods or activities occurring inside institutions as well as private dwellings. Second, representations of space - how space is conceived abstractly through plans, designs, drawings, and other theoretical outlines, all produced by agents of authorities such as engineers, architects, and other agencies. It is a system of signs and codes designed to organize and direct spatial relations. It is a space where agents of authority produce an abstract image of space in terms of knowledge, ideology and culture. Lastly, representational or lived spaces, where one experiences space through senses, memory, and feelings which may also involve writing and art.[29]

Lefebvre's model emphasized the tension between these three spaces as a result of pressures shaping people's lives from above, authorities over their subjects. Lefebvre wrote:

> Space is neither a mere 'frame', after the fashion of the frame of a painting, nor a form or container of a virtually neutral kind, intended simply to receive whatever is poured into it. Space is social morphology: it is to lived experience what form itself is to the living organism, and just as intimately bound up with function and structure.'[30]

Lefebvre drew an analogy between the notion of space and biological forms, in which space is what happens inside a given form. In other words, space is not a pure form, but rather an ensemble of phenomena defining that form. Therefore, if space is always social, not only does society produce things in a space but society's production defines space.

To sum up, my chosen methodology enabled elaboration as to whether concepts of space diminution, history, and politics were initially conceived as linked to one another, and whether this link was understood as fatal. Both diaries expose the micro-history of the Warsaw Ghetto, on a local level but also as part of the Nazi system of ghettos. The analysis of these diaries as representations of the Warsaw Ghetto may be regarded as an additional methodology, which lends great value to the 'interplay between texts (narratives) and life (reality).'[31] Their insights as well as how they described various differences are particularly revealing not only of personal aspects but also in what they chose to describe and what they ignored.[32] The concept of space, in this book, attempts to explore the relationship between the physical space of the Warsaw Ghetto, an area that was formed by tearing apart an already given space, Warsaw; representations of space exercised by German occupants and lived space, how it was conceived within the confined space of the ghetto through the war writings of Emanuel Ringelblum and Reuven Ben-Shem.

In this book, I also allude to the Marxist approach to historiography mainly concerning Emanuel Ringelblum. His socialist views were at the core of the historical methodology which combined on the one hand, Dubnow's methodology with a deeply rooted social consciousness. This he introduced into YIVO (Yidisher Visnshaftlekher Institut, Yiddish Scientific Institute), where he founded the Historical Commission. His work set the tone there and thanks to him the institution became greatly popular among eastern European Jews, who willingly cooperated by providing testimonies, looking up documents and writing their own reports.[33]

By the time war broke out, many Jewish people had been 'trained' to write, which made it easier for Ringelblum to start the *Oneg Shabbat* archive and encourage people to write not only one-time reports but also keep diaries. Hence, a lot of valuable information was gathered, shedding light on intimate experiences of the masses as private individuals, the anonymous, whose voice, according to Ringelblum, had never been heard until then, as well as of a whole society.[34]

Notably, Ringelblum's historical research methodology followed standards characterizing both the schools of microhistory and annals.[35] According to Prof. Samuel Kassow, although Ringelblum used methodology similar to that of the school of annals, neither he nor they were aware of the existence of the other.

Reuven Ben-Shem, an anticommunist, was nevertheless captivated by Jewish history, and it was an imperative source of inspiration in his writings and speeches. Ben-Shem's personal writings distinctly demonstrated the significance of history as a factor affecting one's private life as well as that of others. In this respect, he established a triple link between history, its effect on society and as an abstract notion representing individuals. His unique powers of observation were expressed in detailed descriptions of individuals as well as phenomena. These complement Ringelblum's writings by providing an emotional aspect – Ben-Shem's writings were specific, sharp in their psychological observations and largely uncensored.

Chapter Overview

The book is divided into three parts: the first part addresses the link between politics and history in modern Jewish thought. Chapter one explains the centrality of the concept of history in the Jewish world since the late 19th century, focusing on three important figures, Simon Dubnow

Introduction - A Jewified Space?

whose pivotal role in establishing and disseminating the idea that researching Jewish history was linked to political activism and whose influence on Jewish masses, particularly in east Europe, was cardinal and reached way beyond academic circles.

Reuven Ben-Shem and Emanuel Ringelblum, whose attitudes to history were influenced by Dubnow, exercised this in different ways. Initially political rivals, each of them formulated their own unique historical awareness crystallizing a 'usable past' to help them cope with the challenges of the present.[36] Whereas Ringelblum '... followed in the footsteps of Dubnow, although in tragically different circumstances'[37], Ben-Shem avidly used historical information to prepare the young to establish a Jewish state in Erez Israel (the land of Israel).

The second part consists of chapters two and three. Chapter two addresses Holocaust literature. Dubnow's approach to history democratized methodology in the sense that it gave importance to the voice of individuals by literally encouraging their involvement in writing Jewish history. This developed into a tradition with far-reaching consequences when the Second World War broke out, as many Jews turned to documenting events in different forms. This chapter begins by introducing the concept of Lebensraum (living space) as it was introduced in Nazi occupied territories and the relationship established between geographical boundaries and the phenomenon of bearing witness. Accordingly, different genres of Holocaust literature are introduced, focusing mainly on records produced during the Second World War: primarily diaries, but also testimonies, and *Yizkor Books*.

Chapter three deals with motives to immerse oneself in documentation, particularly during the war, the relationship between testimonies and personal accounts and historical research. This is followed by a discussion of academia's attitudes to witness accounts, initially rejecting them as viable historical resources because of doubts about their reliability.[38] Eventually, testimonials moved from being excluded to becoming an important reference source for historical records.

The third part, 'The Private and Public Spheres' discusses findings from the diaries and interprets their significance in terms of space. Chapter four presents the spatial and demographic formation of the Warsaw Ghetto or what Lebensraum consisted of in Warsaw, namely, how space manipulation introduced by the Nazis affected Jews' living experiences. This is followed by chapters five and six where two main categories are examined under the classification of Between Private and Public Spheres, which discusses the action of writing or what writers say about their own writings and the effect of the armband decree.

Addressing the action of writing, I inspected the political-historical purposes of writing and documenting events, Ringelblum's approach to his own writing, the establishment of the *Oneg Shabbat* archive and his clandestine activities leading to the London BBC radio broadcast, clearly acknowledging the fact that Jews were being deliberately and systematically annihilated. Ben-Shem also alluded to his own writings and their purpose in his diary. Obviously, his observations were more personal but he also related to his aspiration that his diary would be published after the war. It seems that while writing, Ben-Shem envisaged future readers and his words were, at least partly, addressed to them right from the start when he wrote on the first page of one of his notebooks that he wished to have his diary published.[39]

Next, I continue with a discussion about marking Jewish bodies with an identifying symbol, an act which breached their anonymity exposing them and their dwellings publicly. The decree was particularly abusive in Warsaw where a third of its population was Jewish. When it was first introduced, it affected relationships in the city, instantly causing the collapse of norms observed until then, leading to repeated violence on the part of Germans but most notably, by Poles. The impact was so radical that rather than the city being defined as a space, it was the body of Jews that became one.

Chapter seven describes the period when the ghetto was sealed. This chapter, depicting the private sphere addresses what was supposed to stay hidden from the public eye. That is, the reality of life inside dwellings remained primarily private because both writers were reluctant to expose it in their writings. Conversely, the vast majority of ghetto inmates suffered from a lack of privacy and intimacy inside their places of residence. Whereas Ringelblum focused on the public sphere and scarcely offered glimpses into the privacy of people, Ben-Shem's accounts, edited in safety for publication, provided more individual portraits of people he was probably certain were dead. Both writers revealed how life in the ghetto steadily and violently eroded notions of public and private as living conditions in the ghetto made space a chaotic and abstracted realm. What characterized life was that space was an a-utopia or dystopia, a space out of synchronization and opposed to harmonization. The ghetto became a space that was the opposite of lebensraum, a death zone, an area whose physical conditions produced death while its human element thrived through not only physical struggles but also by writing.

Chapter eight discusses the public sphere of the ghetto through the lens of photography. Both Ringelblum and Ben-Shem adopted this notion because they considered it to be the most accurate and objective medium to represent the course of life in the ghetto. Although neither of them had a camera, both strove to provide verbal descriptions to replace images with words. From their point of view, images spoke louder than any other form of representation, which is why many of their descriptions focused on the visual. Thus, the German passion for photography was met with a Jewish response of abiding to descriptions that relied on the visual as representation of the objective and impartial. In this respect, both parties regarded the image as the most loyal and trustworthy means of representing reality.

Nonetheless, the complexity of representation, particularly the visual becomes evident through an analysis of imagery of the public sphere. Indeed, not all German attempts were meant to present Jews as degenerate, but what the Ministry of Propaganda sought to record had a preconceived intention of embodying what they considered deplorable about Jews.

Jewish verbal imagery strove to imitate the visual by refraining from introducing interpretations or emotions and achieved its goal by exposing the effects of denying human beings their means of existence. Meanwhile they also exposed how difficult it was to remain impartial in view of ongoing deterioration. In this sense, Jewish verbal imagery became the missing captions for Nazi imagery.

The last part of this chapter introduces the collapse of human perception introduced in the shops. As soon as liquidation began, shops versus the Umschlagplatz were introduced as two opposing sites: life and death. Shops, which represented life in this newly distorted universe, redefined notions of privacy and public on the one hand, and on the other, life and death. To all appearances, life in shops was deadly yet relatively exhilarating in comparison to the Umschlagplatz. What mattered in shops was being there, as this was conceived as guaranteeing life, not food, which became a secondary worry. Obviously, privacy was a luxury that no one mentioned as in these conditions, it was the communal that offered some comfort despite the difficulties it posed.

Part I

History as a Jewish Identity
The Birth of a Frenzy

I

History Defines Jewishness

Simon Dubnow – A Concept Architect

Modern Jewish historical research started at the end of the 18th century with the *Haskalah* (Hebrew term for Enlightenment), which spread first among the Jews of Germany.[1] Indeed, when Isaak Marcus Jost's first volume of Jewish history was published in 1820, he admitted it had political purposes, to present the Jewish entity as loyal to the state and thus promote the notion that Jews could be integrated successfully into non-Jewish society.[2]

Another important Jewish German historian was Heinrich Graetz (1817-1891) who suggested that Jost had managed to 'reclaim' Jewish history from the hands of prejudiced Christian historians and therein lay the greatest significance of Jost's pioneering work.[3] Mayer claimed that Graetz sought to 'regain a sense of Jewish separateness by revealing the distinct historical path of the Jews.'[4] In many respects, Graetz paved the way for Dubnow who, like him, was concerned with the deep changes Jewish society was undergoing on account of modernity.

One of the most prominent scholars to emerge from the *Haskalah* movement was Simon Dubnow (1860-1941), whose historical research became a beacon to most Jews, especially those from eastern Europe. His research, mostly conducted independently, started a 'dynasty' of prominent Jewish historians who became engaged in gathering documentation and researching Jewish history. Among them were Mayer Balaban, Ignacy (Yitzhak) Schiper, as well as Emanuel Ringelblum, to name but a few.[5] Thanks to Dubnow, prior to the Second World War, almost all Jewish sectors, especially in east Europe, attributed tremendous importance to history. It became a notion uniting the Jewish masses, regardless of their political or sectorial inclinations.

Simon Dubnow – History as a Tool and Politics as an End

Dubnow's historical research intended to find the common grounds of Jewish identity, restore past solidarity and strengthen Jewish community spirit so that it could cope more successfully with modernity. Meyers proposed that by writing about the history of the Jews, Dubnow attempted to recreate the Jewish people. He stressed that this purpose later developed into a national identity in the modern sense; in other words, distanced from religion, a motive that had become central at the end of the 19th century in east Europe.[6]

According to Deutsch, in Russia of the late 19th century, all Jewish political organizations agreed that there was a particular Jewish history and culture, and they all urged Jews to recognize that culture, and develop it, regardless of their political inclination. Deutsch claimed that the notion of a unique Jewish culture as well as history was the only thing all Jewish parties agreed on and identified with.[7]

Reuven Michael suggested that Dubnow, who was anti-clerical, embarked on the road of Jewish history by taking the universal road first, but according to Mahler, Dubnow had actually turned to researching Jewish history because, being Jewish, he was denied access to any government archives, which had prevented him from pursuing his initial interest in general topics. As a result, his first endeavor as a historian was studying the Hasidic movement, a long-standing fascination of his.[8]

In 1887, Dubnow claimed that his passion for universal knowledge came from a national path and not vice versa. Later, Dubnow added in the *Book of Life* (his autobiography) that his aspirations about general literature and universal issues had ended, as in nationalism he had discovered universalism. Indeed, the first fruits of this approach elicited in 1888 a series of articles under the title *The History of Hasidism* that Dubnow, who was then working at the Jewish periodical *Voskhod* (Dawn), started publishing.

In 1890 Dubnow settled in Odessa, where he quickly became part of a Jewish circle of intellectuals such as Asher Ginsberg (*Ahad Ha-Am*) and Hayim Nahman Bialik.[9] At this time, Dubnow formulated his secular theory that attributed the Jewish people's survival to their will to adapt to different circumstances.

It seems the turning point was in 1891, when he published his call to preserve and collect documentation relating to Jewish life. In the Russian Jewish newspaper *Voskhod* (Dawn), he published a 90-page long article entitled *Researching the Whereabouts of the Jews of Russia* where he called for the establishment of a Russian Jewish society. Shortly afterwards, he published in *Pardes*[10], a new journal issued in Odessa in 1892, the Hebrew version of the same article under the name '*Nehapsa Ve-Nakhkera*', (We shall Seek and Research).[11] The call addressed everyone and urged Jews to collect and preserve documentation.

The pamphlet specified what types of documents should be preserved, how they should be collected and what should be copied, etc. In addition, Dubnow emphasized oral sources and proposed the establishment of a Jewish historical society to eventually handle this huge task (a society was indeed established in 1908). The call prompted an important interest in Jewish history and produced an abundance of materials.[12]

'Nehapsa Ve-Nakhkera' included an introduction discussing Jewish history that tried to determine what historical forces made the Jewish people a nation. David Engel posited that the origin of Dubnow's idea that the Jews were a transnational entity had to do with how Jews perceived themselves, that is, as long as Jews universally thought of themselves as one meta-land entity, it was justification enough to regard them as a community.[13]

The first practical germ of Dubnow's historical approach was implemented following the pogrom at Kishinev (1903). A group of Jewish intellectuals in Odessa, which also included Dubnow, Ahad Ha-am and Bialik, not only launched a call for self-defense, but they also appointed Bialik to travel to Kishinev and collect testimonies from the Jews in the area.[14] Bialik was shocked by what he heard from surviving Jews and rather than edit his notes, he reacted by writing a long narrative poem 'b'Ir haHarega' ('In the City of Slaughter') instead. The poem became instantly famous, a symbol of shame as well as '... a new Jewish generation's desire to create its own national history and thereby jettison the degradation of ghetto life.'[15]

The introduction to the planned Russian edition of Graetz's book, *The History of the Jews*, due in 1892, was written by Dubnow under the title *What is Jewish History?*, where he presented the complexity of Jewish history. Just like his predecessors, Dubnow believed that the history of the Jewish people was unique if only for its antiquity.[16] This claim was repeated in his book addressing the philosophy of history: 'To sum up its peculiarity briefly, it embraces a period of thirty-five hundred years, and in all this vast extent it suffers no interruption. At every point it is alive, full of sterling content.'[17]

Contrary to Jost, Dubnow identified distinct features in Jewish history even in the period preceding the destruction of the first temple (586 BC). This period was characterized by unique revelations of spirituality that would only become prominent in the period of the second temple, about 70 years later, a period he referred to as '...the secondary or spiritual-political period.'[18] Hence, spiritual activity became dominant for Jews and eventually turned into a central feature in the nation's life. This is where

Dubnow differed from Graetz as the latter related to the same phenomenon as the embodiment of a religious ideal. In other words, Dubnow believed that the religious ideal became historical consciousness.[19]

Dubnow maintained that Jewish national feeling was rooted subconsciously inside the Jewish soul. Jews experience a national Jewish emotion naturally and the national ideal exists as a conscious factor, while both are united by the historical element.[20] In this respect, history is a reflection enlightening the fate of the Jewish people. The biblical era had already become a source of inspiration for millions of people from various convictions. The second part of the exile would become inspirational once humanity recognized it as the foundation for philosophical and moral revelation. Dubnow emphasized that the revelation of the second part would be discovered by non-believing rational people, who would find in that history the incarnation of moral sublime truth. According to Dubnow, it is then that the raison d'être of Jewish history is to vouch for the unification between Jews and other nations.[21]

Goldin stated that Dubnow was convinced that the situation of Jews was the result of historical developments and therefore, it was impossible for them to assimilate, at least the majority would not. Consequently, Dubnow maintained that Jews had to start a campaign to promote the idea of being given equal civil rights where they resided. His claim was that Jews had become citizens of Europe throughout history because they had been part of it since the establishment of its civilization.[22] Insight about historical developments particular to Jews, encouraged Dubnow to establish the political party *Yidishe Folkspartei* (Jewish People's Party), whose ideology was made public in 1905 but did not appeal to many potential voters.[23]

One of the *Folkspartei* ideas was a demand to establish national communities under the umbrella of one Jewish institution to represent all Russian Jews.[24] In other words, it would grant the Jewish entity autonomy, an idea suggesting that the 'Gola', residing outside the Jewish homeland, was a phenomenon to be continued and only a small number of Jews was expected to immigrate to Palestine.

This notion itself had been presented by Dubnow in his *Letters on Old and New Judaism* published in 1907.[25] The idea became widespread and was adopted by several Jewish parties established before 1906, so that when Dubnow finally announced the establishment of his party, its platform was not innovative and therefore, did not attract many supporters. However, thanks to Dubnow, the idea of a Jewish nationality developing within an existing state was well-rooted among important Jewish leaders such as Ben-

Gurion, born in 1886. Indeed, at the beginning of Ben Gurion's political career, resettlement of Jews in Palestine was conceived as the development of another Jewish community under a foreign regime, in this case, the Ottomans.[26] Only as of the 1930s did Ben-Gurion become known for his views of *Negation of the Diaspora*.

Brenner claimed that Dubnow's historical methodology was purely positivist because Judaism was the highest form of a national movement, precisely because it functioned as a nation even without having its own territory. For Jews, history became the very idea around which the notion of nationality revolved.[27] On the other hand, Dubnow stressed that centralizing Jewish life around community was similar to how a state operated, whereby it was perceived like a state. Dubnow accepted the concept of Jews being a people just like any other European minority residing in Europe. Therefore, Jews, like other communities, were entitled to a certain autonomy within states where they lived.

In 1922, he was granted permission to leave Russia and he settled in Berlin where a large circle of former eastern European Jews already resided.[28]. The translation of his *World History of the Jewish People* into German in the 1920s and 1930s, a series of ten volumes first published in 1896, won him greater fame, and he became renowned as the historian of the Jewish people.

After the founding of YIVO, a Jewish research institute, in Vilnius in 1925, Dubnow became Chairman of its Historical Section. In August 1933, Dubnow left Germany for Riga, Latvia, where he continued to write and when it became clear that war was about to break out, he was offered the opportunity to leave but declined. In July 1941, Nazi troops occupied Riga and Dubnow, with other Jews, was expelled to the Riga Ghetto. Testimonies of the few remaining survivors from the Riga Ghetto, stated that Dubnow repeated to ghetto inhabitants: 'Yidn, shraybt un farshraybt', 'Jews, write and record'.

Apparently, Dubnow was murdered on December 8, 1941, when Jews in the Riga Ghetto were rounded up and led to the Bikernieki (Biķernieki) forest to be massacred. It appears Dubnow was murdered in the city by a former student of his from the University of Heidelberg.[29] Only six days after the liquidation of the Riga Ghetto had begun, were the remaining Jews allowed to bury the dead lying in the streets in a mass grave in the old Jewish cemetery. Among them was Dubnow.[30] Until Dubnow's tragic death, he held on to the idea that Jews were not foreigners. Unfortunately, he lived to witness the collapse of his ideal.[31]

Emanuel Ringelblum – A Brief Account of His Life

Emanuel Ringelblum was born on November 21, 1900 in Buczacz. He was a historian, pedagogue, and social activist. At the time, Buczacz, was a part of the Austro-Hungarian Empire with 60% Jewish residents. As soon as the First World War started, Ringelblum and his family fled the area, ending up in Nowy Sącz, Poland. There he joined the *Poalei Zion* movement, and when the party split in 1920, he joined its left wing.

In the same year, he moved to Warsaw and applied to the faculty of medicine, but his application was rejected by the *Numerus Clausus* enforced at the university. Eventually he was accepted to the faculty of history at Warsaw University.[32] In 1923, Ringelblum, and the historian Raphael Mahler, also a member of *Left Poalei Zion* (LPZ), established '*Historiker Krayz*' (*the Young Historians Circle*) which, at the time, was the first and only forum dedicated to the study of Jews in Poland.[33] Hence, it can be argued that it is hard to separate Ringelblum's political activities from his career as a historian.[34]

Ringelblum continued to develop his competence as a historian when in 1926, he addressed Max Weinreich and Eliyahu Tcherikover to offer his services upon the establishment of YIVO, the first Jewish institution for the research of Judaism.[35] This was a turning point in Ringelblum's development as a historian and scholar, as he set up YIVO's Historical Commission and became its head.

In 1927, he was awarded a 'Doctor of Philosophy' for his dissertation, *Jews of Warsaw from its Earliest History until 1527*, and a year later he was awarded a teaching diploma. For several years, he taught history at the *Yehudiya* Jewish Secondary School for girls. At the same time, his influence in the leadership of *LPZ* grew and with Raphael Mahler, he helped in the initiative of providing *Ovnt Kursn* (night courses) for workers. In addition to publishing numerous articles and pamphlets, Ringelblum published his doctoral thesis in 1932 and in 1937, a monograph about the part Jews played in the Kościuszko Uprising.

In 1930, he began working at the Jewish Joint Distribution Committee (JDC) and his organizational skills helped make him an important figure there too. In October 1938, Yitsak Giterman, the JDC director, asked Ringelblum to go to Zbąszyń, to assist Jewish refugees expelled from Germany but whose entry into Poland had been denied. These refugees were held on the border, in ghastly conditions, in a former military camp in the town of Zbąszyń. Ringelblum's contribution to alleviating the refugees' distress was significant, and he also applied his talents as a

History Defines Jewishness 25

historian, employing YIVO methodology of research to document events and difficulties encountered by these deportees.[36]

When the Second World War broke out, Ringelblum almost immediately started documenting occurrences in the city as well as keeping up with his social welfare work. In the spring of 1940, Ringelblum recruited the first members of what became known as the *Oneg Shabbat* archive whose purpose was to gather every shred of information, and later research the data collected. *Oneg Shabbat* became a one-of-a-kind archive, whose ingenuity is attributed to the outstanding personality of Emanuel Ringelblum. The scope of this archive has enabled the world to become familiar with and aware of the complexity of existence in the ghetto and during the war in general.[37]

Once deportations began, and being a social worker as well as an official employee at Bernhard Hallman's shop,[38] Ringelblum continued his documentation project but with significant difficulties. He wrote brief notes about life during that period mentioning none of his enormous personal struggles. Finally, Ringelblum smuggled his family out of the ghetto in the early months of 1943, but occasionally he would return to the ghetto. In one such visit he was captured and deported to the Trawniki camp. For a while no one knew where he had disappeared, but when it was confirmed he was in Trawniki camp, plans to rescue him led to his being smuggled out in August 1943. Ringelblum joined his wife and son who were hiding with about thirty other Jews in an orangery in Warsaw that belonged to Mieczysław Wolski.

During his stay in hiding, Ringelblum continued to write history but this time, it was not about what was happening in his shelter, but a series of monographs about important people and phenomena in the ghetto that no longer existed. One of the most famous accounts written then was the essay 'Polish-Jewish Relations During the Second World War'. This composition addressed the complex relationships that had formed between Jews and Poles during the war and, unlike other parts of Ringelblum documentation written in Yiddish, this essay was written in Polish indicating its target audience.[39]

On March 7,1944, Ringelblum's hideout, on 81 Grójecka Street, was discovered. All those hiding were taken to prison including Ringelblum, Uri, his son (aged 12), Judith (Józia) his wife, as well as Mieczysław Wolski, the Polish rescuer. All were executed at the beginning of March (probably on the 10th) 1944.[40]

Ringelblum: A Researcher, Social Worker and Political Activist

Already in 1923, while still a student and together with Raphael Mahler, Ringelblum founded the *Yunger Historiker Krayz* whose purpose was to deal with contemporary Jewish-historical themes that concerned understanding modern economic and cultural peculiarities of Jewish society in Poland. This group, set up at Warsaw University was unique and the only one in Poland. Additionally, it was long-lasting, as meetings were held monthly from 1923 until the beginning of the war in 1939. The circle became the basis on which the YIVO Historical Commission relied once founded.[41]

They published two academic journals: *Yunger Historiker* (in 1926 and 1929) which became later *Bleter far geshikhte* (1934, 1938).[42] The journals were entirely in Yiddish, a novelty at the time. This indicated the socio-political attitudes of writers who were not concerned with academia, but with educating Jewish masses about their own history. Yiddish, was intended to make contents accessible to all Jews including those from lower classes for whom Yiddish was the main language in use. Ringelblum attributed importance to the group because he regarded it as a political weapon. Whereas the main purpose was to study Jewish history, the products of such research were to serve the political agenda of Polish Jewry, nationally and socially.[43]

Ringelblum became part of YIVO almost from the start. He and scholars from the *Yunger Historiker Krayz* became invaluable to the institution because the founders were self-taught scholars, such as Tcherikover and Dubnow, whereas Ringelblum and colleagues had tertiary university degrees.[44] In fact, Ringelblum's circle formed the solid academic foundation that was fundamental for the future development of YIVO as an academic institution.

The establishment was founded in Vilnius in 1925 and institutionalized Dubnow's approach to history, based on the concept that Jews must assemble and research their own natural historical resources. YIVO's presence in the Jewish eastern European arena reflected a deep concern for the future of the Jewish people who had experienced tremendous change as a result of modernity.[45] Its purpose was to create a scientific center for the study of Yiddish, Jewish history and the culture of eastern European Jewish communities. Officially, the institute was apolitical; nevertheless, the idea to create such an institute reflected a political concept consolidated previously, namely that Judaism was not only a religion but also a national entity.[46]

In fact, although YIVO operated as a research institute, it had an entrenched political agenda expressed in its initiation of pioneering activities in the Jewish spiritual world, which focused primarily on areas of Jewish history, linguistics, psychology, economics, folklore and sociology.[47] One method of work at YIVO exposing its political agenda was the collection and documentation of history. According to Ringelblum, this was an appropriate political Jewish response to leaving Jews outside history.[48] In his view, if Jews wanted to become part of more important forces in the world, or at least be an entity whose needs were taken into consideration, not only did Jews have to learn about themselves, but it was their obligation to do so because the singularity and uniqueness of Jews was not visible to non-Jews.

YIVO reached out to the Jewish population through bulletins, questionnaires, gathering accounts, youth compositions, and other publications, which created enthusiastic support. While most information gathering was done free of charge, many people, from all sectors, donated money to the institution. YIVO wanted to instill love for the Jewish people by the Jewish people, and the support it received spoke for itself.[49]

In his capacity as head of the Historical Commission at YIVO, Ringelblum formulated the guidelines for the creation of collections of firsthand reports. In this way, Ringelblum created a web of connections from all over eastern Europe whose mission was not only to explore documentation, but to convince people, from ordinary Jews to community leaders, to write their own accounts.[50] Still, at times, Ringelblum was frustrated with the problems he encountered, starting with the total carelessness with which community records and private documents were kept. Despite these setbacks, he was determined to reconstruct the historical picture even by putting together information that was mostly based on testimonies provided by anonymous people, voices that, according to Ringelblum, were silenced until then.[51]

In this he followed similar attempts conducted in the Jewish arena with examples such as documentation that had taken place in Vilnius, known to Jews as *Yerusholayim de Lita* (Jerusalem of Lithuania). During the First World War, a book, *Vilnius Zamlbukh*, (The Vilnius Collection) the first volume of which appeared in 1916, documented life under German occupation,[52] while Khaykl Lunski's (1881–1943) book focused on Jews' day-to-day life in Vilnius during the First World War.[53] This volume became invaluable as it included information, photographs, narratives, and documents collected before the war, knowledge that would have been lost otherwise. The contents of this volume enabled a reconstruction of the past and in contrast, an opportunity to evaluate the magnitude of the loss during the Second World War.

To accomplish his aim of documenting contemporary events, Ringelblum encouraged and persuaded people to become engaged in unfolding their stories, and preserving Jewish history, while he collected documents and accounts from all over Poland, seeing to it that the history of institutions was also documented. Furthermore, Ringelblum was concerned with community leaders' negligent approach to art and architecture. This led him to join forces with different organizations in an initiative to teach the community about preservation, while parallelly Historical Commissions set out on expeditions designed to collect photographs of old synagogues and cemeteries.[54]

Ringelblum considered these important to Jewish life in the countryside whose populations were not interested in Jewish history or archeology.[55] In fact, Jewish sites were never studied, not only in Poland but also in other places. Ringelblum was of the opinion that *Yidisher gezelshaft far landkentenish* (the Jewish Society for Knowledge of the Land) ought to integrate enjoyment (tourism) in the process of gathering information about Jewish sites.[56]

Ringelblum invested enormous energy in encouraging YIVO researchers to take an active part in the proceedings of the Seventh International Congress of Historical Science, which convened in Warsaw in 1933. Their participation resulted in a great accomplishment – recognizing the existence of a Jewish entity.[57] By establishing contacts with historians at large, YIVO registered a triumph, as its scholars were not affiliated to any particular academic institution. Thus, although Ringelblum increased YIVO's influence, unfortunately, this accomplishment did not continue, since with the change in atmosphere, Polish Jewish scholars were not allowed to participate in the Polish representative delegation to the Eighth International Congress.[58]

Ringelblum's work at YIVO was not separated from his political activism. He joined LPZ,[59] a Marxist–Zionist Jewish workers organization. He became a member when he was still an adolescent living in Nowy Sącz but in 1920, when the party split, he made a conscious choice to join its left wing which identified with Communist Moscow.

In the mid-1920s, the LPZ took steps to separate its educational system and established their own unique schools which they named after Borochov. The curriculum was taught in Yiddish and emphasized cognitive skills along with providing students with a sense of security regarding their Jewishness.[60] At the same time, they provided a socialist education and nurtured the notion of establishing a revolutionary society in Palestine.[61]

When Ringelblum was appointed to the Central Committee of *Yungt*, he undertook publishing in LPZ's youth movement two newspapers, in Yiddish

History Defines Jewishness

and in Polish. This was a position that placed him at some risk owing to constant persecution by Polish police.[62] He used his mother's maiden name Munie Heler to publish articles which dealt with Jewish history from a Marxist perspective. These stressed that the study of history was subjective because it was the ruling classes' perspective that dominated research while neglecting to relate to the views of large parts of society not in power. In this way, analysis of old-school history ignored and failed to appreciate the contribution of the masses to society, let alone take their views into consideration. [63]

In 1927, Ringelblum became a member of the managing committee in *Ovnt Kursn,* which sought to provide education to both uneducated adults and youngsters. In an effort to eradicate illiteracy, Ringelblum, together with Raphael Mahler, Bela Mandelsberg and Adolf Berman, formulated a study curriculum for evening classes for working people to attend after work.[64] The curriculum included subjects such as natural science, literature, and history where the committee members' approach to history was manifested, that is, integrating Jewish and general history as an interconnected subject. Lessons dealt with how housing influenced the lives of residents, climate's effects on human societies, diet, and so forth. Ringelblum was deeply touched by the devotion of his students, who attended lessons diligently, often expressing their gratitude for this project despite their busy work schedule and consequent fatigue.

After leaving the World Jewish Zionist Organization in the 1920s, owing to their belief it was 'bourgeois', LPZ sought to rejoin it in 1937. The reasons were that they were worried about the problematic situation of German Jews, the Arab revolt in Palestine and concern that the British would not support the Jews. The challenges awaiting the Jewish people called for a different strategy, that is according to the LPZ, the war against Zionist bourgeoisie could wait until later.[65]

Simultaneously with his other vocations, Ringelblum started working with the American Jewish Joint Distribution Committee (JDC) in the late 1920s. He edited the *Folkshilf* – the journal of the CEKABE (Centrala Kas Bezprocentowych), a network of JDC – sponsored credit societies in Poland, an umbrella organization for credit societies helped by the JDC in Poland. In his capacity as the editor of the *Folkshilf,* Ringelblum published important articles, submitted by people of no special training, about how Jewish communities, from all over Poland, maneuvered in order to deal with economic hardship. Encounters with such lucid insights contributed unique and invaluable information for Ringelblum; first, because they enriched scholarly knowledge and second, because they exposed the complexities of Jewish life in Poland. The years as the editor of *Folkshilf* (1930-1938) reinforced his belief in the intellectual capabilities of the masses while enhancing his intimate understanding of the peculiarities of Jewish social structure in Poland.[66]

Ringelblum's work at the JDC introduced him to Yitzhak Giterman, one of its directors, who greatly contributed to the development of Ringelblum's approach to philanthropy. Whereas traditional charity sought to provide help without referring to the responsibility of those who got this help, Giterman believed in providing the needy with tools to help them manage their crises and perhaps prevent future ones.[67]

Ringelblum's Marxist views were not always congruent with the work he did, (e.g. extending loans to individuals), although this work did suit his sense of social solidarity. As conditions of Jews in Poland deteriorated from 1936, with a growing number of pogroms and boycotts, all supported by the Polish government and clergy, assistance from the JDC became vital, help which was translated into offering loans to protect and restore businesses and individuals affected.[68] By procuring loans and requiring their recipients to act responsibly, Ringelblum turned his efforts into a means of strengthening the community, encouraging its borrowing members to become involved in the country's general economy.[69]

In 1938, Giterman appointed Ringelblum as head of the *landsmanshaft*, a department charged with raising money from former Polish Jews to help those still living in Poland.[70] To solicit such help, Ringelblum published in the *Folkshilf* newspaper heartbreaking accounts of ordinary Jews connected to *kases* (free loan societies), describing the population's great difficulties. The reports he published yielded insights about ordinary people and the wealth of information they could provide about the reality of life in Poland. Since accounts were written by different people with diverse opinions and beliefs, Ringelblum reinforced his perception of Jews being a unique class of their own, seeing how they all made joint efforts to improve the situation, despite their diverse political affiliations and religious beliefs.

It was in Zbąszyń that Ringelblum had encountered what may be considered a prelude to what happened to Jews during the Second World War. In November 1938, Giterman sent Ringelblum to the border town of Zbąszyń, to meet and support Jewish refugees expelled from Germany. According to the Germans, they were considered Polish, but Poland refused to authorize their entry into the country.[71] For over a month, Ringelblum was in charge of refugee support, a task that affected him deeply. In a letter to Mahler, he described his impressions of the situation in the town:

In the course of those five weeks we (originally Giterman, Ginzberg and I, and after ten days, Ginzberg and I), set up a whole township with departments for supplies, hospitalization, carpentry workshops, tailors, shoemakers, books, a legal section, a migration department, and an independent post office (with 53 employees), a welfare office, a court of arbitration, an organizing committee, open and secret control services, a cleaning service, and a complex sanitation service, etc.[72]

The chaos in the refugee camp, Ringelblum's organizational skills and his approach to welfare work is evident from how he organized the camp as an independent separate unit of the town that hosted it. The Zbąszyń experience uncovered the harsh and violent reality of more than six years of Nazism in Germany as well as the antisemitic approach of the Polish government, as he expressed in the same letter to Mahler:

> ... Zbąszyń has become a symbol for the defenselessness of the Jews of Poland. Jews were humiliated to the level of lepers, to third-class citizens, and as a result we are all visited by terrible tragedy. Zbąszyń was a heavy moral blow against the Jewish population of Poland. And it is for this reason that all the threads lead from the Jewish masses to Zbąszyń and to the Jews who suffer there...[73].

Polish government conduct and its cold shoulder, manifested in its unwillingness to assist Jewish refugees, sealed their fate to a large extent. This approach led Ringelblum to understand the depth of the chasm between Jews and Poles, and the message that Jews were not considered part of Polish society, but rather, a separate entity.[74]

During Ringelblum's time there, he collected a huge number of documents as well as oral accounts from displaced refugees. Although materials were lost, evidence of his intention to gather documentation about the deportation to Zbąszyń, is found in a letter he wrote to Raphael Mahler dated, December 6, 1938, where he asked him to collect relevant materials from the Jewish press and English newspapers.[75] Ringelblum's experiences in Zbąszyń served him well later when handling the masses of Jews deported from their towns to the Warsaw Ghetto when war broke out.[76]

Reuven Ben-Shem - A Brief Account of His Life

In his writings, Ben-Shem often referred to Ringelblum as '... mein *ben ir...*' (my townmate), and indeed, just like Ringelblum, Ben-Shem was also

32   *Emanuel Ringelblum and Reuven Ben-Shem's War Writings*

born in Buczacz in the same year, 1900. It seems that sometime during the First World War, he moved to Vienna by himself where he enrolled in the gymnasia *Israelitisch Theologische Lehranstalt*,[77] a modern rabbinical school while becoming a member of *Hashomer Hatzair (The Young Guard)*, at the time, an apolitical group that pledged to create a new Jew, that is, a direct opposite of the Diaspora Jew.

In 1919, Ben-Shem left with a group of *Hashomer Hatzair* members for Palestine, where they established an agricultural farm at Bitanya Ilit. After only a year, he joined another group, *HeChalutz*,[78] that founded kibbutz Kiryat Anavim near Jerusalem. The experience in Palestine left a long-lasting impression on him but in 1921, following his father's murder by Ukrainians, Ben-Shem had to return to Europe and resumed his studies at Vienna University. He graduated from the faculty of philosophy and history in 1923 and, simultaneously, from the Tzvi-Peretz Chajes (1876–1927) Rabbinical School.

Interestingly, despite *Hashomer Hatzair* turning to the extreme left, Ben-Shem being religious and anti-communist continued to be active in the movement until 1925. Then, he joined the revisionists, the right wing, only to leave them too in 1933 and join Meir Grossman, the founder of the *Mifleget Hamedina Haivrit*, Jewish State Party, also considered right-wing. Until the war, Ben-Shem made a living as a teacher, translator, and journalist.

When the war broke out, heavy bombardments convinced the Ben-Shems that it would be best to leave Warsaw. The family with their close friends, the Alters, boarded a train on the night of September 7, 1939. It did not take long for the train to be halted by heavy bombings. When morning broke, the Ben-Shems found they had managed to travel only 30 km. south of Warsaw. The families hired a cart and horse and continued to head south intending to escape to Lublin, closer to the Russian border. They stopped in the town of Łaskarzew, about 75 km. southeast of Warsaw, where they were stuck because German forces entered the town on September 15, 1939.[79]

Both families tried to escape the town, first, to the forest and then to other towns in the area.[80] Eventually they returned to Łaskarzew where they found the Germans had burned to death almost 200 people, mostly Jews but also two Polish families.[81] Eventually, the two families decided to try and return to Warsaw as things got worse in Łaskarzew. In addition, being an anti-communist, Ben-Shem referred to his fear of attempting to reach Lublin, which he thought would soon be under Soviet rule and thus put himself and his family in further danger.[82]

At the beginning of October 1939, the Ben-Shems and Alters managed to find a horse and cart with great difficulty and make their way back to

Warsaw. Ben-Shem recounted that two weeks later, they stopped at Otwock, about 25 km. southeast of Warsaw. Ben-Shem wrote that for the first time in about six weeks they could finally take a bath at a relative's house. At the end of October, they arrived in Warsaw where they found that their flat, at Leszno 66 in the heart of Warsaw, was occupied by an acquaintance and her family who had sold some of their belongings in order to buy food.[83] After some arguments, the Ben-Shems got their apartment back.[84]

The above very brief and concise description of his family's whereabouts during the first three and a half months of the war was put down in a book published by Ben-Shem after the war. The book described in detail the pandemonium in Warsaw, the population's extreme problems, atrocities on the way to Łaskarzew, in the area itself and later when they made their way back to Warsaw.

When the ghetto was sealed, on November 16, 1940, the Ben-Shems flat was within its designated area so they remained there, although like others they had to share. Ben-Shem rented rooms in his apartment to three other people: Rachel Auerbach his cousin, a member of the Police force whose name was Warem and his relative from Gdańsk (Danzig) who was deported to Warsaw in March 1941. When he left, the room was rented to a person named Ziman. Despite the enormous complications of life in the ghetto, the Ben-Shems were relatively well off, which allowed them to deal with the difficulties of food and sanitation.

Like Ringelblum, it seems Ben-Shem started to record events in a notebook that would later become part of his writings documenting life in the ghetto. As previously mentioned, Josef Kermish maintained that large parts of the diary were actually written while Ben-Shem was in hiding. Kermish's conclusions were not only influenced by his personal acquaintance with Ben-Shem but also by the character of texts he examined, which he typified as 'Gothic viewpoints, generalization and the learning of lessons'.[85]

Laurence Weinbaum who wrote about Ben-Shem almost fifty years after the latter's death, concluded that there was not enough evidence to suggest the diary had been written in hiding.[86] However, in December 2018, I found evidence in the original notebook that indeed, Ben-Shem's diary was to a large extent, written in hiding. In February 2020, Bella Gutterman, the scientific editor who had reviewed this diary for publication, told me that there were in fact three different notebooks handed over to Yad-Vashem. This suggests that whereas it is evident one notebook was written in captivity, it is not possible to claim with certainty the same about the two others.

Nevertheless, Ben-Shem's handwritten manuscripts contain additions in several types of ink, directions and referrals, as well as remarks within the texts indicating that this or that part belonged to another page or paragraph. Obviously, the deciphered parts were edited too, probably not only by Ben-Shem. Both the manuscript and the deciphered version were written in Hebrew, a peculiarity, as most diaries were written either in Yiddish or in local languages. Unlike Ringelblum's diary, Ben-Shem's was a personal diary and rich in details about his personal life and that of others. Ben-Shem also provided an abundance of descriptions about life in the ghetto in general and was able to poetically portray particular incidents he witnessed. His language was highly sophisticated and sometimes biblical while his style suggested a large degree of cynicism.

After July 22, 1942, the day deportations from Warsaw began, Ben-Shem went out of his way to secure a job at one of the local shops in order to save his family from the death sentence awaiting those who did not belong to the sector the Nazis referred as 'essential' elements. Ben-Shem ended up at Schilling's shop for carpentry and according to him, without getting a work permit. Clearly, his family too had no permit, which meant having to hide most of the time and certainly during raids.

Life in the shops was extremely harsh and dangerous. It was not only on account of slave work-conditions, but workers were forced to abandon their apartments including belongings, and move to shop allocated housing quarters. These were usually empty flats whose former residents had either been sent to Treblinka, were hiding somewhere, or worked in other shops and were therefore also forced to move out. Apartments were in dreadful condition and often death traps as, at any moment, they could be invaded by the SS or other units seeking to fulfil the quota of deportees to Treblinka.

The Ben-Shems managed to escape the ghetto in February 1943 and found refuge in the village of Pustelnik. Ben-Shem's last page of deciphered documents ends on April 3, 1943, when he and his wife said goodbye to their daughter, Josima, a musical prodigy, who was supposed to be taken into hiding separately. The family was reunited a few days later and went into hiding with a group of other people.

On April 21, 1943, Josima died in the village of Pustelnik and was eventually buried in the yard after the owners, who had wanted to throw the body into a lake, relented: '...under a young tree in a narrow pit, in the same way that children bury their beloved cat or a dead bird.'[87] In an interview with Shoshana Kossower-Rozencwajg (Emilka), she said that she had helped bury Josima in that yard.[88] It is not clear what exactly happened after April 3, 1943, because nothing after that date has been deciphered.

History Defines Jewishness

However, a year after her daughter's death, Pnina, Ben-Shem's wife, died too.

According to Weinbaum, at the end of July 1944, Ben-Shem and others began to make their way to Lublin which had been captured by the Russian army.[89] Once he arrived in Lublin, Ben-Shem became an important member of the Historishe Komisye (Historical Commission) established by Philip Friedman, a Jewish historian, at the end of August 1944.[90] In December 1945, this body became the Central Jewish Historical Commission (CJHC or CŻKH, Centralna Żydowska Komisja Historycza) in Poland with more members including Yosef Kermish.[91]

In his book, Levi Arye claimed Ben-Shem was active in ideas of taking revenge on the Nazis. While in Lublin, a group of Jewish partisans arrived, among them, Aba Kovner.[92] According to Levi, Kovner's leadership created ideas and desires for revenge and in one of those meetings, Ben-Shem initiated the idea of mass poisoning claiming that he had a chemist friend in Warsaw who could provide considerable help. However, when Ben-Shem travelled to Warsaw, he found no trace of that person and therefore, other means had to be considered. It seems that Ben-Shem's participation in these ventures ended once he immigrated to Palestine in 1945.[93]

In early October 1944, the PKWN, Polish Committee of National Liberation, was asked to nominate Ben-Shem as Rabbi, a post that was approved and marked the first time Ben-Shem ever fulfilled this capacity. Ben-Shem was also among the founders of the Zionist party *Ichud* (Unity), but representing the revisionists, the party was outlawed, and Ben-Shem did not participate in the next meeting of the provisional parliament.[94] When Ben-Shem was summoned by the NKVD (The People's Commissariat for Internal Affairs, the Interior Ministry of the Soviet Union), he did not wait and escaped Poland heading for Palestine through Bucharest where he married Ruth Halbersztadt (1913-2007), whom he had met in Lublin.

Ben-Shem and his new wife, together with a large group of other refugees, boarded the 'Transylvania' sailing to Palestine. On October 28, 1945, *Hamashkif* newspaper reported that the ship had arrived in Haifa port and had been admitted by the British authorities. The paper stated that Ben-Shem had brought with him valuable documents about the whereabouts of the Jewish community in Poland during the war.[95]

In Palestine, Ben-Shem rejoined the General Zionists (later to become the Liberal Party) but his political activities remained in the margins. When Ben-Shem was Israel's Cultural Attaché in Argentina, from 1956 to 1959, he published the book *Poyln Brent (Poland Burns)*, which dealt with the three first months of the German invasion of Poland and his whereabouts as a refugee. It seems that much of the content was based on notes written during the war and later edited in safety. Ben-Shem first redacted his notes in Hebrew, then the text was translated into Yiddish, a language he had forbidden to use for the publication of his diary in his will from March 1943.[96]

Ben-Shem settled in Israel in Givat Shmuel, near Tel Aviv. He established a high school called Sokolov Laor in Jaffa and was a lecturer in social sciences. Ben-Shem resumed his literary passion and published several books amongst them: *Me'al Hakvarim Hadomemim* (Above the Silent Graves) subtitled *Kfar Ha'Ichud Treblinka* (the United Village of Treblinka) (1946), which called upon the Jewish people to unite in order to recover from the terrible losses of the war. A children's book, *Ben Chomot Ha'ghetto* (*Between the Ghetto Walls*) (1947), recounted the whereabouts of a girl in the ghetto. The protagonist was named Josima, like his deceased child, and the book was dedicated to her memory.[97] Ben-Shem also published several books about psychology, some of which were adapted for school teenagers. All these books were written in Hebrew.

According to Weinbaum, because of the Holocaust, Ben-Shem established *Efrata*, an organization encouraging birth and objecting to abortions. In Givat Shmuel he established the *Tiferet Israel* (The Glory of Israel) synagogue. Being a liberal at heart, Yoa Rina, his daughter was called to the Torah in that synagogue for her *bat mitzvah*.[98] To this day, such an act is considered unusual and almost sensational.[99] Ben-Shem died at his home in Givat Shmuel in 1980.[100]

Ben-Shem's Activism

From its establishment in 1913, *Hashomer or Hashomer Hatzair*, a Jewish youth movement, was typical of Galicja and its major theme was spiritual, focusing on creating a 'new human being' while acting to reinforce personal traits and discipline.[101] The *Guide to Hashomer Leaders* spoke of the duty to settle in Palestine and be engaged in productive work, although it was not an obligation. During the First World War, Galicja became a war zone and almost half of its Jews fled to Vienna (about 175,000).[102] It was there that news of the Jewish Battalion established in the British army reached members' ears and inspired imaginations.[103] The Vienna period of *Hashomer Hatzair* lasting until the 1920s, was meaningful and even when refugees began to return to Galicja, the Vienna branch remained dominant.

Hashomer Hatzair preached honoring family values, loyalty to religious morality, teaching the young about nationalism, revolting against older generations, training away from home and migration to Palestine. The intimacy developed between group members had romantic traits and became a safe haven for young members, almost like family.[104] In that period, *Hashomer Hatzair* was socialist, not in economic terms but in its spirit of placing group interests above those of individuals. Without being religious, members were supposed to be filled with a religious sense, devoted to the Jewish past including biblical role models, Hebrew language, and education in Judaism.

The first group of pioneers reached Palestine in 1917.[105] Although it is not clear when Reuven Ben-Shem joined *Hashomer Hatzair*, in 1919, he was part of probably the second pioneering group that immigrated to Palestine. The group lived in the Bitanya Ilit commune close to the Sea of Galilee where Feldschuh adopted the pen name of Ben-Shem, which meant son of Shem, as a symbol of his rebirth.[106]

Life in Bitanya Ilit was intense and demanding, both physically and mentally. It became famous for its members' dedication and ideology within the spirit of *Hashomer Hatzair*. They held group discussions that were more like public confessions, straining intimate relationships within the group of twenty-seven people, only four of whom were women.[107] This experience must have been memorable although exhausting. To date, no direct comment related to Ben-Shem's life at Bitanya Ilit was found, probably because he was there barely a year. As previously mentioned, Ben-Shem left, joined *HeChalutz* but shortly thereafter he returned to Vienna.

In the mid-1920s, the leftist radicalization of *Hashomer Hatzair* led some prominent members to leave, including Ben-Shem who was alienated and repulsed by the adoption of 'Soviet Union style' socialism. By 1925, Ben-Shem had officially joined the new Zionist Revisionist movement.[108] However, in 1926, when Ben-Shem became a teacher at the Hebrew *Tarbut Gymnasia* in Kowel, he rejuvenated the local *Hashomer Hatzair* branch, a movement he had officially abandoned in 1925.[109]

Avraham Melamed, a native of Kowel, wrote in the city's memorial book that when Ben-Shem started teaching in Tarbut Gymnasia,

> ...a beautiful and rich period began where students of Tarbut Gymnasia started flocking in large numbers to the '*Ken*' (the 'nest', a chapter which is a branch of a youth movement). This was the 'Ben-Shem' Period. He was a new teacher who arrived in Kowel and had

a hypnotic effect on the youth. Under his influence, many students joined the Ken and also the teachers became interested in it.[110]

Melamed described Ben-Shem's contribution to the movement's revival in Kowel as well as his magnetic personality. Apparently, the time Ben-Shem was there left an indelible impression on the young and contributed to reviving the *Hashomer Hatzair* branch in Kowel.

In the same book Ben-Shem wrote:

> Before noon I was a teacher, in the afternoon, my time, energy, and experience were devoted to *Hashomer Hatzair*... Every Sabbath Eve I went out with the heads of the regiments and groups for a nighttime trek. ... The number of trips increased, and so did the number of participants. ... Lights were extinguished, dogs barked, and Jewish youth trekked through the fields of Poland – Volhynia, walking, taking in the sights, searching, longing, dreaming, learning to strengthen body and soul, learning to wait, to aspire, and to achieve.[111]

Clearly, Ben-Shem took great pleasure in instilling enthusiasm into young scouts' hearts, but also, '... in *Hashomer Hatzair* we inspired intense longing for the land of Israel, the ritual of work, culture, admiring work, singing, respect for society, demand for change, and aspirations for action.'[112]

In 1926, Ben-Shem established a new youth movement whose purpose was to attract youngsters from *Hashomer Hatzair*. He called it *Hashomer Hatzair Hatahor* (*Pure Young Guard*), alluding to his movement being pure and free of socialism, much like what *Hashomer Hatzair* used to be. In 1927, he joined forces with Aharon Kaplan, also a defector from *Hashomer Hatzair*, who had his own youth movement called *Hashomer Hatzair Haleumi* (*Young National Guard*). By unifying the two groups, there were about 50 branches under Ben-Shem's leadership in Poland.[113]

In his article titled '*Zealots*', Ben-Shem claimed that the history of Jews in the diaspora was characterized by continuous internal wars and that the Jewish nation was saved by those who were zealous, ready to sacrifice everything in order to save it.[114] Following this logic, he explained that *Hashomer* was an adequate alternative to the temptation of communism which he referred to as a Rubella plague or the 'red lie', maintaining that the mission was 'to fight those organizations'.[115] In other words, the enemy was not only *Hashomer Hatzair* which had committed to communism but all left-wing movements.[116]

In Ben-Shem's interview in Massuah, he explained that the background for the establishment of *Hashomer Haleumi* was that between 1923-1924, *Hashomer Hatzair* ideology drifted to the left. Ben-Shem emphasized that it was '... left in the sense of those days - it wasn't like it is now. It meant rupture with Jewish nationality and turning to the east, (the Soviet Union). ... Therefore, back then, in 1923, I demanded a change.'[117] He insisted they went back to creating a 'new Jew', and although there was opposition, he succeeded in converting the branch in Krakow which was renamed *Hashomer Hatzair Hatahor*. However, when this branch was removed from his charge, it quickly reverted to left wing ideology and Ben-Shem said it was then that he established the *Hashomer Hatahor* movement which had deliberately removed traces of the old movement by taking the word *Hatzair* out of its name.

Ben-Shem testified that he addressed the General Zionist Organization on the issue but it took them time to realize that *Hashomer Hatzair's* move to the left was problematic because although they remained committed to the idea of establishing a homeland in the land of Israel, it was intended to be structured as a socialist society. In the interview, Ben-Shem emphasized that it was important to build a homeland in the land of Israel regardless of political doctrines.[118] When Ben-Shem said that between 1929-1931 he was simultaneously head of '*Hashomer Haleumi*' and *Betar*, the revisionist youth movement, the interviewer showed astonishment, which Ben-Shem addressed.[119] More than anything, Ben-Shem wanted to unify different ideas and ideologies because what mattered to him was the Jewish entity as such and not social ideologies of any form. He emphasized that he wanted somehow to bridge the gaps between *Hashomer Haleumi* being more left inclined and *Betar* - exactly the opposite. He said: 'In my opinion, *Hashomer Haleumi* should have included all Jewish youth movements apart from *Hashomer Hatzair* because all youth needed three things: Jewish Labor, *Aliyah* (immigration) to Erez Israel and a national Hebrew culture.'[120] Ben-Shem concluded that his approach had always seemed rather extreme and that it had deterred many people. In reply to the interviewer, he said that his incapacity to create one Jewish youth organization for all, may very well have to do with the fact he was also associated with *Betar*.[121]

In his speeches and addresses Ben-Shem continued to be strictly anti-socialist, calling for fierce opposition to such inclinations. According to Heller, *Betar*, became totally opposed to socialism thanks to Reuven Ben-Shem.[122] The latter maintained that anyone who dedicated their life to building a Jewish state in Palestine should have been considered a pioneer (not only those, who in addition to building a home for the Jews, adopted socialism).

Despite its differences with the socialists, *Hashomer Hatzair /Haleumi* never openly confronted the Zionist organization or mentioned their connection to *Betar*. Indeed, they continuously described the development of Zionism as a battle between leftists and pure nationalistic forces, but this never prevented them from joining forces to promote the establishment of a Jewish state in Palestine.[123]

Heller maintained that Ben-Shem's list of recommended books from December 1927, presented guidelines for the cultural education of youth movement members but analysis of this list indicates the absence of a clear ideological orientation. More importantly, Ben-Shem made no reference to Italy's official fascist youth movement although he encouraged the young to become familiar with fighting, yet without specifying who the enemy might be. Heller pointed out that although names of enemies were missing, the left was a target but even in this case, the struggle was supposed to be ideological.[124]

On December 26, 1926, Ben-Shem was elected to the board of the revisionist headquarters.[125] In the meantime, he seems to have been relieved of his duties in *Hashomer Haleumi* while assuming new roles in *Masada*[126] causing a dispute with *Betar*. The controversy concerned ideology, or rather, class differences as *Betar* accepted everyone into its ranks, while *Masada* accepted only secondary school students.[127] In a letter to Ben-Shem, Jabotinsky objected to this kind of rivalry inside the movement and warned Ben-Shem against it. In the same letter, Jabotinsky mentioned that he was against Ben-Shem's initiative to raise money to purchase five airplanes, a plan which had not been discussed with the board first.[128]

Disagreement between Jabotinsky and Ben-Shem grew between 1930 and 1933, when they parted ways. Ben-Shem consistently preached that *Betar's* mission was to fight for a Jewish state, and his willingness to struggle for this cause was subject to his being an active member of the World Zionist Organization. However, when the Organization refused to openly declare its purpose was to establish a Jewish state in Palestine, it led to the final rupture, as Jabotinsky assumed control of revisionist organizational affairs and insisted on leaving the World Zionist Organization. Ben-Shem who attributed great importance to membership in the World Zionist Organization, refused to leave and instead joined *Mifleget Hamedina Haivrit*.[129] In 1935, Ben-Shem established the party's youth movement, *Brith Hacanaim*, which had a similar doctrine to that of *Betar*.[130] Importantly, in 1942 the World Zionist Organization eventually declared its goal to

History Defines Jewishness 41

establish a Jewish state in Palestine at the Biltmore Hotel in New York (the Biltmore Program). Following the Holocaust, in 1946, Grossmann and Jabotinsky's parties reunited and rejoined the World Zionist Organization.

Indeed, it may be safe to claim that what drove Ben-Shem in all his political activities, even before the war, was the notion that Jews were one nation and therefore, political differences should be overcome in order to stay united given the challenges Jews faced. His personal attitude may have been elusive in the years before the war, but after the war, Ben-Shem continued to preach cooperation regardless of political beliefs.[131]

Another of Ben-Shem's activities concerned his being Chairman of the Organizing Committee of the aviation squadron. In this capacity, Ben-Shem and the Chairman of the Jewish Community, President Maurycy Mayzl, initiated buying a plane as a present for the Polish Air Force, which was presented in May 1938. The dedication ceremony was preceded by a service, held at the Great Synagogue on Tłomackie Street where Dr. M. Tauber delivered a sermon.[132] In his book, Ben-Shem alluded to that event stating he was highly satisfied with the gift, and that the airplane was decorated with banners with an inscription: 'A present from the Jewish youth to the Polish army'.[133]

One of the last activities in which Ben-Shem was involved before the war was the 1939 publication of the first volume of a Yiddish encyclopedia, *Jidiser gezelsaftlecher leksikon,* dedicated to Warsaw.[134] In the foreword to this volume, Ben-Shem warned that a dark cloud was hanging over the skies of Europe, which might bring death and destruction not only to Jews but to others as well. The foreword, which ended with an expression of hope for things to come, argued that the presentation of topics was authentic and objective. The foreword ended with the phrase '*monumentum aere perennius*'[135], from *Horace* meaning 'a monument more lasting than bronze,' a phrase used to describe 'an immortal work of art or literature.'[136]

Relationships – Emanuel Ringelblum and Reuven Ben-Shem

Both Ringelblum and Ben-Shem were born in the very same year (1900) and the very same place, Buczacz, Galicia.[137] Years later, in Warsaw, they resided on the same street, Ben-Shem at Leszno 66 and Ringelblum at Leszno 18. Both had been incarcerated in the ghetto, and once deportation started, were shop employees, finally escaping to the Aryan side at the beginning of 1943. Of the two families, Reuven Ben-Shem was the sole survivor.

During the First World War, Ringelblum's family fled to Nowy Sącz while Ben-Shem, on his own, seems to have spent at least the last year of the war in Vienna. In their new residences, each became involved in a Jewish youth movement, Ringelblum in *Poalei Zion*, a politically left-wing party, then still one party, while Ben-Shem became a member of *Hashomer Hatzair*, at that time, an a-political youth movement which he left in 1925 to join the right wing.

In their academic careers both Ringelblum and Ben-Shem were graduates of the Humanities and both wrote their dissertations in history. When the Second World War broke out, both men turned to the pen. From the beginning, Ringelblum set out to write a historical diary whereas Ben-Shem began writing a personal one.

Their cold relationship went back to the days prior to the war which could explain why Ringelblum, who knew Ben-Shem and was aware of his prolific literary work, did not ask him to join the archive team. Ben-Shem's book, *Poyln Brent*, offers a glimpse into their pre-war rapport as he recounted that just before the war, when he had addressed Ringelblum with a request to contribute to the Jewish Lexicon he was writing, the latter did not refuse but submitted nothing by the required deadline.[138]

Ben-Shem bitterly recalled that when he had turned to Ringelblum for help in October 1939, the latter told him that one should support 'productive elements.'[139] Ben-Shem who was genuinely offended and frustrated by this reaction, expressed his indignation in a two-page monologue he wrote years later. He enumerated the activities in which he was involved, ending with an estimation that at heart, it was their political differences that might have explained Ringelblum's refusal to help.[140]

Ringelblum's writings showed that he was well aware of Ben-Shem's activities inside the ghetto. In his diary, Ringelblum mentioned Ben-Shem three times, all unfavorably. The first time was in December 1939, when he wrote that 'The Revisionists, take care of their own, Dr. Ben-Shem and - - had sent a memo on their behalf.'[141] This first mention had to do with Ben-Shem's attempt from November 1939, to address the Gestapo and get their consent for organized immigration to Palestine. Ben-Shem and his friend Abraham Lipman reported to the Joint board, and according to Ben-Shem, Leib Neustadt, David (Daniel) Guzik, Yitzhak Bornstein and Apolinary Hartglas, were contented with the results, while Menachem Kirshenbaum, Yochanan Morgenstern and Emanuel Ringelblum, doubted the value of their efforts.[142] When Ringelblum made this comment, it was related to the fact that as no answer had been received from the Gestapo, the revisionists decided to send a letter again, this time, on their behalf.

Secondly, Ben-Shem was mentioned on May 6-11, 1941 in reference to the '13'[143] because its founder, Abraham Gancwajch, had invited numerous people to a large gathering of about sixty people including important journalists, engineers and doctors, as well as Reuven Ben-Shem and Janusz Korczak. According to Ringelblum, people attended those meetings out of fear or curiosity, and because they believed they could gain something from them.[144] Ringelblum who refused to be involved with the '13', was divided even about Korczak's involvement with Gancwajch. Elsewhere in the diary, Ringelblum criticized Korczak saying he was an 'idler'[145] despite being well aware that Korczak's service as head of a committee for the protection of children, set up by Gancwajch, was crucial and enabled Korczak to get supplies for his orphanage. As for Ben-Shem, he explained his attendance in that meeting by his hope to get employment. Eventually, around February 1942, he decided to cut off ties with Gancwajch because it had attracted negative elements.[146]

Ringelblum mentioned Ben-Shem for the last time in June 1941, again in reference to the job held in Gancwajch's organization, in the youth department in 'First Aid'. In this entry, Ringelblum also mentioned another revisionist who worked with Gancwajch and concluded this remark with: 'Rascals of all parties united!'[147], playing on the famous Communist slogan: 'Workers of the world, unite!' Rather than expressing his reservations about these people, Ringelblum circumvented his criticism and tied the revisionists to Gancwajch's collaborating organization by indirectly referring to moral differences, distorting the famous communist slogan 'Workers of the world, unite!' Weinbaum wrote that Ben-Shem's son, Nekamia, claimed that his father thought Ringelblum detested him for his political views, a possible explanation for employing such harsh words when referring to Ben-Shem.[148]

Apparently, despite efforts Ben-Shem made to approach Ringelblum, he was given the cold shoulder. Hence, it should not be a surprise that Ringelblum was never mentioned in the deciphered part of Ben-Shem's notes. However, it can only be assumed that Ben-Shem did discuss Ringelblum at least once more, in his original diary, during the early days of the war because his book, *Poyln Brent*, probably based on parts of his diary, included allusions to encounters with Ringelblum, all of which indicated that they did not trust each other.[149]

Another important reference to Ringelblum appeared in Ben-Shem's original manuscript and it concerned the discovery of Ringelblum's hideout and death. Ben-Shem wrote that Wanda, probably Wanda Elster, came to visit them in their own hideout and brought the news about Ringelblum and his family's arrest. On pages 338/148, there are two dates, March 10, the assumed date Ringelblum was murdered, but the date was crossed out and replaced by March 8, 1944, after which Ben-Shem wrote that Ringelblum and his family were murdered.[150]

Another link between Ringelblum and Ben-Shem was the latter's cousin, Rachel Auerbach. Although she was not politically active, Auerbach had left-wing leanings and at Ringelblum's request, she joined the *Oneg Shabbat* staff. When he approached her to establish a soup kitchen and document what went on there, she was reluctant at first but consented to take the position rather than escape Warsaw as she had planned. She became a prominent figure among the workers at the *Oneg Shabbat* Archive and during her ghetto period, Auerbach resided with the Ben-Shems. Apparently, Ben-Shem was fully aware of her relationship with Ringelblum just as the latter knew about Auerbach's and Ben-Shem's intimate family ties.

*****

In the introduction to *Writing Jewish History in Eastern Europe*, Alexion and Horowitz stated that it was hard '… to exaggerate the contribution of Simon Dubnow to the popularization of Jewish historiography in Russia and eastern Europe in general.'[151] To discuss YIVO, Cecile E. Kuznitz, used almost the same words: 'The importance of Dubnow's career in laying the foundation for YIVO's work can hardly be exaggerated.'[152] Although each of these researchers emphasized a somewhat different angle, both agreed that Dubnow played a decisive role in uniting Jews around the idea that history defined them and that this awareness led to founding YIVO.

An important aspect in the establishment of YIVO was institutionalizing Dubnow's methodology, thus rendering cooperation between Jewish institutions and ordinary people an interdependent venture. This not only contributed to making Jewish history a national interest, but the combination popularized the study of history while making *zamlers* (collectors) indispensable active participants in the effort of creating the Jewish story by Jews.[153] Thus, assuming individual responsibility over the Jewish experience became a personal rather widespread phenomenon and although most scientific work was conducted by intellectuals, research results were disseminated to the masses in every conceivable format, be it at synagogue gatherings or other forms of organized Jewish activities. The fruits of this cooperation produced various publications including books, newspapers, addressing audiences of both researchers and the masses.[154]

Apparently, Dubnow's impact reached beyond methodological aspects, and went as far as positioning Jewish history in parallel to religious spirituality, as a factor defining modern Judaism. History became the context through which to explain the wrong in Jewish society, in the present as well as the past. The more Jews studied history, the more they felt they could understand the present while relying on that information to create a better future for themselves.[155] In this sense, history became the vertebral column of Jewish political activism in east Europe.

David Engel explained that Dubnow's call from 1891 created a tradition of seeing history as '... less an academic occupation than a popular enterprise uniting all segments of a community in collecting documents and recording recollections...'[156] Importantly, this tradition included gathering oral and written accounts, official and non-official documentation. This approach became rooted in Jewish identity and later formed the backbone of documentation during the Second World War.[157]

Both Ringelblum and Ben-Shem, who grew up in this very atmosphere, were deeply influenced by Dubnow's approach and in their adulthood, the impact of history as a source of inspiration for political activism was embedded in their scholarly and political activism. It appears that what both men had in common was their concern with issues of the hour in Jewish life as well the future, although their interpretations of this situation differed and consequently the routes on which they embarked.

Ringelblum's activities as a historian, social worker, and political activist in Marxist LPZ, were inextricably linked and each nurtured the other. Political emphasis was placed on the structure of society and not where it would be created which explains why Yiddish, the mother tongue of the majority of Jews, was the preferred language. Ringelblum's work with these organizations allowed him to gather valuable information and insights into the plight of Jews and his connections and activities were instrumental scientifically and practically.[158]

Unlike Ringelblum, Ben-Shem was not involved in historical research, but his political activism relied on Jewish history. One of the first practical implementations of history in which Ben-Shem was involved, was joining a group of *Hashomer Hatzair* and immigrating to Palestine in 1919. The impact of that experience was presented in his book *Noce palestyńskie* (Palestinian Nights) published in 1928, where he suggested the land of Israel had electrifying resuscitation capacities for Jews.[159] Ben-Shem's second wife, Ruth, confirmed that the impact of the two years in Mandatory Palestine, caused her husband to adopt his nom de plume, 'Ben-Shem'.

Between 1920-1939, Ben-Shem dedicated his time and energy to preparing young people to realize the dream of establishing a Jewish state. His articles, pamphlets and books published before the war, some in Hebrew, others in Polish as well as Yiddish, showed that for him history was the foundation and tool to draw motivation for political activism aimed at instilling in the young the spiritual-mental base necessary to make Aliyah[160] and realize the final goal of establishing a Jewish state.[161]

It can be argued that Ben-Shem's ideology was above all Jewish, that all Jews, regardless of their political opinions should join forces to establish a Jewish state.[162] He firmly believed that the only solution for Jewish problems in Poland was immigration to Palestine and his energy was dedicated to realizing this plan and inspiring others to do the same. For him, any social doctrines were dangerous deviations and obstacles, because they shifted the focus from efforts to create the state to conditioning its establishment on a certain social structure. This approach dictated that Hebrew should be the first language and indeed, some of Ben-Shem's pamphlets were published in Hebrew.[163]

Dubnow's public call from 1891 to all Jews generated a tremendous change in Jewish society. Indeed, the methodology effectively democratized them by making ordinary Jews an integral part of the rediscovery of the Jewish story. Second, by addressing the entire Jewish public, Dubnow had created a new perspective for understanding the situation of Jews in east Europe in particular, and the new approach was an axis around which dialogue inside Jewish society revolved. Dubnow had shaped a sense of togetherness and belonging to a Jewish space by exploring its history from a man-centered angle.

Creating a 'usable past' through the study of history as a defining cultural concept of Jewish nationality, engineered a new spiritual space. Schrøder Simonsen claimed that 'Literature became a territorial common ground, a portable fatherland in the words of Meyer Waxman, and a meeting place for Jews without a Jewish country.'[164]

She suggested that through literature, Heinrich Heine managed to claim a Jewish space or as she put it 'Heine substitutes ink for bricks to create space for Judaism in cultural Europe.'[165] I argue that the same can be claimed about Dubnow's historical research as well as the application of cultural-social-historical research and narratives that were inspired by his work.

According to Karlip, the spirituality of secular Jewish historians was not only pious in the rabbinical sense but in the same way, favored the spiritual over the material. Indeed, Dubnow's theory suggests that the Jewish people's strength derived from its spiritual force and that Jewish nationalism was dependent on the formation of different cultural centers, which were an elevated form of nationhood, one that relied on its spirituality rather than territory.[166]

Space, then, was a concept in its own right; its study in the modern Dubnow manner meant researching and exploring the living space of Jewish existence. It was at the same time, common but unfamiliar grounds, constructed through historical narratives. It was a medium with the potential to provide ideal conditions for the imagination to enable the construction of social, emotional, and material components of a common social place lending itself to participant interrelationships.[167]

Part II

Literature of the Holocaust

II

Holocaust Diary Writing and Space

Implementation of Lebensraum in Nazi-Occupied Territories

Lebensraum was the principle which guided Nazi policy, based on the idea that the German people depended on acquiring new lands; thus, geography became a central concept in the implementation of Nazi conquest plans, particularly in the east. This meant annexing and making these new acquisitions suitable for Germans' resettlement.[1] This principle, in different stages and forms, guided the Nazis as soon as they came into power, six years before the Second World War broke out.

Lebensraum was implemented according to targeted populations, time, and circumstances, but in relation to Jews the steps taken showed that they contained the seeds of the Final Solution. Yet, despite brutality and torture involved in clearing newly conquered land, Jews found it difficult to identify with the uniqueness of this displacement process something that might have sounded alarming. This book focuses on the whereabouts of the Jewish population, which was eventually to be removed from space entirely without any concessions.

Four unique steps guided cleansing space of Jews to create favorable Lebensraum for the German people. The first: banishment from public spaces. The second: visual identification of Jews applied first in Poland in December 1939. The third: concentrating Jews in distinct areas – in the east, mainly in ghettos; in the west, banishment to internment or transit camps. The fourth: systematic murder of all Jews in specially constructed killing centers in the east. As specified, the Nazis did not necessarily follow all these steps everywhere, or in this order, as decisions depended on local considerations.

German attempts to purify spaces penetrated the most intimate realities of life. One of the first laws introduced on April 7, 1933, was the 'Law for the Restoration of the Professional Civil Service'. It defined Jews as a politically unreliable entity and therefore, banned them from working in any form of civil service. In the same month, another law restricted the number of Jewish students in schools and universities. At the beginning of 1934, Jewish actors were forbidden from performing on stage, while in September 1935, the Nuremberg Laws defined who was considered a Jew based on biological principles rather than religious conviction. These laws denied Jews their citizenship, and forbade any biological relationships with Germans including marriage. In August 1938, it became obligatory for German Jews without Jewish names to add the name Israel (males) or Sarah (females) to their identity cards and passports.[2]

The November 9, 1938 pogrom, known as Kristallnacht ('Night of Broken Glass') was a landmark not only in and of itself, but it also signaled accelerated Aryanization, the systematic confiscation of Jewish property. In 1939, it became obligatory for all Jews to have their passports stamped with the letter 'J', initial for Jew. However, physically German Jews only became visible in public spaces in September 1941, almost two years after Polish Jews were forced to do the same and about six months before the same laws were enforced on the Jews of western Europe.[3] September 1941 also marked the beginning of large-scale deportations from Germany to the east.

If the process of banishing German Jews from the public arena took about six years and identifying them physically lasted from August 1938 until September 1941, that is, three years, the Jews of Poland were forced to undergo this process in three months. The first two steps were implemented almost simultaneously, Aryanization,[4] followed by the decree to don Jewish symbols as of December 1939.

Invasion into the Soviet Union and its satellite states in June 1941, accelerated Nazi Lebensraum and began a new stage in the persecution of Jews. In Lithuania for example, Jews were forced to wear identifying badges as early as July 3, 1941, barely two weeks after the invasion had started.[5] Ghettos were erected at the end of August 1941 and brutal relocation into ghettos was enforced. Murder started even before ghettos were established as Einsatzkommando 9 shot about 5,000 people. According to Kay, it was in Vileyka, Belarus that women and children were included in these murderous acts for the first time. This was a landmark, as from that moment on, anyone who was Jewish, irrespective of gender or age, was systematically murdered.[6] Simultaneously, in other areas of the former Soviet Union, the Nazis did not bother establishing ghettos and introduced a policy of immediate murder using shooting squads.

In 1942, the Jews of western Europe where ghettos were not established, underwent the process of visible elimination from public spaces and were forced to don Jewish identifying badges. Shortly after, in mid-1942, they were gathered in transit camps and soon deported to killing centers in the east. The summer of 1942 turned out to be a crucial point in time for Jews as well as Nazis, as it marked the conscious recognition that cleansing spaces of Jews would be implemented by murdering every single Jew.

Documentation – A Jewish Response

Holocaust Literature

When the Second World War broke out, the Jews' situation in every respect deteriorated rapidly. One response was to embody Jewish experiences through literature, which has been tremendously influential on how post-Holocaust generations have interpreted and perceived the war and its implications. Holocaust literature has come to be known as such, first because of the period it addressed, and second because civilian populations were targeted in a manner not recorded before. The Yale Holocaust Encyclopedia states that Holocaust literature '...consists of all the literary responses to the destruction of European Jewry and other peoples by the Nazi German state and its collaborators during the Second World War.'[7] Holocaust literature is diverse and constitutes a unique body of work comprising different genres such as diaries, testimonies, letters, notes, memories, poetry, prose and more.

Undertaking writing because of Nazi abuse started before the war, particularly in Germany where Jews were targeted as soon as Hitler became Chancellor. As the war began, the phenomenon of writing spread further. According to Dina Porat, one in 7,500 people in Warsaw appeared to have written a diary while in Vilnius the ratio was much higher, one in 2,500.[8] However, considering that diaries were written in other parts of Europe too, only a small fraction survived the war.

David Roskies defined Holocaust literature as a '*Jew-zone*'.[9] He explained that between 1939–1945 two zones existed, wholly independent of any geographical notions: a free zone and a *Jew-zone*. The latter signified that instead of applying to geographical boundaries, the *Jew-zone* related to Jewish lived spaces, that is, people themselves as well as anything connected to them, starting with their personal belongings, and ending with public buildings and cultural assets.

Jew-Zone redefined Jewish lived-in spaces, namely, for Jews it was total destruction and as it turned out, also permanent, thus creating a new form of landscape, unfamiliar to humankind. Roskies claimed that 'Just as fantasy literature pushes the human imagination beyond the boundaries of observable reality, so the wartime landscape requires a new topography.'[10] Roskies noted that what happened in *Jew-zones* was linked directly to the identity of those who were there, and that total destruction became the Jews' lived space. To use Lefebvre words, *Jew-zones* were a '... dominant space...' which were '... invariably the realization of a master's project.'[11]

Another important characteristic identified is that '... Holocaust literature is a resolutely secular enterprise...',[12] stressing that its writers, observant or not, reached out to all audiences which was the reason they, regardless of their education or beliefs, adopted different language patterns as well as western literary forms for their stories to be intelligible to a variety of audiences.[13] Although Jewish lived-in spaces in different geographical regions had been designed for total annihilation, it was from this abstract space that literature of the Holocaust emerged. From areas of no man's land or non-spaces, areas that denied social existence, a new specific and wholly interdependent space was born, that of the narrative, the verbal representation of what a *Jew-zone* meant. In this respect, multiple geographical areas and consequently languages, may be considered one space, as it was within these boundaries, *Jew-zones*, that stories surfaced.

This book discusses Ringelblum and Ben-Shem's diaries; both documents have distinct characteristics for which each may be classified in several ways. Ringelblum's diary appears to match the definition of a classical diary with almost all entries dated, except most of those written after deportations began. It was then that Ringelblum's entries changed into topic-related texts bearing a title with only a few entries dated. However, as Ringelblum's diary was not a personal diary, it may also meet the definition of a chronicle, or even a newspaper, since it sought to record events as they happened.[14] Needless to say, this diary is certainly a testimony as it presents the writer's as well as other peoples' accounts and opinions. Yet, the diary itself was a personal initiative stretching later to the establishment of *Oneg Shabbat*, Ringelblum's ingenuity.

Ben-Shem's writings were structured like a diary as entries were dated. Yet, the text is a deciphered version of three different notebooks and a bunch of notes written on shreds of paper. Legible contents have been edited at least three times, apparently by three different people, one being Ben-Shem himself. While some parts of the deciphered document suggest they were based on notes that were not written as things happened, others appear to be rewritten from notes taken down while Ben-Shem was still in the ghetto. In this respect, although Ben-Shem's text physically looks like a diary, it appears some of the dates mentioned were based, at least partially, on his memory but they were written in hiding, between March 1943 and probably July 1944, when he left for Lublin. Ben-Shem's diary is, therefore, in part a testimony, a memoire as well as a diary.

Whereas Ringelblum did not survive the war, Ben-Shem did, and it appears he was preoccupied with the war until the end of his life, in 1980. On his arrival in Lublin, Ben-Shem was among the first members of the Central Jewish Historical Commission, which started its work in August 1944 and one of whose first activities was collecting testimonials from survivors.[15] Ben-Shem left Lublin sometime in the winter of 1945 and arrived in Mandatory Palestine in October, 1945.

Ben-Shem is an example of a prominent trend that gripped survivors – a writing frenzy that continued increasingly after the war. Rita Horváth, argued that war survivors were exceedingly dedicated to their role as witness bearers, the proof being the enormous number of testimonies that speak for themselves.[16] Indeed, in Palestine, Ben-Shem made unsuccessful efforts to publish his diary but meanwhile, he published short passages, based on his diary, in *Hamashkif*, the newspaper where he worked. In addition to *Poyln Brent,* parts of his diary were also published in Moreshet and Massuah, the last one in 1982, two years after his death. Finally, Yad-Vashem is about to publish a version of Reuven Ben-Shem's diary, more than forty years after his death.

Diaries of the Holocaust as Personal Narratives

Regarding Holocaust diaries, the definition of what may be considered a diary includes in it texts written, in what Goldberg defined as '... the classical form of daily entries or in the more processed form of memoirs and hybrids of chronicle and recollection.'[17] Goldberg clarified that memoires, 'chronicles and recollections' were mainly written in eastern Europe, in hiding, the bulk, from 1943 until the end of the war. In the west, most recovered diaries were written before deportations, when most writers still lived in their homes or detention centers.

Numerous people, adults, teenagers and even children became diary writers. Some of the diaries recovered are complete, whereas others have parts missing or are badly damaged. One exceptionally touching type of diary is that which ended abruptly, generally indicating that their authors met a devastating end. Today, most diaries are kept in archives in Israel, Europe, and the United States, although some remain in private hands. Once in a while, new diaries surface, offering new insights into war experiences.[18] However, to this day, the public is unaware of most recovered diaries because many remain unpublished, such as Reuven Ben-Shem's diary, the case investigated in this book.

What makes diaries valuable is the firsthand point of view they provide close to events. They expose how people understood what went on locally but also in general, information that was based on personal concepts formed by their individual perceptions and upbringing.[19] They reveal the confusion at what they experienced, the seeming senselessness of events, thus allowing readers to explore their physical and mental experiences.[20]

The majority of Jews did not keep personal diaries. Reasons ranged from lack of personal inclination and objective difficulties they faced. Obstacles were similar everywhere, but it was the degree of difficulty that determined whether one could write or not: Impediments included physical hardship, acute living conditions such as hunger, disease, violence, difficulties procuring writing materials, privacy reduced to almost nonexistent and no peace of mind.[21] As expected, fewer diaries were written in camps and even less survived because conditions made it almost impossible to keep or salvage them. David Wdowinski (1895-1970) is one example of a prisoner who while in a camp wrote and rescued his notes. [22]

Other difficulties concerned diary contents, as well as merely keeping one endangered the lives of everyone involved, writers and those who hid them or their diaries. Contents were scrutinized not to include real names or discuss clandestine activities. Ringelblum's diary is an example of secrecy, as while he carefully documented occurrences in the ghetto, he avoided any reference to secret information; the very existence of the *Oneg Shabbat* archive, smuggling reports out of the ghetto or preparations for the uprising remained concealed for the most part. These were plainly referred to in his *Last Writings* after the destruction of the ghetto, when the danger of exposing such information was over.

Changed circumstances separating Jews from general European society had a dual effect: they reduced Jews to a featureless crowd, thus unofficially entrusting diarists with the task of voicing persecuted communities' distress, while this very expression still echoed individual problems diarists encountered as an integral part of the persecuted population. Goldberg maintained that unlike children's diaries, 'documentary-historical' motivation characterized Holocaust diaries written by adults as the role of external-historical events seem to have overwhelmed individuals, shifting the focus from personal to communal.[23] Salek (Calel) Perechodnik and Moshe Maltz's are examples of personal diaries, whose stories represented a communal ordeal.[24]

Some people had kept diaries prior to the war and continued to do so. What makes their diaries stand out is the change of focus, from struggles of individuals to those of a community.[25] Victor Klemperer's diary is an example of a text that changed, as of January 31, 1933, into an account focusing on how occurrences in the public sphere penetrated the private arena. Klemperer showed that banishing Jews from the public German arena, meant a gradual invasion of both public and private Jewish spaces.[26]

It appears that for many, documentation instilled the energy to keep struggling. However, almost all writers experienced ups and downs in their resilience to maintain steady documentation. Helen Berr, explained after a ten-month break, August 25, 1943, that resuming writing was due to her intention to hide her diary. Typically, her personal motives were mentioned only after addressing communal challenges: '... Drancy, deportations and suffering continue'.[27] After another month and a half break, October 10, 1943, Berr clarified that she resumed writing as a response to her sense of responsibility. She felt she had '... a duty to write because other people must know... I am still trying to make the painful effort to tell the story... For how will humanity ever be healed unless all its rottenness is exposed?'.[28]

Interestingly, Chaim Aron Kaplan (1880–1942) also referred to a pendulum in the desire to write. On April 7, 1940, he explained he had not written in a week but even if he had attempted to do so, he would not have had enough time to put everything down. He further argued writing made no difference as he would simply be repeating the same news about '... theft, murder, insults, restrictions and that's it'.[29] His words evoked not only his shifting moods but also an important observation, that life in the ghetto had its repetitive routine and once one became accustomed to it, it was no longer recorded. Indirectly, Kaplan suggested that becoming used to distortion of reality, impeded writing and consequently, drawing conclusions.

Few diaries were written in Hebrew, which was at best a third language acquired later in life. However, when employed, it was because of its significance to the writers. Some of those who kept Hebrew diaries include Chaim Kaplan, Mordechaj Tenenbaum Tamaroff (1916-1943) the leader of the Białystok Ghetto Uprising, Reuven Ben-Shem and Avraham Lewin (1893-1943).

Avraham Lewin was a member of the *Oneg Shabbat* board and Ringelblum's close friend. He kept a diary written in Yiddish, probably started only on March 26, 1942 until June 5, 1942, but recommenced one in Hebrew on July 22, 1942, the first day of deportations from Warsaw. Lewin's language shift was significant, symbolizing the rupture with exile and a conscious decision about future immigration to the land of Israel.[30]

Goldberg characterized that most children's diaries, including Moshe Flinker and Anna Frank's, were private confessions dealing with their inner world. However, even children's diaries reflected one common feature, their inner drive for documentation.[31] Moshe Flinker (1926-1944), a Dutch Jew who fled to Belgium with his family, started his diary in Belgium, in Hebrew. According to Farbstein, Flinker's language choice indicated his struggle to maintain his identity and values using Hebrew to create a reality where the writer was in control of his life. Farbstein noted that this became more evident when Flinker abandoned his habit of entries including both Hebrew and Gregorian dates in favor of Hebrew dates alone.[32]

Anna Frank's diary is without a doubt the most famous diary written by a child. When she received a diary as a present for her 13th birthday, in 1942, she began writing one. Neither was she under direct and immediate threat nor exposed to brutalities evoked in other war diaries written by children.[33] Frank was confined to a room in hiding with her family and others and conditions took a toll on her. Flinker had to assume a false identity, but at home and with his family, he did not have to pretend he was someone else. Both were eventually captured, deported and murdered, Anna Frank in Bergen-Belsen and Moshe Flinker in Auschwitz.

Diaries constitute an outstanding source to learn about the processes leading to the Final Solution. However, the nearest we have to descriptions of actual mass murder operations are mostly escapees' testimonies, whether they survived death camps or Einsatzgruppen shooting squads. One exception was documents written by the *Sonderkommando* (prisoners assigned by the Nazis to operate the death process) who actively took part in the process by giving instructions where to undress, leave possessions, shave victims' heads, leading them to gas chambers, dragging their dead bodies out, pulling out gold teeth, and throwing the bodies into the crematoria.

According to Chare and Williams, although *Sonderkommando* writings were not diaries, they were all characterized by some historical awareness, nuanced or open.[34] Chare and Williams maintained that *Sonderkommando* texts were documents that consciously reached out to the world and they should have been interpreted as such despite their horrendous contents.[35] Yet, *Sonderkommando* writings presented a problem for post-war researchers, as well as survivors, because of the nature of work they carried out in Auschwitz.

This brief review discussed only a handful of diaries chosen because of phenomena they represented, language particularities, time and space –

before or after 1942, at home, in the ghetto, in hiding, in camps or under assumed identity. For many, writing was provoked by the war and began for various reasons ranging from acts of rebellion against extremely severe conditions of German occupation, to a deep sense of bewilderment at what was witnessed and experienced.

However, it can be argued that the notion of diary writing among adults as well as children, stemmed from a strong inclination in Jewish circles to research and study social issues. In her article, Zenderland created a link with the distinct interest of YIVO, in particular Max Weinreich, in the wellbeing of Jewish youth as a major contributor using writing as a tool of self-expression, under the very difficult circumstances of war. Weinreich estimated that the problem Jewish youngsters faced arose not only from their age but most significantly from their Jewishness.[36]

Interviews, Testimonies, Memoires

In contrast to diaries, written while events were taking place and mostly dependent on personal initiatives, testimonials were a deliberate and usually organized activity practiced during and after the war. This does not mean personal diaries did not include testimonials from other people.[37] Testimonials, fundamentally intentional and geared by historical consciousness, sought to gather knowledge, understand and commemorate the effects of the war on Jews. Since mostly organizations collected these accounts, it helped to centralize activities while spreading the idea that personal stories were valuable.

Jockusch traced documentation to a distinctive east European Jewish tradition that had begun in the late nineteenth century and was directly influenced by Dubnow's approach. However, Garbarini argued that Holocaust testimonial literature was part of political efforts to document mass violence similar to volumes seeking to record atrocities following the First World War, such as James Bryce and Arnold Toynbee's, *The Treatment of Armenians in the Ottoman Empire 1915-1916* and *Les Pogromes en Ukraine sous les gouvernements ukrainiens (1917-1920)* (Pogroms in Ukraine under the Ukrainian Government).[38]

Garbarini maintained that how Second World War *Black Books* were edited emphasized the unprecedented nature of Nazi massacres. Nevertheless, these books were not part of any centrally organized initiative, but the result of commemoration endeavors inspired by survivors, which is why each book had its own editor, whose work relied on documentation format and historical accounts employed in such books previously.

One prominent characteristic of these publications was addressing the notion of disbelief, an obvious, widespread approach echoed in volumes published after the Armenian massacre.[39] Garbarini posited that the notion of doubt in testimonies, surfaced too in different genres, such as Primo Levi's *If This Is a Man*. Levi's choice to start his book with allusions to the authenticity of events described therein, echoed attitudes towards atrocity literature, whose contents were largely regarded as witnesses' exaggerations.[40]

Documentation efforts started during the war in various places around Europe including the west. In France, for instance, Isaac Schneersohn (1879-1969), on April 28, 1943, gathered about forty people in an apartment in Grenoble, then under the Italian occupation, to set out on a mission to collect documents about Jewish persecution.[41] Eventually, their materials became essential for the prosecution of Nazi war criminals at Nuremberg and later trials.[42]

In 1943, Ilya Ehrenburg (1919–1967), a writer, journalist and historian, along with Vasily Semyonovich Grossman (1905-1964), a chemist, writer and journalist, began documenting the Nazis' systematic annihilation of Soviet Jewry.[43] Both men were members of the Jewish Anti-Fascist Committee in the Soviet Union and had edited *The Black Book of Russian Jewry*, a particular genre that had been classified as *atrocity literature*. Interestingly, in 1946, Stalin forbade publishing the book, and finally the original version of the book was approved for publication between 1990 – 1993.[44]

In Lithuania, there were several important documentation ventures.[45] Herman Kruk, the Vilnius ghetto librarian who documented events as they were happening, and whose diary had a distinct historical agenda. Kassow observed that Kruk's diary seems slightly more personal than Ringelblum's and this was due to historical developments, when researching Jewish history was a personal quest unsupported by state or university.[46] Kruk's notebooks from the ghetto and Klooga camp in Estonia were recovered after the war.[47] Abraham (Avrom) Suckewer's report was initiated after the war ended as he was encouraged by Ehrenburg, to return to Vilnius to collect survivors' testimonies. In February 1946, Suckewer gave his testimony at the Nuremberg trials against Franz Murer who had murdered his mother and son.

In Poland, there was Ringelblum's archive established in the early days of the war. Undoubtably, this is one prominent example of attempts to create a body of knowledge while the war was still raging. Materials collected were buried in three different places around the ghetto but to this day, only two hiding places have been discovered. The archive ceased to exist after the

Holocaust Diary Writing and Space

final days of the uprising in May 1943, although between August 1943 and March 1944, Ringelblum continued writing monographs and essays about the destroyed ghetto.

Another important documentation venture in Poland was in Łódź where Chaim Mordechaj Rumkowski (1877-1944), the controversial head of the *Judenrat* (Jewish Council appointed by the occupant) ordered Henrik Naftalin, a lawyer, to start an archive as soon as the ghetto was established, February 8, 1940. Chronicles were written daily from January 1941 until July 1944, a month before the ghetto's liquidation. Although Rumkowski was conscious that the archive was becoming a major documentation resource, including eyewitness accounts, he looked the other way and allowed the work to continue.[48] Apparently, Oskar Rosenfeld (1884-1944) and Oskar Singer (1893-1944), who also kept personal diaries, decided at the end of 1943 to add an encyclopedia which included a lexicon of personalities, specific terms and concepts unique to the Łódź ghetto. They explained it was necessary '... lest posterity fails to understand some of the ghetto terminology.'[49]

Most of this material survived having been buried in three different locations. In August 1944, Nachman Zonabend, who was in a group of Jewish prisoners left to clear away the rubble of the ghetto, used this opportunity to secretly sneak into the administrative offices to rescue materials left behind.[50] He hid them in the ghetto post office and when the war ended, gave the materials to the Jewish Historical Commission. Another part, hidden in the cemetery, was burnt by the Germans and a third was found in November 1946 at 13 Lutomierska Street, where the fire department used to be.[51]

Jewish survivors started collecting every possible document they could lay their hands on, following the '... models developed by the prewar YIVO.'[52] Indeed, the establishment of Jewish Historical Commissions around Europe after the war seemed to be a natural continuation of YIVO's approach. Two important factors should be considered, first, the very idea of establishing commissions and second, reinstating YIVO's methodology for documentation and applying it in these commissions. This clearly affirmed that personal accounts were as valuable for their facts and details as historical information.[53]

Clearly, gathering testimonies was at no stage questioned as a primary tool to learn about these events. By the end of the Second World War, this idea was beyond criticism, rather it was the core on which research rested.[54] Moreover, this approach was also adopted in various legal ventures of Nazi criminals' prosecution.

One notable commission was in August 29, 1944, in liberated Lublin. Five survivors, including Reuven Ben-Shem, established the Jewish Historical Commission. Given the dire situation in Poland in general, and that of Jews in particular, the existence of the commission may be regarded as proof of the importance survivors attributed to collecting testimonies.[55]

Felix Tych stated it was not surprising that the first steps to comprehend the scale of the tragedy were taken in Poland, and that this attempt should be regarded through the lens of Emanuel Ringelblum's initial efforts.[56] Still, in 1945, few knew about Ringelblum's archive, but in 1946 and later in 1950, two parts were recovered.[57] Tych made an important observation, that even if those who established the Central Jewish Historical Commission were largely unaware of the proportion of devastation, each was personally exposed to Nazi persecution.[58] Their initial approach was that a true reconstruction of this historical event would be impossible without Jews testifying. Indeed, it seems their most significant achievement was at the Department of Registration and Statistics, which created the *Central File of Polish Jews* and managed to gather 280,000 names of survivors.[59]

Other countries also established historical commissions. On July 1, 1945, an important commission was established in Munich in the American Zone. The American Central Historical Commission (CHC) was headed by Moshe Feigenbaum and according to Boaz Cohen, its role was not only to collect survivors' testimonies, but also to document Jewish life before the war.[60] In addition to 2,250 testimonies, the committee also published a newspaper, *Fun Letstn Khurban* (From our Last Destruction), printed books written by survivors and ethnographical collections of folklore created under Nazi rule.[61]

Nella Rost who worked with the Jewish Historical Commission in Łódź, adopted the model and started interviewing Polish-Jewish refugees in Stockholm in 1946. A similar center was established in France, Centre d'Etude d'Histoire des Juifs Polonais (Centre for the Study of the History of Polish Jews) which also focused on testimonies by Polish Jewish refugees. In Linz, Austria, another commission was established and later, under the influence of Simon Wiesenthal, it focused on assembling evidence against Nazi war criminals.[62]

Finally, we must not forget three important bulks of testimonies: those initiated by individuals, testimonies collected from children and *Yizkor Books*, all ventures characterizing the immediate post-war period. One famous collection is David Boder's (1886-1961), an American psychologist. He arrived in Paris at the end of July 1946 and managed to interview 130 refugees in nine languages. His work is considered among the earliest (if not the first) to have made audio recordings of testimonies.[63]

Jockusch affirmed that historical commissions considered children's testimonies valuable for both future historical research, and rehabilitation.[64] In different CJHC branches in Poland, Maria Hochberg-Mariańska (Miriam Peleg) and Noe Grüss gathered testimonies from children, and adults' accounts about children.[65] Lena Küchler (later Silberman), founder of a Jewish children's orphanage in Zakopane later published interviews she had conducted with some of the children under her care in *Meine Kinder* (My Children).[66] Benjamin Tenenbaum (Tene) (1914-1999) collected hundreds of unique testimonies which children themselves wrote.[67]

What is outstanding is the fact that after the war, so many people still found the energy to tell their stories, as well as document those of others. Significantly, most of those involved in initiating the collection of personal accounts were not historians and had other professions before the war. The war provoked this shift in occupation and had it not been for the war, these people probably would never have turned to documentation of their lives or those of others.

Considering the devastating situation all over Europe and survivors' poor condition, their willingness to address communal responsibilities rather than personal rehabilitation is not obvious. Stemming from cultural historical approaches to testimonial texts, it appears that this frenzy to record should be regarded as an event in its own right. It may be argued that it manifested communal but also individual Jewish awareness of the responsibility to document war events from the Jewish perspective, an obligation and challenge which rested on their shoulders and that preceded addressing their personal needs. Indirectly, testimonies enabled some to track down lost acquaintances thus contributing to filling gaps.[68]

Still, records of the Jewish historical commission in Lublin showed that many refugees had to be convinced to tell their stories to the committee, and that there were discussions about the best way to convince people to testify.[69] Among survivors, some felt that addressing their past was too heavy a burden, especially in view of their harsh present, that is, not only personal physical and emotional desolation but also daily survival difficulties, ranging from finding lodgings to coping with antisemitism.[70] With time, reluctance to testify lessened as more people agreed to do so while others chose to write their personal memories.

Another interesting form of commemoration was *Yizkor Books* (Memorial Books), dedicated to commemorating destroyed communities. According to Gutman, *Yizkor Books*, were the most familiar and accessible form of commemoration and constituted a special category because they were initiated mostly by *landsmanshaftn* (hometown societies of Jewish migrants from the same European town or region). These books were written by contributors who were not professional historians and therefore, they were not error free.[71] For survivors, these were a sort of portable memorial that could accompany them wherever they went, for most indeed left Europe.[72] They had a dual significance: on the one hand, they were a symbolic burial place and on the other, when a tombstone or monument was finally erected, although meaningful in its own right, it gained added significance.[73] The most important part of these texts were lists of names, which preserved each person's individuality not only from oblivion but also from Nazi attitudes to Jews.[74]

Yizkor Books concerned both Ben-Shem and Ringelblum because both had contributed articles to these interesting books in more than one way. Some of Ringelblum's prewar articles were incorporated into the book of Płock, for example, where his research '*The Minute-Book of the Tailors' Union*'[75] was included. Other memorial books concentrated on commemorating Ringelblum, among them Buczacz, his native town,[76] and Warsaw.[77] *The book of Nowy Sącz*, where Ringelblum's family found refuge during the First World War and which was edited by Raphael Mahler, also dedicated an article in memory of Ringelblum.

Ben-Shem himself contributed entries to *Yizkor Books* and his activities in Poland were commemorated in several of them. Texts discussing Kovel's *Hashomer Hatzair* have already been mentioned, but similar passages were added to the book of Tłuszcz, Radzymin where Ben-Shem contributed a passage in honor of Shoshana Kossower-Rozencwajg (Emilka), who rescued him and his family, as well as Emanuel Ringelblum. Ben-Shem also contributed passages he had written to the books of Warsaw and Ozeryany where he and his family had resided.

III

Between Historical and Personal Motivation

Why Write?

Garbarini and Goldberg pointed out that turning to diary writing during the war characterized not only Jews, but also non-Jews. Garbarini quoted Ursula von Kardorff, who published an article in 1942, in which she observed that despite difficulties presented by the war, many people were engaged in writing diaries and this phenomenon was due to the war.[1]

Indeed, during the Holocaust, it appears that diary writing was arguably more prevalent than any other form of writing. As previously mentioned, owing to the special circumstances of the war, the genre of diaries, includes those written contemporaneously as well as writings that were a combination of diaries and memoires.[2] Unlike testimonies, or whether diaries were personal or intentionally historical, writing depended on individual endeavor.

According to Woolf, diaries as a genre developed following the decline in the popularity of chronicles. Until the 16th century, chronicles designed to document the present were the main form of recording history. However, the invention of printing rendered the genre redundant, thus paving the way to more personal documentation.[3] Nevertheless, rather than disappearing, chronicles had actually fragmented into other literary forms more suited to an age of increasing literacy, among them newspapers, diaries, biographies, autobiographies and also historically oriented texts.

Goldberg explained that by the 18th century, diaries were considered a type of self-expression and were associated not only with intimacy, but also socio-political agitation.[4] In addition, great historical changes, on the one hand, mingled with severe personal oppression, on the other, produced personal crises, which translated into diary writing becoming widespread.[5] This explains why during the Nazi era, among Jews and non-Jews, diary writing flourished, including in Nazi Germany.[6]

The reaction of Jews to the vacuum created when the war began was influenced greatly by preconceived world views translated into personal initiatives of documentation. According to Waxman, as soon as Ringelblum realized there would be no help from the free world, his documentation focus shifted to gathering as much evidence as possible.[7] In this respect, Ringelblum, who initially recorded events himself, was not alone. Many people made it their own business to document events through testimony or writing diaries, but Ringelblum's *Oneg Shabbat* was one of few systematic réseaux and even in captivity he endeavored to continue documentation.[8]

In Warsaw, Ringelblum encouraged people to immerse themselves in writing, while he and his *Oneg Shabbat* team did their utmost to collect as many testimonies as possible. In most cases, they found Jews willingly cooperated with them by accepting the challenge to testify, to provide their own written testimonies as well as write diaries documenting their experiences. Samuel Kassow's choice to title his book *Who Will Write Our History?*, which deals with Emanuel Ringelblum and the *Oneg Shabbat Archive*, managed to catch the sense of urgency to record events that had haunted Ringelblum since the beginning of the war.

Scholars, who have discussed changes in documentation purposes, noted that because the persecution of Jews during the Second World War was unprecedented, nothing had prepared them for such eventualities or experiences. In other words, one factor accelerating changes in writing and documenting purposes depended on conceiving the true nature of what Jews were experiencing. Therefore, one concern was how to convey events so that they sounded neither exaggerated nor treated as lies. Sensitivity to the issue was very high because Jews themselves had trouble believing rumors circulating.[9]

Hilel Zeidman (1914-1995) addressed the question and came up with what he considered a solution. He wrote that there were people who had urged him to write while others had dismissed it claiming that there was no point because '… people from the outside would not want to spoil their appetite, disturb their peaceful sleep… and most of all, they would not want to believe.'[10] His solution corresponded to the widespread conception at the time: 'Not to describe but to 'take notes' and 'catch moments' … to photograph them 'while they were still hot'…'.[11] This notion of photography, using words rather than actual cameras became a recurring notion voiced often in contemporaneous texts, including those of Ringelblum and Ben-Shem.

The notion of credibility haunted not only those who lived through the events but survivors too, as they were well aware that many of their testimonies sounded too improbable. One such example can be found in Primo Levi's book, which along with providing a psychological explanation as to why he felt the need to write, he added a vow that his narratives were all the absolute truth.[12] Although concern about authenticity should have disappeared as years passed, and documents as well as research supported Holocaust accounts, the notion of belief remains an issue. Parallel counter-accounts, a phenomenon known as Holocaust denial, try to erode and subvert not only testimonies but also documentation as well as photographs and films taken at the time.

Just like Ringelblum, the historian Yitzhak Schiper who was imprisoned in Majdanek after the uprising in the Warsaw Ghetto, had no question about the importance of documentation. He was cited by Alexander Donat to have said that should the Germans win the war, he was unsure whether what happened to the Jews would be regarded negatively, as history was known to be written by the victors. Yet, he was confident that Jews would get to write the history of that period which he characterized as a history of 'blood and tears.'[13]

Kassow wrote that, unlike Schiper, Ringelblum '… had no doubt that the world would indeed believe…',[14] because it all depended on providing reliable evidence. Ringelblum was convinced that the *Oneg Shabbat* archive was precisely the tool to persuade others, beyond any doubt, that what was documented was reliable information. Therefore, archive members, with Ringelblum at the head, sought to gather as much and diverse evidence as possible including personal commentaries, reports, testimonies, personal diaries and data-based research to write the history of the war from the Jewish point of view.[15]

To tackle the issue of belief, Ringelblum's insistence on procuring contemporary testimonies as well as up to date diaries was especially important.[16] Kassow emphasized that this was because Ringelblum was sensitive to manipulations of memory, and therefore he strove to collect as many contemporary testimonies and diaries as possible, as he considered them to be more reliable sources. In such contemporaneous documentation, he was certain to find representations of reasoning and emotional realities correlating to ongoing events.

On the same issue Schiper and Ringelblum related to how documentation might affect the universal value of the Jewish tragedy. Both agreed that this was not only a Jewish story but Schiper voiced a serious concern that believing Jews would automatically project negatively on the whole human race: '… who will believe us? Nobody will want to believe us as our disaster is the disaster of the entire civilized world…'.[17] Whereas Schiper worried that documentation would project negatively on non-Jews and therefore they would be reluctant to face the consequences of the Jewish tragedy, Ringelblum believed that once the truth was revealed, it would not be treated as only a Jewish tragedy but as a human crisis.[18] It seems that Ringelblum ascribed data he and his team were collecting to conclusive powers that would silence those who did not want to believe. In this, Ringelblum may have shown a somewhat naïve attitude as he ignored emotions Schiper considered to be more powerful than physical evidence, as definitive as it may be.

Zygmunt Bauman also acknowledged that the Holocaust was a Jewish tragedy, but in his opinion, it was not only a Jewish problem or an event that was solely related to the history of the Jewish people, instead it concerned the whole world as 'The Holocaust was born and executed in our modern rational society, at the high stage of our civilization and at the peak of human cultural achievement, and for this reason it is a problem of that society, civilization and culture.'[19]

Although this quote suggests that Bauman agreed that the Jewish tragedy should be a universal concern, according to him, it was Jews as well as the state of Israel that had appropriated the Holocaust thus preventing the world from drawing conclusions-lessons from that tragedy. What is more, in his view, the state of Israel made cynical use of this approach to justify in public opinion controversial political moves.[20] The result according to Bauman was that this attitude estranged non-Jews and prevented civilization from studying the issue as a human tragedy. In this, Bauman blamed Jews for the world's failure to see the Holocaust as a human catastrophe.

Efforts to procure up to date information would prove to be central because those who documented events as they were happening, exposed the process of events, reactions and perceptions leading to total annihilation, without their records being affected by the extermination itself. In other words, in records taken down after extermination, previous events were obscured by the knowledge organized murder was a reality. Such records tended to present this triangular model through the lens of the aftermath. Thus, in representing phenomena that preceded mass-killing, the perception of occurrences was affected by knowledge of the end-result, murder, consequently diminishing in importance that which preceded annihilation.[21] Furthermore, looking back, anything that occurred before organized murder began, seemed relatively minor while becoming a source of criticism as well as self-reproach for not foreseeing the final end in time.

In *Warsaw Testaments* written in Israel, Rachel Auerbach stated:

> Not once did I write that the proliferation of culture and art, the development of spiritual contents, take second place after the Jewish

resistance movement in the scale of ghetto values. Now, I am certain that the movement of culture and resistance are not two different things, but simply two sides of the same phenomenon.[22]

Auerbach's words demonstrate the difference between insights during the war, particularly, ghettoization, to perceptions after the war. While she was living in the ghetto, cultural activities were a part of attempts to survive mentally, but only looking back could Auerbach comprehend that nurturing culture in the ghetto was not only a form of rebellion – claiming a voice, a space, things that Jews had been denied at a growing speed – but also instilled resilience enabling actual resistance later.

Kassow denoted a categorical and distinct difference between diaries and testimonies given after systematic extermination had become a reality. Contemporary diaries offered a glimpse into current states of mind helping to understand how the persecuted processed and deciphered these events.[23] The value of synchronous records lay in their contents, which allowed historians to conceive not only events but how writers felt and what implications these sensations had in choices made.

Garbarini added that the subjective characteristics of diaries were in fact an advantage as they brought authentic voices from the era discussed thus helping to eliminate relativism in historical accounts of the present.[24] To add to this discussion, Michael Bernard-Donals stressed that the uniqueness of the Holocaust lay in the inconceivable developments that made it, in a sense, an a-historic event due to its deviation from familiar historical processes.[25] Therefore, all sorts of contemporary reports had the capacity to expose the confusion, lack of orientation and turmoil experienced by Jews who were experiencing these enormous challenges.

The Nazis wanted to conceal, hide, and eliminate all traces of Jews – their physical as well as their lived spaces. To use Roskies's terminology, after defining and isolating Jew-zones, eradicating them. By writing, Jews reversed Nazi intent as writing carved their lived spaces onto paper thus substituting physical spaces with a verbal universe. Lefebvre stated, 'The uncertain traces left by events are not the only marks on (or in) space: society in its actuality also deposits its script, the result and product of social activities. Time has more than one writing system.'[26] While Lefebvre drew upon the importance of actual physical traces of 'lived spaces', that is, human manifestation of spatial activity, he pointed out that these were not the only forms that left a mark but that writing was another product of lived spaces, a manner in which human experience was abstractly engraved in space.

By mentioning 'time', he called upon the inextricable link between time and space as the production of space happened over time. If this production was written about, it was made timeless, because it elevated it beyond physical space, to another sphere thus enabling a combination of time and manner to render it timeless, hence, 'Time has more than one writing system.'[27]

Writing was indeed a spatial manner of commemoration as those who wrote hoped that words they were putting on paper would serve not only as historical documentation, but also as personal memorials. This was Ben-Shem's declared explicit intention put down in one of the notebooks he began writing in hiding. First, he presented himself and his ancestry. Then, he gave the reason he had decided to start documenting his family's whereabouts, in March 1943. He stated that he was hiding at a Polish family's house, hoping to survive the war and diligently specified what to do with the manuscript if it was found after his death stressing a wish to make the manuscript available for the public.[28]

Documentation as stemming from a historic obligation was a notion that preoccupied Ben-Shem as well as Kaplan. However, whereas Ben-Shem decided to write because of the war, Kaplan routinely wrote a diary for a period of eight years before the war. Nonetheless, On January 16, 1940, Kaplan addressed the change in his writing purpose and referred to a sense of historical commitment that made him regard writing his diary as a moral pledge he would pursue despite the difficulties presented by conditions in the ghetto. He added that he, whom he called '... one of the few 'happy' whose pen was like a fountain',[29] was not deterred by the dangers. He talked about 'sensing'[30] the hour as if he were a seismograph, an 'inner awareness', a 'national obligation' as well as a 'historic obligation' ending the passage that he was certain he had been chosen by 'Providence' to fulfil the task and his notes would serve as '... historiographical material for the next historian.'[31]

In this particular entry Kaplan alluded to several notions motivating his writing and constituting a mélange of personal features, such as being especially prolific and an inner certitude that a higher authority, 'Providence', had assigned him the task. This sense of religious vocation 'fortified' him to fulfil a secular task of documentation for historical purposes. Although Kaplan did not refer to preserving his story for posterity, the name he gave the diary, 'Scroll of Agony', at the beginning of notebook number nine, hinted at its contents and significance. Scrolls, a term originating in the biblical, is meant to refer to their nature as texts written over time. Even as Kaplan attributed great value to history, he tied together the secular nature of history as a discipline to its religious connotations originating in the doctrine not to forget and to pass legacies onto future generations.

In *Numbered Days*, Garbarini reviewed about ninety, mostly unpublished diaries she had researched. She asserted that writing during the war was indeed a spatial activity as pages replaced the progressive decline in physical spaces. Jews' writing was their way of carving themselves an opening that was at the same time, spatial as well as temporal, in the ever-growing chaos of overcrowded spaces into which they were squeezed. Pages replaced missing spaces while becoming a confident, a 'friend' where one could '... make sense of the perils...'.[32] Jews' motivation to write diaries or maintain personal records of different sorts, wrote Garbarini, originated in what was happening to them.

Another central theme of her research was to show that Jews' reactions to their hardships were not identical, on the contrary, they were varied, nuanced and insightful. Garbarini declared, that for her, it was an end of its own to show the '... heterogeneity of the victims, of their experiences of their wartime perceptions and coping strategies.'[33] By analyzing contents of written responses, that is, their diverse conceptual orientation, Garbarini sought to challenge any attempt to reduce victims' cultural reactions to persecution into a single unanimous retort. In this way, she sought to avoid relating to Jews in the Nazi accustomed manner, to portray them as a single mass, as Jews chose many forms of response from writing diaries to cooperating with other documentation projects, letter writing, poems, as well as armed resistance.

Goldberg suggested that 'Stories had the power to situate us within our respective societies and cultures, because the building blocks of the story, such as language, figurative patterns, intertextual connotations, and even the genre within which the story is told are based on the existing practices and structures in the cultures and societies in which we live.'[34] This may apply to Richard Ehrlich, who like other authors, appeared to reinstate jeopardized epistemological framework not only by abiding to its previously familiar rules, but also by leaving a mark, inscribing existence inside the Nazi universe thus sustaining in it the old familiar space of expression.[35]

Indeed, one example illustrating the diversity of reactions is Richard Ehrlich's diary, whose characteristics fall within the genre of a classical diary. Incarcerated in Theresienstadt, his dated entries and letters were addressed to his ten-year-old son Willy, who had been sent to England before the war. Ehrlich's choice to react to events in this manner suggests that writing specifically to his son was meaningful. Garbarini explained that people who addressed their children wanted them to understand what it was like while incorporating educational reasoning into their texts.

She suggested that Ehrlich's text was not only a window into his debate with himself, but that the diary offered insights into evolving purposes of writing and the gap between his intentions and the final result. While Ehrlich attempted to make his account personal and pass both his and his wife's experiences in Theresienstadt onto their son Willy, he realized that his text would be unintelligible to his son if he did not precede the experiences with an objective introduction to Theresienstadt before describing life there.[36] Garbarini pointed to a paradoxical phenomenon, that is, the father becoming aware of the unintelligibility of his writing as it was an unfamiliar universe to his son. The realities both parents went through were not part of anyone's world, let alone their young son's.

Thus, Ehrlich understood that first the alien universe of Theresienstadt had to be decoded for Willy while he was struggling to become accustomed to Theresienstadt. Here another complexity was that he found it difficult to communicate the full scale of the tragedy because he was becoming emotionally detached, a sorely needed survival strategy in that situation. Indeed, the mere effort of trying to make sense to his son, highlights the epistemological gap in knowledge between not only father and son, but also between those who were there and those who were not. It appears it was through the process of writing that Ehrlich was able to regain the sensitivity he avoided and writing bridged this gap.[37] Hence, unintentionally, Ehrlich ended up giving a fairly accurate and objective description of Theresienstadt.

However, creating that separate writing space was not that simple and included perils derived from changes in the language as a tool of communication. Boaz Neumann pointed out that 'In the Nazi language, the gap between the word and the action was rejected.'[38] By this he suggested that the raison d'être of the 'language of action' originated in its capacity to lead to the application of deeds. Apparently, Neumann seemed to allude to the notion that the domain of speech shifted into that of action, thus causing the word to lose its metaphorical qualities. Hence, the worlds of action and speech, separated before, merged into one. Neumann explained that this change in the function of language could be understood as criticism against intellectualism, generally regarded by Nazis as the pointless practice of overusing words.[39] Neumann concluded that the change that had caused the decline of the German language was due to its loss of autonomy as a language, that is, voiding the language of its metaphorical characteristics.[40]

Undeniably, the manner in which language was employed by Nazis not only created new unfamiliar patterns of speech, comprehensible only to them, but the use of language in this way became a devastating weapon against those declared as their enemies, namely Jews. It became a weapon to deceive their victims for whom words remained anchored in a traditional order, thus preventing them from conceiving their true new meaning. In this respect, for Jews, writing and documenting events, using words in their old contexts, before they migrated from the field of semantics to the world of action, acted as a tool to reinstate the old world thus making the new one comprehensible, at least partially, to oneself and others.[41]

This theory explains the role writing had, as diarists used their own cultural tools to reconstruct their space, thus placing themselves inside a familiar framework, in itself, placed in a hostile environment. Whereas the Nazis created and operated in a world of distorted concepts, where the very building blocks of the archeology of knowledge were destroyed beyond recognition, victims' written expression preserved the old order by presenting the twists and perversity of the Nazi universe using the same cultural strategies.

Writing functioned as a rehabilitation space or even cosmos, where what was described was expressed and interpreted in cultural tools familiar to writers. This became even clearer once the wheels of extermination turned, thus making writing even more urgent, because despite physical annihilation, words left behind resurged as life forms of their own. However, using previous language patterns unintentionally contributed to concealing the change in Nazi semantics from the eyes of the recorders themselves, as in this way the process hindered and delayed insights and comprehension of the situation.

Rachel Einwohner examined the differences in Jewish responses in three major ghettoes: Warsaw and Łódź in Poland, and Vilnius in Lithuania. The purpose was to understand variations in reactions and trace their origin. The results showed that the development of the notion of rebellion in ghettoes depended on access to knowledge. Whereas in Łódź no rumors of attempted organized murder reached the ghetto in time, Vilnius was first to identify that the murder of Jews in the Ponar (Ponary) forest was not a local phenomenon. News of this arrived in Warsaw in the winter of 1941-1942 but Varsovians, in particular the older generation, found it very hard to believe these rumors. Einwohner argued that this difficulty in believing may be classified as cultural ignorance.

This was manifested in two ways: people's ability to verify information and the second principle (formulated by Snow and Benford in 1988), referring to people's incapacity to go beyond a certain cultural barrier.[42] Indeed, David Wdowinski wrote that news about organized and systematic murders streamed into the ghetto from the end of 1941. At that point in time, Jews believed this information but they related it to local whims. Things changed when in April 1942, Zwi and Moshe Zilberberg, two revisionist members arrived in Warsaw and recounted the liquidation of the Lublin Ghetto. Wdowinski himself broke the news to Adam Czerniaków (1880-1942), head of the *Judenrat* in Warsaw, who assured him that the Germans had promised nothing like that would ever happen in Warsaw. Then, Wdowinski took the two messengers to Zionist leaders, including Dr. Yitzhak Schiper who reacted saying, 'You Revisionists were always hot tempered...' while declaring that they had the word of Hans Frank (1900-1946) head of the General Government in Poland, that no such thing would occur.[43]

Waxman specified that testifying was first and foremost designed to warn, but added that warning was also a form of rebellion. According to Waxman, testimony provided by Yakov Grojanowski who had escaped from Chełmno to Warsaw at the end of 1941, and whose experiences were recorded in the Ringelblum archive, marked another shift not only in the purpose of documentation, but also in levels of information available to ghetto inmates.[44] Zivia Lubetkin created the link between warning and rebellion to cultural activism in the ghetto. She asserted that youth movements' cultural activism was indeed resistance nuancing this observation by saying that '... as long as we thought that those decrees were meant to dehumanize us, our war was to keep our human dignity, to develop the spirit of rebellion against those decrees. When I say rebellion, I don't mean a particular rebellion but to preserve the human, cultural and social dignity of the young.'[45]

Gutman agreed with this approach and claimed that one should interpret cultural activity as a part of resistance because it came from the same milieu, the youth movements, whose calls for resistance emerged once information about large scale murderous operations reached the ghetto.[46] In this Garbarini proposed that writing, operated as a weapon to resist the Nazis as cultural activity had a symbolic meaning, which later was translated into actual physical resistance. Indeed, Lubetkin confirmed that once Michael Podchlebnik and Yaakov Grojanowski testified about Chełmno, attitudes in the ghetto changed.[47] Lubetkin said it was easier to believe this information because it followed rumors of systematic murder taking place in Vilnius. She stressed that as soon as they heard reports from Łódź, they stopped all cultural activity and '... all our activities were aimed at active defense.'[48]

Auerbach, Lubetkin and Gutman who were all survivors, offer the point of view of time – then, they could not have imagined cultural activities were a corridor leading to active rebellion. In Israel, there was room for perspectives that only time could have produced. Their narratives reflect the complexity of the experienced situations and the burden of living with those memories.

Goldberg criticized the expansion of the concept of resistance into interpreting almost every activity as resistance because it disregarded the traumatic aspects of the very action of writing. He adopted the psychological approach to explain writing as means to cope with personal trauma. Accordingly, attributing to writing the paradigm of an act affirming human existence, interpreting narratives as therapeutically redeeming, as if writing created an inner space where diary writers liberated themselves from destruction and death happening around them, ignored the meaning of writing.[49]

Goldberg suggested that by writing, an author's intention was not really to tell but to show, to achieve as much identification as possible, while warning readers that the testimonies they were about to read addressed the loss of the humane rather than its affirmation.[50] Indeed, in one part of Reuven Ben-Shem's diary, he warned readers before continuing to read the testimony he heard from a so far unidentified person called Platt, about his experiences in Treblinka.[51] The passage stressed not only the dangers posed to future readers by exposure to such information, but also the perils of insanity for the person writing this testimony.

According to Goldberg, the reason bearers of witness warned future readers of the consequences of reading their texts was proof that writers had experienced human disintegration, the crumbling of identity in a most thorough manner.[52] Goldberg's approach suggests that writing diaries was no less an expression of trauma and breakdown and that just as the phenomenon represented self-construction, it also testified to the opposite. In this respect, diaries are complex representations of the Holocaust as they simultaneously express self-affirmation due to disintegration.[53]

Patterson suggested that by writing diaries, writers created a new form of relationship, on the one hand, with the diary itself as a listener and on the other, with the writer as speaker, a dual relationship necessary to recreate life.[54] Davis claimed that contents of Holocaust literature, whether diaries, stories, testimonies, or memoires, and linked directly to real occurrences, depended on listeners. In his analysis of Wiesel's *Night*, the trauma remained locked in, because the witness had no one with whom to share his story.[55] If no one was willing to listen, then tales remained not only muted but also unbelieved. In such cases, testimonies were voided of their meaning as well as their purpose. Thus, Patterson implies that the existence of the event depended on communicating it to others.

Whereas the impulse of modern diary writing has been largely aimed at self-understanding, Holocaust diaries sought the reverse, to document historical events affecting writers. This shift was opposite to the development of the genre that emerged from chronicles and evolved into the personal. In this respect, Holocaust diaries represent a retreat to the genre of chronicles because they documented the external and how it affected not only the 'I', the individual, but also the 'we' as a collective. Thus, one could claim that one typological particularity of Holocaust diaries was the conquest of the outside, external events of personal narratives. In such diaries, it is not the person writing the diary who is reflected, but the one representing other people in the same situation. This feature is especially prominent in places where diary writers experienced 'a routine' in some ways, but the manifestations of that routine were extremely violent, and in themselves required internalization of new unfamiliar codes of conduct and concepts. In these cases, the private, the first person, 'I', became the voice of a group.

Goldberg determined that autobiography during the Holocaust made the 'I' present, but at the same time, the very act of writing manifested the radical limitations of that 'I'.[56] Experienced events were so powerful that they had, on the one hand, merged individuals into one imaginary entity in the same community, while challenging and constantly contrasting the boundaries of private and communal palpitating spaces. Thus, Goldberg concluded that the very usage of the word indicating the self, 'I', in diaries of the Holocaust, actually contradicted the notion, as the 'I' was swallowed by the universal. Not only that, but the uniqueness of a person was destroyed as the experiences an individual underwent, although extreme, were similar to other people's tragedies. This means that even though personal harm was huge, by losing uniqueness, its magnitude shrunk as it was very much like the story of others.[57] This means, what happened to diary writers could be paralleled to a change in the human condition because of becoming an extension of others in the same situation. The private 'I' became 'we' even if this pronoun did not necessarily appear in the texts. Thus, expanding the private sphere by merging it with that of others abstractly enlarged individual boundaries.

Goldberg's theory attempted to explain the traumatic aspects close reading of diaries revealed. Yet, space distortion also appears to explain the reason people became so deeply engaged in writing. Being almost the only

Between Historical and Personal Motivation 77

means of reaction left, it came to signify for them a matter of life and death. I argue that the fact that diarists spoke on their own behalf as well as others, made expression a matter of preserving their existence. In fact, the eradication of human characteristics imposed on Jews was reinstated through the individualization of events by writing, while, at the same time, pouring into their stories social values originating in the awareness that they were speaking on behalf of others as well.

Another role diarists have attributed to their diaries was their apologetic features. Salek Perechodnik's is an example as he started documenting his experiences in hiding, and as a tribute to his wife and daughter. He called the diary 'a confession', and specifically addressed his wife, emphasizing that he was not seeking God's absolution, but his wife's as '...the only person who could have pardoned me although she didn't have to do it.'[58] Perechodnik, tormented by a deep sense of shame and remorse for not joining his wife and three-year-old daughter who had been arrested and deported, addressed his diary to them and, according to Garbarini, at the same time derived individual therapeutic benefits.[59]

Roskies pointed out that what characterizes confessional dairies was their split time zones before the event and in the aftermath. For Roskies, Perechodnik's choice to begin a diary in 1943, when no Jew was supposed to be alive, was an '... act of profound self-awareness.'[60] This document went back in time to terrible choices he had made while confronting present hardships he and others were still living through.

Lewin's reaction to the loss of his wife bears a similarity to Perechodnik's as he reported her loss on August 12, 1942, blaming himself for not following her into the carts going to Treblinka: 'There are no words to describe my agony. I should have followed her, that is, to die, but there is no strength to take such a step.'[61] However, unlike Perechodnik, Lewin wrote while events were taking place, and it is this difference in time that makes Lewin's writing unique as it offers a glimpse into decision making and impossible choices imposed on Jews. This time difference is significant because it is inextricably related to space, both physical and mental. Perechodnik wrote his diary in hiding, thus during a certain routine about events that had taken place about nine months earlier while coping with a grim present. Lewin, however, wrote while he and his daughter Ora were trying to avoid deportations, being on the run themselves.

Significantly, Lewin's manner of dealing with his wife's deportation was by removing himself from the action equation. By omitting the personal pronoun which may point to himself, Lewin evoked the shock he was in, the speed with which he had had to react but it appears that his lack of energy to follow his wife was hidden even from his own eyes by not using the personal pronoun pointing to himself.[62] A month later, on Rosh Hashana eve, September 15, 1942, in a long entry, Lewin went back to the loss of his wife by recording the horrific events that had taken place in the ghetto during the previous week. He compared himself to Mr. Świeca, who had taken only a few moments before deciding to follow his wife and children who were on their way to Treblinka. Lewin wrote that he was confident his wife, Luba would have done the same, but he, on the other hand '... didn't have enough strength to die together, with her, with the one that I loved so much.'[63]

Waxman stated that many diarists such as Lewin expressed vengeful thoughts and emotions as well as debates whether one should judge the whole German nation, or that judicial steps should be taken against individuals alone. After rumors coming from Łódź suggested that young children under the age of ten were hunted and deliberately murdered, Lewin emphatically concluded that whatever happened with Germany at the end of the war, 'Never will the blood of our children be erased from the Cain German people's forehead.'[64]

According to Ben-Shem, indeed, every sense of justice should object to blaming the entire German people for Nazi crimes. However, he claimed it was a fundamental mistake to think this way as the German people would not have been involved in murder, robbery, killing children, torturing thousands if these deeds were alien to their nature. Ben-Shem believed, 'The whole German people is poisoned, it is corrupt, it originates from Huns, and torture, murder and suffocation resides in their blood...'[65] Ben-Shem went on to claim that Hitler came to power because '... sadism and perversity inspire in Germany admiration and a deep flair to taking part in this sadistic process.'[66] As proof, he wrote that at the beginning of the war, '... there were cases among the military and clerks who had reacted humanely...'[67], but that later, almost all of them seemed to be plagued by 'massive sadism'.[68] Ben-Shem, who devoted much thought to the German people, concluded that in the struggle of Germans with their inner nature (he often referred to them as Huns), civilization lost and therefore, the whole German people should be judged and prosecuted.

One prominent aspect of survival was the deep sense of obligation to explain to oneself one's own survival. Why me, why was I saved and not others, what was my duty to the dead? In the introduction to the 2006 edition of *Night*, Eli Wiesel attributed his survival to pure chance and still felt compelled to justify it by giving it meaning, which became his initial motivation to write this book. He went further to say he had '... a moral obligation to try to prevent the enemy from enjoying one last victory by allowing his crimes to be erased from human memory.[69]

Chajka Klinger, who was chosen by members of her youth movement, *Hashomer Hatzair*, to be their documentarist, started her task when she was in hiding after escaping deportations from Będzin. In her first entry on Thursday, August 26, 1943, she wondered if her survival had a purpose. She wrote that her heart wanted to live so as to remember her friends from *Hashomer Hatzair* '... wanted it and they stuck it into my head every day. They wanted someone to remain and tell their story. And why indeed shouldn't they be resurrected on a piece of paper?'[70] In a long debate, Klinger moved from thinking and talking about her lost loved ones to trying to find reasons why she should stay alive. This first entry, written after so much suffering, ranged between a sincere sense of obligation, a debt, a desire to commemorate her friends, and the opposite, to '...throw away the pen...'[71]

Diaries and Testimonies as Historical Sources

For a long time, historical researchers viewed personal records as momentary impressions, or worse, unreliable sources of information. According to Cull, Culbert, and Welch, this was because personal diaries and testimonies were considered propaganda, a term used to refer to information that turned out to be false.[72] Document volumes, which in addition to information, included testimonies about abuse of civilians were considered part of 'atrocity propaganda' and therefore scrutinized for their reliability.[73] Regardless, this remained the preferred genre to discuss such events during and after the Second World War, but since editors of document volumes were aware of their questionable reputation, they used a variety of methods to validate their credibility.[74] Even so, until the 1980s, this literature remained generally mistrusted and therefore outside of the repository of sources in academic historical research.

Indeed, the substantial body of personal accounts available immediately after the war did not automatically belong to the type of sources accepted in traditional modern historical research.[75] Researchers snubbed approaches adopted by YIVO as well as other similar historical schools such as Annals in France and sociological approaches stemming from communist historical doctrines. Eyewitness accounts were considered biased, sometimes indoctrinated and unreliable sources.[76]

Anna Bikont interviewed Prof. Israel Gutman in relation to testimonies about the murder of Jews by their Polish neighbors in several villages in northeast Poland, including Jedwabne. Gutman was quoted to have said that in the early stages of researching the Holocaust, scholars were careful with survivors' testimonies. He explained that these were regarded as inaccurate at best, because a witness could see only part of an event and what one did not witness personally, was completed by hearsay. Gutman expressed repentance for refusing to believe testimonies and said that they (he spoke as a scholar at Yad-Vashem) felt guilty about it.[77] His explanation was that testimonies regarding Jedwabne were rejected as exaggerated because of previous assumptions, also based on what the historian Szymon Datner had published in 1966.

Gutman added that it was his own personal postulation that residents of small towns would find it difficult to commit such crimes, while he falsely assumed that indifference or the willingness to eradicate Jews characterized the population in larger cities. Gutman further stated that the combination of these two factors had prevented him from paying attention to the subtext in Datner's account, which confirmed the allegation made by the few witnesses who survived the massacres in those towns. Indeed, at the time, Datner was under the tight supervision imposed by the Communist government on all Poles, including historians, to control narratives to suit political purposes rather than expose the true facts.[78]

Gutman's interview exposed two important issues: first, automatically labeling testimonies as initially incredulous, and second, that until the 1980s, historiography was primarily based on official documentation because it was considered reliable and as such, objective. This corresponds to the general position in historical research in Israel too, an attitude which was influenced by German approaches to historical research predominant at the time and which, until the 1980s, divided historians at Yad-Vashem too.[79]

Maybe the first crack in this belief can be traced to the controversy around the publication of Raul Hilberg's book, *The Destruction of the European Jews*, in 1961. Hilberg's research which distinctly relied on German official documents, led him to controversial conclusions which stood out particularly compared to information witnesses had provided during the Eichmann trial. It is in light of the trial that one should read Yad-Vashem's repentance for its previous decision to publish the book. Four months after agreeing on the publication of Hilberg's research, Yad-Vashem changed its mind following a heated discussion on the editorial board. Two reasons were given: the first was the fact Hilberg relied almost exclusively on German sources and the second was that Yad-Vashem criticized the book's conclusions which compared the Holocaust to previous historical epochs and Hilberg's poor assessment of Jewish responses.[80]

In 1963, Hannah Arendt, who was sent by The New Yorker to cover the Eichmann trial, infuriated Jewish communities around the world and caused much controversy with her reports from the courthouse. One of her important observations was:

> To a Jew this role of the Jewish leaders in the destruction of their own people is undoubtedly the darkest chapter of the whole dark story. It had been known about before, but it has now been exposed for the first time in all its pathetic and sordid detail by Raul Hilberg, whose standard work *The Destruction of the European Jews* I mentioned before. In the matter of cooperation, there was no distinction between the highly assimilated Jewish communities of Central and western Europe and the Yiddish-speaking masses of the east. In Amsterdam as in Warsaw, in Berlin as in Budapest, Jewish officials could be trusted to compile the lists of persons and of their property, to secure money from the deportees to defray the expenses of their deportation and extermination, to keep track of vacated apartments, to supply police forces to help seize Jews and get them on trains, until, as a last gesture, they handed over the assets of the Jewish community in good order for final confiscation.[81]

Obviously, Arendt's article and later, book, led to passionate discussions because she openly accused Jews of being responsible for their own tragedy. Furthermore, Arendt claimed that had it not been for the cooperation of *Judenrat* community leaders, many more people could have been saved. In addition, she made no distinction between assimilated and orthodox Jews, all of whom, she claimed, cooperated with and took part in the scheme to rob Jews of all their possessions.

In response, Norman Podhoretz blamed Arendt of basing her accusations solely on Hilberg's book, which she herself mentioned.[82] The title of Podhoretz's article, which acknowledged her brilliant intellectual capacities, defined them also as perverse. He wrote that the proof was that the *Eichmann in Jerusalem: A Report on the Banality of Evil* thesis was the result of Arendt self-importance and '...a mind infatuated with its own agility and bent on generating dazzle.'[83]

On behalf of *The Leo Baeck Institute in Jerusalem*, Ziegfried Moses presented Arendt with a formal declaration of war not only addressed to her personally, but also against Bruno Bettelheim and Raul Hilberg both of whom had also suggested that Jewish response to the Holocaust had been passive.[84] Arendt and Moses met in Basel on March 1963, but the result of the meeting did not please either of them. The institute published a public protest but it had no effect on the contents in Arendt's book, yet the mere discussion convinced the *Leo Baeck Institute in Jerusalem* board to research beyond 1933, which they had been reluctant to do previously.[85]

Another point of controversy brought up by Arendt, related to her attitude to witnesses and the contents of their testimonies. She claimed most accounts '... testified to things that, while gruesome and true enough, had no or only the slightest connection with the deeds of the accused...'.[86] Arendt voiced a legal issue that had made it possible to put high ranked officials on trial for the responsibility they bore and on the other hand acquit them, or at least reduce the degree of their responsibility thanks to the same principal. In addition, Arendt also criticized the fact that not only were testimonies irrelevant to the trial but that to begin with, no one was willing or able to vouch for their reliability.[87]

The importance Leopold von Ranke (1795-1886) ascribed to the use of reliable sources, his determination to abide by facts, report them accurately, be honest and impartial set the tone for historical research standards that lasted for over a century.[88] Arendt and Hilberg represented scholars who, following von Ranke's principles, viewed testimonies and for that matter, any personal accounts including diaries, suspiciously and rejected the idea of establishing knowledge by centralizing the role of witnesses. What Dubnow and his followers understood much earlier, particularly after the Second World War, infiltrated into historical research only in the 1970s-1980s, when there was a growing interest in witnesses' stories, particularly in the Social Sciences, psychology and philosophy, manifested in different forms.[89]

Shoshana Felman and Dori Laub's observations contributed to accepting testimonials as viable historical sources. They stressed that testimonies were complex, fragments, rather than statements and because these were provided through language, they were processes of exploration seeking to decipher what one had witnessed.[90] According to Laub, the significance of extermination was the Nazis' success in erasing witnesses' history and in that, shattering their identity too.[91] Laub explained that factual mistakes were not important and what counted was contents that helped to uncover the human aspects of survival, an area to which historians could contribute little.[92]

Saul Friedländer's books, *Nazi Germany and the Jews: Volume 1: The Years of Persecution 1933-1939* (1997) and *Nazi Germany and the Jews, The Years of Extermination: 1939-1945* (2009), were considered groundbreaking for the manner in which the Holocaust was represented. They were unique in their incorporation of testimonies, letters, diaries, and other personal records in addition to conventional historical sources. Friedländer explained that he chose this form of historical narrative because he thought 'segregation' of Jewish history from that of the Nazis was wrong.

Friedländer's approach developed as of 1985, following controversy with Martin Broszat's 'A Plea for a Historicization of National Socialism', which was followed by a series of letters exchanged between the two. One point Broszat made questioned the reliability and objectivity of survivors and their relatives concerning the war, whereas claiming German historians were free of prejudice.[93] In his reply, Friedländer asked Broszat what made German historians, most of whom belonged to the generation of 'Hitler Youth', more objective than Jews and their descendants who had gone through the war.[94] Following this discussion, Friedländer, a Holocaust survivor himself, used his book as a place to give '... priority to the individual voice.'[95]

In his introduction to *Probing the Limits of Representation: Nazism and the 'Final Solution'*, Friedländer referred to the argument between White and Ginzburg concerning the legitimacy of testimonies as historical sources. In contrast to the neutral tone expected in introductions to books, Friedländer's stressed his personal point of view.[96] He wrote that theoreticians of history, namely, relativists, should verify their theories in relation to the extermination of the Jews.[97] However, Dan Stone maintained that despite the attention attributed to theory in historical research, Holocaust research remained essentially positivist and had not produced new theories.[98]

Friedländer's approach shares a similarity with Emanuel Ringelblum in their appreciation of the point of view of the individual. Ringelblum's avid quest for personal records, such as diaries and testimonies, followed the assumption that, first, these documents represented a truth and second, that the personal angle enriched knowledge and added a dimension that would have remained hidden otherwise. He was aware of the fact that the range of information provided by this type of documentation was broad from a local perspective, but at the same time, it was the locality that rendered such testimonials insightful. Ringelblum stressed that although bearers of witness could provide information only from a specific point of time and place, their value lay in their numbers and variety of perspectives that eventually resulted in procuring a comprehensive reliable record representing reality accurately.[99]

Omer Bartov emphatically supports the introduction of personal accounts into historical research claiming that the power of testimony lay in its limited time and locality. That is, the more testimonies, the easier it is to verify the authenticity of the information but more importantly, examine it from different perspectives, which allows a more reliable historical account to be reconstructed.[100] He further elaborated that the process of cross-checking testimonies with other documentation available, such as police records, post war trials etc. could pinpoint the particularities of a locality which in itself contributed to creating a broader historical perspective.

Bartov added that ignoring testimonies, as limited as their scope may be, was somewhat unethical and constituted a historical mistake. First, there was a moral value to any testimony, even if its contents were not supported by other testimonials. That is, the moral value of rescuing a narrative was important in itself and did not depend on confirming its contents by searching for supporting evidence.[101] Second, testimonies could indicate phenomena that would remain hidden if it were not for these narratives. Their importance lay in their ability to draw attention, to look up similar testimonials from other places, which would enable studying issues thoroughly and pinpointing local differences, at all levels, thus exposing different local executions linked to a community where events occurred, contributing to an understanding of a phenomenon.[102]

Garbarini suggested that historical research might be incomplete without diaries and testimonies because the latter provided a more reliable historical image than well-researched and supported historical accounts based on traditional sources. The strength of personal accounts lies in their ability to stipulate the perspective of individual speakers living in an era studied. More importantly, illustrations of abstract notions are inherently embedded in personal narratives, insights that are missing to a large extent from other historical sources. An individual's account about coping with hunger, for example, offers different points of discussion compared to a report about the phenomenon that usually includes numbers, rations, death toll or other formal facts.

Interestingly, as much as official historical sources are seen as trustworthy, the information they include is usually removed from human implications. Official sources take and even distort the very phenomenon they seek to represent accurately because they correspond solely with a certain point of view. In contrast, even if personal accounts are usually related to a limited time frame, location and rather small number of people, their strength derives from their capacity to echo how things were experienced and felt.[103] Or, in other words, how they mirror the effect of a phenomenon discussed in official documentation.

Between Historical and Personal Motivation 85

A good example is one of Ringelblum's most touching passages concerning hunger written on May 26, 1942:

> The social help doesn't solve the problem as it nourishes people for a short time. These people are destined for death anyway and this only prolongs their sufferings without bringing relief because to achieve good results, it has to invest millions of zlotys which it doesn't have. The fact remains that all of those who eat in the kitchens die because the little soup and bread they get for their ration cards cannot sustain them.[104]

A frustrating reality emerges from these pages as Ringelblum put into words the harsh situation of an entire population dying from hunger, and, on the other hand, the helplessness and weakness of the *Aleynhilf (Self-Help)*, forced to settle for offering very little support which in fact, prolonged the suffering of the starving. Ringelblum mentioned products kitchens provided, bread and soup, served against ration cards, food that Auerbach had characterized as having no trace of nutrients, and whose only advantage was that they filled empty stomachs.[105] Auerbach, the manager of the soup kitchen at Leszno forty, agreed with Ringelblum that foods they distributed could save only those who had other means of support, but those who depended on the kitchens alone, were doomed.[106] Most distressingly, Ringelblum emphasized the implied role *Self-Help* was forced to play; rather than offering assistance it tortured the needy.[107]

Later, Ringelblum asked whether to prioritize the elite over others, in an attempt to ensure that some survived. This was followed by other questions touching on the core of his beliefs; what makes one group more deserving than another? What criteria could be valid to make such judgments? This particularly harsh text reflected the predicament of all community work that diligently tried to cope with an impossible situation, yet achieved the opposite effect. Here, Ringelblum was forced to confront the very futility of his convictions, of not only how to conduct efficient social assistance, but also the very notion of its effect. Ringelblum had to indirectly admit the failure to help others, the irrelevance of the concept itself as well as acknowledging that everyone, including he himself, had not really understood where the Germans were leading them.[108]

Two and a half years earlier, Ben-Shem provided a strikingly shocking report about the shape of hunger within the intimacy of family. Just before the Jewish holiday of *Hanukah*, in 1940, two children began to show up at the committee soup kitchen where Ben-Shem worked and hungrily stared at the food.[109] In spite of their evident desire to eat, each time they were offered food, they refused and ran away. Later, Ben-Shem was able to find out where the children lived and with Mrs. Zalzberg, he went to visit the family.

> In an extremely clean and dreadfully cold room, there was a woman sitting at the corner. It seemed as if once she was probably very beautiful as even today her eyes were still sparkling with splendor. Her face features were carved like a statue and in all her bony and scrawny body, there were traces of beauty and aristocracy.'[110]

In the early winter of 1940, barely two months after the ghetto was closed, the lawyer's wife was amongst the growing number of starving people. The story Ben-Shem recounted revolved around episodes of extremes ranging from the expected to the surprising and perverse. The mother, a once beautiful woman, tried to maintain a semblance of dignity by keeping the freezing room meticulously clean. To explain their dire situation, she told the visitors that she had lost her husband six months earlier and that the family had been expelled from their home. Like all other Jews, they too had to move to the ghetto and for a while the family supported itself by selling belongings they had rescued from their home. So far, in the Warsaw ghetto, there was nothing unusual about this story.

However, when she had finished talking, Ben-Shem wrote that they wanted to understand why the children refused to taste the soup and that when they finally relented and ate, they implored them not to tell their mother about it. At this stage, the mother's response shocked the visitors as she exclaimed:

> They tasted?' She screamed in such a strange voice that we became alarmed. Maybe she had lost her mind. ... 'You gentlemen from the committee ... can't understand the sorrow of a woman-mother who ... seeks only one thing, the death of these children without agonizing for too long. We are close to achieving the goal. Today is the fifth day that we tasted nothing, not even water and my greatest hope is that in two days or maybe three, we shall be dead. We will die together and you, you are in the way. Giving the children soup to make their suffering longer! Giving them enough is beyond your capabilities, so why would you torment them and lengthen their sufferings now that we are so close to achieving our goal?.[111]

Ben-Shem's shock derived not from the extreme hunger the family coped with, but by the unexpected change in the mother's countenance and voice, her twisted logic and the fact she had imposed such perverse reasoning on her children. Suddenly, the freezing surgically clean room paralleled the cold and clear reasoning of a woman who seemed to have lost her healthy survival instincts. The sudden reaction of the furious mother changed the nature of the visit into a dive, not only into the intimacy of relationships, but also into a tormented human soul who had deliberately used her authority to indirectly cause her own children's death. If the woman had appeared to have controlled her wits, the soup her children sipped had become the touchstone of sanity, when suddenly and unexpectedly appearances collapsed and devastation surfaced.

Acute hunger followed by humiliation and degradation seemed to have affected the mother's spirit before it broke her physically. In the text, Ben-Shem alluded to the family's aristocratic background as a factor that might have influenced the mother's apparent incapacity to face difficulties, as well as her opting for a passive response instead of fighting back. In this situation, it is the background, her appearance and the spotless house, that screen the mother's insanity. She made her children not only see her at her worst, but also act against their survival instincts while realizing that their own mother wished them dead. Clearly, the children seemed to have been torn between deep respect for their mother and understanding she had abused her authority forcing them to obey and adopt her twisted reasoning.[112]

Although both Ringelblum and Ben-Shem discussed the same phenomenon, Ringelblum's was written from the point of view of a social worker and community leader. His was not a report but a reflective essay echoing the dire situation in the ghetto just as it exposed the deep frustrations of social help, and its workers, who were constantly exposed to the burden of feeding the hungry knowing that their capacity to do so was lacking. While his text managed to communicate the difficulties of *Self-Help* as an institution and understanding that its chosen mode of operation to deal with ghetto problems had failed, it was the misery of individuals involved: social workers, community leaders and the hungry that became less apparent in his narrative.

In contrast, Ben-Shem's text highlighted the intimate dynamics in a family versus the efforts of public kitchens to attend to the hungry. The personal story revealed the catastrophic circumstances where hunger affected individuals as well as family fabric and consequently, society as a whole. In a way, the narrative in Ben-Shem's diary managed to expose the mental effects of hunger as well as the frustrations of *Self-Help*, dilemmas, reasoning, decisions, and human agonies engulfed in that dire situation. The result is that the story of an individual accurately evoked an array of aspects resulting from hunger, thus penetrating into the complexities and reciprocal relationships between *Self-Help* and those it strove to assist.

Both texts communicated the extreme situation in the ghetto but while Ringelblum's discussed the phenomenon itself, Ben-Shem's exemplified it with a personal story. The question is, which one is true? Which one is more accurate? Is it important in this context? How crucial is it whether Ben-Shem's recollection of the discussion represented the exact vocabulary used by the mother? If he misquoted her, did this affect the whole story? I argue that whether all types of testimonies sought to bear witness, understand, decipher the present, or commemorate, is less important when considering their use as historical evidence. That is, the absence of testimonials in historical research risks creating an incomplete representation of the past.

In order to fully understand the implications of Nazi policies, one cannot only recreate a historical narrative based solely on official documents such as representative graphs, dates, orders. Although Ringelblum's text revealed the complexities of social help in that challenging situation, one cannot recreate from his report its significance for individuals. Here, a text, such as Ben-Shem's, managed to represent the reciprocal relationship between the needy and those who helped, domestic complications created, what German orders really meant and the connections between them. Therefore, if a testimony provides information that expands the body of knowledge about a certain phenomenon, it should be considered a valid historical source. Questioning truthfulness of testimonies, versus the authenticity of traditional historical sources is the wrong approach. All sources are written from a certain point of view, including official documentation, and therefore, it is the combination of both that has the capacity to expose the past in a reliable comprehensive manner.[113]

The shadow of destruction or gap in time is evident in written records once annihilation started as everything shrank in comparison to mass murder. Death dominated narratives and personal accounts, as well as historical research thus diminishing in importance other phenomena preceding it. In such narratives, the moral degradation that heralded physical elimination posed a problem to historical research as it affected narratives. The very advantage of history, the fact that historians are at leisure to examine many sources, became a serious drawback when it concerned the Holocaust; systematic murder, hunting down people, annihilating entire families in specially erected sites were phenomena that had never been confronted before.[114]

The spaces to understand these events, that is, how Jews conceived what was happening to them, their conceptual world and reasoning based on a past that did not include such experiences, were factors that made it almost impossible for victims to grasp the present. Historians researching that period must be aware of the fact that so many Jews were tortured and murdered because they had failed to understand what was going on. Historians who do not address the cultural - conceptual gap between victims and perpetrators, present incomplete narratives eventually reflecting that they, the researchers, were unaware of the fact that epistemological gaps were an integral part of the success of annihilation. We now know that this destruction was possible, but victims were unaware that such an outcome existed. That is why what they wrote, said or testified represents crystalized insights into their capacity to interpret at the time, which explains historical events in a more precise manner.[115]

In both Ben-Shem and Ringelblum's writings before the deportations, they applied reasoned concepts of cause and effect, a pattern that reflected their misunderstanding of the Nazis' ultimate goal. Documentation at the beginning of the war, especially among scholars, corresponded to ways of thinking that relied on the pattern of logic and pragmatism. These proved to be misleading and therefore, historians who do not use testimonies of the time, are denied exposure to conceptual approaches constituting the core of what personal records unfold.

The question whether history is an art or a science cannot be settled here. Apparently, the claim that historical narratives, even if they abide by the strictest guidelines to ensure their authenticity and veracity, represent the ultimate truth, is arguable and it is best if they be verified time and again for their reliability. The rate and speed of developing insights renders the story of the past as dynamic in its conception as the rate of time. Therefore, even if such historical narratives are based on valid sources, what counts is how sources are interpreted. In evaluating testimonials, one must take into account that what was considered a reliable historical source was incomplete too. To use the Holocaust as an example, research of this topic has been conducted even though many historical sources were out of reach. Research has been published, books printed, conferences held and other activities relating to historical investigation have taken place, despite the fact that until the beginning of the 1990s, east European archives were out of reach. Similarly, research about the role the Catholic church played during the war took place even though Vatican archives remained, until recently, sealed. In other words, although important historical sources were not available, historians continued their research, settling for what was within reach. In this respect, is there not a similarity between testimonies and eyewitness accounts, forcibly representing a certain locality and historical research that relied solely on a small number of sources to support a theory?

Testimonies and diaries included have their drawbacks, but they do rely on facts. Their narratives are affected by their authors' point of views, not only their beliefs but also where they were physically. However, this is also their strength as they are able to produce micro information otherwise unavailable as well as illuminate experiences from within, together with exposing implications for parties involved. It seems that no one can see everything, not even historians, therefore I argue that in order to provide a fairly faithful image of the past, one should not ignore sources solely because they may be subjective, diaries included. It is these contents that provide historians with ornamentation academic narrative cannot possibly convey. If one is not exposed to on scene particularities, the focus would represent the course of events and unintentionally conceal human phenomena involved, thus rendering the narrative inaccurate.[116] In this respect, neither are historical narratives the embodiment of reliable representation, nor are diaries mere momentary impressions. Moreover, incorporating diaries and other unofficial sources into well-researched historical study may reduce subjective points of view of historians who write with a present understanding about a past they seek to comprehend.[117]

*****

Goldberg argued that cultural chunks namely, language including choices of genre, of a writer's cultural environment had the capacity to root one within the society from which one emerged.[118] Hence, writing involved using one's cultural 'building blocks' resulting in making one's voice intelligible to oneself and consolidating a person's background by creating a space where one used epistemological knowhow to decipher and interpret what one experienced. In the context of the Holocaust, shrinking ghetto space was one crucial element drastically affecting, not only physical, but also mental and emotional spaces. Writing, a typical Jewish reaction to hardship, enabled carving a personal space where events could be presented, discussed, understood or not, a space to sound one's voice in a universe that imposed silence on Jews.

The huge number of records existing today is evidence of David Engel's statement that Jews attributed great importance to writing.[119] During the

War, interest in writing was manifested in private documentation initiatives and in parallel, communal efforts to collect as many testimonies as possible. A surge in records that surfaced after the war, together with growing public interest in personal narratives, created some pressure on more people to become involved in testifying which partly explains why the Holocaust has the highest record of testimonies compared to any other historical event.[120]

During the Holocaust, physical stability was shaken although the degree of turmoil depended on place and period. Nonetheless, what is striking about writings then, is that the urge to write seemed to be strengthened in correlation to how a situation worsened. The question why people immersed themselves in writing endeavors reveals great commitment and urgency, deriving from intrinsic psychological motivations, involving moral and cultural consciousness. Furthermore, examination of these written accounts suggests that each writer was impelled to write for a number of reasons and that these sometimes changed over time according to circumstances.

Some wrote because it was part of their cultural upbringing, but the fact they persevered despite growing obstacles was remarkable.[121] This appears to suggest that through writing, they were able to instill meaning into an activity that no longer addressed themselves, but rather confronted the effects or invasion of the outside world into their personal lives. Other diarists started writing because of the war, as a means of understanding and explaining to themselves what they were experiencing, whereas others wrote to commemorate those who were lost. Some were driven by moral values thus putting tremendous efforts into making sure nothing and no-one would be forgotten whereas others were driven by a pledge to sound a warning and make sure they passed on their stories, whether they dealt with a specific threat or pouring into their texts more educational values.[122]

Documenting while things were happening exposed the processes of bridging epistemological gaps. Writing in the aftermath revealed the difficulties survivors experienced to detach themselves from the past while revealing that gaps in knowledge about their past experiences remained unbridgeable. This exemplifies how the Holocaust had a long-term effect on survivors, a specter that kept haunting them. For them, writing and publishing had, in addition to reasons mentioned before, the value of an evolving perspective over time.

Avraham (Adolf) Berman (1906-1978), the general secretary of Żegota, (Konrad Żegota Committee), a codename for the Council to Aid Jews (Rada Pomocy Żydom) who wrote his memoires in the late 1970s, is a good example of this. He and his wife Batia Temkin, left the Warsaw Ghetto in

September 1942 and led a dangerous and active life on the Aryan side of Warsaw, attempting to help Jews hiding in the city. Berman did not write while he was in the ghetto or on the Aryan side but he was the one who met Ringelblum weekly in his hiding place and collected essays Ringelblum had prepared. Berman turned to writing only a few years before his death explaining it by saying that he felt obligated to do so because his life was drawing to its end and he wanted to explain the mental resources that had enabled him to dedicate himself to communal work before and especially during the war.[123]

Nevertheless, the combination of a thirst for testimonials and changing times have uncovered more stories that people had previously been reluctant to share. According to Omer Bartov, testimonies in general were extremely valuable, including those collected a long time after the war. He noted that survivors who testified immediately after the war were not always willing to discuss their personally experienced humiliation and abuse, because it was extremely difficult for them to reveal their vulnerability through these stories. In other cases, survivors took time to fully grasp what they had experienced and share their insights. In this respect, time became a healing factor as it allowed survivors to find their voice and reveal themselves to themselves, as well as their audiences.[124]

Simultaneously, it took time for testimonies to penetrate the realm of historical research as legitimate resources.[125] The trustworthiness of testimonies versus official documentation was finally challenged by Friedländer when he combined first-hand testimonials with historical narratives. This, concluded Wulf Kansteiner, met with White's argument, that a historical masterpiece was one that succeeded in resolving conflicting centers. He wrote, 'By this standard, the epic struggle among irony, synecdoche, and metonymy that takes places in the pages of *The Years of Extermination* will endure for many generations.'[126]

Bartov added that testimonials were valuable for their capacity to expose facts. They illuminated aspects that could not be found in official documentation and made it possible to understand events from below, from the perspective of individuals. Thus, Bartov suggested that official documentation was not as neutral and objective as initially conceived because these documents too, were products of efforts to imbed messages into official documentation.[127]

One prominent example he provided concerned the rescue of Jews in the Buczacz region by a German official whose name remains unknown. Such testimony illuminated the complexity of the situation on the ground, as Germans reoccupied Buczacz in the early months of 1944 after it had

Between Historical and Personal Motivation   93

been in Soviet hands for two weeks. Bartov claimed that without survivors' testimonies, it is probable that no one would have brought this event to the attention of the public as German officials would have been unlikely to record it and Jews, who were unpredictably protected by a German official, would probably have been murdered leaving no one to tell the story. Therefore, according to Bartov, testimonies were also valuable in their capacity to expose events that otherwise would have remained unrecorded.[128]

Part III

The Private and Public Sphere

IV

Lebensraum – The Spatial and Demographic Formation of the Warsaw Ghetto

Marking Jewish Identity – The Armband Decree

From 1933, Nazi law makers targeted Jews aiming at "purifying" public spaces from their presence. At first, means were taken to intimidate and deter Jews from these areas but later they were visually marked making it unbearable for them to access the public arena. After Kristallnacht, in November 1938, Reinhard Heydrich presented the idea of Jews having to don an identifying badge but, at the time, it was decided against.[1] Thus until 1939, space-wise, attempts to single out Jews in Germany concentrated on Jewish property, personal ID cards and passports but not the human body.

Although Polish Jews knew about the measures imposed on their German brethren before the war, the likelihood that, in the twentieth century, an edict to tag Jewish individuals, like in the Middle Ages, would be introduced seemed inconceivable. Nonetheless, the idea to display a Jewish symbol on the body resurfaced at the beginning of the war.

Hans Frank, Governor-General of the General Government for occupied Polish territories, issued the armband decree on November 23 1939, to be enforced as of December 1, 1939.[2] According to Yisrael Gutman, neither this nor the following edict issued by Fischer (Governor of the Warsaw District in the occupied General Government), specified a reason for introducing identification for Jews.[3] This decree, one of many imposed on Polish Jews from October 1939, was of a particularly shocking nature and had immediate serious consequences on the lives of the Jewish communities all over Poland.

During exile, Jews were used to negotiating with authorities to alleviate pressure and at first, they were convinced that such relationships could be established with the German occupants.[4] However, attempts to cancel the order failed, and until the end of the war, Jews had to identify themselves by wearing badges that varied in size and shape according to local whims.

Because the idea of identifying Jews externally goes back to the Middle Ages, one of the worst periods of persecution in Jewish collective memory, it became a common point of reference for Jews during the Second World War.[5] It supplied them with ample examples of oppression, similar in content and cruelty, to the German occupation.[6] Likewise, the familiarity of the situation provided them with a perspective of how to cope with this and other long-dreaded decrees.[7]

The notion of labeling Jews seemed to suggest that the Nazis strove to erase all individual Jews' human characteristics by stigmatizing them, thus turning them into a faceless entity bearing certain biological features for which the badge became a symbol. It signified that being Jewish was total and unavoidable, at the same time, suggesting that Jewishness was irrevocable and therefore, Jews were no longer sovereign individuals nor human beings, but a faceless collective.[8] This included nullifying their personal and personality traits as well as their human character altogether.[9] It forced on Jews a single identity that de-singularized them as individuals because of their Jewishness.

The imbedded meaning of armbands officially indicated to everyone, Jews and non-Jews, that the marked group was no longer protected by law meaning that their abusers did not face punishment.[10] Although Jews quickly internalized their fragile situation, that their personal safety had been jeopardized, there was little they could do about it.

A Jewish Sphere – The Warsaw Ghetto

Ringelblum wrote that the establishment of the ghetto in Łódź made a huge impression on Jews because no one had expected this in such a large city.[11] In Warsaw, the formation of the closed ghetto started as early as November 1939, when some streets were blocked off by barbed wire, with a sign at the entrance alleging, 'Infection, entry banned to soldiers'.[12]

On November 4, 1939, the *Judenrat*, alarmed by the idea of creating a ghetto in Warsaw, turned directly to General Karl-Ulrich Neumann-Neurode, who had no idea such an order had been issued in his name.[13] This decree was indeed postponed thus creating a false impression that negotiations with the Nazis were possible.[14] Nevertheless, not long after, the Nazis began building walls in different locations, but while Jews had been aware of this for months, they could not imagine the Germans were planning to lock them up behind them.

In April 1940, Ringelblum bitterly used the Nazi term 'quarantined epidemic area' not only to refer to blocked areas, but also to document the erection of walls around what would later become the sealed Jewish ghetto.[15] In May 1940, Ringelblum mentioned the walls on Nalewki and other streets, stating they were regarded as the beginning of a ghetto that would probably emerge unexpectedly.[16] Yet, later on, he noted that it was not clear why walls were being built and estimated that the Germans might be planning to set fire to the ghetto in case of withdrawal.[17] Needless to say, the *Kehilla*, the Jewish Community, was ordered to pay for building these walls.[18]

Unlike the majority of ghettoes in Poland, many of which were deliberately located in the poorest neighborhoods, the Warsaw ghetto was set up across several neighborhoods, and included areas extensively populated by Jewish residents.[19] Standartenführer Waldemar Schön, head of the Resettlement Division of the Warsaw District, said that initially, the intention was to establish the ghetto in Praga, a poor neighborhood across the river, but because Polish authorities claimed it was widely populated by Poles and not Jews, the idea was dropped.[20]

The ghetto's final strange shape reflected German and Polish interests as well as disputes behind the scenes. It was situated in the heart of Warsaw, forming an island in the middle of the city, thus limiting movement of both Jews and Poles. Isolating Jews spatially created a site of Jewish absence formed by cleansing Warsaw of any Jewish presence while rendering the ghetto into an exclusively Jewish space.

Considerations determining ghetto contours did not include the needs of the incarcerated Jewish population. The ghetto consisted of two parts, the larger northern and smaller southern part. They were separated by Chłodna Street, only a short part of which was within the ghetto connecting the two parts through a handful of small, crammed streets. In January 1942, a wooden bridge was built above Chłodna Street, allegedly to ease movement between the two parts of the ghetto.[21]

The wall route caused friction between Poles and Jews, each trying to influence German decisions about it. Ringelblum discussed these difficulties reporting that 'The Poles are using all kinds of scams to increase the number of houses in the Polish quarter. For example, they block the gates of houses facing Jewish areas and they leave open the gates facing the Polish side of the very same houses.'[22] Another case concerned a specific rumor about a Volksdeutsche[23] beer factory owner named Haberbusch, who received flowers for successfully intervening in saving some houses where Poles lived from being included in the ghetto.[24]

Ringelblum's chronicle also included reports about interference from the clergy. He described how Polish priests encouraged people to sign petitions demanding mixed streets, including Nowolipki, which was almost entirely populated by Jews, be left in the hands of Poles, solely because there was a church there.[25] Ringelblum pointed out that Count Roniker had criticized his Polish counterparts stating clear opposition to these Polish maneuvers declaring that in his opinion, Jews and Poles had to work together against the very idea of setting up a ghetto instead of fighting each other.[26]

When the Warsaw Ghetto was sealed, the huge numbers of people inside created a housing problem. On January 20, 1941, Schön stated that the *Judenrat* had conducted a census, claiming there were 410,000 Jews inside the ghetto, but the Germans estimated there were between 470,000 and 590,000, which meant there were on average, 15.1 people per 2.5-room apartment, about 7 people per room.[27]

Kermish and Blumental relied on data published in *Gazeta Żydowska*, according to which there were 1,692 buildings in the ghetto, of which 1,359 were residential apartments and eighty-one factories. This meant that there were, on average, thirteen people per room, whereas on the Polish side, there were seven people per room.[28] This incredible population density meant little to the Germans who continued to dump whole communities into the Warsaw Ghetto. Although Jewish social services immediately came to their rescue, their means of support decreased daily. Refugees, mostly those displaced and evicted from their homes, constituted the smallest, yet most vulnerable group.

At its peak, refugees made up about one fifth of the Warsaw Ghetto population, nearly 100,000 people. The intended ghetto area housed two major groups: refugees from outside Warsaw, and Jews who lived in Warsaw. The latter group can be divided into two subgroups: those who happened to live within ghetto designated borders and therefore could remain in their homes, and those living in areas outside the ghetto borders.

Although people residing within the ghetto borders could remain living there, many of them took in refugees, especially if they were family. But when the ghetto was sealed, the housing shortage forced the *Kehilla* to intervene and make it obligatory for everyone to open their doors and accept strangers into their homes. Ben-Shem, for example, wrote that he had four rooms in his house and had rented three of them to subtenants, among them Rachel Auerbach, his cousin.[29]

The second subgroup consisted of Varsovians who became refugees within Warsaw itself. These people faced great difficulties because they had to find new residences within ghetto boundaries and like refugees from smaller towns, they had to leave almost everything behind and move to the

Lebensraum – The Spatial and Demographic Formation   101

ghetto. Many managed to exchange their own homes with Polish families who were also forced out of the designated Jewish ghetto.[30] However, in many cases, Jewish larger apartments were exchanged for smaller ones without any compensation for the difference.[31]

In addition, some Poles took advantage of the situation and left their apartments within the ghetto in a deplorable state. Jews who were expelled from their homes in the southern part of Warsaw, suffered even more as they were prevented from exchanging their homes, because the south, the richer part of Warsaw, was a strictly designated German quarter. At first, Poles were also ordered to leave their homes in this area, but, later, they were allowed to remain.[32]

On November 16, 1940, the Warsaw Ghetto was sealed and thirty percent of the city's population was locked in a small compound constituting 3.3% of the city's area. According to Wajnkranc, the first weeks were chaotic because ghetto borders constantly changed. She wrote, 'The Community stubbornly fights and negotiates each foot of land, each house ...'. As part of a family, whose newly exchanged flat on Graniczna street was frequently designated inside and outside ghetto boundaries, she described the sensation as if they were '... sitting on a volcano...'[33] Wajnkranc wrote there were people who had to change apartments several times a day, a report corresponding to Ringelblum's, who wrote that he had heard about a man who had to move seven times and another who moved four times.[34]

Ringelblum addressed the issue of sealing the ghetto only three days after it happened. This entry demonstrated the chaos of the day the ghetto was abruptly and without warning closed:

> Saturday, the day the ghetto was introduced was terrible. People didn't know it was going to be a closed ghetto, so it came like a bolt out of the blue. On every street and in every corner, there were German, Polish, and Jewish guards who decided which passers-by were allowed to cross. Jewish women found out that the markets outside the ghetto were closed for them. There was an immediate shortage of bread and other products. Ever since then, there has been a real price rampage. There are long queues in front of food stores... Many items have suddenly vanished from the shops. There is no connection between Twarda and Leszno Streets. One has to go via Żelazna Street.[35]

Ringelblum's entry, in a somewhat prophetic text, introduced some of the most prominent problems that would eventually trouble ghetto prisoners:

movement, means of support and hunger.[36] As it was, Jewish economic activities had been limited previously owing to German decrees imposed in October 1939. Yet, Ringelblum emphasized how isolation by closing ghetto entrances was expected to affect the flow of provisions creating instant shortages of supplies. In addition, any means of making a living were cut off abruptly, which resulted in reducing people to poverty, leading to hunger that only worsened as time went by.

Indeed, hunger struck the ghetto and together with population density, poor services provided by the Warsaw municipality and the *Kehilla* as well as difficulties posed by the Germans, generated a crisis that very quickly became life-threatening.[37] The combination of hunger and poor sanitation translated into an epidemic, mainly typhus, which took its toll on ghetto residents. The numbers of dead soared to such a degree that bodies lay in the streets contributing to creating an inescapable vicious circle affecting ever-growing sanitation problems.

Lastly, Ringelblum's text loudly voiced the surprise and shock created by the realization that the ghetto would be closed. Moderately, Ringelblum's words evoked the conceptual gap expressed in the tremor not only at closing the ghetto, but also understanding that it would remain sealed permanently. Ringelblum was not the only one surprised or taken aback by this. Three days before the ghetto was sealed, Kaplan's diary entry specified his certitude that there was almost no doubt that the ghetto would be closed but owing to '... regional considerations',[38] the ghetto would not be a sealed ghetto like in Łódź. However, his entry from November 17, 1940, suggested that like others, he too was shocked as he had gone to sleep the night before only to wake up in a sealed ghetto.[39]

The fright and surprise were equally prominent in Zivia Lubetkin's testimony at the Eichmann trial: 'One bright day, without any warning, at the beginning of November, if I am not mistaken, the Jews woke up and each hurried to their work but suddenly they encountered the fact that the ghetto was closed, closed with gates, next to which there were German, Polish and Jewish policemen. It was sudden.'[40] Notably, what stood out was the notion of unexpectedness as a meaningful sensation in the experience of having the ghetto sealed. Apparently, it was not only that the Germans lied, as Kaplan put it plainly, but what stupefied Jews was a fundamental realization that their own patterns of thinking, time and again, had misled them into believing the German authorities. Of all testimonies, maybe Lubetkin's, from 1961, stands out as it was given twenty-one years later and her words still echo the shock and sense of astonishment that had gripped the Jews of Warsaw when the ghetto was sealed.

The Sealed Ghetto

Between November 1940 and July 20, 1942, the Warsaw Ghetto public spaces comprised of its streets, the cemetery, the "points" - the infamous refugee shelters erected in public buildings and other institutional buildings, the gates, the only legal opening to the outside world. During its existence, the ghetto bore the closest resemblance to a concentration camp with one important difference, the majority of those interned were families and at least seemingly, ghetto inmates were able to continue maintaining some form of family life.[41] The numbers of residents varied drastically because, on the one hand, Germans forced refugees into the ghetto and on the other, mortality rates rose constantly, particularly during 1941. Engelking pointed out that German data from March 1941 showed that there were about 490,000 Jews inside the ghetto but in the autumn of 1941, the number decreased to 415,000. On the eve of deportation, 380,000 Jews remained in the ghetto.[42]

From July 22, 1942, the ghetto was segmented into three main areas: the first was the remains of the 'small' ghetto in the south; the second was the main shops area in the heart of the former ghetto boundaries; the third, in the northern section of the old ghetto compound consisted of the remains of the ghetto, which had at its south-east corner, the brush maker's shop and in the north, the Umschlagplatz, the deportation area.[43] A major change which occurred in the period between deportations and the ghetto's final destruction, was the abrogation of family as a unit, brutally implemented in shops. This created an unbearable reality, whereby, only approved shop workers were officially allowed to remain, while their families were to be deported.[44]

According to Dan Michman, the policy of ghettoization in Poland was not systematic and its nature was never entirely clarified. However, the mere establishment of ghettos indicated preoccupation with the Jewish question and attempts to find ways of addressing it. Accordingly, Michman proposed that ghettos were one form among others of anti-Jewish measures but not the only one.[45] By the same token, it is not exactly understood what was intended by closing ghettoes especially those erected before 1941 whereas sealing them afterwards became a stage before implementation of the final solution.[46]

Walls or other forms of encirclement erected around ghettos defined both a symbolic and practical private place for Jews. They separated the Jewish population from their non-Jewish neighbors, thus 'cleansing' Polish spaces of a Jewish presence, and in parallel, rendering spaces inside walls into an exclusively private Jewish confinement space. Although ghetto streets were a Jewish public space, they were also the physical and conceptual private sphere of both prisoners and their jailers.

Ambiguously, before the ghetto was surrounded by walls, there had been numerous break-ins into apartments involving confiscation of property and sheer abuse of residents in keeping with the notion that Jewish zones were lawless.[47] However, once the Warsaw Ghetto was isolated, Germans would rarely burst into private dwellings. This situation markedly reversed indefinitely as soon as deportations began.[48]

How ghettos were referred to, echoes their uniqueness. Whereas officially, the Germans in Warsaw, for example, insisted that it should be called a Jewish district, they often alluded to the term ghetto intentionally.[49] According to Weinreich, this was a conscious attempt to mislead public opinion, specifically in the west and intended to camouflage the true plan. Relying on connotation, the word ghetto suggested that it consisted of an effort to concentrate Jews in one place. Second, like in the Middle Ages, it suggested these enclosed communities would continue to have contacts with the non-Jewish population. The blurred associations created because of this terminology were openly refuted in 1941, at the Frankfurt Conference, when Peter Heinz Seraphim specifically noted that in Nazi ghettos, no relationships should be allowed between Jews and non-Jews.[50]

In an attempt to characterize the particularities of the second World War ghettos, Raul Hillberg defined them as 'captive city-states'[51], whereas residents of the Warsaw Ghetto such as Batya Temkin labelled the Warsaw Ghetto 'A City Within a City' while Ben-Shem called it an island of leprosy.[52] Ringelblum reported that people nicknamed the ghetto *Czerniaków's Garden City* (Miasto-Ogród Czerniaków) ironically referring to the head of the Jewish Council, Adam Czerniaków as well as to a neighborhood in Warsaw by the name of Czerniaków.[53] However, according to Ringelblum, ghettos in occupied Poland bore no similarity to those of mediaeval times as contemporaneous ghettos were a deviation from historical development rather than a natural phenomenon.[54] Irrespectively, many Jews, at least at the beginning, welcomed the formation of a closed ghetto in Warsaw as it offered immediate relief from attacks carried out by Poles. They relied on their collective memory as mediaeval ghetto walls also protected their inhabitants by preventing unwelcome elements from entering.

According to Alberto Giordano, Anne Kelly Knowles, and Tim Cole, the Holocaust was a spatial event of great magnitude because it involved various aspects of spatial control, starting with the human body and ending

Lebensraum – The Spatial and Demographic Formation   105

with continents.[55] Tim Cole maintained that spatially, ghettoes were timely places that were part of 'genocidal landscapes',[56] created during the Holocaust. If this observation can be considered accurate in retrospect, of all places of death, initially, ghetto inmates did not conceive their confinement there as life threatening. Paradoxically, despite deteriorating situations in ghettos involving hunger, disease and death, most Jews held on to the concept that it was the least of all evils.

Indeed, even after the ghetto was sealed, Ringelblum echoed this approach when he wrote that even though it was clear from the beginning there would be serious shortages of materials and products, 'In general, the public feels safer' and that if it were not for concerns about lack of provisions and coal, life could have continued somehow.[57] In March 1941, Ringelblum compared ghettos to concentration camps but on June 22-23, 1941, when hunger, disease and death ravaged, he seemed to have relented and wrote twice in two consecutive entries that despite it all, Jews were lucky '...there are walls.'[58]

His observations related to the beginning of the German offensive in Russia and the fierce propaganda campaign against Jews linking them to Bolshevism, which was intended to secure Polish support for Germany against Russia.[59] While ghetto walls protected Jews from assault by incited mobs, extreme shortages of provisions turned them into deadly traps from which escape was almost impossible, if only because, for the vast majority, prospects of finding refuge outside were slim.

Even though German soldiers were barred from entering the ghetto, Ringelblum reported that their presence inside the walls was significant. Many of them took pictures and even filmed indiscriminately, not only in Warsaw, but around Poland too.[60] Ben-Shem noted that 'Despite the ban…, despite the guards… they penetrate the ghetto by force by climbing over the wall or convincing the gendarmes. They smuggled tens and sometimes hundreds of soldiers…'[61]

German soldiers found the Warsaw Ghetto intriguing and many of them wondered its streets taking photographs at will. According to Ben-Shem, some were motivated to enter by prospects of confiscating something from Jews to take back home as presents for their families. In one of his first entries, Ben-Shem reported that in the evenings there were hundreds of soldiers roaming the streets of the ghetto. This was an ongoing phenomenon as their interest spread to exotic aspects of Jewish life. On Yom Kippur 1941, Ben-Shem reported that huge numbers of soldiers prowled the streets and also entered synagogues to watch prayers. Notoriously, German soldiers also flocked to the Jewish cemetery.[62]

Expelled and Displaced - Refugees

The early reports about the "points" that appeared in Ringelblum's diary on December 16, 1939, offer a glimpse into the pandemonium in Warsaw with large numbers of refugees and an ongoing serious housing problem. He wrote that 'Housing conditions for the refugees on five Rynkowa street are horrible, it is impossible to breathe, it is crowded, filthy.'[63] These words written in the third month of the war, discussed refugees, who had fled to Warsaw, at their own initiative, wrongly thinking of Warsaw as a 'paradise.'[64] Ringelblum added that because of their increasing presence in the capital, housing prices rose greatly.[65]

With time, the situation grew worse and Ringelblum's diary entries from 1939 and 1940 indicated how the flow of voluntary refugees was replaced by whole communities the Germans had forcefully and brutally expelled. Refugees' ordeal began with their often violent eviction. Entire families were ordered to leave their homes with permission to take only a few belongings. Eviction orders often were not coordinated with destinations and therefore sometimes convoys with the expelled remained locked up in carts for days.[66]

Robbery, bribery and theft quickly became a 'norm', or at least tolerated conduct in the process if it was not initiated by the local command. These indicated the absence of a preconceived plan mingled with a complete lack of concern for the fate of displaced people. Time and again, it was local Jewish communities that were expected to lend a helping hand while their resources diminished steadily and they too were threatened.[67]

The first displacement order addressed to the SS, stated that the expulsion of Jews was to follow a pattern of concentrating them in larger towns in which there were rail junctions or railroad lines.[68] At first, they planned to create a Jewish ghetto in the vicinity of Krakow, but this was replaced by an idea to concentrate all Jews in the region of Lublin.[69] Prais wrote that in the first wave of displacements, Supreme Commander East furiously condemned these acts of violence. This led Hans Frank to address Himmler and Hitler urging them to suspend these operations.[70] Consequently, Göring ended the first wave of such expulsions in the spring of 1940, but they were soon renewed. Hence, Prais claimed the first resettlement attempt failed because of disputes inside the Nazi regime.[71]

Ringelblum's diary provided numerous reports about the banishment of the Jews from all over Poland. The eviction from Serock, for instance, took place on December 5, 1939, as Jews were woken up at 4 o'clock in the morning and ordered to concentrate in the town's square. Adults and

Lebensraum – The Spatial and Demographic Formation   107

teenagers were chased on foot, to the town of Nasielsk, twenty kilometers away.[72] Once they reached that city, some of the old and sick were executed while the rest were tortured and had to endure body searches for valuables. Then they were uploaded onto trains supposedly to bring them to camps in Germany. According to Arie Mezdelewski, a survivor, the trains traveled back and forth for days in horrendously crowded conditions with neither food nor water. Mezdelewski, a boy at the time, said that his mother could not rest until she managed to bring water from the toilets.[73]

In Płock, the Polish elite was targeted first, but Ringelblum stressed there was no class differentiation concerning Jews, and they were all attacked and robbed. Further details provided showed that Jews' belongings were classified from the most to the least valuable. In December 1939, it was reported that all appliances used by shoemakers as well as tailors were confiscated.[74]

In Chełm, the Germans expelled Jews to the forests (in fact to Hrubieszów) while shooting at them. Ringelblum reported that a few people were murdered.[75] The expulsion of the Jews of Sierpc and Rypin may be considered another example of the chaotic nature of these atrocities. Jews were sent to Grudziądz but there was no room for them, so the Germans sent them back to their original towns. By the time they returned, their homes had been occupied so they were gathered in a camp in the area.[76]

These few examples of expulsions reveal the degree of German obsession with the notion of Lebensraum, which targeted both Polish and Jewish populations.[77] Equally, the way evictions were carried out hints at little planning or concern on the part of the occupant, especially regarding Jews.[78] Separate orders aimed at Jews, and the fact persecution and torture were relentless, demonstrate how this population was singled out from the beginning.

Only once did Ringelblum echo his perplexing observation at the chaos and conduct of the German occupation forces. At the end of March 1940, he wrote that there was turmoil everywhere and if the Germans had combined their current ideology with the sense of organization they manifested in 1914, there would no longer be any Jew alive.[79] Other than this comment, which voiced bewilderment at the inability to elicit the greater plan from what was happening at the time, Ringelblum did not embark on such reflections in writing.

When evicted Jews arrived at their destinations, they were usually dumped onto the care of local Jews. With almost no other choice, "points" were established by relief organizations and the Jewish *Kehilla* to address this pressing issue. If at the beginning, conditions at "points" were somewhat controllable, as soon as the ghetto was sealed, they worsened rapidly due to the huge numbers of refugees and dwindling resources available. Since "points" were usually erected in public Jewish buildings including synagogues, they were, to begin with, unsuitable for habitation, let alone to accommodate large numbers of people, certainly not for long periods of time.[80]

The majority of refugees had no means of supporting themselves and quickly became among the first to starve. At the beginning of 1941, Ringelblum wrote that '... 80% of children wearing rags in "points" are begging for alms in the streets.'[81] In February he added that most women beggars came from there too. As expected, these were pitiful and hopeless circumstances that hastened refugees' deaths. In mid-1941, Ringelblum reported that the highest death toll was among refugees, a fact mentioned again in September 1941.[82]

Being involved with relief activities, Ben-Shem also discussed the horrific situation at the "points". He described a visit to such a center, emphasizing the desolation and despair not only of "points" residents but also that of those who wished to help them.[83] Ben-Shem's house committee decided to lend a helping hand to refugees they had visited a few days earlier by providing them with bread. Ben-Shem remarked that although the committee was aware that a one-time portion of a quarter loaf of bread per person would not do much to help the starving, they had decided to do it all the same because '... there is value in good will too.'[84]

As soon as "point" residents smelled bread, they became frantic and before any of the visitors could react, '... they ("point" residents) decided and not us.'[85] The turmoil was unbelievable, and Ben-Shem wrote that he had thought to himself that such scenes could have only been possible in the Middle Ages. Children screamed, adults shouted, cursed, cried, occasionally having spasms, and there was no way to control the situation, not even when "point" guards hit them brutally with clubs. Ben-Shem attested that he and the others, including the "point" manager were too frightened to intervene and all had tears rolling down their faces.

This episode from Ben-Shem's diary alluded to the enormous efforts made by ghetto institutions, official and unofficial, as well as individuals to help the needy. Attempts to appease suffering, somehow offer moments of relief, were met with the opposite. Instead of comforting, bread for the starving triggered extreme violence making people lose control of their senses. Warsaw Ghetto physicians confirmed these reports. Apparently, starvation had devastating physical as well as emotional and mental effects on people who became irritable, later sinking into apathy.[86] People residing

Lebensraum – The Spatial and Demographic Formation

in the "points" were among the first to die of starvation or disease, and when deportations to death camps began, they were the first to be captured.[87]

After Deportations - Changes in Ghetto Topography

Deportations changed the ghetto's demographics as well as its topography. It was split into several areas and movement between them was prohibited except for those who had special permits.[88] On July 22, 1942, there were about 370,000 Jews in the ghetto. The daily quota for deportations was about 10,000 Jews. Within a month and a half, at the end of September 1942, about 55,000-60,000 Jews remained in the ghetto, half were 'wild'[89] and the rest, 'legal', most of whom were shop workers.[90]

As of July 22, 1942, the ghetto's spatial division consisted of:

A. The northern part of the former ghetto, which had three main sections: the brush makers shop in the south-east, the remains of the central ghetto and the Umschlagplatz in the north.[91] In what remained of the central ghetto, the majority were Jewish Council workers, Jewish police, relief workers and about 20,000 'wild'.

The Umschlagplatz, formerly a train platform used for shipping goods, was converted into a human cargo facility, and formed the departure point to Treblinka. The compound was surrounded by buildings that became short-term detention centers for deportees. Conditions in the Umschlagplatz were indescribable. Rooms were packed with anguished, horrified people who cried, pled and screamed while gunshots constantly added to the pandemonium.

The stench of feces, vomit and urine, together with the unbearable noises, contributed to driving people out of their minds.[92] There were those who sold their belongings, even gold watches for a glass of moldy water, mothers who spat their own saliva into their children's mouths to prevent dehydration.[93]

Henryk Krzepicki testified:

> At the Umschlag, there were only Ukrainians. They beat us awfully. They took the shoes they liked. They searched us for money and watches. In my group on the second floor, they picked out the prettiest girls at night and raped them, shooting some of them dead afterwards. Ukrainians also took several men and women away to the entrance hall and made them have sexual relations in their presence. Then they shot them dead. Similar travesties were staged regularly.[94]

Deportees were forced into extremely packed spaces where any human need, including relieving oneself, was negated. Consequently, the rooms were quickly inundated with horrible smells caused by bodily discharges. People were squeezed together and forced to be physically in contact with others as guards ignored their distress or engaged in further torture, trampling human dignity. Torment lasted for hours, if not days while pressures of bodily needs invaded the mind and impaired self-control capacities.[95]

Ben-Shem also alluded to the Umschlagplatz through the story of Mr. Platt, who was kidnapped on August 5 1942. He was taken to the Umschlagplatz first, then put onto a cattle wagon going to Treblinka from where he escaped and returned to his brother's house in the ghetto.[96] Ben-Shem wrote that Platt had been captive at the Umschlagplatz for at least twenty-four hours and that because he had been to Treblinka too, he used the experience there to say that the Umschlagplatz seemed '… at the most a prologue, an introduction, a corridor, where one witnesses bits of the play but not the play itself.'[97]

B. Even before July 1942, the southern part of the former ghetto was hard to reach despite the bridge over Chłodna street. This area, often referred to as 'the small ghetto', was emptied on August 10, 1942. Its residents were ordered out of their houses within hours and soon afterwards, this part was returned to Polish authorities with the exception of the zone where Többens' shop was located. Until its liquidation, the shop and its workers became an island in Polish territory.[98]

C. The main shop area was at the center of what used to be the Jewish ghetto. This book focuses on this territory, because both diary writers worked in shops located there: Ringelblum at Hallman's and Ben-Shem at Schilling's. This area shared a small border with Polish houses whereas the rest was almost completely surrounded by destroyed, empty houses of the ghetto.[99]

Workshops (Shops) – Ghetto Factories

The establishment of shops in the Warsaw Ghetto was in the best interest of Jews as well as Germans. These were small factories under German ownership set up in the fall of 1941, following the arrival of German entrepreneurs in Warsaw. The latter hoped to make big profits exploiting cheap Jewish labor to meet demands for growing shortages.[100] The Jewish Council was also in favor of establishing these shops as they hoped it would help them cope with poverty, provide the *Kehilla* with funds for maintenance while increasing their capacity to pay Germans for foods allowed into the ghetto.[101]

Lebensraum – The Spatial and Demographic Formation 111

In February 1941, the Germans authorized the *Kehilla* to establish shops but not many Jews were keen on working there because salaries offered were meager. Gutman wrote that Jews opted for other means of support, and even though shop owners attempted to attract workers into shops by offering soup, this did not significantly increase their number.[102] Attitudes towards working in shops changed completely during the spring of 1942, when information about organized annihilation reached the ghetto. Many Jews, encouraged by Germans, made the connection between work and reduced chances of deportation, leading to a growing wish to become shop employees. However, the Germans were no longer interested in increasing the numbers of shop employees and, in June 1942, a month before deportations, only about 70,000 people were registered as shop workers.[103]

As soon as deportations began, demands to be registered at any shop created their own madness. Simultaneously, shop workers became slave laborers and many shops did not provide workers with food. Workdays lasted between ten and twelve hours and conditions were harsh.[104] In addition, laborers had to live in designated communal workshop compounds. The grimmest reality was that workers were accepted as individuals meaning that their families were excluded from the deal and therefore, destined for death. Thus, family members became a part of a new class in the ghetto: the 'wild' having to hide to avoid raids for deportees.

With workshop compounds, people were forced to move to their living quarters without bringing their own possessions. Displacement was conducted hastily and sometimes violently leaving no opportunity to grab but a handful of belongings. What was left behind was claimed by empty-handed others, who either invaded these compounds or were forced into these quarters as they formed another shop's residential compound. Often, apartments assigned to certain shops were in dreadful conditions, especially those from which former residents had been evicted.[105] Equally, no consideration was given to the number of people per shop dwelling and whereas in some cases there was sufficient room, in others, it was the opposite.

During Heinrich Himmler's visit to Warsaw on January 9, 1943, he expressed his dissatisfaction with the number of Jews still living in Warsaw (about 50,000), many of whom were 'wild'. He ordered this number to be reduced, leading to more deportations from Warsaw, attempted on January 18, 1943. From the German point of view, these raids failed because Germans encountered resistance and succumbed to casualties and fatalities.

Following this, Nazis tried to convince shop workers to move voluntarily to factories in the Lublin area. They appointed Walther Caspar Többens who owned the largest ghetto shop, to the position of Jewish deportation commissar. His efforts to persuade Jews to relocate to Poniatowa and Trawniki concentration camps near Lublin, failed. However, after the Warsaw Ghetto Uprising and the complete destruction of the ghetto, in May 1943, all shops moved to the Lublin area.[106] The workers of these workshops met their end a few months later, when between November 3-4, 1943, camps were liquidated, with about 42,000-43,000 people shot in what the Germans referred to as *Aktion Erntefest*, Operation Harvest Festival.[107]

1. Notes on the ghetto underground women couriers, handwritten by Dr. Emanuel Ringelblum. This image is also featured on the background of the cover.

Ghetto Fighters' House Museum, Israel/ Photo Archive, Catalog No. 19214

The historian Dr. Emanuel Ringelblum with his son Uri.

Ghetto Fighters' House Museum, Israel/ Photo Archive, Catalog No. 19212.

3. Yehudit Ringelblum (Józia), nee Herman, Dr. Emanuel Ringelblum's wife.

Ghetto Fighters' House Museum, Israel/ Photo Archive, Catalog No. 2742.

4. A conference of Jewish historians in Vilnius organized by YIVO.
Right and standing: Shmuel Lehman (second), Daniel Lerner, Rafael Mahler.
Left standing: Pinchas Kon (fifth), Rudolf Glanc, Yosef - David Derewianski, Eliahu Szulman and Emanuel Ringelblum.
Seated, fifth from right, Prof. Simon Dubnow, August 1935.

Ghetto Fighters' House Museum, Israel/ Photo Archive, Catalog No. 19197.

5. Josima Feldschuh – Pnina (Perła) and Dr. Reuven Ben-Shem's (Feldschuh) daughter.

Yad-Vashem, Photo Archive, sig. 3384/85.

6. Ruth and Reuven Ben-Shem, Givat Shmuel, Israel, circa 1946.

The Ben-Shem Family Photo Archive

7. Hugging the dog, Ben-Shem's son Kami (Nekamia), Gad Feldschuh, his brother, Rachel Auerbach, Reuven Ben-Shem, Ruth his wife and Yuli (Yoa), his daughter.

The Ben-Shem Family Photo Archive

8. Dr. Reuven Ben-Shem (Feldschuh), Kowel, *Hashomer Hatzair*, 1926. This image is also featured on the background of the cover.

Ghetto Fighters' House Museum, Israel/ Photo Archive, Catalog No. 30011

9. Farewell party in honor of Dr. Feldschuh (Ben-Shem) (second row fifth from the right and sitting) Krakow, 13.8.1927

Massuah, Photo Archive, The Hannah Shlomi Collection, Item ID: 84271.

10. Rachel Auerbach and Hersch Wasser, upon the discovery of part of the buried "*Oneg Shabbat*" archives.

Yad-Vashem, Photo Archive, sig. 3380/745

11. Warsaw, Crowds at the corner of Zelazna and Leszno streets.

Yad-Vashem, Photo Archive, sig.503/1548.

12. Warsaw, Boxes and jars containing the buried "Ringelblum Archives". They were found in the ghetto ruins after the war.

Yad-Vashem, Photo Archive, sig. 1605/17.

13. Announcement of the concert Josima Feldschuh gave in the Melody Palace theatre in the Warsaw Ghetto, 15.3.1941.

The Ben-Shem Family Photo Archive.

At their home in Givat Shmuel: sitting: Reuven Ben-Shem and Rachel Auerbach, behind and standing: Ruth, Ben-Shem's wife.

The Ben-Shem Family Photo Archive.

15. Warsaw, a Jewish policeman directing the traffic between Leszno and Karmelicka Streets, 1941. The photograph was developed by Herbert Paetz. Avraham Haim Topas with his son are standing on the terrace.

Yad-Vashem, Photo Archive, sig. 503/1545.

16. Warsaw, children begging in the ghetto, 1940-1943.

Yad-Vashem, Photo Archive, sig. 933/140.

17. Warsaw, a starving child in a ghetto street, 1941.

Yad-Vashem, Photo Archive, sig. 3186/40.

18. A workshop in the Warsaw Ghetto, October 1940–May 1943.

United States Holocaust Memorial Museum, Leopold Page Photographic Collection, Photograph Number 05540.

19. The historian Dr. Emanuel Ringelblum.

Ghetto Fighters' House Museum, Israel/Photo Archive, Catalog No. 19190.

20. Dr Reuven Ben-Shem after the war.

The Ben-Shem Family Photo Archive.

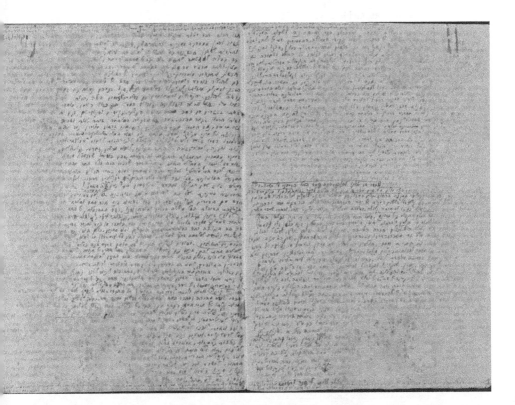

21. A page from Dr. Reuven Ben-Shem (Feldschuh)'s handwritten original diary. This image is also featured on the background of the cover.

The Ben-Shem Family Photo Archive.

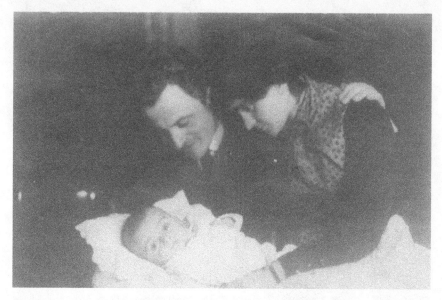

22. Warsaw, Dr Emanuel Ringelblum, his wife Yehudit with their son, Uri, circa 1930.

Yad-Vashem, Photo Archive, sig. 503/7341.

23. Dr Herzl Rosenblum (Chief Editor of Yedioth Ahronoth), Dr Reuven Ben-Shem, Moshe Gold and Elie Wiesel at Be'er Yaacov, Israel, circa 1948.

The Ben-Shem Family Photo Archive.

V

Between the Private and Public Sphere: Documentation

Ringelblum: Writing is Political but Also Personal

In his daily diary, Ringelblum never discussed why he had decided to begin writing nor why he kept a diary until the ghetto was destroyed. Equally, references to *Oneg Shabbat* were rare, but indirectly, he expressed appreciation for and approval of people who kept documenting.[1] It was only in *Last Writings* that Ringelblum addressed his daily records explicitly, mentioning October 1939 as the date he began documentation.

He wrote that subsequently, he had collected documents, and his work at the JDC and Coordinating Committee (supported by SKSS (Stołeczny Komitet Samopomocy Społecznej) had brought him into contact with many people who communicated their harsh experiences to him, information he recorded each evening.[2] Ringelblum added that as time passed and there were enough workers at *Oneg Shabbat*, his daily entries were replaced by weekly and later, monthly entries.[3]

In *Last Writings,* Ringelblum discussed the phenomenon of documentation through personal diaries, characterizing them as '... one of the richest areas *Oneg Shabbat* was involved in.'[4] He added that most of these writers had been murdered and their diaries lost. It is in this context he mentioned his own diary claiming its importance was due to his extensive documentation during the first year of the war, when not many people wrote.[5] According to Ringelblum, an additional advantage was that in his weekly and monthly reports, he was able to incorporate estimations, opinions and discussions about burning issues in the ghetto, including views of various sectors of the Jewish community.[6]

Conversely, this suggests that Ringelblum may have regarded his diary as equal to other personal diaries even though his was intentionally meant to be a historical record. It sounds as if he surmised that other diary writers were also primarily concerned with external events, that is, life in the ghetto and consequently, there was little difference between his and their diaries. Likewise, Ringelblum assumed responsibility for his diary and regarded it as personal in the sense that only he wrote it, and its contents were his concern.

Why did Ringelblum not address the notion of writing a diary while he was keeping one? First, the rapidly deteriorating circumstances in Warsaw probably made it vital to concentrate on chronicling rather than reflecting on actions. Second, although it appears Ringelblum regarded his own diary as a personal venture, its historic nature required no explanation – it was clear. After all, when the Second World War broke out, the realm of writing history as a conceptual mode of response to crisis among Jews was well established, and awareness of the role of documentation appreciated and valued. Hence, it can be deduced that the importance he attributed to recording lay in the mere action. Given the circumstances in Warsaw, fulfilling this enormous task demanded the enlistment of more people. Indeed, this may explain why Ringelblum reported difficulty in recruiting people to work at the *Oneg Shabbat* archive, but he never mentioned anything about having to explain the task to those he wanted to engage.

Indeed, Ringelblum's notes confirmed that the notion of documentation was widespread and that many people had, under their own initiative, decided to record events. In the early days of the war, he wrote that despite the hardships '… advocates of YIVO…'[7] were able to continue collecting materials and recording the present. In contrast, Ringelblum also reported that these same people were also responsible for burning multiple documents, afraid these may lead to their arrest.[8]

In December 1939, he mentioned Rabbi Huberband, his colleague at YIVO and pointed out that the latter was an example of someone who despite being personally affected by the war, continued with his scientific work.[9] Nevertheless, at the beginning, Huberband was so worried documenting might put him in danger, he chose to put his notes inside books as if they were personal remarks. Ringelblum added it had taken him a long time to convince him there was no immediate danger in the act of documentation.[10]

In *Last Writings* Ringelblum discussed once more the two opposing trends, documenting versus refraining from so doing and even destroying documents. He explained that during the early months of occupation, the Germans used to conduct frequent searches that alarmed Jews. However, it turned out, 'The more searches were carried out – and they became more precise and frequent – they referred to something completely different – foreign currency, gold, diamonds …'.[11] By the time the Jews realized that Jewish internal life did not interest the Germans, many had already destroyed books, notes, whole libraries, social pamphlets, etc. In other words, whereas Jewish concerns were based on rational thinking, that the Germans were anxious about political activity threatening their grip in Poland, they were after loot, which explained why homes were constantly raided and plundered.

Irrespectively, Ringelblum did not take confidentiality lightly and was cautious with his notes, frequently coding texts to protect himself as well as others. Many of his entries, particularly during the first year, were camouflaged as letters.[12] On the rare occasions he spoke about *Oneg Shabbat*, such as on January 2-3, 1940, it was in a concise manner and using coded language: '... The young from Kutno (unidentified), the director--, (according to the editor, this may refer to Michał Weichert)[13] and the young Rabbi from the Medical-Social Help (Rabbi Huberband).[14]

According to Gutman, by November 1939, Ringelblum had established the archive and gave it its code name, *Oneg Shabbat*. Gutman argued that Ringelblum sensed that Jews were on the verge of an extremely difficult period and as such, records would be necessary because of the incredible nature of brutalities whose range and pace were unparalleled.[15] However, until the spring of 1940, Ringelblum worked almost entirely alone but the method of documentation changed once more people had been recruited. Ringelblum continued with a less frequent form of synchronic document-ation while the *Oneg Shabbat* team recorded phenomena according to themes corresponding with a historical perspective.

In the circumstances created and despite Ringelblum's distinct political orientation, records were indeed perceived as addressing the wellbeing of the entire Jewish population and not any specific political group. In this respect, Ringelblum's activities were not questioned; because there was a wide consensus about the importance of documentation and creating historical records as a pattern of reaction among Jews suffering hard times.

Ringelblum's approach, which inextricably linked the creation of historical records to understanding current political situations, focused on all Jews, resulting in gathering information almost entirely free of narrow political party interests.[16] With time, Ringelblum became more confident that the *Oneg Shabbat* archive was largely supported by all Jews, regardless of their political beliefs. Still, among archive workers, not one was affiliated with Revisionist parties, longtime rivals of left oriented parties. Gutman quoted Israel E. Biderman who had concluded that Ringelblum's monographs were factual, and his political bias was reflected in the type of topics he sought to investigate yet avoiding interpretations to refrain from imposing his political views.[17]

May 23, 1942, was the first time Ringelblum referred to the difficulties of maintaining archive work, comparing the situation to the early months of the war: '...since Friday, April 18th, we're back to "poor" work. What already exists, must be saved – the method: make a cup of tea and write after the meeting (without the presence of the witness).'[18] The 1939 problems and confusion became a scale in two ways: concern about confidentiality and practicality of being able to carry out the work itself.

The background to these difficulties was events that had taken place in the ghetto a month and a half earlier, when on the night between April 17-18, 1942, the Nazis arrested and murdered fifty-two people for alleged illegal activities. These events were regarded as a landmark in the history of the ghetto and in particular, for the *Oneg Shabbat* workers because it was necessary to reinstate the confidential work patterns to which they had adhered at the beginning of the war.

The fact Jews attributed importance to the arrest and murder of the fifty-two people suggests that once again Jews had fallen into a trap of trying to explain the inexplicable with logical and pragmatic reasons. In this case, it was assumed that political activities had led to the murder, wrongly deducing that refraining from any political engagement would prevent persecution. Ringelblum concluded that they were rather lucky that the archive itself remained in the shadows.

In *Last Writings,* Ringelblum wrote that as far as purpose was concerned, all those who worked for the archive, temporarily or permanently, were '... conscious of the value of the work and its importance for future generations so as to commemorate the tragedy of the Jews of Poland.'[19] This was evident because archive staff and consequently records, grew in scope of topics covered, in both their quality and number.[20]

Simultaneously, a more distinct space was created among the nucleus of this unique group.[21] This was not a geographical space, but a spiritual enclosure that provided the frame, the common cause, that is, documenting ghetto phenomena. Therefore, it was the rationale that bonded people and, in these circumstances, where it was so hard to distinguish between private and public, commitment to one another went far beyond the actual pledge of documentation. Indeed, Ringelblum expressed this in his final words about the *Oneg Shabbat* archive:

> O[yneg] S[habes]did not forget its coworkers. The faithful father and provider was the ailing Menakhem K[on], who saved both Hersh W[asser] and Rabbi Huberband from dying of typhus, who cared about the sick child of Comrade G[utkow]ski, and who greatly aided

Between the Private and Public Sphere: Documentation 117

the writer and the journalist Peretz O[poczyn]ski, who was always suffering from hunger. The quiet dove, Daniel Fligelman, would have died long since had it not been for the constant and affectionate help of our dear Comrade Menakhem. There were countless occasions on which he pressed me to leave Warsaw after the bloody night of April [18], 1942. Every coworker of O[yneg] S[habes] knew that his effort and pain, his difficult toil and tribulations, the risk he ran twenty-four hours a day in the clandestine work, carrying materials from one place to another—that all this was for the sake of a noble ideal and that, in the days of freedom, society will correctly evaluate and award it the highest honor of free Europe. O[yneg] S[habes] was a brotherhood, an order of brothers, who wrote on their banner, 'Readiness for Sacrifice; Loyalty of One to Another; Service to Society.[22]

These final words from the monograph dedicated to *Oneg Shabbat* were written when Ringelblum was well aware that only a handful of his team members remained alive. The obituary nature of this passage is imbued with longing and a deep appreciation of what Ringelblum referred to as 'an order of brethren.' For him, being able to form this group went beyond fulfilling the task of creating historical records. It went into instilling in his co-workers mutual dedication, a sense of family, loyalty to one another as well as the entire Jewish people. The text evidently reveals that permanent *Oneg Shabbat* workers were united not only in their desire to document, but relationships stretched much further, into their private lives. Thanks to *Oneg Shabbat* and despite ghetto conditions, this group became a source of physical as well as mental and spiritual comfort, resulting in the development of strong emotional bonds.

After deportations began, Ringelblum's diary entries reflected how almost unattainable writing became, especially during July-September 1942. Terror at Bernhard Hallman's shop, trying to keep up with his welfare work, the death of so many people he knew, relatives and workers at *Oneg Shabbat* like Rabbi Huberband, Shakhne Ephraim Zagan and Avraham Lewin, to name but a few, left Ringelblum drained of energy and yet committed to writing. Additionally, since many *Oneg Shabbat* workers were under threat or had been murdered, it was infinitely more important for Ringelblum to diligently keep writing. In this respect, there was partial consistency between the last part of his daily diary to his documentation at the beginning of the war - Ringelblum was almost the only one who recorded.

Entries focused almost exclusively on events and phenomena but no longer chronologically. His daily diary, which ends in January 1943, reflected the severity of the situation not only in what he wrote but most significantly in vocabulary and syntax choices.[23] This part of his daily diary was the shortest in time and quantity. The first two entries consisted of lists, which seem like references for later elaboration.[24] When the daily roundups stopped, between the end of September 1942 and January 18 1943, living conditions in the ghetto stayed deplorable and the remaining Jews broken, but Ringelblum's documentation continued. Until December 1942 he added essays, some titled such as 'How Selection was Conducted', untitled or dated entries, sometimes adding dates to titled essays.

Ringelblum's family left the ghetto sometime in February 1943, but he returned to the ghetto several times.[25] During the uprising, though it is unclear when, he was caught and sent to Trawniki. In August 1943, thanks to Teodor Pajewski and Shoshana Kossower-Rozencwajg (Emilka), he was back in Warsaw where he resumed writing, but no longer a synchronic diary, instead, he wrote a series of monographs relating to the ghetto.

Things he could not write about while still in the ghetto, found a place in these notes. The monographs dealt with important people such as the Jewish Fighting Organization's leaders like Mordechai Anielewicz (1919-1943), institutions such as *Oneg Shabbat*, and a long comprehensive review of Polish-Jewish relationships, the only piece in Polish. In this respect, in hiding, Ringelblum created a more traditional historical record having the perspective of a few months' distance.

It seems that the very fact Ringelblum chose to summarize events of the ghetto, ignoring not only his personal situation, but also what still went on in Warsaw after the ghetto's destruction, highlights his approach to the relationship between politics and history; Polish Jewry had been annihilated, it was time for history. Apparently, two factors played a role in this decision. The first, there were hardly any Jews left in Warsaw and whoever was there, remained in hiding, which made it impossible to record their struggles.

Second, he had pledged to write a historical record and not about his personal whereabouts. The situation in August 1943 was such that dealing with politics meant beginning historical research as most Polish Jews had been annihilated, and political activism, at that point in time, was to leave a trace by writing about what had happened.

Conversely, it seems that Ringelblum did not only overlook his personal circumstances of having to live literally underground with more than thirty other people, but that he did not consider this reality, as well as that of many others in hiding, as history worth recording. Equally, it is plausible to

Between the Private and Public Sphere: Documentation   119

assume that Ringelblum regarded documentation of life in shelters as suitable content for private rather than historical diaries.

Indeed, the series of monographs Ringelblum managed to produce during seven months of hiding before his murder, did not hint at the danger he and his family faced; he wrote as if he were already dead but also as if death was no longer a threat as what they were experiencing could hardly be called living. In this way, Ringelblum reintroduced the dividing line separating the public from the private sphere, two spaces, which according to him, should not be intermingled.

Space wise, Ringelblum and other Jews were dead, literally living underground or under false identities – unable to hold onto their true selves. To all appearances, Warsaw was 'Judenrein', free of Jews, thus, Warsaw as well as other areas, had a living space above ground but also in the underworld. Metaphorically, writing in hiding was equal to being outside history, ironically, in the world of the dead, history was no longer needed. Thus, Ringelblum's initial social approach became void as writing history could no longer help Jews politically.

Politics –Ringelblum: On London Radio

Ringelblum discussed the *Oneg Shabbat* archive openly only once in his daily diary and it was in relation to the London June 26, 1942, BBC radio broadcast to which he dedicated only two entries.[26] This radio program followed an earlier one on June 2, 1942 and to which Ringelblum did not refer at all. Apparently, the two entries addressed a new space, which had been until then clandestine, political activity dedicated to informing the outside world of the fate of Polish Jewry.

Although the tone in the June 26 narrative is restrained, Ringelblum's praise for *Oneg Shabbat* and its achievement is evident. He mentioned cities such as Slonim and Vilnius where Jews had been murdered, and that 'For many months we had been asking ourselves if the world was deaf and dumb to our tragedy which was unprecedented in human history.'[27] The palpable satisfaction at successfully smuggling information out, is contrasted with his terrible doubt, mingled with disbelief, that, until then, the tragedy of the Jews remained unknown to the outside world.

Immediately afterwards, Ringelblum openly attacked the Poles and in particular, the Polish leadership, including the Polish Government-in-Exile, for not acknowledging the slaughter of the Jews of Poland: 'We accused the Poles of deliberately silencing our tragedy so that it did not overshadow theirs.'[28] Ringelblum criticized the Poles for exploiting information politically and knowingly "competing" with Jews by entirely ignoring the uniqueness of Nazi attacks on them. Furthermore, Ringelblum's reproach suggests that the Polish Government-in-Exile, once more, did not see its Jewish population as equal citizens precisely because it related to Jews as Poles thus overlooking the fact Jews were singled out because they were Jewish and not because they happened to be Poles.

Obviously, these accusations suggest that information was a political tool for Jews just as much as Poles. The "competition" the Polish Government-in-Exile's was conducting with the Jews demonstrated malevolence on their part, an attitude Ringelblum attributed to Polish beliefs that had they specified the Jewish case, it would have jeopardized Polish interests. Worse, Ringelblum insinuated that choosing not to relate to Jews specifically, ignoring the unusual hardships and torture inflicted on them, allowed Poles to aggravate the image of Polish suffering thus concealing Nazi purposes.

Kassow wrote that the information sent to London was transmitted by the Bund, the only Jewish party retaining a good and stable relationship with the Polish Socialist Party, and which allowed them access to higher levels of the Polish underground leadership ensuring that information reached Allied Forces. The Polish underground used Carl Wilhelm Herslow, Sven Normann and Carl Gustafsson, three Swedish businessmen who lived in Warsaw, to smuggle news out. Indeed, on June 2nd, the BBC reported that 700,000 Polish Jews had been murdered, an estimated number, which according to Kassow, was in reality, at that time, much higher.[29]

Gutman enumerated several reasons for Polish reluctance to publicize accurate information. First, the Poles were afraid that the world's attention would be diverted to Jews and therefore, they refused to make any distinction between Jews and Poles. In their communiqués they referred to the immense tragedy of Polish civilians intentionally omitting the fact these civilians were mostly Jewish. Second, the Government-in-Exile was concerned that the population in Poland might get the impression that they were overly defending Jews and that this would lower its popularity within Poland.

Last, the report mentioning 700,000 murdered Jews related primarily to Jews in eastern Poland, areas that had been annexed by the USSR and conquered by Germany in 1941. Since most residents in those areas were not Polish, the Polish Government-in-Exile did not see itself directly responsible for them. Hence, in their broadcasts, they stressed the part played by Ukrainians and Lithuanians collaborating with the Nazis and as such, the Polish government abrogated responsibility for Jews in those regions.[30]

Between the Private and Public Sphere: Documentation

When Ringelblum mentioned the archive in this context, he indicated that far from keeping quiet, he and others had assigned the material collected for the *Oneg Shabbat* archive additional political purposes, from recording for future research to '… a great historical mission…'[31] equivalent to '… a hard blow.'[32] In other words, for Ringelblum, documentation was a weapon and using it was equal to a striking the enemy in the battlefield.

In this sense, the passage about *Oneg Shabbat* is evidence of the changing purposes of documentation. Whereas compilation of information was initially for future historical research, as soon as it became clear that Jews were being deliberately annihilated, information was also used to notify the outside world about the organized murder of Jews taking place under Nazi occupation. Thus, indirectly, accumulating evidence was active resistance against Germans, as well as an active response to fight inaccurate information circled by Poles.

Choosing to write about the June 26 British broadcast also suggests that it was then that Ringelblum acknowledged the future practical fingerprint *Oneg Shabbat* might have. His satisfaction and relief were plainly expressed when he wrote:

> The O.S. (*Oneg Shabbat*) group …. has alarmed the world to our fate, and possibly saved hundreds of thousands of Polish Jews from extinction – obviously, this would be proven or refuted only in the near future. … all our work and exertion, our commitment and continuous terror, have not been in vain. We have struck the enemy a hard blow.[33]

Ringelblum used the phrase 'We have struck the enemy a hard blow' twice in the same passage, sharpening how highly he regarded this mission and the results of the continuous and diligent efforts to alarm the world. Equally, this passage showed Ringelblum and other Jews' frustration at the notion that no one seemed to know about their systematic murder. Refusing to resign to this implication that the world did not care, his words demonstrate that Jews preferred to think their tragedy remained unknown, which encouraged them to risk themselves and smuggle information out.

Ringelblum was not naïve and whereas no real ambiguity can be traced in the former text, on June 30 1942, he distinctly expressed despair and, how despite wanting to be hopeful, he was also rational. Previously he had omitted his frustration at the realization that the Allied Forces were aware of atrocities. Here, and to somehow offset the impact of such a realization, he tried to explain it by comparing the murder of Jews and non-Jews,

180,000 in Rostov and the same number in Kiev, asking, 'Why should the world be shocked when everyday rivers of blood flow in battle fields.'[34] Surprisingly, the initial answer he gave was still the same: 'Only now did we understand this silence. London simply did not know.'[35]

Yet, a sentence later he wondered, how it was possible to think that '… London simply didn't know…'[36] when the news about the murder of a hundred Jews in the Pawiak (a prison inside the ghetto) reached London a day after it happened. Clearly, this narrative seems to reflect Ringelblum's inner conflict that swiveled between hope and desolation. Logically, he knew that London had the information long before his report arrived. Emotionally, he was unable to give up on the thought that there was some logical reason for the apparent indifference to the fate of Jews. Although Ringelblum admitted he could not explain this discrepancy, the rest of the discussion indicated he preferred to stick to the approach that the disseminated information could still affect the future of the remaining Jews.

One should bear in mind that Ringelblum's open discussion of this activity in his diary was unusual and somewhat risky even though then, he was the only one in control of this document and what he recorded was not intended to become public at that stage. Nevertheless, this entry insinuated the degree of political activity taking place behind the scenes, involving the Polish underground, cooperation with other political parties that were not natural partners for Ringelblum and the LPZ, as well as the efforts invested in the corridors of the British government by Jews in England, most notably, Szmul Zygielbojm (1895-1943) whom Ringelblum mentioned in this passage, as well as others.[37]

Further, Ringelblum discussed public opinion inside Germany expressing hope that when they became aware of the existence of places such as Chełmno, they would firmly object. He further noted that 'So far the press and the radio have kept silent',[38] a situation he understood as the German media was controlled by the Nazis. Notably, Ringelblum makes a clear distinction between the Nazi armed forces and the German public whom he refused to believe was aware of the massacres. To prove that there was such a difference and that his hopes were not unfounded, he wrote about a rumor concerning the liberation of Jews from Ostrowitz who were already inside a train cart. Ringelblum concluded by saying that if this incident really happened, it might be proof that '… a new era was about to start',[39] and that it was thanks to dissemination of information.

As much as the June 30, 1942 entry shows Ringelblum's satisfaction at being able to smuggle out the reports, it also expresses self-reproach, that is, deceiving himself into believing that no one knew about the Jewish tragedy. In a somewhat restrained manner, he also clearly gloated at being able to force the Polish Government-in-Exile to publicly acknowledge the uniqueness of the Jewish issue. This was followed by considering the possible impact this might have in Germany, a text reflecting Ringelblum's hopes mingled with sober reasoning expressed in the ending, that the longer the war lasted, the slimmer Jews' chances of survival were.

These two passages offer a glimpse into a range of issues that preoccupied those incarcerated in the Warsaw Ghetto, most prominently, a deep sense of isolation and abandonment. Ringelblum and Jewish prisoners in the ghetto could not understand how it was possible that their tragedy remained unnoticed.

At first, Ringelblum explained this by suggesting it was due to Polish tendentious reports. The second justification introduced a comparison, the murder of Jews versus that of others, asking whether Jews' blood was redder than that of Russian, Chinese, British soldiers and others.[40] The third excuse was '...the eternal answer...',[41] hinting at antisemitism, a pretext that was immediately dismissed. Finally, Ringelblum tried to claim that information simply had not reached London, a claim he refuted instantly.

Most importantly, Ringelblum mentioned that people in the ghetto feared German retaliation after this program, but apparently, there was no such reaction. Lastly, now that the news about the Jews had become known to everyone, Ringelblum reported that people were interested in the reaction of the German public, but there was no indication of this in the diary. On the contrary, apart from these two entries, Ringelblum did not mention the radio program, *Oneg Shabbat*, hopes this broadcast stirred or not, nor the disappointment that followed.

Reuven Ben-Shem – Writing is Personal but Also Political

For Ben-Shem, a prolific writer, the experience of writing without clear and evident prospects of publication must have been challenging. Like Ringelblum, an opinionated social activist who did not refrain from expressing his views publicly, he did not keep a diary before the war. Regardless, since he had not been involved in any documentation ventures previously, keeping a diary, which to begin with, originated in extreme historical pressure, was demanding.

In the analysis of Ben-Shem's diary, I relied almost exclusively on his deciphered document. As it is an edited text, it means that the reasons for starting a diary or writing one did not necessarily appear in the original version. That is to say, these discussions, all or some, may have resulted from the process of editing in safety rather than representation of contents in the original, with one exception. In one of the notebooks' first page, which presumably constitutes the beginning of documentation in hiding, Ben-Shem addressed readers directly.

In February, 1943, Ben-Shem and his family were smuggled out of the ghetto and went into hiding in Pustelnik. About a month later, Ben-Shem started what appears to be a diary that sought to document his whereabouts from the beginning of the war. The first paragraph directly addressed anyone who might stumble upon his manuscript. He began by stating his name, pseudonym, ancestors' names (including a claim that his mother's family, Lippa, were descendants of Rashi),[42] and the region from whence they came, Stanisławów (now Ivano-Frankivsk), east Podolia. He further wrote that he, his wife and daughter, dressed like Poles, probably referring to typical rural clothing '... armed with Polish identification...'[43] went underground hoping to be saved from annihilation '... the head of the demons of all times declared on us.'[44]

Ben-Shem added that he wanted to record his family's 'adventures' because they were among the few survivors after the 'First Destruction of the People' adding in brackets that there were two 'Temple Destructions'[45]. Hence, Ben-Shem drew a poetic parallel between the destruction of the land of Israel, and the Holocaust, a word not yet in use then, to refer to the annihilation of Jews during the Second World War. The date, March 1943 (written in words) was noted, adding that entire Polish families were facing a death penalty if Germans found Jews hiding on their property. The statement/testament ended with a series of requests imploring future trustees of his notebooks to fulfil:

'To make it known where I, my wife and daughter were killed and to grant us proper Jewish burial.

Notify my family (all are Feldschuh) in America about us and also my brother Gad Feldschuh in Tel-Aviv, (I do not dare to wish such a thing) but they might want to move my bones to Eretz Israel, where I worked —) and about which I have dreamt during the best years of my life ...'

Publish these notebooks on one condition, in all languages except Yiddish...'[46]

Much like other diarists, this manuscript entry projects Ben-Shem's sensations that the war years, with the intensity of events, were equated to a lifetime. Although Ben-Shem declared the immediate purpose of writing was to inform his relatives about their story or history during the war, he also regarded their war experience as representing what happened to the entire Jewish people. By coining the term, the 'First Destruction of the people', Ben-Shem tells us his family was one amongst a mere 100,000 Jews, who for the time being, survived the annihilation of 3,500,000 Polish Jews, and that he was almost certain they were not likely to survive the war and chances to tell their story were slim unless he documented it.

Ben-Shem's choice of the word 'adventures' to describe what the family had undergone in the previous years, sounds somewhat inappropriate as it implies some degree of free will. Initially, 'adventures' seems to belittle the gravity of situations experienced, as if he was trying to convey meanings of threat, surprise and stupefaction while lending it qualities of an audacious journey.[47] In that sense, 'adventures' may seem to be misrepresenting not only the family's ghetto experience but also that of all other Jews incarcerated in the ghetto.

Was Ben-Shem attempting to convey concisely the degree of danger, unexpected turns and loss of control over one's life they had experienced, or did he use this word cynically? Does 'adventures' attempt to create a total separation between what came before and Ben-Shem's present, hiding, as if he regarded the here and now to be stable? Is it possible that Ben-Shem was proposing a comparison, that being motionless and concealing any signs of life, was the reverse of an adventure? Apparently, the new period, living in a nook underground which implied that no signs of life were to be visible was opposite to adventurous, seemingly because it was about being still, pretending not to exist.

Next and most importantly, Ben-Shem asked that, if possible, they took care of their burial as well as publish the manuscript.[48] Discussing publication indicates that already during the war and before actually starting the process of documentation, Ben-Shem understood the universal value of his account and consciously wrote with an eye on a potential reader. This means that this story may have addressed his family first but also an undefined audience, suggesting that special attention had to be given to contents - what to omit, what to write and how.

The implications publishing his diary might have also explained his order, that '... before publication, names have to be changed because I don't want to hurt anyone and as I will not be alive, my observations might wound a person's self-esteem--'.[49] As already noted, the manuscript, being illegible, does not allow one to determine whether in the original Ben-Shem adhered to this rule selectively or not. However, in his deciphered diary, edited almost twenty years later, some names were openly stated while others remained obscure, and I can only assume that the reason had to do with whether they or their relatives survived.

As for the request not to translate the document into Yiddish, Ben-Shem explained that:

> ... it (Yiddish) was not its fault but our parents and ancestors who have dragged the language from the Rein to the rest of Europe, Poland and now this language has the same sounds as German. And to its rings – the German language, our parents, brothers, children, relatives and all of our people perished.[50]

Regardless of the war experiences and contrary to Ringelblum, who was an avid Yiddishist, Ben-Shem was an enthusiastic Hebraist. For Ringelblum Polish was a threat because it signified detachment from Jewish society and a tendency to various degrees of assimilation. In contrast, Ben-Shem and his wife, Pnina, both originally from east Galicja, where Yiddish was largely spoken by Jews, seem to have chosen to refrain from using Yiddish at home, which was the reason their daughter, Josima only spoke Polish and a little Hebrew.[51]

Throughout his diary, Ben-Shem did not explain once why he wrote in Hebrew, an unusual choice as the language was the third for most Jews of eastern Europe, including Ben-Shem himself. The local language was generally acquired as a second language once a child was exposed to the world outside home. Most children, particularly boys, were exposed to Hebrew in their early years at Jewish pre-schools. Their knowledge of the Hebrew alphabet made it easier not only to cope with reading the bible, prayers, etc., but also with reading Yiddish as it used Hebrew letters. The paradox was that although many could read Hebrew, most could not understand modern Hebrew as it was not a daily spoken language for the vast majority. Thus, writing personal diaries in Hebrew was the least natural choice.[52]

An incident in early December 1942 demonstrates Ben-Shem's ambiguous approach to Yiddish. He recounted that he was approached by parents whose children survived the great deportation and wanted him to organize classes for them. This request triggered a debate about which language to employ for this purpose, a discussion that offers a glimpse into his attitude to Yiddish. Eventually, it was decided that the children would

Between the Private and Public Sphere: Documentation   127

study without books, although there were plenty left behind. Ben-Shem explained that there was no point in teaching them in Polish because '... if anyone survived, who would remain in Poland.'[53] Yiddish, essentially, a German language was according to Ben-Shem, out of the question as the death of Jews was accompanied by the sounds of the German language and the similarity to Yiddish made it unbearable to Jewish ears. He felt that the crimes committed using German, in speech and in writing, consequently contaminated Yiddish. However, Ben-Shem did not explain how the issue was resolved but it can be assumed that eventually, even without books, studies were conducted mostly in Yiddish as this was the main language spoken.

As previously mentioned, Ben-Shem's first entry in the manuscript indicated that out of the three notebooks at Yad-Vashem, at least one was written in hiding. That notebook started with his will, followed immediately with him recounting his family's whereabouts from the first day of the war. As it is not possible, at this stage, to tell the notebooks apart, it is equally difficult to determine how much of the manuscripts' contents were based on previous notes written while he was in the ghetto or whether what we have now represents reconstruction of life in the ghetto conducted in hiding. Indeed, information in the deciphered diary suggests that when Ben-Shem left the ghetto, he had taken with him some of his notes.

Furthermore, Ben-Shem addressed readers directly several times. The first such reference appeared at the end of December 1940:

> I don't know whether this notebook with my notes, will ever reach the eye of a reader, although I would certainly like that to happen. It is hard to say whether I will get to see the day my diary is published or if others would like to publish it when they find it after my death. In any case, I note my impressions including those which apparently seem worthless and trivial and give them a place here. May the reader, if such ever exists, forgive me for not sparing him any misfortunes or descriptions of sorrow we have gone through. Every detail is important, the world should know, remember and engrave it on its memory so as to draw the proper conclusion.[54]

The passage was presumably written after a *Hanukah* party that took place at the Ben-Shems' house in December 1940, during which his daughter Josima, played the piano and a nice sum of money was collected from guests for the house committee.[55] Assuming this passage was actually written in 1940 and copied unchanged in safety to the typed version, it contained an indirect address to potential readers to whom he explained the rationale underpinning the detailed style of his diary.

The text depicted a hypothetic situation sometime in the future when contents were read by an anonymous reader and to whom the writer apologized for his detailed style. This imaginary internal dialogue was designed to makes it clear that under any circumstances, the author would like his text to be published, whether he survived the war or if the notebooks were found after his death.

The imaginary dialogue continues with an apology for not sparing readers, '... a single difficulty..., description of sorrow ... Every detail is important, the world should know, remember and engrave it on its memory so as to draw the proper conclusion.'[56]

The passage, which appears quite early in the diary, highlights Ben-Shem's focus of attention, details including 'impressions' as well as an educational purpose. These, details and education, were linked to one another as the they would allow readers to draw conclusions and learn lessons. Ben-Shem considered specifics meaningful and essential because they revealed what the big picture concealed. Exposure of the sordid details enabled an understanding of the unprecedented nature of events and thus, drawing accurate conclusions, a process possible only if one were exposed to what had happened in full.

This address was followed not by descriptions of ghetto life but his own assessment of Germans. He stated that the latter had crossed every possible '... line, concept and human perception ...',[57] a statement followed by a long, furious passage in which he declared himself an authority on history but had never before heard about such atrocities. Ben-Shem stated that it was this that made it so important to document events in detail as the Germans, whom he called 'Teutons', had challenged '... human perception.'[58]

According to Ben-Shem, 'Furor Teutonicus',[59] the term Romans used to describe the Barbarian tribes that invaded their empire repeatedly, was '... a compliment in comparison to the truth.'[60] This passage employs extremely sharp vocabulary, terms and concepts to describe Germans, including comparisons between them and many other European nations, none escaping the whip of his language, all of which were designed to convince future unknown readers that Ben-Shem's evaluation of the unparalleled nature of attacks on Jews was based upon his personal body of knowledge of the history of the human race.

In fact, in many ways, this address to readers along with his lengthy explanation about, on the one hand, his expertise as a historian, a '... Dr. in Philosophy specializing in history...'[61] and a person for whom '... the paths

Between the Private and Public Sphere: Documentation 129

of history...were as clear ... as the paths of the ghetto...',[62] do not function as much to assert his authority as to lead readers into a time tunnel opening with scenes from the early era of civilization designed to prove that the Germans, this time, were worse than their ancestors. He also added another criterion for judging Germans, in comparison to the infamous pogroms in Russia, Ukraine, and Poland, none, concluded Ben-Shem, was comparable to what Jews had endured during this war.

Whereas the previous dialogue with readers attempted to explain the rationale of documentation, Ben-Shem's other addresses did not. Two prominent imaginary discussions with readers, addressed the notion of veracity, a concern preoccupying many writers. One entry was personal and concerned a performance his daughter gave at the Melody Palace in the ghetto, a performance, he assured readers, which was outstanding.[63] Intimately, Ben-Shem seemingly confided in readers that these were not simply the words of a loving father, and as proof, he quoted what had been written in an article published in *Gazeta Żydowska*, March 21, 1941.[64]

The other address concerned rumors circulating in the ghetto about systematic murder taking place in occupied Soviet territories. On this occasion, March 26, 1942, Ben-Shem wrote that he had not written for a long time because he wanted to confirm the rumors before recording them in his diary.[65] Hence, reporting about precaution with documenting unfounded information, Ben-Shem assured readers that the news he was about to expose, was accurate. This suggested that the news was so shocking that its authenticity had to be verified prior to publication.

One heartbreaking entry related not merely to writing, but the importance these writings had in his and his distant cousin, Rachel Auerbach's, lives. Around July 20th, 1942, just before the deportations began, Ben-Shem wrote in his diary about the silence and emptiness that had suddenly engulfed the ghetto once it became clear to everyone there was no way to stop the deportations.

> I came home. 'Shiva'.[66] Everyone is sad, their heads lowered, the eyes wide open, looking to the distance and the depth ... each one looking at the other as if they were already dead ... My relative and I began to take care of our soul mates. She packed all of her writings including her printed articles into one bundle and tied them up very well. I also packed my books, my writings and newspaper articles from different periods, tying them up and writing on the top using a chemical pencil: books and manuscripts belonging to R. B. S., Dr. F. (Reuven Ben-Shem, Dr. Feldschuh), Beware not to burn! Donate

to the Hebrew University in Jerusalem! My relative wrote on her bundle: R. R. A (Rachel Rokhl Auerbach) – Donate to YIVO, Vilnius, or the University in Jerusalem. She added this (the University in Jerusalem) after I explained that YIVO's fate would most probably be similar to ours if it had not happened already. We looked at our life products as if they were our most favorite child, the produce of blood, hearts, brains and mostly our longings. We added another address on the other side using a pen and we put them in the basement of our room, in the most distant corner, between two bricks we placed our treasure, maybe ...our memory will not be wiped out forever and will not be lost in oblivion... With dry eyes and calm movement, we fulfilled this duty of our souls and went upstairs.[67]

In the passage, Ben-Shem created a parallel between two ceremonies, *Shiva* and the packing of his and Auerbach's writings to which Ben-Shem referred as 'our soul mates' thus drawing another parallel between flesh and blood relatives to those of the soul. Ben-Shem used inclusion to discuss his writings because they were relevant parts of his life.[68] To emphasize their importance, he used vocabulary equating their significance to that of his family. Personifying books and writings as 'our soul mates', he sharpened their presence in the text and thus granted them a status elevating them to a degree no less important than his relatives.[69]

Shiva, which takes place after a burial service, in this case preceded the death of the people who were sitting at home stunned by grief and fear. Yet, *Shiva* was simultaneously taking place while Auerbach and Ben-Shem prepared their writings for burial. Their collections were packed meticulously and with great attention, each parcel carefully closed and on each, an address was inscribed, full of hope that if not they, their writings at least would get to Erez Israel. Notably, the difference in addresses also highlighted a difference between the two, Ben-Shem wanted the Hebrew University to get his writings, whereas Auerbach, first of all, thought YIVO would be a suitable home for her writings highlighting her attachment to Emanuel Ringelblum with whom she worked closely.

Clearly Ben-Shem, as well as Auerbach, ascribed a great deal of importance to their writings. These were their '... most favorite child, the produce of blood, hearts, brains and mostly longings.' However, while burying one's writings might have ensured their survival, the same could not be said about people. In this context, it is words that had a chance of survival whereas people, still alive and upstairs looked '... at each other as

Between the Private and Public Sphere: Documentation   131

if they were already dead...' This passage stands out also because in February 1943, once both Ringelblum and Ben-Shem left the ghetto, they too would hide in holes in the ground, buried alive hoping to emerge among the living.

*****

For Ringelblum and Ben-Shem, writing and documenting seem to have been the most obvious space to turn to once the war broke out. [70] The evident choice was only reinforced as the situation deteriorated, leaving hardly any room for debate or hesitation, as unfamiliar, extraordinary in their brutality, surprising and indigestible events unfolded before their eyes. Documentation turned out to be remarkably important because it exposed the enormous scope of devastation imposed on Jews, as well as the pace at which events occurred.

For both, recording events chronologically was a novel experience. Ringelblum had kept a contemporaneous diary only once and for little more than a month, in 1938, when he was in Zbąszyń. To the best of my knowledge, Ben-Shem, had most probably never kept a diary before. Whereas for Ringelblum, in general, documentation was a rooted practice yet only for the second time contemporaneous, for Ben-Shem this was a new venture he must have felt compelled to execute.

The passages examined sought to understand if and how both writers adhered to the traditional Jewish response of recording and what each of them said about their own writing. Apparently, their writings show that neither felt this reaction required deliberation as circumstances and the visceral nature of life in the ghetto called for documentation. In this respect, both Ringelblum and Reuven Ben-Shem's diaries are genuine Jewish responses to crisis.

To begin with, Ringelblum declared his intention was to produce an unbiased record and refrain from interpretation. For him writing was obvious, because he had been involved in historical documentation for many years prior to the war. Only once *Oneg Shabbat* members dealt with the facts, collected testimonies and documented details, did Ringelblum move from factual daily documentation to more reflective essays. And yet, being able to continue documenting during the war was demanding not only because of how long incarceration in the ghetto was, but also because of the nature of events to be recorded.

By establishing the *Oneg Shabbat* archive, Ringelblum seems to have created for himself a more comfortable workspace. Being a historian, he thrived on creating a historical body of knowledge observing primarily its research rules. When he categorized *Oneg Shabbat's* work according to themes and areas of interest studied, he could dedicate himself to summaries and reflections in his daily diary instead of recording current events. Thus, his personal notebook ceased to be a classic documentary diary, and as of 1941, became a summative-reflective journal.

Simultaneously, Ringelblum himself became the audience for reports and research others presented to him before these were documented and hidden. This ensured his reflections were relevant as they were based on up-to-date information collected from a variety of sources and streaming constantly from *Oneg Shabbat* employees. In this respect, despite the change in practice, Ringelblum's remained a pure diary.

This changed as soon as deportations began, because circumstances prevented Ringelblum from writing daily. Indeed, between July and September 1942, there were only a few entries containing outlines of topics seemingly designed for later elaboration. Around October 1942, writing became steadier and contained essays related to themes characterizing life in the ghetto, untitled dated notes as well as titled entries which had dates, the last one bearing the title of 'The Ten Tribes' from December 15, 1942.

When Ringelblum was smuggled out of Trawniki in August 1943, he resumed writing but it was no longer a daily diary, but a tribute to the annihilated Jews of Warsaw. Instead of referring to his situation, hiding underground with about thirty-seven other strangers, Ringelblum returned to the process of synthesis he and his comrades had started in the winter of 1942. Whether he sensed that the fate of the handful of Jews who had managed to escape the Nazis and remain alive in hiding was unworthy of attention, or that the unmatched events of the ghetto years had cast a long shadow over the ongoing persecution of Jews, remains unsettled.

Surprisingly, Ben-Shem too reflected little on his motivation to write. In his manuscript, it may have been only the opening in March 1943. However, in the deciphered diary, there were several direct addresses to readers, but only one related specifically to what drove him to write. Unlike Ringelblum, Ben-Shem's diary was personal, he survived the war and deciphered the diary in order to publish it. These may have been the reasons creating his need to turn to readers occasionally, dialogues that were not necessarily present in his original manuscript.

As previously stated, except for one notebook, it is unclear when Ben-Shem wrote his other notes. However, the huge body of documentation he left behind, leaves room to suggest that he was obsessed with writing. Ben-Shem began editing his manuscript almost twenty years after the war and chose to begin the deciphered part in November 1940. It contains dated reports, but some of the dates appear to be wrong. This implies that at least some of these dates were estimations added later, and therefore mistaken. In other words, although some passages seem authentic, as if they were copied from notes originally written while he was in the ghetto, other entries do not.

Most prominent is the second half of his diary that began with the deportations, July 20, 1942, two days before the first convoy of Jews was deported to Treblinka. From here until February 1943, when Ben-Shem and his family left the ghetto, he filled 319 pages, documenting the last six months in the ghetto, when the family belonged to Oskar Schilling's carpentry shop. The lengthy descriptions of living conditions, events, and terror were so extreme and horrifying that it seems almost impossible Ben-Shem could have recorded anything simultaneously.

Although shop work was considered lifesaving, the reality of life there was far from it, particularly during deportations when actions were carried out against Jews working in shops (officially, these raids ended at the end of September 1942 and resumed for a short time in January 1943). Constant round ups, terror, and the hunt, especially for women and children, could not have left any room for consistent documentation. At best, one could write occasional notes. Hence, it can be assumed that Ben-Shem's extremely detailed descriptions of the horror in the shops, were reconstructed in hiding and then copied entirely or partially to the deciphered diary.

In 2010, Yad-Vashem received the original handwritten manuscripts from Ben-Shem's family. The notebooks were scanned but there does not seem to be consistency in the order. Pages attached to a notebook were scanned in this way, while others were more difficult to place. However, one notebook began with what sounded like a testament and was therefore scanned as the first page. Large parts of the manuscript are illegible as some pages have water stains or tears, the handwriting is extremely small and dense, and it seems Ben-Shem added later notes in almost every empty space. Evidently, the original manuscripts went through some editing which makes it difficult to determine what was added later and when.

Once Ben-Shem arrived in Palestine, in November 1945, he started working at *Hamashkif*, a revisionist daily newspaper where he published extracts from his diary. In 1957, Ruth Ben-Shem wrote that when they were stationed in Argentina, her husband showed his diary to the writer Yehuda Prishewski, who was so impressed that he recommended translating it into Yiddish and publishing it.[71] Apparently, Prishewski had in mind the Jewish audience in Argentina who were Yiddish rather than Hebrew speakers.

It is assumed that copies, in Hebrew, of September-October 1939, which were found in the possession of the family were part of the blueprint translated for the publication of *Poyln Brent*, into Yiddish, a language Ben-Shem himself had instructed not to use for the publication of his diary. The book was never translated into any other language and had only one edition. It appears that the publication of the book in Argentina encouraged Ben-Shem to try to do the same with the entire diary in Israel.

In the early 1960s, Ben-Shem was helped by Lilly Goldenberg, who would come to their house and work on the diary. Apparently, manuscripts 2-4 were prepared by Mrs. Goldenberg before the deciphered part was typed. Simultaneously, it appears that Yad-Vashem itself seemed to have been involved in attempts to decipher the diary and prepare it for publication.[72] The work was never completed, and the project was abandoned.[73] To his final day, Ben-Shem tried to interest different people in publishing his diary, but failed.[74] Recently, Dr. Bella Gutterman from Yad-Vashem has edited the diary and it is due to be published shortly.

Finally, although documentation was second nature for Ringelblum, several factors made it unique: the daily documentation which lasted for such a long time – during the three and a half ghetto years including having his records, at least briefly play a role in world politics, documenting in Trawniki and finally documentation in hiding for about seven months. For Ben-Shem, apart from being engaged in almost daily documentation, there was also the outstanding effort to reconstruct the past while he was in hiding, decipher parts of his diary in safety and striving till his death to publish his story.

VI

Between the Private and Public Sphere: Armbands

The Body as Space

In his book *The Production of Space*, Henri Lefebvre raised the question whether '... the body, with its capacity for action, and its various energies, can be said to create space?'[1] Though his answer was positive, he restricted it by saying that before bodies produced space, that is, created materials and products, such as tools, or before they produced themselves by '... drawing nourishment from the realm'[2] or even influenced other bodies, '... the body with the energies at its disposal, the living body, creates or produces its own space; conversely, the laws of space, which is to say the laws of discrimination in space, also govern the living body and the deployment of its energies.'[3]

Lefebvre's approach determined the relationship between the body and 'laws of discrimination in space'[4] as interdependent on one another. The body must obey the 'laws' of space and it is within this realm that production takes place. Using this model, it is possible to say that imposing armbands on Jews did not only become an additional discriminatory law but shaped an entirely different social setting that excluded Jews but at the same time centralized their role in this new space.

Accordingly, armbands are a criterion to investigate how enforcing the decree was treated in the writings of Emanuel Ringelblum and Reuven Ben-Shem. That is, how their written documents presented the decree, how they conceived its role, and whether donning armbands altered city residents' experiences as agitation of their space. Additionally, it is important to determine whether there are traces of a conceptual link between marking out Jews and their extermination, or signs of a deeper insight as to the nature of the idea itself.

The assumption is that armbands, being a spatial-visual element, 'conquered' the space because of their disturbing multiple messages, making their presence impossible to be ignored or avoided by provoking a radical change in dynamics and relationships within the city. This new discriminatory bigoted law shattered the previous delicate balance between Poles and Jews. Armbands affected equilibrium not only between people involved but also the mutual space they occupied. From this point of view, analyzing reactions to armbands is expected to illustrate rapports established between different factors in the space: armbands as a focal point to examine how they influenced Jews who wore them, their Polish neighbors, and German conquerors.

Briefing About Armbands in Both Diaries

There is a significant difference in how the topic of armbands was treated in the diaries under discussion. Ringelblum, who began documentation as soon as the war started, related to the horrendous effect of the armband decree as it was happening. In contrast, Ben-Shem's writings, of which the deciphered part began in November 1940, a year after the decree was issued and whose deciphered diary was dictated/rewritten when he was living in Israel, contain few references to armbands. Although it is possible that the original diary included more such mentions, the fact remains that in the final editing process, these allusions, if they existed, were omitted.

Nevertheless, the fact that the deciphered part of Ben-Shem's accounts hardly included allusions to armbands is in itself informative and fundamental to this discussion. By the time Ben-Shem arrived at his hiding location, March 1943, where according to his testimony, he started documentation, the affront and danger of having to display armbands had long since declined in importance in comparison to the violence and atrocities to which Jews were subjected in the ghetto.

In his hideout, in great danger and under the influence of those years in the ghetto, in particular the last six months as a shop worker, Ben-Shem's writings offered a relative point of view influenced by the perspective of time. That is, the life-threatening events that challenged ghetto inmates physically, emotionally, and mentally affected Jews far more than the affront of having to put on armbands.

Furthermore, when Ben-Shem edited the deciphered diary, he chose to begin in November 1940, when the importance of the Jewish symbol as a nuisance, gradually diminished. This conscious decision may reflect Ben-Shem's estimation that atrocities in the closed ghetto were more critical to communicate and therefore, he skipped the first year of occupation when the insult of having to don armbands was significant.

In contrast, Ringelblum's diary contents are eye-opening because they exemplified how armbands created a fundamental change in the fabric of life, especially during the period of September 1939 – November 1940, when officially there was no ghetto in Warsaw, at least not a sealed one. Ringelblum's almost daily documentation revealed that once Jews started displaying armbands, December 1939, it had an inciting effect not only on German forces but also on Poles. Apparently, the reaction of Poles affected Jews far more than the violence carried out by Germans of whom it was expected.[5]

Interestingly, whereas Ringelblum mentioned armbands more than fifty times during the first year of the war, they were mentioned less than thirty times between November 16, 1940 and July 1942 when deportations from Warsaw began. Moreover, of the cases mentioned, only five related to abuse connected to armbands, while in the first year, the vast majority of armband reports discussed friction directly linked to donning them. Lastly, from July 1942, until the last entry in Ringelblum's daily diary, January 1943, armbands were mentioned only five times, and none addressed violence.

Ben-Shem has fewer than ten references to armbands in his deciphered diary which covers the period of November 1940 – April 1943. Out of these, only once were armbands inextricably linked to hostility. The issue concerned the execution of eight people who were found outside ghetto walls in November 1941, a period notorious for intense starvation which forced more and more people, including many children, to smuggle food into the ghetto. The Germans reacted by issuing a decree threatening Jews with death if they were caught outside ghetto walls, hoping to deter people from becoming involved in smuggling.[6]

Both Ringelblum and Ben-Shem dedicated a whole passage to that execution and treated it as a landmark in developments in the ghetto. Ringelblum stated that the crime committed by the eight arrested people was that they were found outside the ghetto walls, a version supported by Kaplan.[7] Ringelblum's detailed report about this affair and the reactions it provoked, concluded that the execution did not discourage people from attempted smuggling, which continued as usual. Smugglers claimed that despite the risk, it was the only way to avoid certain death from hunger.[8]

According to Ben-Shem, however, the reason for the execution was that they were without their armbands. This was an implausible reason as the eight executed Jews had been caught on the Aryan side, where they would not betray their identity by keeping their armbands on.[9] It is possible that the time that elapsed since this happened contributed to Ben-Shem's confusion and he must have mingled the explicit threat that Jews were forced to identify themselves externally with the 'additional crime', smuggling foods.[10]

In another entry dated February 1941, Ben-Shem mentioned armbands in comparison to yellow badges against which he expressed strong feelings. This was recorded when a member of the Jewish Council from Łódź arrived in Warsaw. The scene described had no movement; on the contrary, everything was immobile and passive:

> In the evening, scenes from the ghetto of the Middle Ages appeared before our eyes. A man from Łódź with a yellow badge just like the one worn by Jews in the Spanish ghetto, in Germany and in other European countries.[11]

This depiction highlighted a still and silent image, a frozen scene that immediately transferred into one's preexisting associations in the mind. Rather than the real scene, the active space became the spectator's mind, where the yellow badge provoked an array of connotations drawing one from the present, back in time to the Middle Ages. To show how much he was sickened, Ben-Shem added that '… in comparison to the badge, our tie (the armband) seems aristocratic….'.[12] Bitterly he added that the purpose of the armband was not only to repulse Jews' neighbors but also to make Jews disgusted with themselves.

Indeed, other than Ben-Shem's two allusions to armbands, it appears that like Ringelblum, the decline in the importance attributed to armbands was directly accorded to the growth in the ghetto's life-threatening problems: hunger, disease, death, and higher rates of random and arbitrary violence within ghetto walls. Even more crucial, because Poles were, in general, prevented from entering the ghetto, attacks carried out by Poles on Jews with armbands ceased. In this way, Jews were spared not only from numerous attacks but also from the sensation that their neighbors were turning against them, feelings that had shaken them up.

Simultaneously and without any relation to armbands, inside the sealed ghetto, behind the walls, gendarmes, guards, and soldiers showed fewer and fewer constraints or morality, giving way to capricious violence, which became an acceptable and even encouraged norm. It seems that senseless cruelty was not only a routine in the ghetto, but that German high commanders as well as the Gestapo were not at all troubled by the conduct of their soldiers.[13] In such circumstances, it is little wonder that attention shifted away from armbands to life-threatening issues.

All Jews Are Equal

The Jewish community of Poland, and certainly the Jews of Warsaw, were a multifold and incredibly diverse community with a large number of Jewish political parties, youth movements, religious and secular sectors.[14] On December 1, 1939, when the armband decree was enforced, it signified, to them and others, that they were considered an invariant identical collective. Visualizing their Jewishness had actually cancelled out their traits as individuals, eliminating any personal features, innate or chosen but also the human characteristics of the entire Jewish entity.[15]

Goldberg emphasized that displaying a badge still observed a certain metonymic distance between the symbol and one's body.[16] Simultaneously, while this metonymic detachment was observed, the mere action of labeling drastically contracted Jewish living spaces. The different processes of marking had eroded human traits reducing Jewish human beings into a multitude of 'it', merely Jews, defined by the badge which acted as a signifier.[17]

One result was that Jews sensed that they were equal, to use one famous saying by Abraham Rubinstein, a comic fool in the Warsaw Ghetto. The edict to mark Jews had, in reality, grasped the Jewish population of Poland in a unique and immediate manner. Physically free, they were effectively prisoners jailed by their marked bodies. They were free hostages, recognizable to all and conspicuous in space. In this way, their marked bodies were turned into spaces of their own, walking bodies subject to the whims of anyone and everyone.

Rubinstein, a beggar who roamed the streets of the ghetto and probably arrived in Warsaw around 1941, expressed authentically how Jews felt before the ghetto was sealed, when armbands changed their lives in the city, as well as after the ghetto was closed when all had to succumb to the same fate. Rubinstein used to entertain passersby with exaggerated body gestures, jokes, and sayings of which, '*Alle gleich—urm un reich!*' ('All are equal -poor and rich!') became famous.[18] Rubinstein's aphorism probably originated not only in his personal observations of what was going on in the ghetto but also widespread socialist notions inspired by Marx's communist doctrine. Nevertheless, equality in the ghetto was a bitter deviation and explains how Rubinstein's saying, which seemed to capture the unique singularity of the situation of Jews in the ghetto, caught on.[19]

To explain Rubinstein's saying, Goldberg called upon extreme class differences evident in the ghetto, lack of food versus abundancy, hunger, and associated troubles such as disease, begging, smuggling, degradation, versus decadent lavish parties and depravity, which had struck the ghetto from the beginning. This disturbed many including Ben-Shem, who despite being openly anti-communist, expressed his deep sense of indignation at what he was witnessing in an entry from the end of 1940:

> A new and interesting phenomenon in our ghetto! You could pass from one end to the other and two extremities stab you in the eyes: hunger and satiation. On the one hand, the dying and bloating because of hunger and on the other hand, potbellies filled with everything that is good.[20]

Bernard Goldstein, a leader of the Bund (a Jewish socialist organization) also addressed extreme differences between poor and richer Jews in the ghetto:

> The sword of the Nazi extermination policy hung over all Jews equally... a social differentiation arose in the ghetto, setting apart substantial groups who had the means even under those infernal conditions to lead a comparatively full, well-fed life and enjoy some kinds of pleasures.[21]

Like Ben-Shem, he stressed the irony of class differences among Jews owing to economic background, versus equality in their situation, all Jews were one common condemned class.

Indeed, Dreifuss explained that initially, there were many socio-economic differences in Jewish society before the war. However, when the ghetto was sealed, there were rapid changes in the structure of this society because of extreme shortages of everything, changes that made it impossible to speak about the Jewish community of Warsaw as one entity. At first, the lowest class in the ghetto was made up mainly of refugees, about 100,000 people, who either had been forced into or escaped to Warsaw. Yet, over time, better off Jews were impoverished and joined the poor.[22] From Ben-Shem's testimony dated May 1942, he wrote that he had been added to the list of those who were supported by the American Jewish Joint Distribution Committee. The new situation seems to have embarrassed and frustrated him, a sentiment voiced in a cynical narrative where he enumerated the various titles and degrees he had been awarded, some of which were: Rabbi, Doctor of Philosophy, gymnasium professor, translator, editor, journalist, writer; to which the status or title of 'supported' was added.[23]

Gutman's observation is crucial in this discussion, as he pointed out that after the war, there were historical narratives about extreme class

Between the Private and Public Sphere: Armbands   141

differences in the ghetto distorting the picture as researchers tried to determine the phenomenon of inequality in the ghetto using sociological criteria formulated to study normal healthy societies. Gutman emphasized that condemning Jews may be understandable among people who had experienced the war themselves, in particular, those who had experienced life in ghettos, but it was unacceptable when it concerned historical narratives written after the war and whose lens could have been much wider than that of ghetto inmates.[24]

Ringelblum, whose communist political inclination certainly made him more sensitive to social issues, was also preoccupied by the phenomenon of extreme inequality. The entry from January 7-9, 1940, appears to convey a deep sense of chaos, frustration, and profound feeling of injustice. Ringelblum's conflicting emotions and sense of entrapment emerged when he wrote:

> Jews without bands were taken to the police station for three days. The moral issue of wearing the armband or refraining from it, solidarity. The enemy punishes for donning a dirty band. The community prepared printed bands. They faded away as soon as it rained. There are embroidered armbands and even ones made of silk. Even here – class differences. There is a star of David that is sewn on the existing one. It is obligatory to put it on the sleeve, if not, punishment. People hide the armband with handbags using all kinds of tactics.[25]

In this passage, he raised two aspects: class differences and fellowship. That is, Ringelblum was convinced that all Jews, without exception, should put on armbands as a token of their solidarity with one another and because, to the Germans, Jews were all the same. The text raises issues of morality and solidarity in relation to the continuous hunt for Jews around the city while exposing the perils of movement in a previously safe space and heated discussions in the Jewish community about how to address the armband edict.

Clearly, Ringelblum believed that solidarity was important, and therefore, armbands should have been worn by all Jews courageously. The narrative suggests that he was reproaching those who tried to evade it, indicating the controversy within the community about strategies adopted in order to ensure, on the one hand, the safety of commuters and on the other hand, kinship, notions that were already showing signs of erosion from the inside. Thus, Ringelblum echoed here two problems, marking Jews affected relationships within the community, but the pressure was on individuals who were held personally responsible for dealing with consequences on their own. It seems that Ringelblum offered a strategy, that is, ensuring that everyone abided by this decree, as a means to fortify the emotions of individuals first.

An extreme example of disobedience was Janusz Korczak, who repeatedly refused to put on an armband. On November 20, 1940, a few days after the ghetto was sealed, Ringelblum reported that Korczak had been arrested because he had no armband on his sleeve.[26] According to Ringelblum, Korczak declared, at his trial, that he had never worn the armband and had no intention of doing so in the future.[27] He remained in prison for several months and according to Gutman, was finally released under the false observation that he was insane.[28]

Who were those who risked walking about without an armband? Was it only those with 'good looks'?[29] A close examination of this text does not betray the identity of evaders, only Ringelblum's firm reproach. A glimpse into the predicament of Jews was expressed in a more compassionate manner in Ludwik Landau's diary. He alluded to the Jewish dilemma whether to display armbands and concluded that both options were dangerous, and that Jews found themselves between Scylla and Charybdis, an impossible choice.[30]

Armbands also exposed class differences through difficulties obtaining bands which met German demands. Ringelblum's sensitivity to the issue is evident in his criticism manifested, armband-wise, in problems obtaining long-lasting armbands. On the one hand, the *Kehilla* provided poorly made armbands that faded when it rained, an issue putting those displaying them in danger. On the other hand, those who were better off could afford to acquire 'proper' armbands, and in this way, be more protected from harassment; yet, by so doing, they forcibly exposed those with lower quality products to persecution.

Hence, his criticism is tripled: first, against those who instead of facing and coping with the decree, chose not to put on armbands, thus, rather than showing solidarity with the community, cared only about themselves. Second, the more affluent who used durable armbands, indirectly exposing to harassment those who depended on poor-quality armbands provided by the community, thus testifying to, if not lack of solidarity, their indifference to the vast majority of the community. Third, criticism of the community whose armbands were defective and if displaying one was not risky enough, their poor quality played into the hands of the Nazis who deliberately looked for excuses to pick on Jews.[31]

The idea of equality seemed to have engulfed a lot more than class differences as the edict to identify Jews erased all differences between them,

Between the Private and Public Sphere: Armbands 143

for outsiders as well as Jews themselves, because they understood that labeling them curtailed and undermined their human characteristics.[32] The distortion of the term equality and its abnormality became so rooted in ghetto folklore that according to Ringelblum, there was even a theatre play produced about the topic bearing this title.[33]

Goldberg suggested that Rubinstein's cry may also have conveyed the idea that the same fate awaited everyone, death.[34] In 1941, the situation in the ghetto deteriorated at a staggering rate, and a huge number of people died from hunger and typhus. Between June 1941 and April 1942, the rate of death was between 4,290 and 5,560 per month, preventing individual burial.[35] The large number of dead, the inability to provide decent burials, along with a fundamental approach in Judaism deriving from the verse 'You are dust, and to dust you shall return',[36] corroborated the notion of equality in death. It seems that this conception went beyond biological reality and referred not only to the Jewish faith but also fate. Differences between people were leveled in death and no Jew was to be exempt from it.[37]

In October 1942, Ringelblum wrote a bitter but brief passage entitled: 'Why', where, bewildered, he lamented the murder of 300,000 residents of the Warsaw Ghetto in Treblinka. At the end, he added that only groups such as the '13', workers and burial societies (also collaborators), community officials (they refused to cooperate with deportations and their participation was stopped), retained special badges because 'All other armbands were cancelled. All Jews were equal.'[38] Ringelblum, once more, repeated the well-entrenched notions of *'Alle gleich'*, an idea that condensed the gist of the common fate of Jews, all of whom were equally destined for death.[39]

Visual Shock

Once the armband decree was enforced, Jews had no choice but to obey and display them. Those who looked Jewish, could be identified easily even without armbands, while those who did not, still had little choice in the matter, because their identities were known to their immediate and sometimes also distant surroundings.[40] In fact, only if one was able to distance oneself from one's immediate environment, happened to look Polish and overcame difficulties of concealing one's identity, was there a chance to mingle in Polish crowds.

Abusing Jews started in the early days of occupation, particularly in smaller communities. This included expulsions, robbery, theft, harassment, humiliation, beatings, and cold-blooded murder.[41] Ringelblum reported such crimes in Warsaw as early as October 1939, but at that stage, it was the reports from outside Warsaw that were more alarming.

The beginning in Warsaw seemed relatively calmer, which explains why cases of violence against Jews were conceived as random rather than organized. For instance, in an entry dated October 4, 1939, Kaplan documented many cases of attacks inflicted on Jews by Germans, including one of the first notable events, food distribution to residents of the city, before armbands were implemented. Kaplan wrote that when it was a Jew's turn, they would push him/her away without food.[42] At this stage, Kaplan pointed an accusing finger at individual soldiers but not at the high command, although he did blame them for turning a blind eye. Still, as long as Jews were not marked out, some were able to avoid attacks, because Germans in particular, found it difficult to identify them. This changed in December 1939 when armbands exposed all Jews to everyone, giving insinuated but clear permission for persecution, sometimes using armbands themselves as an additional pretext for violence.[43]

A month of heavy air raids on Warsaw left its mark on the city. There were entire or partly ruined streets everywhere, and consequently, numerous refugees.[44] The addition of armbands to the already changed landscape of Warsaw, estranged the city even more. To all appearances, displaying armbands had contributed to defamiliarizing the space. Abruptly, the volume Jews occupied in Warsaw appeared to be quite stunning. According to a census taken in April 1940, there were 395,025 Jews in Warsaw which constituted 30.1% of the city's population.[45] This meant that every third person in Warsaw was Jewish and unlike before, they were all visible.

First reports about armbands appeared in Ringelblum's diary almost as soon as they were introduced. These suggest that the altered scenery of the city preoccupied everyone and created a raft of emotions. From the Jewish point of view, their sudden conspicuousness in space created a trust crisis, primarily, with their Polish neighbors rather than the Germans, though the nature of German harassment certainly took them by surprise. Ringelblum reported how walking around the city had become a hazard because Jews were targeted by Germans but most alarmingly, Poles as well.

Indeed, attacks by Poles posed a greater problem as Jews had not expected them; on the contrary, Jews anticipated their support. The result was that because streets had become unsafe, many Jews refrained from leaving their homes, or avoided walking in non-Jewish areas. Even peddlers gave up trying to sell their goods on Polish streets. Kaplan wrote that although there was no formal ghetto then, these new conditions led Jews to create a ghetto of their own, unintentionally, by avoiding Polish streets and concentrating in more Jewish areas of the city.[46]

Havi Dreifuss stressed that during the first year of occupation, the armband became a criterion according to which Jews determined and evaluated relationships with Poles. Her research revealed a complex image as in their diaries, Jews, apparently, filtered out what they wrote about Polish aggression towards them and when they did write about it, they ascribed it to negative elements in Polish society while stressing that these did not represent the majority.[47] Dreifuss claimed that the attribution of violence to marginal Polish individuals or groups reflected a Jewish conceptual strategy, 'comforting interpretations', that enabled them to better cope with their growing sensation of unease and alarm at the conduct of Poles while continuing to regard Polish society as a whole, positively.[48]

Ringelblum's diary content consistently demonstrated this trend, which is supported by other testimonies. Adolf-Abraham Berman, a Zionist activist in the Jewish underground, one of the leaders of Zegota (the Polish Council for Aid to Jews) and Ringelblum's close friend, wrote in his book about severe attacks by Germans against Jews, especially religious Jews. In a quite lengthy passage, he added that Polish assaults on Jews were not only conducted by organized gangs, but that these attacks were encouraged by Nazis. He characterized their attacks as having pogrom features, a notion Kaplan also used to describe such incidents.[49]

Things were even more nuanced, yet complicated, between Jews and Poles as Ringelblum reported that Poles turned to Jews, seemingly in wonder, and asked why they were obeying the armband order.[50] The first such report was written between December 10-11, 1939, when Ringelblum quoted the following: 'Poles say to Jews: 'Why are you donning the bands?'[51] From the position of this quote in the text, the impression it conveys is that it was not connected to anything that preceded or followed. Its importance comes from its content as well as being among the first mentions of Polish reactions to the visual changes in the city's landscape.

The second time the perplexity of Poles was mentioned was on December 22, 1939: 'Voices of support from the Poles. We are writing down the names of those who point at Jewish businesses and houses. - - tell us, why are you wearing the band, take it off.'[52] To begin with, the proximity of these two reports, ten days apart, suggests that in the early days of enforcement, Poles' criticism of Jews for being 'over obedient' was not rare. Furthermore, the fact Ringelblum noted this criticism in his diary, may hint that not only was he personally sensitive to it, but that such comments were rather frequent. Regardless, these contents appear to indicate that in Polish society there was a discussion about the manner in which Jews were forced to appear in public, a debate that seems to have been at least partially critical of Jews.

In the first entry, Ringelblum did not mention that Poles were considering the risks of disobeying orders, but quoted what may have been the exact wording of their question: 'Why are you donning the bands?' This direct quote suggests that Ringelblum was voicing his own criticism of Poles because he understood that the question was not as innocent as it sounded, and in fact, implied that although Poles knew what Jews risked by disobeying, they ignored the stakes. In other words, asking that question suggested a condescending approach and a hint that Poles were really saying that had they been forced to wear armbands, they would have reacted differently. Furthermore, this remark showed that armbands had not only visually separated the two entities, but that Ringelblum suspected Poles were quick to set themselves apart from the Jewish population.

The second passage began by emphasizing that Poles were showing empathy to the predicament of Jews, yet the following sentence pointed to the complexity of the situation. Seemingly unrelated, Ringelblum stated that he and others were '... writing down the names of those who point at Jewish businesses and houses.' The very fact Ringelblum plainly wrote that Poles were denouncing Jewish property to the Germans, meant that some Jews concealed their identity by not marking their businesses as they had been ordered.[53] This seems to imply that Ringelblum was indirectly suggesting that Polish strategy, not to don armbands or mark businesses, was a tactic already adopted by some Jews. Hence, Ringelblum may have insinuated that on the one hand, Jews had come up with such ideas before and that Poles were stereotyping Jews unjustly as over-obedient while collaborating with Germans to expose those Jews whom they had advised not to wear armbands or mark their businesses.

In the following sentence, Ringelblum repeated the apparent friendly advice: '... tell us, why are you wearing the band, take it off.'[54] Unlike the previous entry, this does not appear to be a direct quote but the style suggests there was a casual approach conveyed by the phrase 'tell us', followed by a rhetorical question, '... why are you wearing the band?' and almost blunt advice, '... take it off'.

A closer inspection of this entire passage and the manner in which it is organized, may denote that, first, it was important for Ringelblum to acknowledge Polish sympathy for Jews. Second, some people whose identities were not revealed, cooperated with the Germans pointing out Jewish residences and property. Third, Ringelblum and his colleagues

Between the Private and Public Sphere: Armbands 147

reacted by documenting names of these informers and expected to prosecute them after the war. Fourth, that Poles criticized Jews for obeying occupant orders, thus showing little understanding or identification with their neighbors.

How the text is arranged hints at a phenomenon Ringelblum noticed, a distressing development in the relationships between Jews and Poles. His efforts not to jump to conclusions were expressed by declaring firstly that the Polish population showed empathy with Jews. Immediately afterwards he provided a negative example of close cooperation between Poles and Germans against Jews. However, just as Dreifuss observed, he did not state who informers were, but described their actions, including steps Jews took against them. In so writing, Ringelblum revealed that these people were Polish.

The fact the text was followed by the sentence '... tell us, why are you wearing the band, take it off,' continues this tendency to minimize the Polish element in the text. Ringelblum seemed to say here that Polish advice to remove armbands was unnecessary for several reasons. First, some Jews had adopted this tactic themselves. Second, by reporting such advice, the text evoked reproach to Poles whose advice appeared simplistic and did not read the situation clearly. Poles knew that people were fined if their armbands were not the right size,[55] or if they did not put them on,[56] whereas others were beaten up for the same crime,[57] some were arrested for exhibiting a dirty armband[58] and there were even cases of death.[59]

Not only did Poles demonstrate that they had misjudged the situation, most probably, deliberately, but even if Jews chose not to mark their possessions or bodies, what good would this do if their neighbors were showing Germans who Jews were. The text also exposed Ringelblum's possible inner conflict as he struggled to understand contradictory reactions within Polish society and at this stage, only implying that a gap may have been forming between Jewish and Polish populations.

If at this early stage, Ringelblum did not accuse Poles directly of abandoning Jews, he did so more openly about a year later, between November 29 and December 2, 1940, after the ghetto had been sealed. Being under the false impression that Jews of Belgium and France had been forced to exhibit yellow badges, he stated:

> They say that in Antwerp when they enforced the Jewish badge, the whole population wore it and because of that the decree was cancelled. The same goes for Paris. There, they ordered Jews to walk on the road itself (not on the pavement). The French also did it and

caused the cancellation of the edict. The Poles did not behave in this way. On the contrary, the word 'Jude' (a Jew, in German) is often heard.[60]

If at the beginning of this entry Ringelblum appeared resigned to the fact that Poles had not behaved like their counterparts in Belgium and France, at the end he clearly accused Poles, stressing that their behavior was the opposite. Moreover, he added an explanation to his comment 'on the contrary', that is, not only did Poles refrain from acting like the Belgians and French, but they adopted the German term for Jews, 'Jude'. Apparently, Ringelblum seems to suggest that embracing the German phrase for Jews indicated that Poles had approved and accepted German attitudes towards Jews and not only in relation to the armband.

Another aspect of visibility was invisibility or deceit. At times, German insistence on making all Jews noticeable and recognizable had some peculiar results testifying to how useful armbands could be. Ringelblum reported on March 6, 1940 that he had heard of some Poles donning armbands to pass as Jews and thus avoid being sent to Germany as forced labor.[61] For economic purposes, the same practice was adopted after the ghetto was sealed, and those who wanted to continue doing business with ghetto inmates, were reported to have worn armbands before entering the ghetto.[62]

This information acts as a scale representing benefits and drawbacks to displaying a Jewish symbol. Before the ghetto was sealed, Poles preferred to risk abuse, if only to evade being deported to work camps in Germany. But after, putting on an armband inside the ghetto and mingling in the marked crowd, although still dangerous, offered chances of making some profits. Equally, these reports also highlight Nazi obsession with exterior identification, that is, even though ghetto inmates were all Jews, they had to display armbands, apparently, not in order to be identified, but as the mark of Cain. Conversely, because this mark functioned more as a symbol of humiliation, it did not pose as much danger as it had before the ghetto was sealed or otherwise, it was unlikely Poles would follow this path.

The following anecdote illustrates, yet again, deceit in what Ringelblum reported about the notorious German soldier, Josef Blösche or Frankenstein, as Jews nicknamed him.[63] Frankenstein, who was mentioned in Ringelblum's daily diary only twice, and not until 1942, was one of the most well-known though dreaded characters in the ghetto. The two cases related to Blösche's impersonating a Jew by displaying an armband on his sleeve during German operations to prevent the smuggling of foods into the ghetto.[64]

The first entry mentioning Frankenstein was dated May 30, 1942, and described one in a series of terrorizing Nazi activities as of April 1942. This is an unusual report in which the language Ringelblum used was untypically highly emotional, designed to explain the reason Josef Blösche was given the epithet 'Frankenstein': '... because he looks and acts like the monster from the film of that name. He's a bloodthirsty dog who kills one or two smugglers every day. He just can't eat his breakfast until he has spilled the blood of a Jew.'[65]

Intriguingly, Ben-Shem's diary provided specific examples of Frankenstein's iniquity using rather similar language: '... sometimes he eats his breakfast instead of at eight, at ten or even eleven because he had not had a chance to kill a Jew earlier.'[66] The language similarity might suggest that Ben-Shem and Ringelblum's narratives echoed voices of the ghetto. Regardless, this description stands out, first, because the language used to explain the reasons for his odd nickname, Frankenstein, and justification for this choice deviated from standards set by Ringelblum himself. In other words, sticking to facts rather than interpretation, and certainly refraining from expressing any evaluation.

Second, an inspection of the daily diary showed that although Ringelblum had recorded events of sadism and degradation before, until May 1942, he had ignored Blösche in his accounts. This denotes that the man's conduct was even more perverted than other ghetto jailers, and Ringelblum may have thought that since Blösche's comportment was a deviation even from Nazi debasing behavior norms in the ghetto, his example was not typological and therefore, not worth mentioning. On the other hand, mentioning Frankenstein so late in the diary could suggest Ringelblum might have been more careful with Blösche's case until then because he had strongly vehement emotions towards the man, feelings he exposed when he eventually wrote 'a bloodthirsty dog' or '... He will not eat his breakfast until he has spilled Jewish blood first.'

Third, introducing Blösche by his nickname Frankenstein, and accompanying it with a clarifying description, requires explanation. In general, descriptions of atrocities related to actions, anonymous perpetrators and victims. Here, what is remarkable is the personal address, mentioning Blösche's name openly, which hints that his actions against smugglers diverged from sadism to the political realm. In other words, it seems Blösche is mentioned here specifically because his vicious conduct coincided with political actions that Ringelblum estimated would be researched in the future.

Apparently, Ringelblum was envisioning that after the war, his notes would serve to study events in the Warsaw Ghetto and therefore, it was essential to provide background and introduce Blösche as an individual. This stands out because as long as Blösche's brutality was within the range of the pervert – his conduct was even outside Nazi already degraded norms – it was not 'important' enough. Once Blösche's 'imported his standards' into the realm of the political, traversing the line separating personal caprice from accustomed standards of behavior, Blösche lost his anonymity and 'gained' a place in Ringelblum's diary.

The second entry which mentions Frankenstein, June 11, 1942, appears to be an attempt to rectify the previous outburst. Ringelblum's language is more balanced although he repeats Blösche's purpose and method, finding smugglers by impersonating a Jew. Despite being aware that Frankenstein was involved in crimes committed against Jews,[67] ascribing reasons to justify these actions, in a composed and balanced report of the man's doings, somehow seems to mend the wrong, that is, returning to highlighting facts rather than emotions.

Humor was another manner of dealing with sentiments about the situation in the ghetto, and indeed, Ringelblum's diary contained an abundance of jokes about serious issues including the armband. One such joke was that Nalewki street had become Hollywood as it was full of stars. Obviously, Ringelblum was referring to the fact that Nalewki Street, at the heart of the Jewish area, was full of Jews donning armbands with the star of David at their center.[68] An echo of this joke can be found in the title of Bernard Goldstein's testimony (1947) about his experiences in the Warsaw Ghetto, 'The Stars Bear Witness.' Space-wise, the allusion to Hollywood stars emphasized the comical bitter point of view, the area was indeed inundated with stars but none of these 'stars' looked like one.

Another joke from May 1942 was imported into the ghetto by Jews from Germany who were deported to Warsaw. They confided to Ringelblum that they had interpreted the letters on their badge, 'Jude' (Jewish), as initials of 'Italians Und Deutschlands Ende', that is, the end of Italy and Germany…[69] By turning this humiliating symbol into a sort of prophecy about the destruction of their enemies, converting the deliberately embarrassing message of the word 'Jude', German Jews seemed to have been able not only to set themselves apart from the atrocities the Germans intended for them, but also extract a secret force from their interpretation of these letters. Their reading appears to have instilled in them energy to bear their conspicuousness by ascribing an opposite meaning to the very letters that were supposed to degrade them. Furthermore, distorting the original meaning of the word 'Jude' served also as a meaningful act of defiance about which their enemies remained in the dark.

Feelings – About Jews and Converts

In his diary, Ringelblum's pledge to objectivity is evident in his attempts to choose unbiased language and contents as much as possible, manifested mainly in reporting actions rather than emotions or commentary. In the early days of the war, most reports were balanced to an extent that contents required some effort to expose the repercussions of events described.[70] In contrast, when direct or hinted emotional effects were present, they did not act as information fillers, but became holes of their own as they mirrored and highlighted a general absence of such aspects in the majority of documentation, where sentiments were insinuated through concrete descriptions of actions or reactions, both still in the domain of the visual. In other words, what was seen rather than interpretations of scenes.

However, on one rare occasion when mentioning feelings explicitly, Ringelblum referred to his personal experiences, twice in the same entry. Both these personal accounts appeared inside a passage documenting numerous violent incidents against Jews attacked by Germans and Poles. The entry dated January 29-30, 1940 stated that a day earlier, Polish gangs were ransacking the streets of Warsaw and they '... were dragging people out of carriages, beating them up using whips and lashes.'[71] Ringelblum named five especially busy streets in Warsaw where this had happened and said that the same had occurred in other streets as well. Immediately after this, Ringelblum noted that Germans had murdered 160 (in fact, 120) Jewish Polish prisoners of war in Bug Wlodawski.[72]

The description of his personal experiences came in the same entry and right after these incidents. However, it is uncertain whether both personal attacks occurred on January 30, 1940, a date Ringelblum specifically noted, at least for the first attack he suffered. Context-wise, mentioning the precise date, may be related not only to Ringelblum's desire to be historically accurate but an attempt to draw a distance between grave events he had recorded earlier to what he himself had undergone. Yet, a transparent line separating these events also functions as a criterion for understanding, on the one hand, the significant amount of violence, and on the other hand, personal implications for its victims.

In the description of the first attack, he began by stating he had had a difficult day because while he was walking in the Saxon Garden (Ogród Saski) and owing to his armband, he had been attacked by Polish teenagers, to whom he referred as hooligans, and had hardly been able to escape. The text reads:

> Today, the 30 (January 1940), I experienced a difficult day. In the Saski Gardens, there was a Polish hooligan gang, 14-15 years old who saw me and my armband. With my last breath I managed to escape them. The path was empty, there were hardly any people there.[73]

The syntax Ringelblum used enables us to detect how difficult this encounter was, how this incident was a personal landmark for him. The report itself is quite short and concise: beginning with the date, he created a dramatic pause that may indicate levels of alarm and fear that gripped the writer as well as a possible emotional personal crisis. Ringelblum continued not with an orderly description, but by summing up his emotional experience, a personal evaluation, 'I experienced a difficult day.' The description suggests that the experience itself had not lasted long and yet, the fact Ringelblum characterized the whole day as difficult hints at the event's impact, which apparently overtook his entire day, dominating any other occurrences while distorting the sense of time as a direct consequence of intense emotions provoked by this traumatic encounter.

Additionally, he did not mention that he had been attacked by the boys, instead he wrote there were teenagers in the park. He did not say whether or what they had said or called him. He did not even mention that they had chased him trying to catch him. What was provided was the encounter itself, the eye contact: he saw them, and they saw his armband, but what happened to his ability to evade them in between these moments was not specified. He concluded by saying, 'The path was empty, there were hardly any people there.' Thus, Ringelblum informed readers that there had been few witnesses to his humiliation while also hinting that the few who had been there, did not intervene.[74]

Immediately afterwards, Ringelblum wrote about another personal incident he had experienced. A certain woman, to whom he referred as a 'madwoman', had the habit of raging in the streets of Warsaw attacking and beating up Jews suddenly and unexpectedly.[75] Ringelblum added that she led a group of teenagers with whom she carried out these assaults. This is followed by telling readers that several people had been severely injured, because hooligans had attacked them and snatched someone's coat. It is here that Ringelblum once again referred to himself saying that he too had been affected as they had tried to grab his hat but thanks to his 'quick legs...'[76] he had managed to escape. He added that after this incident, his friends nicknamed him Kusociński.[77]

Notably, in this report, the emotional aspect was not revealed directly but illustrated through actions. What makes this text subjective is the fact

Ringelblum referred to himself as part of the event described. Furthermore, it seems that the somehow relieved tone of this report may explain its presence here. Unlike previously, this time, Ringelblum appeared to have been satisfied with his performance, and certainly less affected. The reason may lie in the fact that Ringelblum mentioned he was jokingly called Kusociński, and if in the previous incident, at the Saski Gardens, he specifically wrote that there were very few people in the park, here there were witnesses to his rapid reactions. Seemingly, mentioning his newly earned nickname, Kusociński, served to restore his own unease about being intimidated and humiliated by teenagers.

These two incidents recorded about himself certainly did not conform to his habitual pattern of documentation, but their importance derives from this deviation. The personal angle sheds light on the writer's inner space, where emotional turmoil created disorientation because of senseless violence. It is the exposure of the concealed world of feelings that lends meaning because it allows readers to generalize the significance and effect violence had had on victims in general.

If Jews were in a difficult position with regard to their obligation to don armbands, converts found the decree even more challenging as it reinstated them mentally, symbolically and effectively, into a community they had previously chosen to abandon. According to Nazi authorities in Poland, converts were to be considered Jews, which meant that restrictions placed on the Jewish population applied to converts too.[78] The community of converts found it difficult to accept this, especially because most of them had willingly and consciously converted to Christianity years before the war and being pushed back into a community with whom they did not identify any longer, felt like an offence.[79]

The fact Ringelblum recorded in his diary how Dr. Israel Milejkowski characterized converts may imply agreement with his analysis of their predicament.[80] According to Milejkowski, converts tended to have an inferiority complex among Christians and a superiority complex towards Jews.[81] In relation to armbands, Ringelblum's diary evoked converts' difficulty as soon as the decree was enforced. Their particular situation was presented as primarily psychological and resulting from having to assume an identity they had rejected previously. This means that by addressing the issue of armbands among converts, an act that complicated their lives significantly, Ringelblum was able to evoke a self-identity crisis forcibly accompanying the implementation of this decree.

On the one hand, Ringelblum showed empathy with people who found it difficult to cope with their newly imposed status as Jews, but on the other

154 *Emanuel Ringelblum and Reuven Ben-Shem's War Writings*

hand, he could barely bring himself to be impartial when addressing condescending attitudes towards Judaism and Jews. In an entry from December 5-8, 1939, for example, Ringelblum noted that converts found it enormously difficult to accept armbands calmly, resulting in cases of suicide, a phenomenon that was more widespread among them than Jews.[82]

In contrast, Ringelblum was cautious when alluding to cases of converts' antisemitism, such as in the case of a man called Brajerson whose address was given in full, Warsaw, 32 Elektoralna street.[83] Ringelblum wrote that although the man's daughters were fervently antisemitic they too were forced to put on armbands. From the way this case is presented, it may be safe to assume that Ringelblum had a grudge against them. Not only did he record their story by mentioning real names, but he also provided their address, as if he was making sure that whoever read his text, knew the exact identity of the person discussed. While this suggests Ringelblum's personal lack of sympathy for the family, the absence of adjectives in the description of the daughters, rather than alluding to an objective presentation of facts, appears to gloat at their fate, having to move around with armbands. In fact, it seems that without saying it plainly, Ringelblum suggested the girls were punished for their attitude towards Jews while insinuating that their tragedy, was of their own making and had to do with their antisemitism.

A comparison between entries relating to Jews and converts showed that complications caused by armbands were evoked for Jews through descriptions of movements and actions but when discussing converts, what was addressed was their identity crisis, which was an additional impediment. In this way, Ringelblum acknowledged the particularity of converts who, by being forced to assume a Jewish identity, were actually experiencing an existential crisis.[84] This implies that Ringelblum insinuated that although Jews were forced to externalize their Jewishness, when converts were forced to do so, it involved loss of orientation as they were uprooted not only from their physical space of choice, but also from their inner space, namely, their identity of choice.

Converts' predicament was not only painful for them, but also for Christian clergy, to whom they turned in their desperate attempts to be exempted from decrees aimed at Jews.[85] Such efforts failed, and Ringelblum reported a case involving cheating, betrayal, and complete disregard for European civilized cultural behavioral norms, which shocked Poles and showed that Germans had no regard for them or the Christian clergy. The incident concerned twenty families of converts, who had Count Roniker speak on their behalf. At the German's request, the latter presented Germans with a list containing converts' names and addresses, having been assured that their request to reside outside the ghetto would be considered seriously. However, according to Ringelblum, a short while later, all these families were arrested and moved into the ghetto.[86]

Professor Ludwik Hirszfeld, a famous microbiologist and serologist who was also a convert, was among those forced into the ghetto. In his memoires, he wrote that he and his family had never worn armbands until he was tempted into registering with the Main Custodial Council, which tried to help Christians and non-Christians who had done Poland outstanding service. They attempted to be exempted from the armband decree and recruitment into forced labor, but immediately after they received this exemption, all registered families were arrested. Hirszfeld wrote that on February 26, 1941, police forces arrived at his house and his whole family was forced into the ghetto without any of their possessions.[87] In fact, it was because they had registered with the Catholic organization that the Germans had their exact names and addresses and, unceremoniously, they were all seized and sent to the ghetto.

*****

Henri Lefebvre stated that space was firstly, one's personal body, and only afterwards, its 'mirror image or shadow.'[88] According to him, the production of space was the result of human activity in a space where social practices took place within a certain compound and in a certain time. Nonetheless, the social realm is formed in the interaction of the body, or what Lefebvre referred to as: '... the shifting intersection between that which touches, penetrates, threatens or benefits my body on the one hand, and all other bodies on the other. Thus, we are concerned, once again, with gaps and tensions, contacts and separations.[89]

Ringelblum and Ben-Shem treated the issue of the Jewish symbol differently because its effect on Jewish lives depended on time and place. Therefore, the armband's predicament in Ringelblum's contemporary diary is mentioned many times more than in Ben-Shem's deciphered version beginning in November 1940. Regardless, both diaries managed to convey the fragility of the situation, or that fine line discussed by Lefebvre, the 'intersection', that precise but undefined point, where the body meets its environment, where experiences are formed, where Jews ran into others but also into themselves.

Prominently, the 'intersection' in Ben-Shem's diary brought into the discussion a new factor, the realm of the mind, when eye contact with the yellow badge on the Jew from Łódź, began an inner reaction of associations. In contrast, Ringelblum's diary revealed physical events, movements, unfolding situations, how people interacted in space, thus producing it, creating a sociological arena.

In encounters with others, armbands created an invisible triple barrier: between different populations in urban areas, individuals and their surroundings, and individuals and themselves. This sudden emergence of a visual Jewish identity into the space, had far-reaching consequences. Obeying the order, they expected to be harassed, but if they did not, they risked fines, imprisonment and even death. Their visibility signified their identity and that they were not protected by law, which accelerated routine revelations of humiliation and violence.[90]

This new situation required Jews to sharpen their ability to read reactions, predict problems, weigh their own responses, and foresee encounters with others. In short, Jews had to expend energy on conducting their daily lives renouncing automated performance that characterizes ordinary lifestyles.[91] Accordingly, their daily lives became extremely difficult as every ordinary activity turned into an ordeal thus forcing Jews to reconsider their habits and calculate their movements carefully to avoid hostile encounters.[92]

Initially, the problem of Jews was making them visible. Ringelblum presented actual actions while generally avoiding interpretations as subjective experiences. In this way, before ghetto walls were erected, rather than creating separate areas for Jews and non-Jews, armbands visualized the excluded while effectively indicating that their bodies were forfeited.[93] In other words, Nazification of spaces excluded Jews, but simultaneously created abstraction of borders. Thus, restrictions on Jews formed a paradox, as although symbols signaled limits, they provoked the collapse of moral, physical and emotional boundaries leading to expanded spaces of chaos.

Ringelblum's reports essentially projected the armband's significance, how people felt about it and how they coped with it but through action. In his entries, he spoke of solidarity with, and commitment to, the Jewish community while also exposing how hard it was to meet these standards of comradeship. The predicament of converts was almost solely exposed through attention to their psychological strivings rather than practical difficulties, which were similar to those of Jews: confiscation of property, personal assaults, etc. On their issue, Ringelblum revealed his personal sensitivity, as it was converts' emotional state that singled them out.

On a personal level, Jews had to show a great deal of courage, swallow their pride as well as resign themselves to violence. Individuals' struggles

Between the Private and Public Sphere: Armbands 157

were most prominently expressed in how Ringelblum addressed issues of personal experiences when he himself was a victim of violence. His personal emotions, some explicit and some insinuated, may serve as criteria for the interpretation of the subjective effects of occurrences and how they were imprinted on one's mind.

Indeed, the armband offence was above all private as it affected one's self-esteem and body. According to Boaz Neumann, the concept of Jews being marked, derived from the Nazi obsession with the idea that Jews had been polluting German existence and therefore, were a menace that had to be exposed. Being forced to wear armbands made Jews similarly experience their own bodies to how Nazis experienced them, that is, as a foreign body within the German people's body.[94]

Helene Berr, who lived in Paris where the decree was enforced in June 1942 (in France, it was a yellow star), wrote, 'I suddenly felt I was no longer myself... that I had become a foreigner...'[95] If for Berr the Jewish symbol felt like a personal estrangement, for Yitskhok Rudashevski, from Vilnius. it felt like a hump, as though '...I had two frogs on me.'[96] For Ruth Kluger, a child at the time, walking to school wearing a *Judenstern* felt like stepping into a battle zone where she was subject to looks as well as occasional abuse.[97] The armband was a real worry as it differentiated the Jewish population, while forcing it to become aware of its imposed identity relinquishing one's personal choice.

Placing individuals in the spotlight and making them stand out physically produced a sharp sense of intimidation accompanied by a change in perceptions of one's own being, physically, emotionally, and psychologically. Reports from marked people suggest that one's personal physique became unrecognizable as exposure made them stand out, yet simultaneously yielded an inward desire to shrink and disappear from the space in which they stood out against their will. This meant armbands made individuals as such unnoticed, but in parallel perceptible as a symbol.[98] This subjective shift between the real and the sensed translated into a feeling that one's size grew while invisible space surrounding one's body shrank, the bigger and more noticeable a person felt, the smaller the imaginary space around one became.[99]

If the Cartesian approach states that existence derives from the fact that people are thinking beings, the Jewish symbol nullified personal identities, thus preventing their carriers from claiming any other identity. The philosophical principle introduced by Descartes, '... *Je pense, donc je suis...*,[100] maintained that thinking defined the essence of what human beings were. The Nazi decree clearly challenged this affirmation by alleging that the physical body was the essence of existence rather than thinking capacities.

Jacques Lacan, the French psychoanalyst and psychiatrist, suggested that Jews were forced to regard themselves through the eyes of others who defined them. Emmanuel Levinas related to this when he recounted how Jews were regarded by passers-by outside prisoner camp gates but '… the strength and wretchedness of persecuted people, reminded us of our essence as thinking creatures…'.[101] That is, the look of a passer-by was what defined Jewish prisoners as 'a gang of apes',[102] but the effect of this mirror reflection, the gaze of the others, was what helped them recall who they were. Forcing a Jewish symbol on Jews, not only denied their rights effectively but also made others stare, a gaze that robbed Jews of their right to self-determination as human beings and individual entities. Jews were literally made to assume and accept the image others had of them.

By creating a physical identifier, the Nazis caused spatial turmoil changing spatiality by contravening balance. This created immediate changes in the city's space as mixed zones turned into areas of frequent verbal and physical friction while increasing the flow of Jews into more Jewish areas, which consequently cleansed Polish areas of Jews before the actual ghetto emerged.

The repulsion evoked by armbands was well documented in Ringelblum's daily diary, but he did not seem to attribute to their introduction more than a deep sense of insult. On the contrary, insisting upon solidarity, he suggested everyone put on the armband despite the dangers they posed, according to him, a non-lethal peril. The mere fact that he brought up and discussed the notion of solidarity in relation to armbands suggests that had he attributed deadly qualities to exhibiting them, he probably would not have urged people to do so.

Even when annihilation became a reality, Ringelblum could not look back, examine, or conceptualize that the seed of the idea was in the introduction of armbands. After July 1942, and although the concept that cold-blooded murder was possible had sunk in, gaps between occurrences in the ghetto and the human ability to conceive them abstractly, seem to have prevented Ringelblum from regarding the notion of marking as predicting death. Then, singling out Jews with a physical feature remained, at most, a symbolic act indicating no Jew would be exempt from hardship, but initially not as an element that designated annihilation.

The contents of Ben-Shem's writing also showed that the link between the Jewish symbol and death was not established. As already mentioned, the only debate in Ben-Shem's writings concerning armbands was the surfacing of the menacing Middle Ages yellow badge sewn onto the clothes of a man from Łódź. Ben-Shem's reaction to the yellow badge remained closely tied to his preconceived notion of the Middle Ages, an idea that did not change. His attitude in this entry hinted that, like Ringelblum, the hardship and shame the Jewish symbol provoked were overshadowed and even erased in comparison to the experiences they underwent in the closed ghetto, particularly during the traumatic period of deportations.[103]

Elie Wiesel (1928-2016) recalled that in the spring of 1944, the yellow badge decree was introduced in Hungary, for the first time. Initially, his father belittled its significance, a reaction that, at the time, comforted the young Wiesel. Years later, in his book *Night*, Wiesel wrote that looking back, he realized the yellow badge turned out to be 'lethal',[104] an insight he could only have reached after having gone through the experiences of the Holocaust.

According to Jean-Gerard Bursztein, when events themselves were unfolding, Jews could not have conceived that by referring to them with nouns such as 'rats' (as in the 1940 propaganda movie '*Der ewige Jude*', the Eternal Jew) or forcing on them the typological names of Sarah and Israel, Nazis were literally changing Jews from humans to objects, so that although they were human in form, they were not in characteristics.[105]

Bursztein further claimed that Jews were unable to perceive that nullifying their civil rights equated to denying their essence as human beings, and therefore, they found it difficult to imagine that it would lead to their extermination. Accordingly, their blindness derived from their inner belief in the sanctity of life.[106] Apparently, cultural concepts were not the only factors creating this blindness, but practically, marking Jews, diverted focus to formulating daily survival strategies, rather than reflecting on the decrees' significance.[107]

Finally, it seems that armbands changed the face of Waraw. Indeed, it made Jews visible and this visibility created a sheer transparent barrier around each of them individually and all of them as a group. Yet, this barrier did not protect them. On the contrary, it was the Jewish symbol that enabled and encouraged violation of boundaries, blurring limits as if the marked Jewish body itself became a space to be used, produced, created, and eliminated. By making one's ethnic affiliation visible, it established an equation of removing personality from individuals, thus creating a faceless collective. This effect was reversed once more, since while individuality was disregarded in favor of ethnic collectivity, coping with the visual element was individual, thus making the struggle personal rather than communal.

VII

The Private Sphere

Aspects of Privacy - Within the House – An Uneasy Space

Cultural signifiers in one of Ringelblum's jokes accurately illustrated the deteriorating situation in the ghetto: 'Allegedly, in a letter from America, they asked us if we ate as if it were Yom Kippur, our houses were like a Sukkah and we dressed as if it were Purim.'[1]

This joke, which appeared in Ringelblum's diary two weeks after the ghetto was sealed, seems to summarize the dire situation in the ghetto by alluding to three different Jewish holidays while managing to contextualize these harsh realities into an intimate cultural and historical space, without minimizing their poignancy. Yom Kippur (the Day of Atonement), a Fast day, relates to lack of food as well as craving it. A Sukkah, a temporary shelter, is erected during the holiday of Sukkot and commemorates provisional fragile dwellings Israelites used during their forty-year journey in the desert after escaping slavery in Egypt. In this context, it refers to the deplorable living conditions in the ghetto. Purim refers to masquerading, thus evoking not only the shocking situation of clothing but also that people's appearance had changed beyond recognition.

Ringelblum's joke conjures imagery originating in intimate Jewish culture to refer to very serious shortages of food, housing, and clothing whilst enveloping these realities with a Jewish flair. These cultural clues or codes, namely, Jewish holidays, create a narrative that conveys meaning to both writer and readers by common cultural association.[2] Their connotations allude to memorable historical contexts, thus placing the current disaster in a long line of past events, which at the same time make the situation comparable and thus, contextualized within Jewish tradition, while relying on the embedded notion that everything is temporary, and Jews would survive this too.

These three categories of food, housing, and clothing make it possible to understand the relationships between individuals' deterioration and the effect this ruination had on society. Hence, what will be examined is the degree to which households in the ghetto were able to provide shelter and comfort, a refuge from the outside world, as a means of exploring notions of privacy and intimacy that are central to maintaining well-balanced human beings.

Indeed, it appears that what was initially conceived as private, like lodgings themselves, family units, and relationships within families, were challenged because of the unique conditions in the ghetto.[3] Apparently, how Jews were forced to reside caused an immediate erosion of boundaries and blurring of borders, not only between the private and intimate versus the public, but also between the outside and inside, thus significantly affecting both private and public spheres as well as human experiences.

In the analysis of these two diaries, it is difficult to draw a line between the private and public. A prominent reason is that both Ringelblum and Ben-Shem related to concepts of privacy and intimacy in a manner reflecting conventions of what was conceived appropriate for discussion, thus avoiding topics that Berl Lang referred to as 'the sequence of 'S's', namely, 'Sex, Shit, and Status.'[4] That is, contents in these diaries represent distances the writers imposed on themselves in choices they made of what to record. Thus, when it concerned private residences, both seldom referred to these issues explicitly, yet these were insinuated when relating to the public sphere. Even discussions of the public arena were expressed cautiously, giving precedence to general phenomena rather than providing detailed specifics.

In the case of Ringelblum's diary, the private arena is hardly mentioned at all. As previously noted, Ringelblum's diary provided extensive reports during the first year of the war, but these focused on what was going on in the public realm: cities and their streets illustrated by documenting individual cases. Likewise, he recorded penetration of the outside into the inside when individuals were affected by invasions of their private spaces. Records seem to deliberately avoid any reference that might lead to identifying people.

For instance, in September 1940, he noted that on Śliska Street, water had been thrown onto furniture to damage it and that at night, water was also spilled onto beds.[5] These actions affected individuals' living conditions inside their homes, but Ringelblum's description maintained distances by providing the names of streets involved, while even omitting the identity of the perpetrators, who were involved in vandalizing Jewish property as a caprice, leaving readers to assume they were Germans.

Importantly, Ringelblum's diary contents moved further away from mere factual daily reports from 1941 onward because *Oneg Shabbat* staff had grown, and the task of documentation allocated differently. Ringelblum stated what areas were of interest to *Oneg Shabbat*, thus, shedding light on what he and his team considered Jewish spaces, such as monographs about cities and towns painting the whereabouts of entire communities, from the beginning of the war to their end, all written in accordance with specified guidelines. These were: '... economic life; the relationship between Germans and Poles and the Jewish population; the *Kehilla* and its activities; social welfare; important episodes in the life of communities, such as the Germans' arrival, pogroms, expulsions, and acts of atrocity committed during Jewish holidays; religious life; work and issues that were connected with it...'[6]

Ringelblum, whose text showed an almost obsessive determination to present what he considered to be a solid objective historic image of events, did not undervalue personal stories as converging with this approach. In his review of *Oneg Shabbat*, Ringelblum wrote that private diaries were a special area of interest he was very keen to preserve because what characterized them had to do with the fact that '... everyone wrote and mainly diaries...'[7] Still, his interest in these personal stories came from their potential to serve as sources from which to draw conclusions about the social rather than individual arena.

Nonetheless, it is possible to reconstruct the private sphere from Ringelblum's diary because of his descriptions of the public sphere. What he recorded in his diary, referred to visible life, what he saw in the streets, heard from people and information he was able to gather from different sources. It was his reports about visible life in the ghetto that worked as a mirror to the private. When he wrote about a mother who had hidden her dead child so as to benefit from his food ration card, or when he reported that on Wołyńska Street, rats were nibbling at corpses that had been lying untended for several days, one could draw conclusions about what preceded these public revelations.[8]

Questions such as how hunger had affected the mother's emotions, whose craving for food had overshadowed her grief for her lost child, thus refraining from burying him, her previous struggles to support both, how physical deprivation shaped morality can be deduced from the brief facts provided, that a mother hid her child's corpse. By the same token, the report about rats nibbling bodies enables readers to picture a household where everyone was probably too sick and unable to attend to one another. These portraits of the results, the effects of living conditions, moments when what happened became public knowledge, allow us to imagine the domestic realm preceding these outcomes.

These examples demonstrate that what was supposed to remain behind closed doors burst out into the open, as living conditions imposed on ghetto

The Private Sphere

residents turned privacy into a luxury constantly eroded until its disappearance. The fact that otherwise private scenes were exhibited in public was because circumstances inside houses were so grim that they leaked from indoors to outdoors rendering them public, thus visible to everyone and consequently, describable.

Ringelblum and Ben-Shem seem to have regarded writing about specific people wrong, but how they implemented that approach was different. For Ringelblum, avoiding discussions about the private sphere, originated in the very concept of what historical narratives were, that is, the focus was on society, not ordinary individuals. As a historical diary was to be studied by future researchers, what mattered historically was the issue or event, not the identity of the people involved. Second, Ringelblum wrote his diary as things were happening and writing about other people's personal affairs was indiscrete and unethical, private matters of the living were not meant for historical research. Besides, in case notes were discovered, information about people could pose a danger.

When the ghetto was destroyed, and Ringelblum resumed writing in hiding, his approach changed owing to circumstances. His notes from that period were meant to commemorate important members of a community that had almost completely vanished and yet, even these monographs did not evoke detailed personal portraits of the private realm for previous reasons. Accordingly, what was emphasized was unique social contribution and achievements.

As for Ben-Shem's diary, his offered a clearer glimpse into the private sphere, but during the two and a half years before deportations began, he too did not devote large parts of his diary to life inside households, including his own. This changed in the six-month period he and his family were slave workers at Schilling's shop. As previously noted, almost half of Ben-Shem's diary addressed his frightful experiences at Oskar Schilling's carpentry shop and his descriptions of existence at the shop, almost the only permitted form of life in the ghetto after deportations began, which mirrored stories of others in shops.

Conditions for shop workers totally denied the notion of family or personal needs. This meant people were accepted into shops according to their work capacity, and no other considerations mattered. One was considered a shop worker as an individual regardless of whether one had a family or not. The implication was that the majority of women and children were considered illegal in shops and therefore, constantly hunted for deportations. Laborers were allocated living quarters where they had to live whether there was enough room for everyone. This terrifying existence was extremely difficult and was not unique to Ben-Shem's family. That is why his descriptions of life in shops, although referring to his own family, represent the story of others including Ringelblum, who worked at Hallman's but wrote nothing about his struggles.[9]

In this respect, although Ben-Shem provided a detailed description of forced households, it was, in fact, not private at all. What his family underwent denoted what other families experienced in all shops as life in shops denied any privacy or any recognition of a domestic existence. What seemed to be reports about the private realm, were actually reports about its absence. It was these bizarre spatial circumstances that permitted Ben-Shem to discuss issues that remained in general unrecorded, that is, two out of the three 'S's': Shit and Status.'[10]

This was possible because living circumstances in shops were more communal than private, rendering discretion considerations pointless. Everyone, irrespective of sex or age, was exposed to the torture of individuals before their eyes. Therefore, what may have been considered intimate had lost its poignancy as experiences were public. The fact torment was communal converted the intimate, the personal experience into a public display of the innermost, which in turn, enabled its exposure without any regard to privacy.

However, because what is analyzed here is Ben-Shem's typed version, his writings show that several of the reservations that had preoccupied him before, were no longer important. There are real names in Ben-Shem's typed version, and it is plausible to assume that when writings were edited, he was certain these people were no longer among the living. In other cases, people's identities were not revealed, perhaps because he was aware they had survived or had surviving relatives. In Ben-Shem's case, it appears that distance in time and place had certainly altered the notion of what was considered discreet and ethical.[11]

The meaning of privacy changed in the ghetto and was redefined following changes to spaces designated for residence. In October 1940, Ringelblum reported that since the *Kehilla* had listed all apartments in the ghetto, prices had stabilized, enabling more people to find accommodation other than "points". The lucky, who remained in their own apartments, sought acquaintances as their subtenants before the *Kehilla* forced them to have their homes invaded by displaced people.[12] This reality worsened once the ghetto was sealed and apartment shortages became an even greater concern when waves of displaced Jews were constantly thrown into the ghetto.[13] Indeed, housing and refugees remained a serious concern of ghetto life throughout its existence.[14]

The Private Sphere

Apartments were crammed with people even in more affluent areas of the ghetto but the number of people and initial conditions depended on the economic resources of occupants. Thus, Janina Bauman's family who came from a well-off background was given a two-room apartment she shared with family and acquaintances. She, her mother, and Sophie (Zofia), her sister, occupied one room while two other people occupied the smaller room and another person lived in the corridor. In comparison to others in the ghetto, these were considered fairly good conditions.[15]

Wajnkranc and her family were not that lucky. They moved to a three-room apartment they had exchanged with a Polish family. In addition to the hardship of parting with their old apartment, the Wajnkrancs had to settle for a room in a smaller apartment than they had before, on Wspólna Street, and whose occupants were not related to them. Wajnkranc wrote that her father whom she described as a sworn optimist, hushed complaints about the new situation consoling everyone by stressing that this apartment was better precisely because of its small size as it would allow them to clean it more easily and save on heating costs.[16]

Shortages in housing were a permanent concern not only for residents but also if one wanted to maintain some sort of routine for children. In an anecdote in Ben-Shem's diary from 1942, he wrote that he had approached the Dicksteins about hiring rooms for a school he intended to establish.[17] The family, who had in their possession a whole school building, decided to give up their own room and move into the kitchen to benefit from the rent.

Conditions in the ghetto became even worse when electricity was cut off and water pipes exploded, with the Germans carrying out no maintenance while preventing Jews from attending to these issues. One particularly gruesome aspect of the lack of electricity surfaced at the end of February 1941, when Ringelblum reported the Jewish hospital owed 60,000 zloty to the electricity company. What he wrote exemplifies the predicament created as 'An operation is performed in the Jewish hospital … Officials from the electric company come in… Dr. Borkowski asks five minutes to complete the operation. "It doesn't matter," says the electric company official, "So there'll be one Jew less". The operation was completed by candlelight.'[18] The text speaks for itself as doctors faced the vicious remarks made by people from the Polish electricity company while having to perform professionally in such inhumane conditions.

Criticizing the *Kehilla*'s poor organizational capabilities, Ringelblum addressed its failure to provide means to warm houses. He stated that there were three things desperately needed in the ghetto: coal, gas and electricity.

Ringelblum wrote that, for several weeks, apartments had no gas and electricity was available only for a few hours a day. This implied that it was impossible to heat houses and even if one had food, cooking was also unfeasible. A glimpse of effects these shortages had on the private sphere was echoed in Ringelblum's complaint that since there was no gas and there was '... electricity only at certain hours, between ten at night and seven in the morning...'[19] no one had the possibility to have even one glass of hot water.

Reports of shortages in basic needs can be found too in Ben-Shem's disturbing and distressing descriptions of a visit to his friend, Avraham Lipman's apartment. Ben-Shem described a narrow and dark room where the walls were painted in colors '... that inferno-painters must have dipped their brushes in...,'[20] a rag separating the Lipmans from their neighbors, and how 'In the house, it is colder than in the street, ... The windows covered, Lipman's style, namely, wall maps of Europe and other countries...,'[21] in addition to a three-legged table from which anything put on it, slides off. Ben-Shem described how he '... entered the room, stumbled rather, because the darkness prevents one from stepping confidently...'[22]

An explanation of the strange manner in which Lipman covered his windows can be deduced from Bernard Goldstein's memoires where he referred to a severe shortage in materials to repair windows. He wrote about a whole industry that ghetto residents developed as a result of acute shortages in raw materials, glass in particular. Indeed, glass became a much-desired commodity, which was the reason many Jews became glaziers. As there was no glass in the ghetto, windows were either boarded up with wood or by putting together small pieces of glass to make panels that were large and stable enough to cover windows.[23]

Apparently, Lipman's household was too poor to afford wooden boards, and instead they used maps. Ben-Shem wrote that '...the wind and the cold here were rude and paid no attention to this concrete defense and shamelessly entered the unheated room...'[24] Ben-Shem's picturesque but ironic and sarcastic narrative personified the wind and the cold's behavior, calling them 'rude', as they 'paid no attention' to barriers comprising wall maps which he cynically referred to as made of 'concrete'.

Ostensibly, other annoyances in the ghetto were noise and constant movement. Large numbers of residents created constant commotion and movement in and out of apartments. Not only did several families occupy one apartment, but since Jews were banished from economic life and schools were closed, everyone was indoors. To lessen the tension resulting from the turmoil, even before it became obligatory to state the names of

The Private Sphere 167

apartment residents on front doors,[25] people had come up with a similar idea to cope with disturbances caused by visitors. Thus, in Wajnkranc's diary, she explained that when they had settled into their new apartment within ghetto premises, and a third family moved in, she wrote on the door 'Schonberg, ring once, Wajnkranc – twice; Arzojcen – three times.'[26] It is plausible to assume that what Wajnkranc recorded about this system to find the 'right' person was customary in many apartments around the ghetto.

Although Wajnkranc did not complain about the practice, apparently this was a new phenomenon to which all had to adjust. Lefebvre proposed that people's first means of experiencing a place, before conceptualizing it was through the senses. He wrote that 'For it is by means of the body that space is perceived, lived- and produced.'[27] Could this explain, even partly, why Wajnkranc had added a seemingly small detail such as this in her memoires? It is hard to say, but it seems that noise pollution was an issue in apartments. Ringelblum's diary also echoed this nuisance when he wrote that one could not find peace and quiet in apartments as people were endlessly knocking on both the apartment's doors.[28] Like Wajnkranc, the fact Ringelblum brought up this evidently insignificant detail may indicate how upsetting and imposing on one's often already shaken up senses the phenomenon was.

However, the worst of the dwellings were the "points" where many refugees lived. Between 1939 and 1942, a hundred and eighty "points" were erected, some of which closed and others that existed until deportations began.[29] Located in public buildings, people were put where there was space, usually in large halls with no adequate facilities that Lea Prais described as overcrowded and uninhabitable.[30] Joshua Perle (1888-1943) described the "points" as '... a desolate hole, a filthy, neglected place where healthy people shared their beds with typhus patients, where the living lay shoulder to shoulder with the dead, where people wished they were dead a hundred time a day.'[31] Refugees' 'private' residences were often the mattress under one's body or worse, the space one's body took on the bare floor, often having to squeeze together.

Ben-Shem illustrated their distress as he wrote that his house committee, which according to him was considered efficient, '...got a present...,'[32] to help "points" residents from the former cinema on Pańska street. He wrote that he was:

> ... speechless, there is no ink in my pen, no energy in my brain to describe the scenes I witnessed, if God had at all meant such scenes to be presented by people ... There is no doubt that these people were

born and died or weren't born at all but are the dead whom he had sent to an exhibition so that people see different sorts of corpses, the fruit of the angel of death's labor.[33]

This report from June 8, 1941, and which exemplified the physical distress of these people, suggested nothing about the lack of privacy. Obviously, as Prais maintained, privacy was not a pressing issue since physical conditions had reduced people's needs to the most basic, food, and food alone.[34] Like Perle, Ben-Shem's text evoked that "points" residents were barely alive.

The Production of Space - On Intimacy and Self-Restraint

Overcrowded ghetto apartments, and consequences of life imposed on their residents, rendered the notion of a lack of privacy which, although annoying, were less central to what preoccupied people, namely difficulties in sustaining themselves. Hunger became a constant source of worry and prominent factor together with the spread of contagious diseases, particularly typhus.[35] In August 1941, Ringelblum reported that there were about 7,000 sick people in their homes, but only about 900 in hospitals. He explained this disproportionate number with what he had heard from Dr. Israel Milejkowski, who claimed patients were dying of hunger and not disease. The latter suggested that weakness caused by hunger prevented healing and was, in fact, the cause of death.[36] Indeed, according to Roland, only 219 calories a day per person, 9.2% of the required rate for survival were allocated to Jews in January 1941, whereas by August 1941, rations had dropped to 177 calories (7%).[37]

Even before the ghetto was sealed, hunger was a rapidly developing problem and this issue occupied more and more space in Ringelblum's diary while the gravity of descriptions became even more apparent. In December 1940, Ringelblum addressed the issue, writing, 'A solemn impression is created by shop windows that are full of hallahs, rolls and other good things. They agitate the hungry.'[38] Two weeks later, writing almost the same sentence, he added more details to explain shop windows' depressing effect, that is, that beneath their windows, poor people lay crying for help while in houses there were multitudes with bloated bellies while, many perished in refugee shelters every day.[39] Prominently, this time, when the human factor was added, the poor lying under shop windows were contrasted with the satiated, so the meaning of hunger became more evident yet remained impersonal. In line with this principle, Ringelblum chose to report the scientific-social aspect of his discussion with Dr.

The Private Sphere   169

Milejkowski thus avoiding the personal. That is, his description relied on
revelations of the phenomenon in the public sphere while ignoring
personal implications.

These reports reflected difficult social circumstances also pointing to
class inequality, a topic Ringelblum found specifically distressing.[40]
However, ravaging hunger was quickly followed by a greater concern, the
rise in the death toll. In his reports, Ringelblum discussed this alarming
phenomenon by addressing individual cases as well. In an entry from
March 1941, he wrote about a father and son who lived in his building and
had died on the same day because of hunger.[41] In August 1941, Ringelblum
discussed Wołyńska Street where entire families were dying and '... it so
happens that the last one to die in the family remains untouched until the
neighbors smell his body's stench.'[42] Ringelblum added that since adults,
particularly men, died first, there was a considerable increase in the number
of orphans. He concluded by writing, 'If things continue at this rate, the
"Jewish question" will soon be solved in Warsaw.'[43]

The fact men seemed to be more susceptible to typhus appears to relate
to both hunger and a weaker capability to deal with mental hardships of
ghetto life.[44] This affected families and altered traditional roles inside family
units, as the burden of coping and keeping families together including food,
shifted to women. Indeed, the vital role women played in the ghetto did
not escape Ringelblum's watchful eye and on June 10, 1942, he wrote, 'The
future historian will have to dedicate an appropriate chapter to the Jewish
woman during the war. She will occupy an important page in Jewish history
for her courage and endurance. It is thanks to her that thousands of families
have been able to surmount these frightful times.'[45]

Rather than express insights about dramas that must have taken place
indoors, as a professional historian, Ringelblum turned to generalizations
based on private cases and observed that in addition to men, young children
also seemed to have been more prone to death. Ringelblum's report was
that of a social worker, an activist, a person deeply involved in the life of
the ghetto. Although in this entry, he provided specific addresses where
described cases occurred, narratively speaking, he remained distant.
Information he provided allowed a peek into the lives of those who were
struck. The image was of entire households, where people became totally
helpless, too sick and mentally affected to attend to themselves or seek
rescue for themselves and their loved ones.

Passages focusing on observations made by individuals about their own
subjective perceptions explain not only their personal angles but also offer
insights into the effects of hardship on the larger group. Lefebvre suggested

that the first step in the production of space was relationships established between the body and space on an individual level, that is, 'Before producing effects in the material realm (tools and objects), before producing itself by drawing nourishment from that realm, and before reproducing itself by generating other bodies, each living body is space and has its space: it produces itself in space, and it also produces that space.'[46] If this was what was necessary to ensure production, Oskar Rosenfeld wrote on May 10, 1942 that the ghetto was a unique place, an exception to the rule of growth as people were locked up in '... decaying houses with just enough air to vegetate',[47] and that they could not produce anything because there were no materials to do so. He concluded by saying that this terrible scarcity resulted in changing humanity as they lost the will to live and 'No philosophy can help here.'[48]

When Ringelblum alluded to the smell emerging from dead bodies in apartments, the effect he discussed related to the nuisance such smells caused. Once a source had been discovered, the immediate reaction was to remove it. In this scenario, odors functioned as a lead, as well as indicator of decay. In this sense, removing the source of the stench, indeed worked as a solution, yet eliminating the smell by neutralizing its source offered only temporary relief, a brief separation between the here and there, but without suggesting repair of any sort.

The smell of a decaying body also offered but a glance into the heart of a special problem in the ghetto – ceaseless attempts to avoid abjection, that is, to maintain separation between filth, decay, death, bodily discharge, etc. and cleanliness, life, self-control. To use Mary Douglas's theory, although the home has its own set of restrictions, it still protects the individual from what Douglas referred to as '... voyeurism and intrusive scatology.'[49] This was the total opposite of the situation in the ghetto where so many people lived together in small spaces that allowed no privacy even for the most intimate bodily functions.

According to Lefebvre, 'If sensual rapture and its antithesis exist anywhere, if there is any sphere where, as a philosopher might say, an intimacy occurs between 'subject' and 'object', it must surely be the world of smells and the places where they reside.'[50] When Janina Bauman wrote, 'A warm smell of freshly baked bread wafting from a gate we passed by, almost made me faint...',[51] she alluded to loss of control, as if her bodily needs conquered her mind by accessing her senses because of the smell of bread. Her words evoked frustration not only at a lack of food but also her body's uncontrollable reaction, the feeling of faintness, provoked by the penetration of an invisible but detectable odor from the outside into her

The Private Sphere   171

senses and mind ending in abjection, in the collapse of boundaries. Julia Kristeva suggested, 'The abject has only one quality of the object – that of being opposed to I.'[52] In other words, smell behaved as an invisible realm unexpectedly linking the outside, the body, and the inside. What was under the skin, the invisible, triggered one to lose the 'I' because it made borders and restrictions collapse and therefore converge. In Bauman's experience, it was brief as only for a moment did the 'I' and the opposite, abjection, uncontrollable bodily functions merged so as to erase the boundaries between mental and bodily functions.

Ben-Shem's diary referred to the effects hunger had inside family space, and how it turned people against one another. One such case concerned Avraham Lipman, Ben-Shem's friend. In his diary Ben-Shem wrote that he happened to witness this incident because he accidentally came to visit only to find everyone in a deplorable situation. Ben-Shem understood from what he was told that Lipman had succeeded in exchanging some of his precious books for bread and took this 'treasure'[53] home. His wife and son were in bed trying to warm themselves in their frozen apartment, while he left the bread at home and went outside to fetch a glass of hot water for tea. In the meantime, his son '... smelled the bread and without saying a word, pretended to go to relieve himself and in no time, managed to swallow all the bread.'[54]

A short inquiry revealed that Lipman himself had nibbled on the bread on his way home, and that what remained was a mere quarter of the loaf of bread which was what his boy had secretly eaten. When Lipman returned and realized the bread was gone, he immediately suspected his wife of this offence, and therefore he attacked her both verbally and physically. Although it turned out that it was his son who could not resist the tempting smells, Lipman kept yelling at his wife and at the same time tried to soothe the boy who was crying bitterly. Ben-Shem wrote that the crisis was resolved by finding another piece of bread thus calming everyone down.

This incident linked shortage and false abundance together – an inability to warm water with the deeply affecting appeal of the wonderful smell of bread. Even more evident poles were exposed in this narrative, as according to Ben-Shem, Lipman's apartment was located at the end of a courtyard above toilets and characterized by a 'sour' smell unmistakable even from the outside.[55] In this clearly stinking environment, the intense odor of bread overcame all other bad smells and allowed this aberration from the expected. Namely, a father who rather than control himself, had eaten parts of the bread and a nine-year-old boy who was well aware of the scarcity of bread, knew this piece was meant for all three of them, but whose

172   *Emanuel Ringelblum and Reuven Ben-Shem's War Writings*

senses prevented him from resisting the alluring aroma, all of which ended with a violent ugly feud.[56]

Ben-Shem preceded this incident with a description of Lipman's dire financial situation and how he tried to provide for his family. Apparently, Lipman possessed a huge library of about 3,000 books that he '... lovingly took care of neglecting everything, his wife, the house...'.[57] Having no other means of support in the ghetto, Lipman decided to sell his books. Ben-Shem wrote, '... in the morning he eats Nietzsche, for dinner two volumes of Keyserling and for supper Le Petit Larousse of which some has been left for the next breakfast'.[58] The analogy between books and food stands out as revenues used for buying food came from selling books. Lipman deprived his soul, substituting food for thought with actual food.

On the struggle between the animalistic and sublime, Ringelblum brought up a conversation he had with a refugee who had gone hungry for a long time. The man confessed that hunger had consumed him to such a degree that he could not concentrate on anything else but his craving for food. This had gripped him so intensely that he had trouble thinking about even bathing himself. Ringelblum's encounter served as a concluding argument in his attempt to explain reasons for Jewish apathy. According to him, hunger had made people listless, which was the source of their silence and passive behavior as their minds were fixated on food, leaving them little energy to revolt.[59]

The body's surrender to its basic survival instincts, leading to boundaries being erased and ending in total abjection, was exposed in Ben-Shem's testimony about his wife's attempt to sell their fur to a Polish policeman. Pnina was accompanied to the Lustman's home where she was left to wait in a dark room. Ben-Shem wrote that his wife said her nostrils were immediately hit by smells of human feces and she became terrified as she could see nothing in the dark, not even the door she had been led in through. An old man's voice suddenly asked who was in the room and she immediately recognized it. It was the father of the family who advised her to light matches as there was no electricity. In the light, Pnina witnessed a frightfully memorable image. 'Inside a stable filled with dry horse manure and human feces, partly already dry and partly not, there were bodies lying in the corner, not people, but skeleton-like bodies.'[60]

The family, moved to tears because Pnina had recognized them, explained that their condition was due to the death of the mother and illness of their daughter. In order to save her, they had sold everything they had, including all their clothes, which was why they were lying in bed, naked with nothing but a filthy blanket to cover them. The family concluded by

The Private Sphere

173

saying that '...until today, we didn't die, because dying requires strength too.'[61]

The abominable state of this family's abjection reflected the infiltration of disintegration and collapsing social order into intimate spaces. In this sense, the spatial situation, the lived space in the ghetto appeared to penetrate the family unit: not only did families collapse as an entity, but their current condition suggested that they had lost their capacity as a sheltering unit bordering on animalistic existence. No one, except the son, whose first name was concealed, seemed to have kept his senses, could physically function. Yet, the manner he used his vitality did not suggest it was aimed at helping his family, rather, he appeared to take care only of himself. Furthermore, by bringing Pnina into his family residence, knowing how dire it was and on the other hand, being aware of Pnina's background and her living conditions, the young Lustman appeared to have lost his social sensibilities and shame. Was he not aware of his family's condition? Was he not sensible enough to realize that one did not leave a stranger in one's house literally in the dark?[62]

In this narrative, Ben-Shem appeared to imply a reciprocal influence and intrinsic link between physical spaces and humans who occupied them, one reflecting the other.[63] In a state of total abjection, private space, the semi-stable or room, appeared to be nothing but a tomb-like space containing the barely alive bodies of the family. The narrative hints that this lived-in space with its human inhabitants was a somewhat prophetic or allegoric description of ghetto existence. The family no longer functioned as such because mutual care appeared to have disappeared, bodies themselves, naked as if they had just been born or were already dead, taboos broken with both males and females lying naked and worse, they were a father, brother and sister-daughter, all together in a lawless universe.

The whole scene echoes Dante's *Inferno*, suggesting disorientation of mind, space, and body, as if chaos had been reinstated. Nazi conceptualization of Lebensraum into family units serves here not only as a scale of shock but also of relief. Shock, because even in the harsh reality of the ghetto, the degradation these people experienced was extremely unusual. Relief, as being faced with such a repugnant situation, one was comforted that in comparison, one was relatively well off.

Bernard Goldstein's diary presented another aspect of abjection. He was privileged to have a room to himself owing to his position in the Bund. In his memoires he recounted that he was surprised to be approached by a seventeen-year-old girl who lived in the same apartment seeking his advice. She told him she was in love with a boy called Kostek and that the couple

174 · Emanuel Ringelblum and Reuven Ben-Shem's War Writings

wanted to consummate their love. She asked whether that would be an immoral act because they were not married and Goldstein assured her that there was nothing wrong with it, although he wondered why she had confided in him so openly. When the girl did not leave his room immediately, Goldstein wrote that it had dawned on him that she was asking him to lend them the room because there were no opportunities for intimacy in the crowded ghetto. Goldstein pretended it was his idea to lend them the room and make it possible for the couple to meet intimately under the pretext that he needed her boyfriend's personal reports about activities in the ghetto, which was how they were able to fulfil their love. Goldstein added that both of them had died in deportations.[64]

The Outside Goes Inside

As much as abjection characterized the situation inside homes, it was in many ways parallel to what was happening on the outside. Indeed, the ghetto was characterized by desolation in the private and intimate sense, blurring of boundaries – physical and mental, mirroring the public sphere. Rather than being a refuge, the private arena was dominated by constant movement between the inside and outside, that is, it was repeatedly penetrated by the outside and due to loss of control, it diffused from the inside.

One peculiar form of flow was through sounds and voices that pierced the inside. Lefebvre suggested that the means by which people related to space was through their senses.[65] Of all these senses, hearing was the most prominent as it served as a mediator between the body and the world.[66] In the ghetto, as such, sounds had a crucial role because they were a constant irritation streaming in from the streets and invading apartments. Ludwik Hirszfeld, a bacteriologist and serologist, who was also a convert, strikingly alluded to this issue by writing about the dramatic difference between ghetto streets, '… a pit of hell – disgusting odors and screaming people…'[67] and the welcome silence engulfing the church courtyard where he lived. The man who was forced into the ghetto, nevertheless lived in better conditions, in the presbytery of All Saints' Church on Grzybowski Square, which was within ghetto premises.

While sounds of screams, shouts, cries, and a never-ending turmoil of people characterized daytime hours, at night, what permeated houses were the voices of crying children and beggars who took no notice of curfew hours and continued wandering the streets hoping to get some food. In one report, Ringelblum appeared to have been particularly angry when he

The Private Sphere   175

wrote, 'Frozen children have become a widespread phenomenon…',[68] contrasting this with the festivities in the ghetto held during *Children's Month,* whose posters were used to cover the bodies of dead children lying in the streets.[69]

Although Ringelblum's subtext criticized the incapacity of households (when such existed), ghetto institutions, whether the *Kehilla* or Jewish self-help, more than anything, the text evoked his own pain provoked by this complex situation. Still, the impersonal text reads:

> A special kind of beggars are those who beg after nine o'clock at night. When you stand at the gate, you suddenly see new beggars you have not seen before. They walk in the middle of the street and ask for bread. The majority are children. In the silence around, the cries of these hungry children-beggars are terrifying and shocking, and as tough as you are, you will eventually be forced to throw them a piece of bread for otherwise, you will find no peace at home for your soul.[70]

Children's cries penetrating the inside of houses made the connection between the outside and inside inseparable and intolerable, thus adding to the deep sense of guilt of those inside apartments. Typically, Ringelblum did not speak of the Germans' responsibility for the situation yet, untypically, he evoked the personal effect the ghetto's routine had on one's mental resilience. In this context, his text is revealing because it almost sounds as if he was criticizing beggars rather than addressing an alarming phenomenon. Thus, his choice of words allows a peek into the constant erosion of all ghetto inmates' mental and emotional capacities.

In this case, Ringelblum's historical discourse showed the states of mind of those who recorded as an indication of their inability to cope relatively well. In other words, documenting meant one was a master of one's reasoning and emotions, as without them, one would be unable to perform the task. However, the structure of the text suggests that looking at others and writing about them created estrangement between recorders and what they recorded. Intrinsically, the emotions aroused by a writer's perspective presenting the relationship between the outside and inside, acted as a piercing look through a crack.[71] What Ringelblum exposed here was another burden consisting of helplessness and guilt at one's powerlessness mingled with repugnance towards the phenomenon as such.

Not only did sounds penetrate private dwellings but also the cold. Ben-Shem wrote:

, ... in the houses of the poor, everyone is in bed. They never leave them as there is no coal to light a fire. ... they lie there and not only those who have not yet sold their duvets. ... Those in the "points" also lie down all day long in one place, covered only with rugs and torn up cloaks... trembling, frozen.[72]

Ben-Shem was referring to the situation in many houses where not only was there no coal to burn, but windows were missing, a situation Bernard Goldstein explained well.[73] On the effects of the cold, on the inability to regard one's homes as a refuge, Ben-Shem wrote in November 1941,

... if the cold is terrible and frightening in middle class Jewish houses, it is crueler in beggars' houses. I spoke to some of them (beggars) and they explained that the cold was worse than hunger. If one was hungry, one could go outside, beg and when successful, get some coins ... and at least for a few minutes it eases...[74]

They added that begging for coal was not an option as one could never get the sum of money required to buy or beg for the coal itself.[75] Ringelblum related to the same issue in January 1942, writing that refugees in the "points" were freezing to death because there was insufficient coal while coffee shops could get coal to warm their spaces and therefore '... the number of freezing is huge, and it is a daily phenomenon.'[76] Interestingly, although both writers discussed the same phenomenon, Ringelblum's text was depersonalized, yet, he conveyed social injustice by comparing heating in coffee shops to those freezing in their places of residence. Whereas Ringelblum emphasized social gaps, Ben-Shem addressed the same topic by individualizing reports and voicing what beggars had observed about it being worse than hunger.[77]

Even during a few moments of happiness within one's household, the outside remained a threat and a penetrating point of reference for the private sphere. One such episode was recorded in Ben-Shem' diary and concerned Passover Eve, 1941, Friday, April 11. Ben-Shem wrote that for the holiday, he had received Matzot from several sources: a friend, the journalists' union, and as he was listed as a Rabbi, from the *Kehilla* as well. These came with other products necessary for the Passover meal, including an egg and wine. This unusual abundance was extremely gratifying, and Ben-Shem wrote they were preparing the 'seder' meal as if neither 'the demon'[78] nor 'the devil'[79] was lurking on their doorstep.

Ben-Shem described a beautiful image of a family gathering during one of the most important events of the Jewish calendar, Passover, celebrating divine intervention to free ancient Jews from slavery in Egypt. When he came back from synagogue, his home was filled with happiness, excitement and wonderful smells: 'In the kitchen my wife and relative 'make noises' (originally in inverted coma) and from the kitchen, the smells of the Pesach (Passover) soup with *kneidlach* (soup dumplings) and the smell of wine...',[80] distinct odors smelled once a year, which filled him with contentment while serving as a mental and spiritual bond to the past.

He wrote how listening to his daughter singing and that of the others who joined her, transported his mind to Passover Eve at his father's home, thinking about the probability that the house might have been destroyed, but comforting himself with remembering that the 'tune' did not die as '... the tune exists in the heart of every Jew religious or not ... in the warehouse of his soul...'[81] and was sung once more around their table. This year, he declared, each prayer verse, including the blessings, were read more emphatically, making an analogy between their present confinement in the ghetto and slavery in Egypt. 'I mumbled 'commemorating the departure from Egypt' (originally in inverted commas) and with all my heart, I participated in the exodus from Egypt and in all the exoduses of my people from trouble to the open, from slavery to salvation.'[82]

Ben-Shem's texts conjured the warmth of the inside versus the outside where '... he reigns... the angel of death's friend' (written in Yiddish) using more adjectives and descriptions to evoke the abhorrent Hitler, but without mentioning his name, '... he reigns, one millimeter from the windows but here, in the room, my home's rooms, he has no control.'[83] These were contrasted with the exact opposite: 'Here purity reigns, pure love... family friendship... Here angels sit and enjoy the joy of happiness that their will created... despite the obstacles ... they enjoy the bliss of their souls that were not depressed even now, by him and in the ghetto.'[84]

The contrast, the binary opposites between the here and there, Passover of 1941, was not only between the inside and outside, but between two different worlds. The world of Hitler, characterized by evil and the world of innocent human beings whose mental resources sustained them, despite circumstances, strong and worthy of the title 'angels'. That evening seemed to have restored biblical order as there was a clear and distinct separation between good and evil. The microcosm in his home reached far beyond the ghetto, into ancient Egypt and the Exodus the Almighty had supervised attentively.

In this text, Ben-Shem recreated a thread that led from early Jewish history through his father's household to the present in the ghetto. In this way, while the description of the holiday may appear to suggest the inside was a shelter from the outside, it also illuminated temporary apparent serenity, on the one hand, while forming a bridge of memory to other Passover eves, as well as antiquity when the Israelites were saved, thus instilling hope for the present.

Choosing to include and provide great detail about this event in his diary appeared to allow Ben-Shem to form, by their inclusion, not only facts and what related to them, but also evoke the end point of his life story. The prominence he gave this event in that particular period became a focal point of reference for the opposing realities of serenity with which he imbued his text. By choosing to discuss Passover 1941, Ben-Shem was able to establish a narratological opposing pole that enabled him to sharpen contrasts, not only with the world outside his door, but also link it to other historical events in the Jewish calendar, to draw hope and a positive perspective for the future. Here, there were three spaces: the desolation of the ghetto, the inside of his home and the memories and associations instilling fortitude against the perils they experienced.

VIII

The Public Sphere

Ghetto Public Spaces – The Visual and the Truth

Once the walls were erected, the notion of Jews being visible – the ability to distinguish them in a crowd – was supposed to have lost its poignancy. In the reality of the Warsaw ghetto, the armband indeed stopped being such an important concern as all ghetto inmates were Jewish, and almost everyone had to wear it. Still, the idea of visibility inside took on a different perspective, as within the Ghetto, the problems were life-threatening: hunger, disease, and death. Rather than armbands, what characterized Jews externally was little and ragged clothing on ill-looking, scrawny people. In this way, the visual of Jews no longer depended on armbands, instead their physiques became a sign, a visual representation of their acute condition and consequently, their identifying mark.

The pledge to truth is a recurring theme in diaries as well as testimonies during and after the war. In this respect, both Ringelblum and Ben-Shem's texts were no different although their points of departure to ensure reliable information were not the same. Of great pertinence to the present discussion is the nature and intent of both texts and future purposes they were to serve. The end determined not only how their diaries were written but consequently influenced choices both made about what to record.

As might be expected, because Ringelblum intended his diary, and later the archive, to embody a historical point of view and be studied by historians, his emphasis was on methodology designed not only to ensure objective and accurate depiction of reality but also eliminate doubts. Initially, Ben-Shem's private diary, at least the deciphered version, indicated his intent to publish but his attention to accuracy did not rely on a systematic methodology. Rather, his was based on his personal experiences and various sources ranging from letters, hearsay, or actual discussions with people involved. That said, because Ben-Shem deciphered his diary in safety and several years after the end of the war, he was in the position of knowing about the veracity of at least some of the events he had learned about indirectly and which he included in his diary. Hence, the urge to provide conclusive proof of occurrences diminished because by then, more was known about the war, which contributed to lessening the dread of not being believed.

Apparently, their primary reason for writing was a profound urge to record what was happening, ensuring texts included facts to produce objective narratives. Both held photography in high regard for its authenticity, yet both were not as naïve as to think that photographs and film necessarily reflected the truth. They were only too aware of how Nazis manipulated reality using photography. In their attempts to produce these faithful depictions of the historical development of the ghetto, both Ben-Shem and Ringelblum attempted to imitate the image verbally using photographic discourse as a means to represent the true state of affairs, and contradict German propaganda that used actual images.

Lefebvre noted that photography was the act of exposing or illuminating phenomena through a sign.[1] Yet, inherently, photography had a flaw, its quality of fragmentation forcibly distorted reality, if only for its capacity to disintegrate space. He noted that illusion and inaccuracies were to begin with, part of '... the artist's eye and gaze...'[2] Alongside this observation, he emphasized that the nature of a photographer, whether compassionate or cruel, went beyond the limitations of the medium. In this sense, what Ringelblum and Ben-Shem achieved by textualizing images, appears to accentuate what Lefebvre argued, that is, going beyond the '... clarity, readability and plasticity...'[3] by means of their text imagery.

Indeed, since its invention, in the late 19th century, photography had gained popularity and became more accessible to the masses. Although it remained rather expensive to own a camera in the 1940s, the practice itself became more and more popular and was largely considered a faithful account of the real world.[4] In the ghetto, neither Ringelblum nor Ben-Shem had a camera, but both expressed numerous times that they viewed photography as a powerful and reliable medium of documentation.[5]

Diligently they documented what occurred in the ghetto, often employing terms related to the world of imagery and photography, such as photo, sight, vision, spectacle, or play. Not only this, but even without using such words explicitly, both diaries contain many descriptions emphasizing the visual and attempting to create in readers' imaginations a certain mental image that would duplicate reality accurately. Although for both the notion of photography was often associated with attempts to provide impartial reports, it is this approach that revealed a more hidden notion, that is, the fear that words may not be enough to provide a full picture of the complexity of existence in the ghetto.[6]

Not once did Ringelblum use terms that related to photography to emphasize the level of impartiality workers of *Oneg Shabbat* strove to archive. He explicitly emphasized 'Multi-sidedness was the main principle of our work, objectivity was the second guiding principle, we wanted the whole truth to be reflected in it, bitter as it might be, our photographic reports are authentic and not retouched.'[7] Hence, referring to 'Multi-sidedness' meant that the aspiration was to gather information from different sectors, classes, age groups, and locations, yet refraining from talking to people from the *Kehilla* because of their frequent contact with the Gestapo. The idea was to have them write about the same subject because it was the subjectivity of their points of departure that guaranteed an authentic image that would emerge once all these testimonies were studied scientifically.[8]

To achieve this, Ringelblum wrote that they wanted the same events to be described by a great number of people so that '... by comparing the different documents, the historian would not find it difficult to reach the kernel of historical truth and reconstruct the actual course of events.'[9] Ringelblum emphasized that *Oneg Shabbat* workers stuck to the truth as they were promised that no material about people who were still alive would be used and that records were solely for historical purposes. Therefore, the approach writers adopted had to ignore their fear of Germans as well as the *Kehilla*, so that the pictures they formed would be of value to future court trials as reliable evidence after the war.[10]

Further proof of incontestability was provided by Ringelblum who emphasized that despite the atrocities Jews suffered, they did not turn a blind eye to acts of kindness on the part of Germans and Poles and put them down in writing as well. Once again, he pointed out, '...we must be objective even when it relates to our sworn enemies so as to present an objective picture about the relationships between Germans and Jews.'[11] Ringelblum added that the same approach was to characterize their descriptions of Polish-Jewish relations.

Ringelblum and Ben-Shem's regard for imagery and photography was an attitude shared by many. In his diary, Ringelblum noted that because it was impossible to get out of the ghetto, schoolteachers had to settle for pictures and postcards to teach children about Warsaw, thus exemplifying how photos were viewed as direct portrayals of reality.[12] Similarly, he pointed to September 26, 1940, as a date when German newspapers sold around the ghetto for more money because they contained pictures of destruction caused by bombardments in Germany. The manner in which Ringelblum reported this is noteworthy: he provided the information as a fact without interpretation, that is, refraining from exposing the intense appeal these pictures of destruction must have held for those who bought these newspapers. Thus, it is possible to indirectly understand how popular these images were by mentioning that sales that day were better.[13]

If postcards and newspaper photos were conceived as faithful representations of the present, so were personal photographs. Indeed, beggars in the ghetto used their own pictures to draw attention to the past, as evidence of the effect the war had had on them. In their diaries, the writers echoed this trend when they documented begging whose unique feature was the notion of now and then, or pictures as mirroring the before. Ringelblum wrote about a person who had previously been a prisoner in a camp and as a means of arousing pity and getting help, he would show people his picture from before, when he looked '... nice, fresh and healthy.'[14]

With his friend, J.J. Prapus, Ben-Shem prepared a list of sixty-five different categories of begging, classified according to tactics beggars adopted to persuade passersby to help them.[15] Category fifty-nine, 'Snapshots', concerned photos. Ben-Shem described a typological scene of a scrawny woman with a swollen face, who had a photograph of a beautiful woman next to her. Ben-Shem wrote that as men were 'eternally' interested in women, they were drawn to take a closer look at the picture but once they approached it, they realized that the woman sitting on a bunch of rags was in fact the same person in the photo.[16]

Category sixty suggested that this practice became known for its benefits to users, which was the reason many embraced the same strategy and it soon spread like '... mushroom after the rain.'[17] Named 'idyll', category sixty consisted of a variation of the same theme and discussed a tactic implemented by families when one or both parents staged an idyllic picture: '... the father and the mother in the middle, the children behind or at their side, and next to them in an enlarged photo from one or two years before the war, the exact same group, with big smiles, their faces radiant with contentment, satiation and serenity.'[18]

Ben-Shem testified that such sentimental scenes managed to achieve their goal because they reminded people of the importance attributed to family life in Jewish culture. In positioning the family of the present in the same way they had posed for the camera in the past, they were trying to reconstruct the past visually and mentally. This calculated tactic relied on the assumption that the extreme change in circumstances would arouse passersby's interest not only because they would take pity on them but because anonymous crowds were all experiencing the same difficulties. Thus, these photos mirrored one's personal yearning for the before.

The three types of photos used, postcards to familiarize children with Warsaw, newspaper snapshots of ruin in Germany and old photos that beggars used to arouse interest, appear to have a similar intent and purpose.[19] All consisted of contrasting ideas; while all referred to a grim present, some projected it with reality, such as the case of destruction in Germany, while the others represented it with nostalgia.

If photos were conceived as an accurate replica of the actual state of affairs, they also exposed a sentimental yearning for a past, denoted by imagery that no longer existed. If anything, these photographs failed to convey a truthful reproduction of the world. Warsaw of the postcards was a distortion of the present in the same manner that the ruins of Germany were mere fragments of the situation in Germany. These images visualized a much-desired illusion, a thriving Warsaw that no longer existed, devastation in Germany imparting prospects of liberation, and beggars who deliberately used their old private photos to survive, depending on emotions of pity they aroused in others.[20] Here photographs were a means not to represent reality but to instill hope for a future relying on wishes.

Point of View – Propaganda – Das Ghetto, 'Documenting' Jews

According to David Welch, the term *propaganda* became synonymous with lies and therefore, pejorative because of Goebbels' actions during his office as head of the Propaganda Ministry.[21] By 1939, the activities of this body against Jews were well known not only to the public in, but also outside Germany. Indeed, invading German forces were followed by photographers and film crews documenting in picture and film the course of the war. Materials were used for news bulletins, newspapers and propaganda purposes.[22]

These units also circulated in the Warsaw Ghetto from the outset, and Ringelblum reported their work as early as the spring of 1940 when there were severe clashes between Jews and Poles in Warsaw, violence referred to by some researchers as pogroms.[23] Rather than film events, German propaganda squads staged scenes to suggest that German forces were protecting Jews from rioting Polish mobs.[24] This phenomenon was not unique to Warsaw, as Ringelblum reported other such scenes filmed in Łódź.[25]

Between 30 April and 2 June 1942, a German film crew appeared in the Warsaw Ghetto. Jonas Turkow (1898 – 1988), an actor, stage manager, director, and writer, pointed out that almost all filming crew were pilots, and some were dressed as civilians. Turkow added that all their restaurant bills for food and drinks were covered by the Jewish council.[26] The filmmakers' intentions and visions remain unclear to this day, but according to Ringelblum, everything filmed was staged, clearly suggesting it was not the truth that they were after but distorted versions of it.[27] One such example is provided by Avraham Lewin who referred to the filming as 'bacchanalia',[28] and recounted how his wife was stopped on the streets on her way to work so that German film directors could film her being nicely dressed.[29]

Drawing on Lefebvre's observation that a serious flaw of photography was its inherent quality of manipulation by fragmenting reality, it appears German filmmakers used this characteristic to produce a movie that integrated into directed scenes, authentic shots of life in the ghetto thus managing to attribute it with a semblance of authenticity.[30] Apparently, it was quite successful as when the film was discovered immediately after the war, it was judged neutral because there was no documentation to accompany it and to suggest that contents were not authentic.[31]

One falsified scene Ringelblum mentioned showed a Polish policeman grabbing a child intending to hit him but then 'in no time, a German emerged, held the Pole's hand saying that it was not permitted to hit children.'[32] Ben-Shem wrote about another staged scene at the cemetery. As the Germans had forbidden burials to be conducted for several days, a huge quantity of corpses accumulated in the cemetery shed thus enabling filming the situation at its worst '…without showing not even once the main cause, which forced half a million people to live in a few streets surrounded by a wall and without air to breath.'[33]

He also reported demands made on the *Kehilla* to supply the German crew with scenes of a circumcision, a wedding, etc., clearly indicating there was a hidden purpose, and Ben-Shem added that even those who were 'blind'[34] could see it was not innocent.[35] Like many others, he reported an exceptionally disturbing scene in which men and women were forced to undress and have sexual intercourse in a *mikvah* (Jewish ritual bath). After filming was over, one man committed suicide, while two women became ill, and one lost her mind.[36] This particular event horrified many, which explains why it was mentioned in numerous diaries, such as Rachel Auerbach's,[37] Chaim Kaplan's,[38] Ringelblum's, and Bernard Goldstein's diaries, to name but a few. The latter stated that the purpose of driving naked Jewish men and women together and filming them was to show the depravity of ghetto Jews.[39]

The movie 'Das Ghetto' was discovered in 1950, and for years, it was taken as authentic footage representing life in the ghetto.[40] Accordingly, it

The Public Sphere   185

was used to learn about the Holocaust without realizing it was a staged version of the truth when ghetto Jewish inhabitants were forced to become actors in the movie.[41] The discovery of two other reels in 1998 by Adrian Wood, a British researcher, had a tremendous effect on the scholarly interpretation of 'Das Ghetto' as the new reels footage clearly showed filmmakers and directors accidentally entering one another's shots.

These reels contained similar scenes to previous ones but had multiple takes showing German cameramen and S.S. guards in the background while others were shooting. These reels provided solid evidence that many of the scenes of Jews living in the Warsaw Ghetto were merely staged propaganda, and this discovery confirmed testimony of these incidents appearing in numerous diaries.[42] Yael Hersonski, the director of *A Film Unfinished*, dealt with the new discoveries and exposed Nazi lies. She wrote,

> What was shown were scenes of starving people, dying people, a mass grave. When it focuses on the victims, and you decontextualize it, it becomes material for the mourning process, and you stop thinking about the origin of these images - because the context was changed.[43]

That is to say that the fact the movie had neither soundtrack, nor any documentation, had initially opened it to interpretation as one had to rely on pictures alone.[44] In addition, because only parts of the movie were available, it was easier for experts in many fields to accept it as authentic footage.

Silent films and photographs reveal that as reliable as images may appear, they become devoid of meaning without explanation. In other words, without a context to accompany images and filmed footage, interpretations can be falsified. In this respect, what one sees depends on what one says about it and this is where language and sight meet.[45] Conversely, Hersonski went as far as comparing the Ringelblum archive to imagery ' ... like a still photo. It is the frozen present of writing.'[46] Yet, Hersonski pointed out that even Ringelblum was aware that scholarly writings did not have the skills to authentically communicate what happened.

A Film Unfinished contains raw footage of the later reels showing staged scenes such as a dinner party that allegedly proved how Jews lived an extravagant life and well-dressed Jews who were forced to bypass corpses lying in the streets. Another famous scene was described in Czerniaków's diary on May 3, 1942 as:

At 10, the film crew from the propaganda office arrived and proceeded to take pictures in my office. A scene was enacted of petitioners and rabbis entering my office, etc. ... a nine-armed candlestick with all candles lit was placed on my desk.[47]

This invented scene suggests that the director had specifically a Christian audience in mind as he made sure there were typically familiar Jewish symbols regardless of the occasion. The scene, filmed in May, showed an impossible event from the Jewish point of view, as nine-armed candelabras are lit only during *Hanukah*, which falls in winter, usually during December.

Hersonski was quoted as saying that she had been taken aback when she watched the newly discovered reels because she realized how much evil there was in the idea of staging such scenes. This also made her question the value of movies shot from the point of view of perpetrators and the value of photographed history because what appeared to be authentic may indeed be far from it.[48] In this respect, the newly discovered reels carry a warning against simplistic interpretations of historical visual records. That is, even if the low technological capacities of the 1940s prevented manipulation on a high level, when intent intervened, distorting reality was conducted either by staging or editing.[49]

As previously mentioned, the thirst for photographs preoccupied German soldiers from the beginning of the war. This was at first encouraged but after the invasion of the USSR, when it became known that mass murder events were photographed, orders were issued to ban photography.[50] However, this did not stop soldiers from taking pictures. In Warsaw, German soldiers who were stationed in the vicinity of the city flocked into the ghetto to do just that, take pictures.[51] Springer-Aharoni gave several examples of photo collections created by soldiers, some of which were certainly antisemitic while others, such as those taken by Joe Heydecker, an anti-Nazi soldier from PK 689 of the propaganda unit stationed in Warsaw in the winter of 1941, which have been interpreted to show empathy with those photographed.[52]

Of particular interest was the Jewish cemetery in Warsaw as herds of 'tourists' streamed to the area along with film squads, all of whom came with a specific intent to witness incredible scenes of death first-hand.[53] Ringelblum noted in May 1941, that the daily death rate rose to a 150 a day and therefore, 'Groups of visitors inundate the cemetery incessantly: the military and private people. The majority do not show any sympathy with the Jews. On the contrary, some of them think that the death rate is too low.

The Public Sphere

187

Some take all kinds of pictures. The shed, where dozens of dead bodies are brought during the day, arouses special interest.'[54]

The more time passed, the more pressing the issue of the dead became. The ghetto had changed and if many beggars occupied its streets, many of them died in the streets too. 'It has become a daily spectacle that in the middle of the streets people lie faint or dead. It doesn't make any impression at all',[55] wrote Ringelblum at the end of February 1941. Between June and August 1941, as typhus claimed more victims, the quantity of dead increased, not only did many die in the streets, but many others were moved into the street, so as to avoid paying the taxes the community demanded for burials.[56] Ben-Shem added that dead bodies were collected and brought for burial in mass graves and that in the summer particularly, the smells coming from the cemetery were so horrible that one had to hold one's breath. He pointed out that in addition to taxes, the burial company wanted for the removal of the body, they were also after their clothes, a precious commodity needed by those who were still alive.[57]

By July, the scale of the dead was so large that the majority remained anonymous as they were found on the streets with no indication of their identity. Ben-Shem wrote that undertakers struggled to cope with the burial of so many people and therefore everything was done in haste, paying little attention to rituals. According to Ben-Shem, the only thing observed was a separation between men and women before pushing them into mass graves.[58] Later, Ben-Shem added that in addition to conducting burials, the cemetery attendant, Avraham-Moshe Posner, made sure to take photographs of the dead, which were developed and kept in albums.[59]

Apparently, the relationship between repellant and extraordinary astonishing sights in the cemetery and owning a camera had a power that Suzan Sontag characterized as transforming '… one person into something active, a voyeur: only he has mastered the situation.'[60] Thus, the ghetto became a spectacle, a show exhibiting sights never experienced before by anyone: inmates, prisoners, or visitors. The attention the cemetery received involved voyeurism, and taking pictures appeared to have replaced language with photographs as a means to control representation of an indescribable truth that only an image could embody.[61]

Helmut Gernsheim characterized the uniqueness of photography as being the only language that was understood everywhere by everyone and this linked all nations and cultures.'[62] This appears to be particularly accurate in the ghetto where human eyes witnessed the unprecedented out in the open, as if they were contemplating hell.[63]

Most photographs, including those from the Warsaw Ghetto, were not taken by its residents as few had cameras, let alone film or facilities to develop them, not to mention the fact that it was simply forbidden for Jews to photograph or film.[64] This particular interest in the frightful scenes at the cemetery raises the question of purpose. Photographs of characters in the ghetto, the immense number of bodies in the cemetery, as well as allusions to Nazi soldiers photographing the ghetto and the dead, filming squads in the ghetto, as well as pictures that were taken by the cemetery attendant Posner, contained, to begin with, hidden meaning that required deciphering.

Why did soldiers take photographs at the cemetery? Why was the film crew so keen to film the cemetery? Why did they bother to invent even more sinister scenes than the ghetto offered in abundance anyway? These questions also preoccupied those in the ghetto, which is why almost every document recording the ghetto alluded to the film squads and Germans walking around the cemetery and taking pictures.

On May 14, 1942, Kaplan referred to the obscene scene at the *mikvah* as a 'sick phantasy' while Auerbach asked herself why they were filming the cemetery scenes. 'Let them film! Let them film as much as possible! Let there remain a film testimony of the destruction they brought on four hundred thousand Jews! ... For many years to come, the faces, the eyes, will go on crying silently telling the truth... Let the multitude of beggars be immortalized ...'[65] Auerbach answered her own question by pointing to the dual effect of photographs, even if Germans intended to hurt and humiliate Jews, photographic footage would eventually turn against them and expose the truth. At some point, Ben-Shem wrote that the cemetery was like a '... border panopticon ... a living fair of death'[66] where grief became a spectacle some of the 'tourists'[67] rejoiced in watching and even documenting, leaving mourners to look on helplessly at how their sorrow had rendered them and their dead a mere attraction.

Thus, a triangular relationship was created between voyeurs who were photographers, that which they captured with their cameras and a third party, those who were forced to become photographic subjects, sometimes actors and always watching the watchers. In this context, it appears that what Bernd Hüppauf proposed was rather accurate, that the act of photography was part of the murder because it produced images of its own doing. Hence, they rendered the spaces where such actions took place into foreign, spaces where there were no limits of civilization, the incarnation of abstraction and abjection.[68]

The Jewish Point of View

Ben-Shem explicitly addressed photography when he wrote:

> ... it is a pity that it is forbidden to take pictures because it is worthwhile to follow the footsteps of the ghetto and its rhythm. Literally chaos with one exception, in the beginning, out of the chaos a world was created but from this chaos a disaster will occur...[69]

If Ben-Shem had a camera, how would he show this chaos? And who can guarantee that others who saw these pictures or films would refer to what they saw as chaos? If he had not drawn an analogy, would the cultural message of creation and destruction be manifested in viewers' minds? On the other hand, how authentic and accurate was this observation, referring to what was going on in the ghetto as chaos?

Indeed, Ringelblum, Ben-Shem and others, without any photographic means, used the pen as a camera to represent details designated to form a faithful image of reality. Ben-Shem and Ringelblum used words, language, to create mental pictures, enabling others to decipher their meanings from their personal points of view. In their case, it was verbal expression that formed pictures in context. In fact, a paradox resulted as both considered photography to create a conclusive, reliable and objective tool to provide proof, yet it was the use of words as a device that rendered their imagery truthful.[70]

The visibility of hunger on the streets was unavoidable; it was not only apparent but also active as beggars employed all kinds of strategies to get help, starting with adopting a certain act and ending with snatching food out of people's hands. Begging characterized views of the ghetto from its earliest days. In November 1940, Ringelblum stated that there was not yet hunger in the ghetto but what annoyed him was visible prominent discrepancies, social gaps, between a growing number of beggars and apparent abundancy. In December, he pointed out that many beggars were lying beneath shop windows, whereas in January 1941, he reported food snatching for the first time.[71] This last incident was contrasted with extremities of life in the ghetto, that is, Gancwajch, the founder of the '13', and lavish parties he threw in the ghetto. Ringelblum wrote that at the hotel Britannia, on 18 Nowolipie Street, the '13' had opened a club that was in fact a brothel.[72]

Ringelblum's reports conveyed the imagery of chaotic scenes on ghetto streets by reporting what appeared to be important information in the same way he had done before the establishment of *Oneg Shabbat*, that is,

190   *Emanuel Ringelblum and Reuven Ben-Shem's War Writings*

emphasizing events themselves. In an entry from 31 December 1940 to January 17, 1941, he put together the following:

1. A report about opening a night club at the Britannia hotel stressing it was actually a brothel.
2. Four cases of bread snatching.
3. Hunger intensifying and next to almost every house entrance, there were people of all ages screaming and pleading for help.
4. 'On the other side'[73] (the Polish) they said that if one wanted to have a good time, they should go to the ghetto. Ringelblum mentioned numerous performances house committees organized (to raise money to help the needy).

The above short remarks, from a long entry, encompass various reports: negative portrayal of the club, a new phenomenon on the streets – food snatching, a reason explaining begging, and finally, mentions of a rumor circulating on the Polish side and facts of ghetto life that may explain the origin of this rumor. Scrutinizing the nature of this concisely written combination of facts one after the other, suggests the chaotic but dynamic course of life in the Jewish ghetto as well as projecting a reverse mirror to how events in the ghetto were conceived by different parties.

Extravagant festivities held by the '13' stood out in opposition to performances conducted by house committees taking these opportunities to raise money to provide for the growing number of impoverished. Both institutions stood out, not only in their raison d'être, but also because one was appreciated while the other despised and yet both were only partially understood by outsiders, the Poles. There is no doubt that not many Poles were aware of the differences between the two institutions and perhaps the rumor Ringelblum mentioned was not as prevalent as he thought in Polish society. Still, putting this in his diary leaves room to assume that Ringelblum was personally offended not only by the comparison, but more likely by how little understanding or identification Poles showed with Jews' circumstances.

Parties and performances in the ghetto, also stand in contrast as they formed a frame, each at one end of the text, while between them, Ringelblum wrote about hunger: cases of food snatching and almost every house entrance occupied by numerous beggars. Barely three months after the ghetto was sealed, hunger became so rampant that ghetto residents, rather than stay indoors, went outside to seek help. Intriguingly and somewhat poetically, reports about parties also framed the two following details provided about begging – parties as a black frame around reports

The Public Sphere   191

of poverty and misery. The combination of all four items presented here works like a camera lens focusing and distancing to supply a truthful and comprehensive image, a visual representation created by words.[74]

Ringelblum's linguistic choices indicated a change in the pattern of begging. To refer to food snatching, he reported what he had been told using the neutral active voice, 'someone counted'.[75] This implies that an anonymous person had reported to Ringelblum, but the word 'report' itself is not mentioned. The linguistic structure signifies a change of spirit among beggars to which Ringelblum added an explanation, hunger had intensified. 'Next to almost all houses and near entrances, there are humans rolling on the ground, people, women and infants begging for help.'[76] This desperate, but active and even violent atmosphere was conveyed by using, on the one hand, descriptions of active reactions: counting, snatching, with the impersonal form to discuss people who were 'rolling on the ground' suggesting their helplessness. In this way, the chaotic nature of ghetto streets was reflected in the appearance of actively hungry people contrasted to those who were either too weak or not as aggressive to adopt the practice.

Ben-Shem approached this phenomenon more or less at the same time as Ringelblum, the end of January 1941. He wrote that food snatching had become a plague and affected weaker women in particular. His manner of reporting was to present several anonymous cases as if they were a recurring movie.

> A woman, minding her own business went out holding a bag, and in the bag, there was bread she had got in return for food ration tickets or bought for her children. The snatcher jumps on the tip of his toes and approaches her slowly, then, like a cat, he attacks. In no time he grabs her bag off her hands... sticks his ugly and filthy hands inside... takes out the bread at a miraculous speed and before anyone can shout or call for help, he has already run away.[77]

Like Ringelblum's text, this passage was all written in the neutral present active voice using broken up series of actions in rather short phrases, one after the other. In this way, the snatcher's speedy but calculated actions were conveyed by introducing one sentence fragmented into twelve sequenced actions giving the text a dynamic nature while creating a mental picture of an act in slow motion. This pattern of description was repeated several times in his diary with variations.

The following passage addresses the viewers' point of view who described and interpreted the reaction of a snatcher who was caught:

They catch him. Him, yes, but the bread, no one can remove it once he snatches it as he bites into it with his teeth and chews it so quickly that all the measurements of velocity in physics may be considered nothing next to this. They catch him, but the bread, no hero would be able to take it from his hands and teeth. They hit him brutally, a Jewish policeman is quick to come, they hit him with a rubber club ..., he is pushed to the ground or he falls and he puts the bread under his body, holding it frantically, chewing and sticking his teeth in it. They roll him in the garbage, kick him, hit his head in the teeth, blood pours, but no one can grab the bread. He chews, chews and swallows, swallowing whole pieces, a quarter of a loaf of bread in one go. It seems the body is weak --- he has no strength to breathe, but heroes will not rise up against him. And if sometimes a policeman succeeds by brutal beatings around the head and teeth, to tear the bread away from him, another snatcher arrives and soon the rest of the bread is in his mouth... [78]

Much like Ringelblum, the language Ben-Shem used did not refer to an isolated case but to a pattern of behavior that characterized street scenes in the ghetto. Words created a mental moving picture of a single typological and repetitive shot, characterizing a new phenomenon that had spread in the ghetto. Descriptions stressed on the one hand, a snatcher's insurmountable power that did not derive from good physical condition, whereas on the contrary, their source was their great body weakness instilling them with unpredictable energy that seemed to have emerged from the dwindling mental resources of a physically extremely weak person.

Here too, the passage is in the present tense consisting of short sentences depicting a series of actions, achieving an effect of speed, haste and despair in both victim and snatcher. Whereas Ringelblum's text mentioned the number of times the snatching phenomenon was spotted, what manages to project the notion of recurrence is Ben-Shem's text, whose narratives focused more on movement in space, was emphasizing repetitive movements in that space. In this respect, time and space formed an integral part of the narrative, which consequently produced a mental image of what was described in words.[79]

Ringelblum's imagery suggests he was less interested in providing an accurate image of an isolated case but wanted to point out a phenomenon that more specifically might affect the image of life in the ghetto. Ben-Shem's imagery, although not traced to a particular event or individual built a coherent image of a prototype that developed into an archetype. Ben-

Shem and Ringelblum's descriptions both presented a phenomenon but if Ringelblum's reference to food snatching created a sense of action on the part of snatchers, Ben-Shem's managed to convey the notion that snatchers were amongst the weakest and what motivated them was acute hunger.

How both Ringelblum and Ben-Shem portrayed extremes in the ghetto emphasized seeing for themselves and categorizing what they saw. Within this framework, both appeared to be passive viewers, but their singularity was their capacity to categorize and map a phenomenon through an entire scene.[80] Whereas Ringelblum talked about a general development and not a particular case, Ben-Shem conveyed this idea by describing a particular image that served as a model to which other nuances could be integrated.

Ringelblum also addressed the issue of piercing hunger so acute it destroyed all mental sensitivities among the hungry, who were so fixated on devouring food that not even severe violence could stop them from eating.[81] Like Ben-Shem, the issue was addressed in general, as a recurring phenomenon in the ghetto. However, occasionally, Ringelblum mentioned a particular case, but his narrative approach still suggested the incident was not unique but rather typological. He wrote: 'A sight: a woman snatches a bagel from a woman peddler, and she hits her, pulling her hair but the other doesn't respond, she doesn't feel the blows, she satisfies her hunger.'[82] Despite the somewhat detached tone, it can be deduced that this incident somehow shook Ringelblum up, otherwise why would he try to be even more impersonal than usual by opening his narrative with 'a sight'? Could this unusual opening not suggest his feelings about the witnessed scene?

Viktor Frankl made a comprehensive remark about an almost total lack of emotion as a result of hunger. He attributed the reason for this apparent numbness, to being reduced to 'primitive life' because of endeavors to remain alive.[83] Bernard Goldstein pointed out that food-snatchers '…were a special category…' because they were the incarnation of two opposites, desperate nonetheless powerful. Like the cases described above, food snatchers' unexpected drive came from their grave situation, and it was anguish that enhanced their determination.[84]

Neutral, passive language and discourse patterns used by both writers added a dimension to descriptions of corruption resulting in a sense of habit and custom. Using the same structure for food snatching alongside suggestions of a pattern stressed that in food snatching, there were real observers and those observed. By watching, viewers were turned from mere spectators to active observers whose responsibility was manifested through recording what they had seen without stepping into a scene and becoming involved, thus creating a relationship between snatchers, onlookers and writers, all participants in the same scene.

Alongside visual emphases in the diaries' descriptions and in addition to the projection of mental images, the graphic verbal representations testified to the total collapse of personal and social order as well as civilization and humanity's rapid disintegration. The descriptions, including portraits of individuals and moving imagery of scenes, projected a chaotic sense of space perception mingled with disorientation.

Simultaneously, opting for verbal-visual representation appears to reflect the degree of intimacy both diary writers allowed themselves to insert into their descriptions of distress. In other words, by focusing on scenes and views, both Ringelblum and Ben-Shem not only rendered what was described into typological imagery but also avoided the explicit abject nature of what was witnessed.[85] Drawing on Keilbach theorization, I argue that attempting to typologize verbally what is seen produces a similar effect. By lending too much importance to visual descriptions that may be interpreted as 'objective', one renders the described subject into a type and by that the writer becomes an agent of de-personifying of victims. Sticking to the visual preserved shreds of human dignity for described subjects, while maintaining a certain detachment, as if the writers were merely uninvolved viewers.

Narrating facts about so many people displaying distress publicly also rendered public spaces into an arena abundant with visual invasive spectacles never seen before in such severity and quantity. Although visuality corresponded directly with the wish to present reliable images, it also contributed to safeguarding the writers from being threatened by these very sights. In this respect, photographic-like observations turned those whose images were recorded into 'others', that is, part of suffering multitudes, distant subjects, whose existence was sufficiently far away, while simultaneously continuing to pose a threat for those recording their presence in this space.[86]

Lefebvre explained this psychological phenomenon by proposing that although

> ... the Ego is liable to 'recognize' itself in the 'other', but it does not in fact coincide with it: 'other' merely represents 'Ego' as an inverted image in which the left appears at the right, as a reflection which yet generates an extreme difference, as a repetition which transforms the Ego's body into an obsessing will-o'-the-wisp. Here what is identical is at the same time radically other, radically different...[87]

If indeed reflected imagery helped to create a demarcation line between the 'I' and the other, it was thanks to reverse reflections creating a distinct difference, which in turn, separated and protected the writers. Maurice Blanchot explained this separation by claiming, 'To write (of) oneself is to cease to be, in order to confide in a guest – the other, the reader, entrusting yourself to him...'[88] Indeed, both writers attributed a quality of objectivity to visibility because of its ability to guarantee one remained an active viewer, yet whose involvement was manifested only by choices of what to watch and document.

Nonetheless, an additional aspect was that such descriptions reflected the visual, but since they concealed personal contexts of what was documented, they became very much like actual photographs, which meant this verbal imagery also had to be deciphered.[89] Regardless, both diarists, in their own way, while relating to mortifying and alarming exhibitions of misery in more general and impersonal ways, occasionally traversed the threshold of the emotional. Their personal involvement appeared in textual lapses illuminating the relationship between the 'I' as witness and 'I' as recorder manifested in the infiltration of personal emotions into their narratives.

The Inside Goes Outside

In documenting the public display of misery, both Ringelblum and Ben-Shem visualized the dire and deteriorating situation in the ghetto, that is, revelations of varied forms of despair breached all boundaries. For the growing number of beggars, it became clear that desolation had to be exhibited outside, as their only chances of survival came from exposing their condition openly. Those who were still in control came up with various tactics designed to gain attention and get help. Beggars whose health had deteriorated or were less energetic were usually less active and sufficed with less conspicuous forms of begging. The most pitiful were those who were on the verge of death, openly exposing mortifying scenes. Either way, the ghetto streets were inundated with phenomena that were new and strange to the public sphere.

In February 1941, Ringelblum enumerated several categories of acts performed by street beggars, ranging from using one's talents to elicit emotions of pity to portraits of themselves in better times:

> Beggars ply their trade in different styles: the cantor from Pułtusk along with his assistant stand and he, trills *El Male Rachamim*[90] and

other prayers. Another one gives whole sermons, walking quickly as if someone was at his heels while waving his arms back and forth as if he were on a Bimah[91]. A mother was begging for help and had her child next to her, a child who turned out to be already dead. Children aged three and four collect charity in the streets, and it is extremely appalling. Some beggars practice all sorts of theatrical poses to make the biggest impression possible.[92]

Ringelblum began with a general introduction to what he was about to describe, strategies employed by beggars to gain attention and help. In contrast to his usual impersonal style, Ringelblum began by describing a tragi-comic scene of a cantor who, rather than praying/singing in synagogue, did it in the street. Even though the cantor's name was not given, revealing his city of origin probably identified the individual and possibly his assistant too. By mentioning the prayer, *El Male Rachamim*, there is room to believe that Ringelblum suggested the prayer drew people's attention while indicating that the cantor's repertoire revealed his strategy, appealing to people's emotions. This rather long and very moving prayer must have struck many chords around the ghetto and drawn attention in streets where death ravaged. If by naming the prayer, Ringelblum had intended to criticize the cantor's obvious appeal to emotions, it seems that mentioning it indicated that he might have been implying unintentionally that the prayer affected him too.

The portrait that followed, a preacher giving entire sermons as if he were in a synagogue, reinstated the impersonal tone. This was done not only by refraining from any sort of identification but also by adding a comical zest to his description, emphasizing his quick speech along with exaggerated movements. This narrative may be suggesting that the preacher appeared somewhat disoriented, thinking he was in a synagogue rather than a street. This manner of narration can be interpreted as a methodical break, emplotment, a constructed artifact, which stresses the bizarre yet comical as a literary device to pave the way for the following two somber images: a mother dragging her dead child and hungry toddlers roaming the streets begging for charity.[93]

It is in the narrative of the last image, child beggars, where Ringelblum expressed his emotions explicitly by writing it was an appalling image. If child beggars made Ringelblum deviate from his custom of refraining from emotional display in documentation, no such obvious reaction can be identified when he wrote about the mother who used her child's dead body to entice people into giving her charity.[94] Nonetheless, his personal reaction

The Public Sphere 197

to the mother and child was folded into details of revealing the child was actually dead. From this information, one can understand that, from the mother's point of view, she had produced the desired effect of drawing attention, yet it is thanks to this attention that someone inquired and it became clear that the child was dead. With such concise and impersonal imagery, it is unclear who checked on the child, whether it was Ringelblum himself or others. Still, what is apparent in this narrative is the drama that must have taken place, which had led not only to discovering the child was dead but understanding the appalling physical and mental state of a mother who had probably lost her wits, if not worse, to use her own child's body in this way.

The effect produced by the last two images seemed to fade away when Ringelblum ended this sequence of imagery with a somewhat conclusive statement that seeks various practised theatrical poses to have greater effect.[95] Narratively speaking, the last sentence appears to draw an end, to close the window on the emotional effect street scenes provoked in the writer, at least on that day. Notably, no particular place is mentioned, and only once does Ringelblum write the word 'streets', all contributing to enhancing the typological characteristics of these public scenes.

According to Ben-Shem, in May 1941, there were about 100,000 people on the verge of starvation in the ghetto. As previously mentioned, Ben-Shem and his friend Prapus, diligently classified sixty-five different types of begging named according to strategies beggars employed to get people's attention and help. He enumerated three categories of those he claimed had acquired certain habits: door-to-door or street begging, relying on passersby's kindness. The second group consisted of those who performed some artistic acts such as singing, individual musicians or whole orchestras, choirs, and soloists whose repertoire ranged from an entire artistic program to singing songs in English, Polish, Yiddish, and Hebrew. This category included reciters, pantomime, or real actors and in total, Ben-Shem referred to about eighteen different artistic performances. Finally, there was a category including all kinds of pretenders with twenty subcategories such as those who faked a stroke, fainted, imitated an epileptic fit, cursed, blessed, or attempted to hypnotize others by staring at them wildly.[96]

Both writers provided moving portraits of distress, but occasionally, they managed to raise a smile. Such was the case when Ben-Shem described in category thirty, families who originated from outside of Warsaw with a large number of children 'incongruent with their wealth.'[97]. He wrote about such a family wandering the streets and having identified a rich man in the distance, they would block the width of the street and the head of the family would introduce his wife and offspring graciously, as if they were royalty. Ben-Shem wrote that this was not a successful tactic, but it usually affected women, more than men, who would eventually give them something to appease their own conscience.[98]

Although they presented the comic in their texts, neither writer viewed the situation lightly. On the contrary, the declining state of ghetto inmates was moving as it accentuated and heightened a deep sense of helplessness. Nevertheless, it may very well be that as their descriptions provided real street images, bitter humor hid a desperate sense of despair on their part while contributing to enhancing the distance necessary to fulfil the task of documentation.

If indeed those described became an incarnation of otherness, those who wrote about them were allegedly on the other side. Yet the mirror effect in the ghetto was much more complex. Onlookers, some of whom were Germans in different capacities, 'better off' Jews, some of whom, like Ben-Shem and Ringelblum, wrote about what they saw but remained an armlength away from becoming beggars themselves. A third element in this relationship was the 'actors', that is, beggars themselves, whose efforts were directed at being seen and noticed rather than hidden.

In this sense, beggars turned visibility into a means of survival as they strove to stand out. In so doing, they too became observers of those whom they considered others, that is, Jews in better conditions than they were, people whom they examined carefully as they weighed up prospects of success in enticing them to help. Rarely did Ringelblum mention non-Jewish onlookers, but Ben-Shem referred to them more often. Nonetheless, even his allusions to Germans were not directly linked to scenes of extreme physical and emotional distress exhibited by huge numbers of beggars. Both Ringelblum's and Ben-Shem's poignant photographic reports of street scenes appeared to concern the writers not in relation to whose fault it was but as a constant burden on their senses. This explains why Ringelblum hardly interjected himself into the text while Ben-Shem seemed to do so with no particular concern as to appearing unobjective.[99]

Mary Douglas claimed that home protected individuals from intrusion by hiding possible encumbrance.[100] All of Ben-Shem's examples represent the chaotic reality of the ghetto, where people were constantly on the move between indoors and outdoors.[101] In the ghetto, dwellings hardly protected anyone, which was why many left the fragile safety of their residences to achieve the opposite, to be seen and noticed as a means of survival. Flocking outside emphasized an ambiguous situation of a dead-end because neither the outside nor the inside offered any relief.

The flow to the outside exposed everyone to difficult-to-watch phenomena, forcibly imposing themselves on everyone's already shaken nerves, rousing deep concern evoked by what was conceived as a mirror effect of oneself.[102] Likewise, these invasive and distressful sights constantly made people feel guilty because they could not help more. Even worse, Ringelblum and Ben-Shem revealed how begging and misery encompassed abomination, resulting in growing chaos that engulfed almost every aspect of ghetto life. The deliberate public exhibition of distress of those whose deplorable situation, acute sense of urgency and desperate attempts to survive, had driven them to the streets as a last resort.[103]

Both writers focused on Jews rather than on the interaction between imprisoned Jews and their jailers. Hence, both writers referred mainly to interactions among Jews themselves, avoiding almost entirely the dangers awaiting from random and deliberate violence perpetrated by Nazi patrols in the ghetto. In other words, the image of the struggling multitude on the verge of death, some of whom concocted schemes or adopted tactics to be seen and recorded in one's memory, were solely addressed to other Jews from whom they could only hope to get help. In so doing, they imposed their public displays of distress on Jews, which not only created a visual tremor but also shook the very foundations of civilization by exposing outside phenomena involving breaches of privacy and intimacy or abjection.

What was articulated with difficulty about beggars, was more openly exposed when it concerned the dead. Ringelblum observed in May 1941, '... death has reached such levels that it literally rolls in the streets. Children are no longer afraid of death. In one courtyard, children amused themselves by tickling a body.'[104] Around April 1941 Ben-Shem reported 'Lately it has become the custom to literally die in the streets... Twelve hours is all it takes ...'[105] This is the beginning of a passage where Ben-Shem described in great detail the dying process. People were often moved and '...of all times, it is then that they buy him a cake or bagel and stick it in his mouth...'[106] When a person died, Ben-Shem wrote that people used newspapers to cover their faces, placing four stones at each corner to prevent the paper from moving. In November 1941, once the epidemic became more and more widespread, Ben-Shem wrote about breaching boundaries: 'In normal times the dead are apart, and the living are apart, a separation that does not exist anymore.'[107]

These passages alluded not only to the degree Jewish culture and religious observation had been affected and violated but also to spatial changes. Ben-Shem's descriptions of the process of death in public conveyed a deep sense of misplacement mingled with disorientation of both the dying as well as the writer. Rather than the dying spending their final hours at home or hospital, they underwent this process in streets under the gaze of everyone in the vicinity.

This degradation of the dead was not only an esthetic issue but a profound violation of Jewish culture and religious conventions. Observing clear separation between the dead and the living is a strict requirement of Jewish law and customs.[108] In Jewish culture, the dead are considered to be defiled and strict separation between the living and dead is observed by all, whether religious or not. Ghetto streets exposed the complete opposite as people lay dead in the streets while ghetto authorities were unable to keep up with the high mortality rate.

Collapse of Human Perception - The Shops

On July 22, 1942, physical spaces in the Warsaw Ghetto changed abruptly and violently. One major and crucial change was that until then, families had been able to remain together and maintain some shred of familial routine, but once deportations started, this collapsed. If one was a Jew incarcerated in the Warsaw Ghetto, there were three main routes life could take: deportation to Treblinka, which was what happened to most Warsaw Ghetto inhabitants. Although some tried jumping off running trains, few attempted to do this and fewer succeeded in this venture.[109] The second escape route was fleeing the ghetto, an almost impossible mission that offered slim chances of survival, particularly when it concerned more than one person, let alone families.[110] The third option, accessible to a limited number of people, was finding employment in one of the shops, a possibility involving almost exclusively adults, usually men.[111]

Those who remained in the ghetto had to choose a survival strategy, and one widespread approach was hiding or trying to find ways to render their presence legitimate. One unusual scheme, for instance, was contracting false marriages to people with life-saving certificates. Another group, which initially thought they were protected, were the shop workers' families who were at first exempt from deportations. This policy quickly changed with women and children hunted down for deportations, which forced them into hiding.[112] As mentioned, when it was harder to fulfil daily quotas, even men with valid papers were taken away.[113] Regardless, anyone allowed to remain in the ghetto, whether one was a shop employee or had another kind of permit, was in fact postponing an already finalized death sentence.

Both diary authors worked in shops, and their writings revealed how every familiar notion was distorted while boundaries of space and time blurred, consequently becoming significant oppressive factors, seriously affecting their writing capabilities too. Interestingly, while half of Ben-Shem's diary was dedicated to his experiences at Schilling's, Ringelblum wrote relatively little about shops in general and almost nothing about Hallman's where he was registered, let alone his own personal difficulties there. It is the little that he wrote about shops and their workers that implied hardships including his own.

Notably, during the great deportation, Ringelblum almost entirely stopped recording events and the few entries, written between July and September 1942, consisted of several outlined notes consisting of short sentences or points for future discussion. One can find phrases such as 'Tens of thousands joined the shops', or 'evacuation and displacement', 'apartments facing the street', all indicating an extremely stressful situation that did not permit immersion in writing, not only because events were alarming but also because they were rapid and surprising.[114] His phrases were more than revealing, full of hints, gaps and most of all silence, an incapacity to put into words what was witnessed. In this sense, Ringelblum's discourse goes against literature as it abandoned the tally in favor of reserve and suppression, thus opening the way to imagination.[115]

As a *Self-Help* worker, Ringelblum was better informed about what was going on in all three isolated parts of the ghetto.[116] Given the circumstances, when he resumed writing, his attempt to refer to the ensemble of historical phenomena in the ghetto resulted in most of his entries after September 1942, to focus on subject matters: The Umschlagplatz – What It Looked Like, Resistance, How Selection Took Place?, etc., titles given to his accounts. Nonetheless, coherence in these later essays mostly comprised of restricted impersonal language demanding readers to make special efforts to fill in missing information and decipher implications.

In contrast, out of Ben-Shem's seven hundred pages of deciphered diary, over three hundred were dedicated to shops, a period of six and a half months. As noted, Ben-Shem's manuscript suggested that most of his account was written in hiding, with this period in the shops overshadowing the hardships of the previous two and half years in the ghetto. Indeed, life at Schilling's and for that matter, all shops, was so incredibly strenuous, it is understandable Ben-Shem could not have written then.[117] In that respect, what Ben-Shem revealed about the course of events in the shops explains why despite Ringelblum's initial historic aspirations, it was an almost impossible task to document at that time, and so what he managed to record should be regarded with awe.

In other words, distorted existence, especially during deportations, contained many surprises and unexpectedly speedy developments that left little time for reflection and/or recording. This also affected language as its powers of depiction were impaired in light of unfamiliar phenomena to which one was exposed.[118] Although Ben-Shem expressed a number of times that he was stupefied and remained speechless, his reports were detailed yet reflected his difficulty to find the right terms, and also the struggle to explain the harsh reality of shops. That being said, the experiences at Schilling's, and all shops, not only shed light on a strenuous existence of all Jews in shops but also explains why almost half of his diary is dedicated to this relatively short period.

It is noteworthy that although the diary writers managed to temporarily secure their families' lives by hiding them at the shops where they worked, soon, they became targets for roundups and deportations. Whereas Ringelblum's position as a *Self-Help* worker and an employee at Hallman's secured his temporary immunity, his family was not exempt. As for Ben-Shem, during the first months of deportations, and although he worked at Schilling's, he had no official permit. That is, every raid at the shop put not only Pnina and Josima at risk, but having no papers, Ben-Shem was in danger too. Finally, he received his yearned for official S.S. stamp on September 18, 1942, a few days before the first wave of deportations ended.[119]

Ringelblum and Ben-Shem's entries about the perplexing nature of time and space demonstrated the perverse cosmos created in shops. Not only did the character of events and their speed impose constant attention demanding reaction, but it put conceptual perceptions at stake, as events constantly transgressed understanding and the very belief that shops could protect from annihilation.[120] Thus, new epistemic values emerged, that immediate and real threats of torture and death, inhumane life conditions were less important than shops' capacity to save Jews from being sent to the Umschlagplatz. The exertion needed to survive the shops marked a significant thematic shift in diaries. Echoing what people were forced to endure at the Umschlagplatz and trains heading for Treblinka, shop compounds seemed palpably safer and lifesaving while creating a new scale of contrast of what constituted human endurance.

Redefining Human Concepts

During June and July 1942, the belief that shop workers might be saved, a notion encouraged and spread by the Germans themselves, created a ferocious race to become shop workers. Abraham Lewin referred to the phenomenon as 'Shopomania,'[121] conveying the feverish atmosphere in the

The Public Sphere · 203

ghetto created by people desperately trying to be accepted at a shop. Ringelblum addressed growing restlessness in the ghetto and reported pandemonium in Warsaw, specifying what one needed to do to be awarded the position of vital employee. Not only did people wanting to work have to bring their own tools (including sewing machines) but in the spring of 1942, they also had to pay 500 zlotys.[122]

The issue of work tools was not a new requirement, according to Perez Opochinsky, who documented the development of shops in the ghetto from the winter of 1941. He wrote, for instance, that in May 1941, a shop specializing in sewing underwear was established and only employed those who brought their sewing machines. At first, Jews did not understand the purpose of this requirement, but when some wanted to quit working at a shop, it became clear that although they were allowed to leave, they were unable to retrieve their sewing machines.[123] However, in the reality of June 1942, urgency to work forced people to agree to anything if only to be saved, which obviously made possessing relevant tools a treasure.[124]

Ben-Shem wrote that in June 1942, Jan Többens, one of the owners of a shop on Leszno Street, held a small party for his employees. On raising a toast, he said, '...I hereby formally announce that... you will remain the last...'[125] Ben-Shem reported that this announcement was received by a mixture of applause and dismay as he and others,

> ...understood the tone of the speechmaker who was not laughing or kidding at all, nor was he even astonished. He simply stated what he was authorized to say, that is, because of their good and efficient work, the Jews working at his shop would get a prize... the extension of their lives for a while... but in the end everyone would be shot.[126]

According to Ben-Shem, whereas some in the audience cheered when they heard Többens's statement, others understood the nuances, including a blunt and open declaration about the future awaiting Jews. Ben-Shem said that their shock was not only because Többens seemed to have accepted this as a natural development but the information seemed to confirm their worst fears while remaining an inconceivable possibility. It was this disbelief that led people to turn to the Jewish Council to inquire about the veracity of these rumors. The *Kehilla* officials replied that the Germans told them to '...mind their own business and refrain from thinking about what Germans intend to do...'.[127] *Kehilla* officials scolded callers and claimed that such reports frightened them and Ben-Shem noted angrily that they were

204   *Emanuel Ringelblum and Reuven Ben-Shem's War Writings*

totally wrong and naïve because they had failed to perceive the irony of what the Germans were saying.[128]

Ben-Shem sarcastically wrote that shops were a safe haven, using the term 'paradise',[129] while explaining that they '... would grant us life for a certain time.'[130] His frustration was expressed by his claim that shops were a divine creation, as if '... an opening appeared, an eye of a needle, He gave, and through it, Jews would thread their elephantine survival hopes.'[131] Ben-Shem's metaphors voiced the fragmentation of space of conceptualization. It correlated directly with the actual shrinking size of space allocated to Jews, while alluding to time as interdependent. That is, for Jews space depended on time and was parallel to life existing only in the shops. This 'paradise'[132] was, in fact, the size of 'an eye of a needle'[133] versus the volume of Jews' hopes which were as large as an 'elephant'.[134]

His chosen vocabulary suggests the impossible options Jews faced. These challenged their understanding and capabilities to make conscious choices, as every decision had impossible consequences. Chances of survival by becoming shop workers were scarce, as Ben-Shem's words exemplified, paradise and divine creation, they were not. He asked '...Is there a way out of this hell?'[135] and the answer was obvious to him because, in that circumstance, choosing a hellish existence in shops at least offered some hope. These contradictory characteristics of shops were referred to in Kabalistic terms as Ben-Shem spoke about an 'opening'[136], a rescue route provided by the divine. Still, he immediately suggested that this opening was an inner force, hope, equal to belief, which instilled in Jews the vitality needed to keep fighting for survival and endure that obstacle too.

The narratives shifting from one end, paradise – or heaven to hell – vividly demonstrate relativity and loss of orientation. Shops were hell just as they were 'heaven' as they allegedly secured life, but in hellish conditions and prospects for the future. This incongruity was also employed by Nazis in their euphemisms, as Friedländer explained about Treblinka, where the path leading to the gas chambers was called Himmelstrasse, the road to heaven, a passage ornamented with thick branches, separating it from its surroundings.[137] Simone Gigliotti corroborated such contradictions, quoting Isabella Leitner's memories of her approach to the Kisvarda Ghetto in Hungary. A day before deportations from that ghetto were due, she wrote, 'The ghetto suddenly seems beautiful. I want to celebrate my birthdays for all the days to come in this heaven.'[138]

On the first day of deportations, Ben-Shem illustrated what Lewin called 'Shopomania'. When large numbers of police ransacked the ghetto, he was desperately trying to obtain documents that might save his family. On July 21, 1942, Ben-Shem wrote that together with JDC officials, Daniel Guzik, Yitzhak Gitterman and General Zionist activist, Menachem Kirszenbaum, they went to Többens's shop managers to obtain more permits. When Ben-Shem left Többens empty-handed, he described how time became a burden because every moment counted.[139] Rushing through the chaos in ghetto streets, he wrote, 'I mustn't wait…'[140] as he was being hunted by the Jewish police who demanded he go with them to the Umschlagplatz. '…Sweat covered my body and wet my shirt. At that moment, I saw myself lost and my family buried.'[141] Even though Ben-Shem talked his way out of this, his account reflected a shift in time and space caused by the alarming situation. While in his mind, Ben-Shem felt time had stopped as he saw himself dead, it started racing again when he was released and had to hurry to avoid being captured once more.[142] If the arrest made Ben-Shem, in his mind, cross from the world of the living to that of the dead, his release seemed to have thrown him into the turmoil in the streets created by the round-ups, while desperately trying to reach a space where there was still time – allegedly that in shops.

Jewish Compounds – Work Area and Housing

Despite the differences between the diaries, both expressed the constant sense of confusion directly linked to unsafe premises and the pace of adjustment imposed on shop workers. The assertion that despite overwhelming circumstances in shops, there was life, became a notion frequently contrasted with the fate of those who had been murdered or were held in inhumane conditions at the Umschlagplatz. The relationship between the inside and outside consisted of a series of contradictory spaces. On the one hand, shops were imagined as a safe haven, and on the other, the realities of existence in shops, constantly refuted this idea and thus posed an unbearable emotional and conceptual burden on shop workers. In this respect, diary writers not only had to adapt, but also invent new concepts to process the situation.

Life in a constantly raided space had a significant impact not only on those who were captured but also those who were not, as these experiences left them frantic, either devastated because their own flesh and blood were among those captured, or because they had witnessed these scenes.[143] In December 1942 and in what seemed to be notes for future elaboration, Ringelblum concisely wrote 'The tragedies of the families: thousands of men without women, there are men who do not know what the point is to

206 *Emanuel Ringelblum and Reuven Ben-Shem's War Writings*

go on living. ... the disaster of women who had numbers. They counted the numbers and lined up. Those without numbers were saved.'[144] His short sentences, which provided no evident imagery and relied on common knowledge known only to those who were there insinuated the consequences, that is, after the raid, what was left were people who carried on through inertia alone.[145]

The 'what happened' was not reveled in Ringelblum's text, but was reported in Ben-Shem's diary:

> They open the gate and they move the workers' wives before us. Each holding her child in her hands or arms... a whole row of women and children are led to their slaughter before their husbands' eyes... Each one moves and is looking for her husband as if she wishes to part with him for the last time. And the husbands who watched their wives and children moving before their eyes, wanted to jump out of their rows: 'Havale, Etale, Sarale, Roshika, Rivke'! 'Chaim, Moshe, Herman, Yakov!' were the calls heard from the men to their wives and from the women to their husbands. Policemen forced the men to stay back so as they could not jump towards their loved ones. A whole line passed and endless calls: 'Hava, Breyne' 'Moshe, Bernard'... A whole procession of women and children led ... (in the original) to slaughter before their husbands eyes.
>
> This is probably what a meeting in Hades looks like, a depiction of a meeting of souls in hell. - 'Zamek!' Nadel's wife cried and sent him a farewell look, as if it was a complaint, dismissal, disappointment. So many personal feelings and scandals were hidden in that stare that I shivered at that peek.[146]

Even though Ben-Shem used language of imagery to describe the procession of women and children who had been arrested and led to the Umschlagplatz, the addition of voices, together with his language and syntax, projected his point of view into the text, that of extreme agitation. Ben-Shem, whose wife and daughter were not among those caught, recounted a situation beyond imagination, for those whose families were captured, as well as for he who witnessed this and wrote about it. Irreconcilable visions dominated his speech, repeating 'A whole procession of women and children...',[147] the names called out loud and the desperate looks between wives and husbands and vice versa. Shops were compared to hell, mentioned twice, once using Hades' name and then explicitly.

Ben-Shem's text called upon cultural imagery from Greek mythology, the story of Eurydice and Orpheus. His narrative arrangement recalled the disappearance of Eurydice through the scene of wives of whom there was only a glimpse before their departure from one hell – the shops, into another – the Umschlagplatz. The short encounter of looks and gazes evoked Orpheus' forbidden gaze at Eurydice. His music was represented by the cries of wives and husbands about to lose one another forever, and their looks were as Orpheus' forbidden look as they were forced to move on.[148]

It was not only shops that were raided, but dwellings too. As previously mentioned, shop workers were forced to move to residential blocks allocated to shops. People had to leave their homes and abandon most of their possessions, settle in other people's apartments, many of which belonged to those who had already been deported. Almost all these apartments were in terrible shape, crowded, dilapidated, unsanitary, and without any privacy.[149] Sometimes, apartments were empty, but many were not.

Indeed, Ringelblum discussed how the Germans did not take into consideration any factors that may have hindered their purpose. They took no notice if allotted apartments had residents still living in them, who were ordered to move out brusquely and cruelly. Ringelblum recounted cases when 'They gave half a day to move out...'[150] mentioning the fact that unlike other shop owners, Hallman, where he worked, treated residents humanely: instead of throwing them out, he talked to house committees and arranged gradual relocation from these apartments.

Of an encounter with what might be his own future, Ben-Shem wrote on August 18, 1942, that he was charged with preparing an apartment given to Schilling's shop. It was hard work consisting of clearing rubble and readapting the space for a family. He explained that two weeks before, these apartments had been raided violently and their residents deported to Treblinka: '...for the first time in my life I entered apartments whose owners had been kidnapped or killed ... in each flat a different lifestyle ...each object still warm... In many apartments, we found tables set, cooked food in the kitchen...'[151]

In the days that followed, a closer encounter occurred as Ben-Shem and his neighbor were preparing a flat they had been allocated. He wrote that he had stayed in the apartment all night, becoming intimate with its previous owners by going through belongings left behind. '...I read his papers, certificates, his diary, and the man became close to me... and he too was kidnapped and did not have the chance to fulfil his dream... Pasensztajn (the neighbor) and I ... are destroying the order the man had put in his flat ...'[152]

Shop workers were not only directly threatened in dwellings in which they were supposed to live as well as in shop compounds themselves, but had further encounters with death because they were forced into the space of others, whose destiny had been murder. Ben-Shem expressed this when he wrote, 'Now Pasensztajn and I will inherit from him. Who knows for how long...'[153] Ben-Shem lines about 'destroying the order...'[154] mirrored how disturbed he was by making his own arrangements in the dwelling, as if he too had committed a crime. Not only was he intruding into someone else's space, violating his belongings by touching them, throwing out unnecessary possessions, but in so doing was erasing the little that was left of that person's existence.

How Ringelblum described shops provided a macro of various phenomena they encompassed. He noted that although being a shop worker was conceived by the vast majority of Jews as a refuge, in as much as they were a 'life certificate', they were also a trap. The complexity of this existence was contrasted to the status of the 'wild', who were forced to invade empty houses and maintain a clandestine existence.[155] This discrepancy between the two modes of subsistence might be regarded as clear evidence of how desperate people had become and why prices to be accepted into a shop soared, about 2,000 zlotys.[156] However, as Ringelblum wrote, 'If the shop ceases to exist, they will lose the right to live.'[157] When he wrote 'they', it obviously included himself.

With the chaotic existence in shops and in an attempt to protect women and children, many workers avoided going back to their dwellings in the evening and started sleeping in factories thinking this would better protect them from unexpected raids.[158] Nonetheless, as time passed, it became harder to provide the daily quota of Jews for deportations.[159] Therefore, shop raids became more and more frequent and involved the cooperation of shop owners. In this regard, Ringelblum specifically mentioned Hoffman and Brauer, who contributed their share to the manhunt.[160] To fulfil the daily quota, not only were women and children, who were mostly 'wild' in danger, but shop workers themselves became a target and little notice was paid as to whether workers had proper documentation or not.[161]

On August 24, 1942, while working at a shop, Ben-Shem wrote that shots had been heard but contrary to their initial instincts to run away, one of the shop foremen ordered them to keep working as there were Ukrainians watching them from the roofs. Ben-Shem talked about '... the air literally trembling'[162] describing how, frozen with fear, they had to retain a semblance of working while watching out of the corner of their eyes. Accidentally, Ben-Shem pounded a nail into his finger, but he dared not

The notes of public and private spheres were fundamentally modified

stop working for fear of being noticed. Then the 'murderers'[163] conducted a selection. The Ukrainians '...smiled at us a hunter's smile...'[164] making a slight movement with their fingers and they ran into the houses to search for those who were hiding. Meanwhile, Josima and Pnina were hiding with many other women and children under a huge saw inside the shop. The selection lasted three hours, with all workers standing out in the sun and watching.[165] Ben-Shem described how people who looked older tried to look robust to avoid deportation. Ben-Shem concluded by saying that although a hundred people were taken to the Umschlagplatz, 'Today, there is hardly any wailing in the shop... They took the old and husbands whose wives and children had already been taken on Black Friday. Now, there was no one left to cry or mourn the kidnapped.'[166]

*****

The notions of public and private spheres were fundamentally modified even before the wall separated Jews from the city, as relationships were characterized by repeated disruption of boundaries. To expose this mélange, the third part of the book was divided into the three following categories: Between the Private and Public Spheres, the Private Sphere and the Public Sphere. The sections dealing with what the diarists said about their records and the part dealing with the armbands were classified as Between the Private and Public Spheres.

Writing, predominantly a secluded activity and mostly conducted in private, was nevertheless the product of being involved in the public arena. Ringelblum and Ben-Shem's writing ventures were intended to record actual occurrences rather than anything else, and therefore, the action of writing and its purpose depended on prior social interaction. In the case of Ringelblum, it was even more typical as from the beginning, his diary was meant to become a source of information for researchers. As for Ben-Shem, his was also meant for other eyes and was written with the idea it would one day expose his family's whereabouts to others. Although writing was a private activity, because it dealt with documentation of the course of life in the ghetto, it constantly shifted from the inside to the outside – it required observation and recording.

Regarding armbands, once the decree was issued, Jews became instantly estranged, as they stood out in the public arena, signifying they were entities whose boundaries could be traversed.[167] In this way, Jews wearing an armband were subject to abuse personally but it was because they were identified as part of a shunned group. In other words, external identification isolated individuals and made them exposed publicly to harassment because they represented a discriminated against group. Their ordeal in such encounters was public, but attacks were personal.

At first, many believed the introduction of ghetto walls would reinstate some personal safety, but it soon became clear that even in isolation, this new Jewish compound was open to breaching and crossing more borders as there were no limits observed for Jews, not when it concerned their bodies, private or public spaces.[168] Thus, the private and public spheres, up to one's flesh, quickly lost their initial boundaries allowing the introduction of chaos.

Ben-Shem and Ringelblum exposed how squeezing large numbers of Jews into so called dwellings predetermined their end through hunger and disease. Conversely, the subsiding domestic domain became a mirror to abjection in both the public and private spheres. That is, as the private realm offered little refuge, the streets of the ghetto were flooded with the distressed, who while exposing their broken spirits and bodies, sought help. Thus, none of the spheres offered protection from exposure to intimate-personal phenomena, which disrupted people's own sense of ego, concepts of spatial recognition and consequently, prevented adjustment.

The diarists echoed the sensation of the ghetto becoming nowhere, no place, while also voicing their disbelief and loss of words in view of the realities unfolding before their eyes. Ringelblum avoided almost exclusively discussion of occurrences inside dwellings, not as a phenomenon or by introducing individual cases. From Ringelblum's diary, one could infer about personal struggles from reports concerning the public arena, where the drama was visible to all.[169]

Apparently, Ben-Shem, probably due to the period his diary was edited, was less cautious about introducing personal portraits. Most prominently, he wrote once about the Lustmans whose hardship was discovered by his wife, and quite a lot about his friend Avraham Lipman and the pitiful situation to which he and his family were reduced. In both cases, the acute and dire shape of their households was visible, accentuating the link between lacking sustainability means as a factor leading to the obliteration of physical and moral boundaries and the destruction of the fragile fabric of family relationships.[170] The visceral characteristics in descriptions, dirt, smells, and sights, exposed the degree of violation of what was human and the nature of penetration into people's personal-social spaces, affecting the material, emotional and sensory.[171] Apart from these cases, few of Ben-Shem's friends or acquaintances were mentioned by their real names. Notable are his references to Auerbach, who was his subtenant but whose name was never mentioned – instead, he wrote 'my relative', revealing no other personal details about her.

Ghetto apartments and "points" were directly affected by what took place on the outside. Inside, there was little peace, not only because apartments were crowded, but also as there was constant outside activity almost twenty-four hours a day. In their dwellings, people had to pull themselves together to tolerate the outside chaos penetrating their private spaces. The invasive sounds coming from crying children were particularly distressing as they aroused emotions and remorse mingled with a sense of guilt about not doing enough to help.[172]

With rapidly declining resources, the dreadful lack of materials created impossible circumstances on a personal level. Although conceptual alterations in the private sphere were reflected in Ringelblum and Ben-Shem's diaries in different ways, it seems that both authors' writings functioned increasingly as a means to reinstate the old conceptual world when phenomena that were supposed to be public or private were just that, separate.

Time and space in Warsaw Ghetto shops functioned almost as air bubbles, a cosmos in a space undergoing a process of liquidation. Slave-laborers experienced life as constant torture, particularly during deportation waves, as survival in shops was anchored to a certain place, shop compounds, which were time-limited.[173] Prominently, during that period, experiences altered sensory capabilities consequently distorting notions of orientation and time to which shops were particularly linked. Belonging to a shop came at a price, as the status of laborers robbed people of the little control they previously had over their lives, becoming totally dependent on shops for work, dwellings and existence.

Squeezing people into the pressure cooker of shops allowed the Nazis to bend time and space in opposing directions, which produced new values, including conflating and confusing what was generally perceived as public or private. This distorted both victims' perceptions of reality and the very idea of what a human being was, consequently affecting their human nature.[174] The relationship between people's reactions to space disintegration and Nazis' manipulation of rationality, played a decisive role in disaggregating knowledge and understanding of the world, to thinking that death sentences might be negotiable.[175]

With little choice, and unable to predict or understand Nazi logic, Jews followed while many of them persisted in holding onto rationality in a world cynically taking advantage of this.[176] Yet, clinging to rationality was simultaneously a vital survival strategy, allowing people to assume they were still human and had some control. Thus, although shops and their living compounds primarily signified a deviation from familiar norms, Jews wanted to conceive these spaces as justifying their purpose. By creating such recognizable grounds, Jews were led to believe in the logic of their twisted subsistence.

However, whenever the trap-like qualities of this allegedly normal routine became apparent, basic notions of existence were challenged. Endless terror eliminated boundaries between life and death, dwellings and shop compounds, and the total disregard for family ties. Thus, a unique universe emerged where everything was familiar yet alien. In this sense, it could be claimed that Nazi success was based on parodying basic human certainties and perceptions.[177]

There is a correlation between the historical event of enclosing Jews into ever smaller spaces using rapid, recurrent, pitiless, and astounding attacks, and how diary entries represented these. Ringelblum's brief notes provided verbal snapshots of sights or movement versus Ben-Shem's detailed accounts written in hiding, but both indicated that one important aspect of life in Jewish spaces was silenced almost completely – writing.

It appears that Ringelblum went out of his way to continue recording the course of life in the crumbling ghetto and shops, but phenomena encountered made it almost impossible to cope. Ben-Shem's notes and the large volume he dedicated to shops confirm, on the one hand, the difficulties to cope when one was there, and on the other, the everlasting imprint of this incredulous time. Obviously, the contents of his reports speak for themselves, it was impossible to record and document anything in those circumstances. Their different writing styles voiced the utter shock that gripped everyone and prevented people from reacting or properly reflecting in these circumstances. Even during more stable periods in shops, the course of life remained strenuous and left little scope for writing. The murder of 300,000 Jews from Warsaw, the shop experience and the second deportation on January 18, 1943, left people disillusioned and searching for ways out. Indeed, both families escaped the ghetto in February 1943, each to a different hiding location.

Conclusions

The quest to find a 'usable past' or form insightful lessons in what is referred to as *Historia magistra vitae (est)* became a deeply rooted traditional Jewish response affecting both Emanuel Ringelblum and Reuven Ben-Shem. Close examination of their diaries suggests their writings during the war acted as a Jewish space: for Ringelblum, raw material for future research; for Ben-Shem, a personal historical record. Using diary scrutiny, narrative analysis, close reading techniques, and relying mainly on Lefebvre's *The Production of Space,* showed that language functioned as a spatial vehicle to introduce order into chaos and enabled understanding of relationships between what was described.

Lefebvre's model, which rests on three interdependent factors, consists of first, spatial practices concerning physical activities taking place inside and outside. In Warsaw, this meant isolating Jews and cutting off any dialectical relationships with their surroundings, leaving them dependent on German occupation, which allocated almost nothing to Jewish existence. The second, representation of space consisted of an abstract demonstration of the physical. It was made up of restrictions, including decisions about shape, structure and accessibility. Residents were denied vital survival materials, not only food and other essential commodities, but also restricted movement. The third, lived spaces related to people's sensual experiences and feelings, including writing and art.[1] The lived space of Jews in the ghetto was menacing in every respect, a no man's land where anyone could act out their whims on Jews. This methodology, namely, the combination of literary investigation techniques with Lefebvre's theory, allowed me to address the question of gaps in comprehension including verify patterns and ways of drawing conclusions from events.

The writings were scanned for evidence that the diarists had understood Nazi manipulation of space as paradigmatic historical and political steps leading to annihilation. In this sense, documentation or writing historical observations and diaries was their response to declining physical space designed to create a historical and political counter-paradigm or claim back lost space, an action steeped in traditional Jewish reactions.

However, initially, Jews did not conceive of space manipulation as a life-threatening political and historical paradigm. The two diaries showed that it took Jews some time to understand the connection between the Nazi historical and political paradigm of space shrinking and the final goal of organized murder. In fact, although life conducted in the ghetto was often considered deadly, this was attributed to deliberately meager conditions provided for Jewish survival. In other words, death was conceived as a result of conditions and not mere incarceration in confined spaces.

The diaries also revealed that challenges of space manipulation were not addressed as such, and Jewish responses did not derive from spatial changes but related first to acute shortages in materials and later, extermination. An absence of precedents to Nazi actions impacted Jews' conception of the Final Solution. Lending importance to the relationship between space quality and its effect on Jews led to the creation of a correlation between living conditions in the ghetto and the growth of written documentation including the *Oneg Shabbat* archive.

Equally interesting was the question of whether and how the two writers conceptualized historical events taking place. That is, if documentation reclaimed denied Jewish spaces, did writing create a space through what was intended to be erased? When space diminished, when deportations began, perspectives changed because despite extreme shortages of food and other supplies to ghetto inmates, these felt secondary as downsizing living spaces implied that life itself was negated. Simultaneously, with space reduction, writing was affected conceptually and effectively. As previously mentioned, incredible events in the ghetto forwent privacy and at the same time, pressured people to the end of their tether. In such conditions, it was not only almost impossible to write, but to most people, it seemed superfluous vis-a-vis surrounding atrocities and urgency to find ways of surviving despite the realization that writing had to continue as it replaced actual spaces.

The more time passed, the more evident the end – extermination – became. Still, despite information streaming into the ghetto from the outside, and although both writers appear to have grasped the idea of annihilation logically, emotionally, and mentally, it remained incomprehensible. This is reflected in the way in which both addressed the topics for discussion and what they said about their reasons for documentation. Most interesting is how their understanding of events and hidden motives are reflected in their interpretations of historical events to which they referred. Their bewilderment is especially prominent in passages where they expressed self-reproach for their own misunderstanding.

The first part of the book addressed interconnected ideas, the relationship between history and politics, a spiritual or even cognitive space of action where historical research was regarded as raw material for political activism. Many Jews viewed this bond as holding the key, on the one hand, to explaining their current situation and, on the other hand, to finding possible solutions to mend wrongs. This approach had a significant impact on both writers. While Ringelblum's diary was historic, Ben-Shem's was personal. Yet each document uniquely echoed the complex association between the individual and communal through history's invasion into one's intimate existence.

The second part of the book discussed the effect of Dubnow's approach to historical research on all Jews under Nazi occupation and how Ringelblum and Ben-Shem were not alone but a part of a much larger trend of Jews who assumed personal responsibility for documenting occurrences during the war. This part of the book focuses on how Jews developed this notion of personally undertaking accountability for their history. Regarding Ringelblum and Ben-Shem, this was especially important because although both men were bibliophiles, neither had kept diaries before the war. Still, both felt compelled to do so when the war started. Although writing seemed to function as a predictable response given their professional careers and background, the uniqueness was embracing the idea of writing diaries rather than other forms of documentation.[2]

The third part of the book addressed the private and public realms and their representation in the diaries as expressions of the link between historical and political activism on the one hand and, on the other, how writing claimed back spaces denied to Jews. Conceptual gaps victims experienced, along with frequent changes in thinking patterns as exhibited by the Germans, made it challenging for Jews to comprehend events around them [3].While Jews struggled to adhere to a traditional conceptual framework, the Nazis disrupted every familiar notion. In this sense, the Jewish traditional response of documentation became a goal almost in its own right as it reinstated order into deliberately disordered spaces. Paradoxically, by putting events onto paper, the act of writing deciphered madness making it a comprehensible, although still an inconceivable development.

However, it seems that writing, a highly valued notion, became distinctly dependent on space shrinkage. When space was reduced beyond the point of Jews being denied their humanity as a paradigmatic approach, that is, when officially no significance was lent to the notion of family, when individuals were solely "meat" for deportations or slave labor, when their flesh and blood ceased to count, most individuals were unable to resume life. In this respect, it was not only the physical annihilation of so many, but to those who remained alive, the torture, loss, and helplessness killed them while still breathing. In other words, the creation of the ghetto universe, followed by the process of shrinking it, led to reducing spaces to the boundaries of one's body thus killing people before they were physically dead.

As both writers' most preferred prism was photography, recording life in the ghetto as if it had been filmed and photographed, texts were analyzed accordingly. This proved challenging when it concerned the private sphere since the notion of visibility was not consistently used. Beginning with an examination of what the writers said about their diaries, it appears that what was important was to represent occurrences in the ghetto in the most loyal fashion. Nonetheless, whereas Ringelblum elaborated on his methodology emphasizing the means employed to achieve authenticity through words functioning as a camera, Ben-Shem expressed his aspiration to represent the ghetto faithfully but provided no methodology. Since the diary was initially written to tell his family what he had undergone, Ben-Shem appeared to rely on his reputation as proof of his texts' veracity. Interestingly, Ben-Shem's references to his political affiliation are almost entirely missing from his deciphered text, as if there was no such activity at all. It is possible the reason was that the majority of his writings were done in hiding, when the notion of large-scale organized murder was a reality, making all previous political rivalries insignificant.

The private sphere was not revealed in Ringelblum's diary, whereas Ben-Shem occasionally provided details about certain domestic households, some discussing specific people, although these details concerned particular incidents. The fact people's privacy was observed by not writing about them directly made it difficult to understand the nature of the living spaces from the text itself. In this way, the relatively few incidents provided by Ben-Shem became a reference, a means to ask questions about people's private lives, details at which Ringelblum hinted but did not describe. When Ringelblum wrote about the fact that entire families perished and sometimes it was only the smell that led people to discover a last family member who had died, he avoided not only identifying details but also any reference to dramas that had taken place in that household. Therefore, Ben-Shem's accounts of the Lustmans, for example, provided a point of reference, a scale by which to imagine what domestic spaces were like, physically, emotionally and psychologically.

Questions we may ask about other people could also be relevant to both men's households. Indeed, Ringelblum excluded his private life and

Conclusions 217

difficulties from his diary, whereas Ben-Shem discussed his family a number of times, also referring to his self-image that had been affected by his inability to provide for his family. In this sense, Ben-Shem's diary allowed a glimpse into private households making it possible to conclude about experiences on individual and familial space levels. It appears that neither regarded the private sphere as history, which was another reason such information was totally absent from Ringelblum's historical diary while present in a limited manner in Ben-Shem's. This may also explain why neither of them attempted to check how much the private realm was affected by the public realm and whether one reflected the other.

Lefebvre claimed that in the relationship between the outside and inside, it was the outside that influenced how the inside was organized because the outside embodied the rules governing space. He suggested that psychoanalyzing space would reveal what he referred to as 'bourgeois space', that is, separation to the point of repression between the intimate and extrinsic. Examination of the Warsaw Ghetto hints at a strong influence of the outside on the inside, yet, what was created was the reverse of 'bourgeois space' as the ghetto was by definition, an obstructive place designated for Jews and consisting of disciplinary restrictions aiming at ruining Jewish spaces. In this way, it appears that ghettoes, including the Warsaw ghetto, were geared to exhibit how degenerate Jewish existence was.

In writing about public spaces in photographic terms, a close reading of texts revealed a paradox. As well as presenting a surgical image of the ghetto, the writers managed to avoid the personal and replace it with a typological representation of an array of phenomena, starting with different forms of begging. Hence, the privacy of the individuals described was preserved as rather than referring to them personally, they became representatives of a phenomenon. In addition, the act of photography enabled viewers to remain emotionally distant. This was not always successful as some cases were too touching and tragic, as exemplified by the case of beggar-children Ringelblum and Ben-Shem mentioned more than once.

Nonetheless, their efforts also projected Nazi efforts to do the reverse, that is, their photographic documentation of the war was meant to represent Jews in the worst possible light. This included staging scenes as if Germans protected Jews, or the later attempts to produce a documentary about the ghetto, a film that was anything but documentary, because it included an assortment of staged footage to portray Jews as complete degenerates.

Space disintegration was manifested most blatantly when the ghetto was torn to pieces, leaving three separate and distinct compounds whose nature had drastically changed. Alongside physical spaces, conceptual ones emerged, opposing yet similar, new in their purpose and form: the Umschlagplatz and the different shops. The former represented death, and the latter, allegedly life, although tortuous.

Lefebvre spoke about the parallel and mutual relationships between the outside and inside emphasizing the importance of separating them. Shop compounds represented the opposite, where there was no separation, particularly during the great deportation. Existence was on a razor's edge because people were literally hunted, first outside shops, and very quickly inside, too. Human relationships such as family were abolished altogether as men were regarded as a sheer commodity. Fear of death drove people, the 'wild', mainly consisting of women and children, and the 'legal' to stick together, sleep in shops, hide their existence in a desperate attempt to hold onto life. This aberrant existence in shops led to the collapse of any notion of visibility as apparency was no longer attempted, parallel to obliterating any humane traits of Jews.

Pressure on Jews who remained in shops was reflected in both diaries. First, despite clear understanding that annihilation in especially erected sites was taking place, both writers expressed gaps in their perceptions as these developments seemed inconceivable, and therefore, unpredictable because nothing in history could have prepared them for it. Furthermore, if either diarist assumed he was writing notes for future use, it dawned on them that these may be futile as not only would they not survive, but all Jews would die. This realization gave these diaries another dimension. If they were previously conceived of as claiming a Jewish space, the notion that no one would remain alive robbed them of their initial purpose as a historical record, let alone as documents serving as a source for future political improvement. It became meaningless when no prospects of the future were expected. In this way, written records rather than representing life in the ghetto, became testimonies to total annihilation.

What this book shows is the relationship between visibility and spatiality as introduced by the Nazis and Jews as well. The concept of Lebensraum consisted of defining what should appear in space and what should be banished. Just as it had been important to make Jews visible by forcing them to wear armbands, for example, it was this same visibility that became intolerable and led to their liquidation. This did not happen before their visibility had been exposed most degradingly, exploiting them in every sense, starting with satisfying Nazi fantasies about Jewish pervasiveness to making them subsist in inhumane conditions, turning them into slaves, and finally murdering them. This series of mirror effects created in Jewish zones helped Nazis to internalize the foreignness of Jews, as boundaries between the inside and outside were abolished in different ways.

Lefebvre also theorized the body as a space. Allusions in the diaries, particularly Ringelblum's, revealed that before the establishment of a closed ghetto, Jewish bodies were treated as if they were spaces. Armbands isolated personality, reducing it into one collective identity vis-à-vis others and making Jews living targets for all and whose physical boundaries could be breached at will. Armbands immediately set Jews and Poles apart, creating a clear division and at the same time, nullifying the human characteristics of those wearing them. Even though this symbol of being Jewish was a constant irritant, the fact it was mentioned much less once the ghetto was established, hinted at the decline in its invasive qualities because regardless of armbands, the ghetto was no man's land but it offered some protection.

Ringelblum and Ben-Shem relied on visibility, but their documentation testified they were not lured into this trap of appearances. They showed how squeezing humans into a cage-like existence while depriving them of vital resources did not reflect on Jews in particular but on any human beings in the same circumstances. Whatever mirror reflection the Nazis tried to introduce, their texts exposed the distorted and perverted aspects of such attempts. If the Nazis abolished boundaries by relating to phenomena in the ghetto typologically, Ringelblum's narratives as well as most of Ben-Shem's were able to reestablish dignity. The surgical gaze they adopted was able, on the one hand, to preserve individuals' anonymity while on the other hand expose what people had been reduced to. The same effect was achieved when they refrained from discussing private households and yet recorded how they suffered in the ghetto. Adhering to what was visible in their texts was able to mirror the private, also because many strove to be seen and noticed; being visible turned out to be a means of survival.

The diarists examined clearly manifested tensions between the urge to record and avoid violating and humiliating those they were recording. Close scrutiny of the relationships introduced between space and visibility, in relation to aspects of the public-private, personal-communal, and intimate-extrinsic, provided unique and valuable points of view to further understand the nature of experiences during the Holocaust and their spatial significance.

Nazi policy nullified boundaries, deliberately creating chaos within Jewish spaces, which was characterized by nihilism, turning these into frenzied boundaryless containers. By denying separation or even keeping up appearances, pushing people to exasperation, the very idea of lived spaces collapsed as the humane in people crumbled. The texts, or rather their act of writing, initially originated from a favored typical Jewish reaction to hardship since the late 19th century when Dubnow first formulated this theoretical approach to documentation. For Ringelblum, embarking on this venture of recording, choosing the diary format, including its developments, was linked not only to the abundance and speed of events but also to his declared historical purposes. For Ben-Shem, it appears that the mere existence of the deciphered version of his original diary indicated the degree to which the six years of the war had haunted and marked his life before because it was seen through the prism of the war, and after, as a consequence of the war.

Irrespective of their differences, the texts revealed the tension between memory and history. Ringelblum wrote for the sake of history, but the nature of events confused history and memory, especially in his *Writings in Hiding*, when practically all Jews in Warsaw had disappeared. Ben-Shem appears to have been compelled to write because of memory, to be remembered, and after the war, for the sake of history as testimonies received more and more attention as historical records, and as a memorial.[4] In this sense, the personal and communal met as the history of individuals, at least during the Holocaust, confounded and conflated with that of community.

Ultimately, the attempt to record the whereabouts of Jews during the war through verbal photography as the ultimate means of objective representation showed that the term objectivity was understood differently by each of them. Thus, to get a better picture, combining Ringelblum's scientific approach with Ben-Shem's emotional and psychological observations, produced more precise imagery of the ghetto. Indeed, Ringelblum himself was well aware of the deficiencies one narrative could create, and in this respect, the amalgamation of both in this book, serves Ringelblum's methodology, to have many people with different approaches write about the same event so that in the end, a more faithful report emerged. Still, if photography cannot do without descriptions, Ben-Shem's narratives may be regarded as the missing captions of Ringelblum's concise and condensed narratives.

Endnotes

INTRODUCTION

1 Emmanuel Ringelblum, *Diary and Notes from the Warsaw Ghetto, September 1939 - December 1942*, Vol 1, Jerusalem: Yad-Vashem, Ghetto Fighters' House, 1999, (Hebrew), p. 212-213.

2 Reuven Feldschuh (Ben-Shem), *Testimonies, Diaries and Memoirs Collection*, Record Group 0.33, File Number 959, *Deciphered Diary*, Jerusalem: Yad-Vashem Archive, (Hebrew), pic. 30.

3 Ibid., pic. 30.

4 Ibid., pic. 30.

5 Hannah Arendt, 'Understanding and Politics, (The Difficulties of Understanding)', in *Essays in Understanding, 1930-1954, Formation, Exile, and Totalitarianism*, Jerome Kohn (editor), New York: Schocken Books, 1994, p. 307, 318.

6 Boaz Neumann, *The Nazi Weltanschauung, Space, Body, Language*, Haifa: Haifa University Publishers, 2002, (Hebrew), p. 98. Neumann discussed gaps in knowledge prisoners in Auschwitz had shown regarding grasping the notion that senseless murder could take place. Indeed, it seems that many Nazi actions reposed on that gap, not only as manifestation of their plans but also as a deliberate mode of operation including surprising their victims. In this manner, Nazis hoped to achieve a sense of superiority as well as rob their victims of the possibility to comprehend and react accordingly. Nazis implemented disorientation as a tactic against their Jewish victims, leaving the latter stupefied, thus gaining a wide enough margin to achieve control.

7 '*Yevanim*', For a Jew, (ancient) Greeks represent religious and cultural opposites. This notion developed following decrees enforced by Antiochus IV Epiphanes (king of the Seleucid Empire), which forbade Jewish religious practice and sparked the Maccabean Revolt, focusing on refusing to worship the Greek gods.

8 Reuven Feldschuh (Ben-Shem), *Deciphered Diary*, pic. 30.

9 Ibid., pic. 30.

10 Catherine Kohler Riessman, 'Narrative Analysis', in: *Narrative, Memory & Everyday Life*, Nancy Kelly, Christine Horrocks, Kate Milnes, Brian Roberts, David Robinson (editors), Huddersfield: University of Huddersfield, 2005, p.

3. Riessman explains that structural analysis emphasizes how the story is narrated, which implies that language is central in this kind of research.

11 Amos Goldberg, 'The Victim's Voice and Melodramatic Aesthetics in History', *History and Theory*, Vol. 48, No. 3, Wiley, Wesleyan University, Oct. 2009, p. 236-237.

12 Rachel Auerbach, *Warsaw Testaments: Encounters, Actions, Fate 1933–1943*, Tel Aviv: Moreshet, Mordechai Anielevich Memorial, Workers Library, 1985, (Hebrew), p. 59. Auerbach wrote that looking back, the warning signs of the fate awaiting Jews were there. She blamed herself and others for refusing to acknowledge them. The way I see it, at the time, they were unable to conceive what these signs meant as the conclusions seemed implausible.

13 Out of these pictures, 87 are shredded or erased notes and a copy of Anka Grupińska's article summing up her interview with Shoshana Kossower-Rozencwajg (Emilka).

14 Because these files end on April 4, 1943, the last date which appears in the deciphered file, I assume these notes were prepared as raw material before typing.

15 Samuel D. Kassow, *Who Will Write Our History? Emanuel Ringelblum, the Warsaw Ghetto, and the Oyneg Shabes Archive*, Bloomington: Indiana University Press, 2007, p. 148. According to Kassow, especially during the first year, Ringelblum's daily diary seemed more like a memo notebook for future research.

16 Moshe Kol, 'Dr. Reuven Ben-Shem [Feldschuh]', *Massuah, a Yearbook on the Holocaust and Heroism*, no. 9, pp. 44-45, Tel Aviv: Massuah, April 1981, (Hebrew), p. 45. Kol wrote that Ben-Shem told him he had begun writing the diary in the ghetto itself on shreds of paper, as small as a match box.

17 Emmanuel Ringelblum, *Last Writings, Polish-Jewish Relations, January 1943-April 1944*, Jerusalem: Yad-Vashem, Ghetto Fighters' House, 1994, (Hebrew), p. 304. In a letter Ringelblum wrote to Rephael Mahler, November 14, 1938, he asked Mahler to collect information from newspapers about Zbąszyń.

18 Emmanuel Ringelblum, *Diary and Notes from the Warsaw Ghetto*, p. 423. On December 5, 1942, Ringelblum wrote an essay entitled 'Why Did They Leave 10% of the Warsaw Jews?' He claimed that many believed the purpose of leaving 10% of the Jewish population in Warsaw alive was not economic but derived from political and propaganda considerations.

19 Interview with Nekamia Ben-Shem, 17.6.2017.

20 Emmanuel Ringelblum, *Last Writings, January 1943-April 1944*, p. 3-22. The *Oneg Shabbat* Archive, or the Ringelblum Archive, was an underground archive established in the Warsaw Ghetto in order to document life during the war. In *Last Writings*, Ringelblum began the essay about *Oneg Shabbat* by explaining the name: 'The origin of this strange name is that the meetings of the group were conducted on Saturday and therefore, we named it, for confidentiality reasons, *Oneg Shabbat*.' Ringelblum wrote that he had

Endnotes 223

established the first 'building blocks' for this archive in October 1939, a period that according to him, was characterized by fear of persecution for political reasons.

21 Amir Haskel, 'Dr. Reuven Feldschuh [Ben-Shem] and The Archived Diary', 18.9.2011, (Hebrew), accessed, 20.6.2020. https://meyda.education.gov.il/files/noar/yoman.pdf. Accessed 13.03.2017. Haskel is a Brigadier-General and a Holocaust researcher.

22 Joseph Kermish, 'Margined-notes to Ben-Shem's 'Note-Book', *Massuah Yearbook*, Vol 10, Kibbutz Tel Yizhak: Massuah, 1982, (Hebrew), p. 52. In this article, Kermish wrote that Ben-Shem had written most of the diary in hiding.

23 Itzchak Zuckerman ('Antek'), *Those Seven Years 1939–1946*, Hakibbutz Hameuhad and Bet Lohamei Haghetaot (Ghetto Fighters' House), 2010, p. 253. Zuckerman wrote that during the Uprising, he was positioned at Ben-Shem's empty apartment, where he found his hidden archive that contained various documents including letters from Jabotinsky. According to Zuckerman, these documents were most interesting to read. Indeed, Ben-Shem alluded to his and his cousin Rachel Auerbach burial of documents as soon as deportations from Warsaw began [see: Reuven Feldschuh (Ben-Shem), pic. 324]. However, it is unclear what exactly had been hidden or what he chose to take with him when he left the ghetto in February 1943 (see: Reuven Feldschuh (Ben-Shem), pic. 636).

24 Reuven Feldschuh (Ben-Shem), *Testimonies, Diaries and Memoirs Collection*, Record Group 0.33, File Number 959, *Manuscript* 1, Jerusalem: Yad-Vashem Archive (Hebrew), pic 2.

25 Gabriela Spector-Mersel, 'Mechanisms of Selection in Claiming Narrative Identities: A Model for Interpreting Narratives', *Qualitative Inquiry*, 17(2), Sage, 2011, DOI: 10.1177/1077800410393885, p. 172-174.

26 Catherine Kohler Riessman, *Narrative Methods for the Human Sciences*, USA: Sage, 2008, p. 107.

27 Ibid., p. 59.
See also: Gareth Williams, 'The genesis of chronic illness: narrative reconstruction', *Sociology of Health and Illness*, Vol. 6 No. 2, 1984, p. 177. I used Gareth Williams's approach 'narrative reconstruction' for the analysis of the texts.

28 Catherine Kohler Riessman, 'Narrative Analysis', p. 2-3.

29 Henri Lefebvre, *The Production of Space*, UK: Basil Blackwell, 1991, .p. 38-39.

30 Ibid., p. 93-94.

31 Sigurður Gylfi Magnússon, 'A West Side story and the one who gets to write it', in Sigurður Gylfi Magnússon and István M. Szijártó, *What is Microhistory? Theory and Practice*, New York: Routledge, 2013, p. 134.

32 Sigurður Gylfi Magnússon, 'Postscript: to step into the same stream twice', in Sigurður Gylfi Magnússon and István M. Szijártó, *What is Microhistory? Theory and Practice*, p. 152.

33 Samuel D. Kassow, *Who Will Write Our History?* p. 9, 81.

34 Ibid., p. 269.

35 André Burguière, *The Annals School, An Intellectual History*, USA: Cornell University Press, 2009, p. 63.

36 David G. Roskies, *The Jewish Search for a Usable Past*, Indiana University Press, USA: Indiana University Press, 1999.

37 Samuel D. Kassow, *Who Will Write Our History?*, p. 386.

38 Laura Jockusch, *Collect and Record! Jewish Holocaust documentation in early postwar Europe*, New York: Oxford University Press, 2012, Kindle edition, locations 552, 876.

39 Reuven Feldschuh (Ben-Shem), *Manuscript 1*, Jerusalem: Yad-Vashem Archive (Hebrew), pic 2.

CHAPTER 1

1 Michael A. Mayer, *Judaism Within Modernity: Essays on Jewish History and Religion*, Detroit: Wayne State University Press, 2001, p. 35-36. According to Mayer, the idea of progress convinced a growing number of Jews to 'convert' their beliefs, and adopt the notion that progress was the incarnation of messianism, that science rather than religion was the force that could redeem the world, including the Jews.

2 Ibid., p. 55-56.

3 Ibid., p. 53-54. According to Mayer, Graetz was no less interested in claiming the research of Judaism from non-Jews, who at the beginning of the 19th century, remained under the influence of anti-Jewish Christian theology rather than science. Mayer mentioned Jacques Basnage, a cleric and Hannah Adams whose history '...was an argument for the truth of Christianity.'

4 Ibid., p. 59

5 Raphael Mahler, 'Dubnow's Method and His Jewish Historiography Achievements', in *Historians and Historical Scholarship, Selected Lectures from the 7th Convention for the Study of History (Hanukah 1962)*, pp. 93-116, Israel: The Israeli Historical Society, 1977, (Hebrew), p. 94.

6 Michael A. Mayer, p. 59-60.

7 Nathaniel Deutsch, 'When Culture Became the New Torah: Late Imperial Russia and the Discovery of Jewish Culture', *The Jewish Quarterly Review*, Vol. 102, No. 3, Summer 2012, p. 460.

8 Raphael Mahler, 'Dubnow's Method and His Jewish Historiography Achievements', p. 95.

9 *Ahad Ha-Am* (1856 – 1927), was an essayist, and one of the leading pre-state Zionist thinkers. He is known as the founder of cultural Zionism. *Ahad Ha-Am* was his pen name and it means 'one of the people', chosen from Genesis 26:10. Hayim Nahman Bialik (1873-1934), was one of the pioneers of modern Hebrew poetry and a prominent thinker.

Endnotes

10 Pardes, was a Jewish literary anthology edited and published by Yehoshua Ḥana Rawnitzki.

11 Reuven Michael, *Jewish Historiography from The Renaissance to the Modern Time*, Jerusalem: The Bialik Institute, 1993, p. 368.

12 Simon Dubnow, *YIVO Encyclopedia*, https://yivoencyclopedia.org/article.aspx/Dubnow_Simon, accessed 7.11.2017.

13 David Engel, 'Dubnow, on the Particular and Universal Elements in Jewish History', *Zion*, Vol LXXVII no. 3, Jerusalem: The Historical Society of Israel and the Zalman Shazar Center, 2012, (Hebrew) p. 311.

14 Laura Jockusch, *Collect and Record!*, locations, 544, 552, 576.
See also: Kristi A. Groberg, 'The Life and Influence of Simon Dubnov (1860-1941): An Appreciation', *Modern Judaism*, Vol. 13, No. 1, Oxford University Press, Feb., 1993, p. 71-72.

15 Monty Noam Penkower, 'The Kishinew Pogrom of 1903: A Turning Point in Jewish History', *Modern Judaism*, Vol. 24, No. 3, Oxford University Press, Oct. 2004, p. 209.

16 Reuven Michael, p. 369.

17 Simon Dubnow, *Jewish History: An Essay in The Philosophy of History*, Philadelphia: The Jewish Publication Society of America, 1903, p. 11.

18 Ibid., p. 23.

19 Reuven Michael, p. 369.

20 Ibid., p. 369.

21 Ibid., p. 370.

22 Semion Goldin, *Letters on Old and New Jewry: Dubnow's Nationalism in the Russian and Polish Contexts, Zion*, Vol LXXVII no. 3, Jerusalem: The Historical Society of Israel and the Zalman Shazar Center, 2012, (Hebrew), p. 334.

23 Vladimir Levin, The *Folks-Partey* of Simon Dubnow – A Study of Failure, *Zion*, Vol LXXVII no. 3, Jerusalem: The Historical Society of Israel and the Zalman Shazar Center, 2012, (Hebrew), p. 363.

24 Ibid. p. 360.

25 Ibid. p. 364.

26 Dimitry Shumsky, 'Zionism in Quotation Marks, or to What Extent was Dubnow a Non-Zionist?', *Zion*, Vol LXXVII no. 3, The Historical Society of Israel and the Zalman Shazar Center, 2012, (Hebrew), p. 371.

27 Michael Brenner, *Prophets of the Past: Interpreters of Jewish History*, Princeton: Princeton University Press, 2010, p. 98.

28 Simon Rabinovitch, 'The Dawn of a New Diaspora: Simon Dubnov's Autonomism, from St. Petersburg to Berlin', *The Leo Baeck Institute Yearbook*, Volume 50, Issue 1, Berghahn Books, January 2005, p. 272.

29 Ilya Ehrenburg and Vasily Grossman, *The Complete Black Book of Russian Jewry*, New Brunswick, USA: Transaction Publishers, 2009, p. 388. According to Captain E. Gekhtman, who presented this information, Dubnow would

occasionally give lectures in Oriental Studies outside Berlin. He gave such lectures at the University of Heidelberg where Johann Siebert studied. When the war broke out, Siebert became head of the Gestapo in Riga. According to the report, Siebert used to tease his old professor on several occasions. When the round ups started, Dubnow was pushed out under the prodding of two Germans and he saw Siebert outside. The latter '... bared his teeth in smirk...' and shot him. Dubnow was 81 years old.

30 Ibid., p. 391.

31 Jacob L. Talmon, *The Riddle of the Present and the Cunning of History*, Jerusalem: Bialik Institute, 2000, (Hebrew), p. 95-96.

32 Samuel D. Kassow, *Who Will Write Our History?*, p. 24-25.

33 Ibid., p. 58.

34 Samuel D. Kassow, 'The LPZ in Interwar Poland', in: Gitelman, Zvi (editor), *The Emergence of Modern Jewish Politics, Bundism and Zionism in Eastern Europe*, pp. 71-84, Pittsburgh: The University of Pittsburgh Press, 2003, p. 77.

35 Samuel D. Kassow, *Who Will Write Our History?*, p. 81.

36 Ibid., p. 102.

37 Victoria Nizan, 'Politics and History in Emanuel Ringelblum's War Diaries. Emanuel Ringelblum between the Two World Wars', *Journal of Global Politics and Current Diplomacy*, no. 4, Issue 2, Centrul pentru Dialog European şi Diplomaţie Culturală (Center for European Dialogue and Cultural Diplomacy) (DEDIC), April 2016, p. 17.

38 Small German operated factories.

39 Samuel D. Kassow, *Who Will Write Our History?*, p. 334

40 Namysło Aleksandra, The story of the 'Krysia' Bunker, August 2017, *Polin, Museum of the History of Polish Jews*, accessed 20.3.2021. https://sprawiedliwi.org.pl/pl/historie-pomocy/historia-bunkra-krysia.

41 Samuel D. Kassow, Introduction, in Robert Moses Shapiro and Tadeusz Epstein (editors), *The Warsaw Ghetto, Oyneg Shabes-Ringelblum Archive, Catalogue and Guide*, Bloomington USA: Indiana University Press, 2009, p. xvii.

42 Samuel D. Kassow., *Who Will Write Our History?*, p. 59.

43 Ibid., p. 60.

44 Ibid., p. 82.

45 Ibid., p. 78.

46 Ibid., p. 51-52.

47 Jeffrey Shandler, (editor), *Awakening lives, Autobiographies of Jewish Youth in Poland before the Holocaust*, New Haven and London: Yale University Press /YIVO Institute, 2002, p. xiii.

48 Samuel D. Kassow, *Who Will Write Our History?*, p. 8

49 Ibid p. 79-80.

50 Ibid., p. 81.

51 Ibid., p. 83.

52 Ibid., p. 10.

Endnotes

53 Khayk Lunski, *Characters and Images from the Vilna Ghetto Written in Turbulent Times*, Vilno: Farlag fun dem fareyn fun di yidishe literatn un zshurnolistn in Vilne, 1920, (Yiddish).

54 Samuel D. Kassow, *Who Will Write Our History?*, p. 84-85.

55 Ibid., p. 9, 85. Kassow wrote that non-Jews showed little interest in Jewish history and when they did, they often distorted it (p. 9).

56 Ibid., p. 78.

57 Ibid., p. 83.

58 Ibid., p. 84.

59 LPZ was founded at the turn of the 20th century by Dov Ber Borochov (1881–1917), after the Bund, a secular Jewish socialist movement, a trade union as well as a political party, had rejected Zionism in 1901. The Bund focused on culture as the glue of Jewish nationhood, which was also the reason why they rejected Zionism.

60 Shimon Frost, *Schooling as a Socio-Political Expression: Jewish Education in Interwar Poland*, Jerusalem: Magnes, 1998, p. 137.

61 Ezra Mendelsohn, *Zionism in Poland: The Formative Years, 1915-1926*, Jerusalem: The Zionist Library, 1982, p. 149. p. 186.

62 Samuel D. Kassow, *Who Will Write Our History?*, p. 35.

63 Ibid., p. 38.

64 Ibid., p. 36.

65 Samuel D. Kassow, 'The LPZ in Interwar Poland', p. 74.

66 Samuel D. Kassow, *Who Will Write Our History?*, p. 100.

67 Ibid., p. 90.

68 Ibid., p. 98.

69 Ibid., p. 99.

70 Victoria Nizan, 'Politics and History in Emanuel Ringelblum's War Diaries', p. 27

71 Deportation of Jews who resided in Germany to Zbąszyń was a response to Polish legislation from March and October 1938, which addressed cancellation of passports to Poles living outside of Poland. The law was aimed at the numerous Jews living in Germany, and whom the Polish state was afraid would return to Poland because of the Nazi regime. In response, the German authorities expelled Jews of Polish origin to Zbąszyń

72 Emanuel Ringelblum, letter to Raphael Mahler, Śródborów, December 6, 1938, in Yitzhak Arad, Yisrael Gutman, Abraham Margaliot (editors), *Documents on the Holocaust - Selected sources on the destruction of the Jews of Germany and Austria, Poland, and the Soviet Union*, Jerusalem: Yad-Vashem, 1981, p. 123-124.

73 Ibid, Śródborów, December 6, 1938, p. 123-124.

74 Emanuel Ringelblum, *Diary and Notes from the Warsaw Ghetto*, p. 306.

75 Emanuel Ringelblum, letter to Raphael Mahler, Śródborów, December 6, 1938, p. 123-124.

76 Victoria Nizan, 'Politics and History in Emanuel Ringelblum's War Diaries, p. 29.

77 Weinbaum Laurence, 'Shaking the Dust off, The Story of the Warsaw Ghetto's Forgotten Chronicler, Ruben Feldschu (Ben-Shem)', *Jewish Political Studies Review*, Vol. 22, No. 3/4, pp. 7-44, Fall 2010.p. 11. Weinbaum states that this information is based on Ben-Shem's own biography. However, another document written by Ben-Shem, suggests he had graduated from the rabbinical seminar when he was 17 years old.

78 *Hehalutz, HeChalutz, He-Chalutz* or *Chalutz* was a Jewish youth movement which later became an umbrella organization of Zionist youth movements. They trained their members for life in agricultural settlements in Palestine.

79 Reuven Ben-Shem, *Poyln Brent*, Buenos Aires: Tsentral-farband fun Poylishe Yidn in Argentina, 1960, (Yiddish), p. 275, p. 138.

80 Ibid., p. 178, 185. Ben-Shem mentions the villages of Sośninka (p.178) and Sobolew (p.185).

81 Ibid., p. 187. Ben-Shem wrote that the Germans had set fire to houses and when people tried to escape, they shot them back into the burning buildings.
See also: Emmanuel Ringelblum, *Diary and Notes from the Warsaw Ghetto*, p. 27, 81. Ringelblum mentioned twice atrocities in Łaskarzew but none seem to refer to what Ben-Shem had written. Ringelblum wrote that more than twenty people were murdered in Łaskarzew. In another incident Ringelblum wrote that several months earlier, twenty seven people in Łaskarzew were ordered to dig a hole into which they were shot. One was injured, survived, went back to the city and reported the event. It could be that Ringelblum was talking about the same event and what he added in February 1940, were additional details he might have obtained later. However, in that entry, the two reports were not linked.

82 Reuven Ben-Shem, *Poyln Brent*, p. 217.

83 Ibid., p. 241-242. In fact, the whole book describes the first four months of the war starting with the dreadful bombs shed on Warsaw, the flight to the south and the return to Warsaw.

84 Ibid., p. 243

85 Joseph Kermish, 'Margined-notes to Ben-Shem's 'Note-Book', p. 52.

86 Laurence Weinbaum, p. 19.

87 Rachel Auerbach, *In the Outskirts of Warsaw*, Tel Aviv: Am-Oved, 1954, (Hebrew), p. 183.

88 Anka Grupińska, 'Ja myślałam, że wszyscy są razem, Z Emilką „Marylką' Rozencwajg (Szoszaną Kossower), łączniczką żydowskiego i polskiego podziemia, rozmawia Anka Grupińska' (I thought that They Were All Together, Anka Grupińska Talks with Emilka 'Marylka' Rozencwajg (Szoszana Kossower), a liaison officer of the Jewish and Polish underground), *Tygodnik Powszechny*, no 18, 6.5.2001, accessed: 30.3.2021.

Endnotes

229

https://www.academia.edu/11008478/Shoszana_Kossower_Ja_my%C5%9Bla%C5%82am_%C5%BCe_wszyscy_s%C4%85_razem.

89   Laurence Weinbaum, p. 24.

90   *Hamashkif*, 10.4.1945, 'Dr. Feldschuh wrote 11 notebooks about the Jews' situation in Poland During Nazi Occupation', (Hebrew). https://www.nli.org.il/he/newspapers/hmf/1945/04/10/01/?&e=————-he-20—1—img-txIN%7ctxTI———————1, Accessed 21.3.2021. The newspaper stated that Ben-Shem was head of a committee designated to help the survivors.

91   Natalia Aleksiun, 'The Central Jewish Historical Commission in Poland', in: Gabriel N. Finder, Natalia Aleksiun, Antony Polonsky and Jan Schwarz (editors), *Making Holocaust Memory*, Vol 20, USA: The Littman Library of Jewish Civilization in association with Liverpool University Press, 2008, p. 75

92   Aba Kovner (1918 – 1987), a poet, writer, and partisan leader. He is famous for his manifesto published on January 1, 1942 which identified the Nazis' plan to kill all Jews categorically urging Jews to rebel.

93   Arye Levi Sarid, *The Moreshet Journal,* The organization *Revenge* – its History, Image, Deeds – part A, no. 52, pp. 35-43, April 1992, (part A), (Hebrew).
Ruth Ben-Shem, (née Halberstatdt), *The Days of My Three Lives*, p. 103. The manuscript was written by Ben-Shem's second wife, Ruth, and for now, it remains unpublished. Sharon Ben-Shem Da-Silva, kindly let me read this manuscript.

94   Hanna Shlomi, 'The History of the 'Ichud' – The United Democratic Zionist in Poland on the First Year of their Existence', August 1944-1945, *Zionism Collection*, 20, 1996, p. 191-192. Shlomi wrote that Gustaw Alef-Bolkowiak, the Representative of the Polish authorities, had advised Ben-Shem to leave Poland.

95   *Hamashkif*, 28.10.1945, 'A Branch Plucked out of the Burning [Zechariah, 3, 2], Fighters, Jews Arrived to the Shores of the Land of Israel, the Transylvania Immigrants in the Haifa Port', (Hebrew), p. 4. Accessed: 21.10.2020. https://www.nli.org.il/he/newspapers/hmf/1945/10/28/01/?&e=————-he-20—1—img-txIN%7ctxTI————————1.

96   Laurence Weinbaum, p. 27. Although Weinbaum stated he was unsure whether the book was based on notes taken in that period, a few months before resuming my research, Sharon Ben-Shem Da Silva found a part of the manuscript Ben-Shem prepared for the publication of the book.
See also: Reuven Feldschuh (Ben-Shem), *Manuscript 1,* pic. 2.

97   Reuven Ben-Shem, *Between the Ghetto's Walls*, Tel Aviv: N. Twersky, 1946/1947, (Hebrew).

98   A *bat mitzvah* is a coming-of-age ceremony for girls.

99   Laurence Weinbaum, p. 28.

100 Ibid., p. 8-9.

101 Elkana Margalit, 'Social and Intellectual Origins of the *Hashomer Hatzair* Youth Movement, 1913-1920', *Journal of Contemporary History*, Vol. 4, No. 2, Sage, Apr. 1969, p. 28, 34.

102 Ibid., p. 29.

103 Morton H. Narrowe, 'Jabotinsky and the Zionists in Stockholm (1915)', *Jewish Social Studies*, Vol. 46, No. 1, Indiana University Press, Winter 1984, p. 9. Jabotinsky, who would later become the leader of the Jewish right was for Ben-Shem, a revered leader until 1933 when their differences could no longer be bridged. The issue related to Ben-Shem's objection to Jabotinsky's decision to quit the World Jewish Congress.

104 Elkana Margalit., p. 38, 40.

105 Ibid., pp. 34-35.

106 Daniel Kupfert Heller, *Jabotinsky's Children: Polish Jews and the Rise of Right-Wing Zionism*, Princeton: Princeton University Press, 2017, p. 48. See also: Ruth Ben-Shem, p. 107. Ruth Ben-Shem confirmed the origin of his name was being the son of Shem, Noah's eldest son.

107 Glenda Abramson, *Drama and Ideology in Modern Israel*, Cambridge: Cambridge University Press, 1998, p. 85.

108 Daniel Kupfert Heller, p. 49.

109 Laurence Weinbaum, p. 11. In his article, Weinbaum brought testimony from Ben-Shem's former student, Shimon Goldstein, who remembered Ben-Shem trying to erect a cell of *Betar*, the Revisionist Zionist youth movement.

110 Mordechai Melamed, 'Reflections about *Hashomer Hatzair*', in Eliezer Leoni-Zopperfin (editor), *Kowel: Testimony and Memorial Book of Our Destroyed Community*, Tel Aviv: Arazi Publishing, 1957, (Hebrew), p. 310-311.

111 Reuven Ben-Shem, 'Around the City', in *Kowel: Testimony and Memorial Book of Our Destroyed Community*, p. 71.

112 Ibid., p. 68.

113 Daniel Kupfert Heller, p. 49.

114 Reuven Ben-Shem (the Board), *Guidelines of Hashomer*, Warsaw: *Hashomer Hatahor Haleumi* in Poland Publications, Bulletin no. 1, December 1927, p. 4.

115 Ibid., p. 6.

116 Daniel Kupfert Heller, p. 49-50.

117 Reuven Ben-Shem, interview, Massuah International Institute for Holocaust Studies, Tel Yitzhak, file 7442 , AR-T-002-17, archive 2/17,ע/ tape 3, 27.10.1971, p. 1.

118 Ibid., p. 2.

119 Ibid., p. 4. The interviewer asked Ben-Shem twice for these details as if he was not certain he understood, and then added the remark, '...you played both sides of the fence...' a statement, to which Ben-Shem agreed adding that his vision was to have one united organization, which was why he paid no attention to doctrine nuances.

120 Ibid., p. 5.

See also: '*Hazfira*, 'A New *Shomerit* Organization in Poland', 20.01.1927, (Hebrew), p. 4. https://www.nli.org.il/he/newspapers/hzf/1927/01/20/01/

?&e=————-he-20—1—img-txIN%7ctxTI—————1, accessed, 13.7.2020. The newspaper published the news that the movement was created and introduced its new doctrine, amongst others that the movement was to prepare the young for immigration to the land of Israel and that any form of settlement they chose was acceptable.

121 Reuven Ben-Shem, interview, Massuah, p. 2.

122 Daniel Kupfert Heller, p. 47.

123 Ibid., p. 47.

124 Ibid., p. 77

125 Chen Ben-Yerucham, (Merchavia Melech Hen), *Book of Bethar, Volume I (To The People)*, Tel Aviv: Jabotinsky Institute Publishing, 1969, (Hebrew), p. 234.

126 Ibid., p. 294. Masada was a student organization that supported revisionists ideology. They were rivals to *Betar* which caused clashes within the revisionist party.

127 Ibid., p. 294.

128 Ze'ev Jabotinsky, a copy of a letter Jabotinsky addressed to Reuven Ben-Shem (Feldschuh) and Mr. Rosenblum in London, 11.2.1931, file 1118., Jabotinsky Institute, Tel-Aviv.

129 Rafael Medoff, *Militant Zionism in America: The Rise and Impact of the Jabotinsky Movement*, Tuscaloosa Alabama: The University of Alabama Press, 2002, p. 18. Meir Grossman (1888-1964) was a noted Zionist leader, prominent journalist, and former member of the Jewish Agency Executive.

130 Laurence Weinbaum, p. 13.

131 *Hamashkif*, Dr. Feldschuh in the Newspaper of Journalists: The Survivors Testimony – Unity to Redeem the People', 11.11.1945, (Hebrew), p. 4. Accessed 22.7.2020. https://www.nli.org.il/he/newspapers/hmf/1945/11/11/01/?&e=————-he-20—1—img-txIN%7ctxTI—————1.

The same news item appeared in *Hatzophe* (Watchman), 'A Call to Unite in Order to Be Saved', on the same date. The report presented parts of Ben-Shem's lecture given at the Moghrabi Movie Theatre in Tel-Aviv, where he told the audience about the war. He concluded by saying that 'We must be the generation of salvation and learn how to fight to totally change our political status in the world in order to prevent another Holocaust of our people in the diaspora.'

132 Głos Gminy Żydowskiej. Organ Gminy Wyznaniowej Żydowskiej w Warszawie, maj 1938 r., nr 5, ('Voice of the Jewish Community. Organ of the Jewish Religious Community in Warsaw', May 1938, No. 5), 'Uroczystość przekazania pierwszego samolotu eskadry im. młodzieży żydowskiej Armii Polskiej' (The ceremony of delivering the first airplane named after The Jewish Youth of the Polish Army), (Polish), p. 121-122, accessed 18.10.2024. file:///C:/Users/User/Desktop/G%C5%82os%20Gminy%20%C5%BBydowskiej%20_%20organ%20Gminy%20Wyznaniowej%20%C5%BBydowskiej%20w%20Warszawie.%20R.%202,%201938,%20nr%205.pdf.

See also: Laurence Weinbaum, p. 14, 37-38. Weinbaum wrote that at the ceremony, Ben-Shem expressed the Jewish commitment to Poland even though they aspired to establish a Jewish state in Palestine.

133 Reuven Ben-Shem, *Poyln Brent*, p. 23.

134 Nachman Meisel, 'From week to Week', *Literary Journal*, 20.01.1939, (Yiddish), p. 30. Accessed, 20.6.2020.
https://www.nli.org.il/he/newspapers/ltb/1939/01/20/01/article/16.2/?e=———
—-he-20—1—img-txIN%7ctxTI————————1.

135 Dr. Reuven Feldshuh (Ben-Shem) (editor), *Yiddisher Gesellschaftlicher Lexikon in Poyln, (Lexicon of Jewish Society, Poland I, Warsaw)*, Warsaw: Yiddisher Leksigraphisher Verlag, 1939, (Yiddish).
Laurence Weinbaum, p. 38. In that footnote, Weinbaum stated that in an interview he conducted with Nekamia Ben-Shem, November 28, 2009, the latter said that his father was contemplating the option of publishing additional volumes in cooperation with a writer called Getzel Kretzel, but the venture was finally abandoned.

136 Merriam-Webster Dictionary accessed: 26.3.2020. https://www.merriam-webster.com/dictionary/monumentum%20aere%20perennius#:~:text=%3A%20a%20monument%20more%20lasting%20than,work%20of%20art%20or%20literature.

137 Laurence Weinbaum, p. 10.

138 Reuven Ben-Shem, *Poyln Brent*, p. 275.

139 Ibid., p. 300

140 Ibid., p. 274-275.

141 Emmanuel Ringelblum, *Diary and Notes from the Warsaw Ghetto*, p. 43.
Reuven Ben-Shem, *Poyln Brent*, p. 318 - 324. Ben-Shem wrote about attempts to get permission from the Gestapo to leave Warsaw and his encounters with the relevant personnel at the Gestapo offices in Warsaw.

142 Reuven Feldschuh (Ben-Shem), *Poyln Brent*, p. 333.

143 The group Thirteen network was a Jewish collaborationist organization in the Warsaw Ghetto. The Thirteen took its name from the address of their main offices at 13 Leszno.

144 Emmanuel Ringelblum, *Diary and Notes from the Warsaw Ghetto*, p. 280.

145 Ibid., p. 294.

146 Reuven Feldschuh (Ben-Shem), *Deciphered Diary*, pic. 133. With Gancwajch's help, Ben-Shem organized six courtyards in which he established kindergartens.

147 Emmanuel Ringelblum, *Diary and Notes from the Warsaw Ghetto*, p. 291.

148 Laurence Weinbaum, p. 16-17.

149 Reuven Ben-Shem, *Poyln Brent*, p. 275.

150 Reuven Feldschuh (Ben-Shem), *Manuscript 1*, pic. 221.

151 Natalia Aleksiun, Brian Horowitz, Introduction, in Natalia Aleksiun, Brian Horowitz and Antony Polonsky (editors), *Polin, Studies in Jewish Jewry, Vol.*

Endnotes 233

29, *Writing Jewish History in Eastern Europe*, Portland Oregon: The Littman Library of Jewish Civilization in association with Liverpool University Press, 2017, p. 8.

152 Cecile E. Kuznitz, 'YIVO's "Old Friend and Teacher": Simon Dubnow and his Relationship to the Yiddish Scientific Institute', *Jahrbuch des Simon-Dubnow-Instituts (Simon Dubnow Institute Yearbook)*, Vol. xv, Leipzig: Vandenhoeck & Ruprecht, 2016 p. 478.

153 Ibid., p. 478.
See also: Joshua M. Karlip, 'Between martyrology and historiography: Elias Tcherikower and the Making of a Pogrom Historian', *East European Jewish Affairs*, 38:3, Routledge, 16 Dec 2008, p. 263.

154 Cecile E. Kuznitz, 'YIVO's "Old Friend and Teacher": Simon Dubnow and his Relationship to the Yiddish Scientific Institute', p. 479-480.

155 Samuel D. Kassow, *Who Will Write Our History?*, p. 8.

156 David Engel, *Historians of the Jews and the Holocaust* (Stanford Studies in Jewish History and Culture), California: Stanford University Press, 2010, p. 127.

157 Guy Miron, *To Be a Jew in Nazi Germany, Space and Time*, Jerusalem, Israel, The Hebrew University Magnes Press and Yad-Vashem, (Hebrew), 2021, p. 228, 232. Miron pointed out that the Jews' thirst to learn about the past originated in the need to deal with the present. This need was manifested during the Second World War in the increased tendency to write personal journals. That is, history became wider as it extended from the communal to the personal.

158 Samuel D. Kassow, *Who Will Write Our History?*, p. 49-103.

159 Reuven Ben-Shem (Dr. Feldszuh), *Czerwone dusze (Red Souls)*, Warsaw: Perły, 1932, (Polish), p. 117.

160 *Aliyah*, means in Hebrew 'ascent' or 'going up', a common Jewish term to refer to immigration to the Land of Israel.

161 Eliezer Leoni, 'From Poor Education to the Hebrew Gymnasia, The History of the Hebrew Education in Kowel', in Eliezer Leoni-Zopperfin (editor), *Kowel: Testimony and Memorial Book of Our Destroyed Community*, p. 148-149. Although Leoni was not among Ben-Shem's students, he admired him and characterized Ben-Shme as the type of the 'new Jew', that is, Erez Israel was at the center of his activity.
See also: Aharon Levi and Mordechai Blorai, 'Hashomer Hatzair', in Eliezer Leoni-Zopperfin (editor), *Kowel: Testimony and Memorial Book of Our Destroyed Community*, p. 300. The two wrote that in 1926, Ben-Shem's students from *Tarbut* school joined them and brought a whole new spirit to their group.

162 Reuven Ben-Shem, 'Around the City', p. 67. Ben-Shem recounted that when he was a teacher at '*Tarbut*' school, he re-established the group of *Hashomer Hatzair*, a movement he had left earlier. He wrote that what was important for him was to instill in the youth the idea of establishing the Jewish state.

234   *Emanuel Ringelblum and Reuven Ben-Shem's War Writings*

163 Ben-Shem Reuven, 'The Principles of *Hashomer Haleumi*', Warsaw, Iyar (May-June), 1929, Circular number 23/89. File: AR-A-019-29, computerized: 17396, Massuah, Tel Yitzhak, Moshe Kol's Collection. In this pamphlet for the members of *Hashomer Haleumi*, Ben-Shem formulated thirteen principles to guide the movement. In almost each of these principles, Ben-Shem made various allusions to the idea of establishing a homeland for the Jewish people while principle nine, declared upon 'a Hebrew renaissance'. The pamphlet was published in Hebrew.

164 Cecilie S. Schrøder Simonsen, 'A Spatial Expansion of a Pocket-Size Homeland: Heinrich Heine's Construction of Jewish Space', *Partial Answers, Journal of Literature and the History of Ideas*, Vol. 14, no. 2, Baltimore: John Hopkins University Press, Jun 2016, p. 303-304. This approach of substituting ink for bricks continued later with writing community commemoration *Black Books* after the Holocaust.

165 Ibid., p. 318.

166 Joshua M. Karlip, p. 260.

167 Guy Miron, *To Be a Jew in Nazi Germany, Space and Time*, p. 244. Miron concluded that the Nazi policy of banishment which shrank Jewish spaces physically and timely (the option to plan a future) gave way to treating the past as space by its expansion which sometimes acted as comfort but also as a menace.

CHAPTER II

1   Wendy Lower, *Nazi Empire-Building and the Holocaust in Ukraine*, Chapel Hill, USA : University of North Carolina Press, 2005, p. 28.
See also: Max Weinreich, *Hitler's Professors, the Part of Scholarship in Germany's Crimes Against the Jewish People*, USA: Yale University Press, 1999, p. 72-74. Weinreich wrote that during 1935, a Reich Agency for Space Arrangement (Reichsstelle für Raumordnung) as well as a Reich Board for Space Research were established. These bodies were engaged in implementing scientific methodology into a study of how to change landscapes. This seemingly innocent research contributed to the spread of the popular approach that the east was historically German and that once these lands were conquered, German settlers would be entering into a 'vacuum', which could be shaped at will.

2   United States, Holocaust Memorial Museum, Timeline of Events. On August 17th, 1938, the law required to add the names Israel (males) and Sarah (females) to identity cards of Jews whose first names were not Jewish. In 1939, all Jewish passports had to be stamped with the letter 'J' in red. Source: United States Holocaust Memorial Museum, https://www.ushmm.org/learn/timeline-of-events/1933-1938/law-on-alteration-of-family-and-personal-names, accessed, 23.3.2019.

Endnotes

3   The shape of the Jewish symbol was not uniform and depended on local authorities. In Germany, the symbol was a piece of yellow cloth cut in the shape of the Star of David and with the word 'Jude' in the middle.

4   Barbara Engelking and Jacek Leociak, 'Chronology: September 1939-May 1943', in Barbara Engelking and Jacek Leociak, *The Warsaw Ghetto, A Guide to the Perished City*, New Haven: Yale University Press, 2009, p. 37. In mid-October, for example, different kinds of bank accounts belonging to Jews were frozen and one was allowed to draw a weekly amount of 250 zlotys while limiting the overall sum any Jew could have in cash to no more than 2,000 zlotys.

5   Yitzhak Arad, *Ghetto in Flames, The Struggle and Destruction of the Jews of Vilna in the Holocaust*, Jerusalem: Yad-Vashem, 1980, p. 55.

6   Alex J. Kay, *The Making of an SS Killer, The Life of Colonel Alfred Filbert*, 1905-1990, UK: Cambridge University Press, 2016, p. 57.

7   James E. Young, 'Literature' in Walter Laqueur, (editor), *The Holocaust Encyclopedia*, New Heaven and London: Yale University Press, 2001, p. 393.

8   Dina Porat, 'The Vilna Ghetto Diaries', in Robert Moses Shapiro (editor), *Holocaust Chronicles Individualizing the Holocaust Through Diaries and other Contemporaneous Personal Accounts*, Hoboken, New-Jersey: KTAV Publishing House, 1999, p. 158.

9   David G. Roskies and Naomi Diamant, *Holocaust Literature, A History and Guide*, Waltham, Mass: Brandeis University Press, 2012, Kindle edition, location 545.

10   Ibid., location 552.

11   Henri Lefebvre, p. 165.

12   David Roskies, 'What is Holocaust Literature', in Eli Lederhendler, (editor), *Jews, Catholics, and the Burden of History, Studies in Contemporary Jewry*, An Annual XXI, New York: Oxford University Press, 2005, p. 201.

13   Ibid., p. 201.

14   Samuel D. Kassow, *Who Will Write Our History?*, p. 172. Kassow pointed out that Yiddish was the traditional language for community chronicles, the same language Ringelblum used in his own war diary.

15   Natalia Aleksiun, 'The Central Jewish Historical Commission in Poland', p. 75.

16   Rita Horváth, 'The Role of the Survivors in the Remembrance of the Holocaust, Memorial Monuments and *Yizkor Books*', in Jonathan C. Friedman (editor), *The Routledge History of the Holocaust*, USA: Routledge, 2011, p. 472. Horváth mentioned over 1,000 *Yizkor Books* and 100,000 testimonies.

17   Amos Goldberg, 'Jews' Diaries and Chronicles', in Peter Hayes and John K. Roth (editors), *The Oxford Handbook of Holocaust Studies*, USA: Oxford University Press, 2010, p. 398.

18   Claire Rosen and Robin Schulman, 'How an Astounding Holocaust Diary Surfaced in America', *Smithsinian Magazine*, editor's note: 30.10.2018.

https://www.smithsonianmag.com/history/astonishing-Holocaust-diary-hidden-world-70-years-resurfaced-america-180970534/, accessed 15.1.2019.

19 Alexandra Garbarini, 'Diaries, Testimonies, and Jewish Histories of the Holocaust', in Norman J. W. Goda (editor), *Jewish Histories of the Holocaust, New Transitional Approaches*, New-York, Oxford: Berghahn, 2017, p. 99.

20 Marian Turski, 'Individual Experience in Diaries from the Łódź Ghetto', in Robert Moses Shapiro (editor), *Holocaust Chronicles Individualizing the Holocaust Through Diaries and other Contemporaneous Personal Accounts*, Hoboken, New-Jersey: KTAV Publishing House, 1999, p. 119.

21 Zoë Vania Waxman, *Writing the Holocaust: Identity, Testimony, Representation* Oxford: Oxford University Press, 2006, Kindle edition, locations 558, 561.

22 David Wdowinski, *And We Are Not Saved*, Jerusalem: Yad-Vashem, 1986, (Hebrew), p. 144. Wdowinski was in eleven camps and miraculously his notes were saved. The original diary was written in Hebrew in Latin orthograph and began on September 18, 1944 until October 18, 1946. It is unclear whether Wdowinski wrote before, but his records were from the last four camps, Vaihingen and Wasseralfingen (parts of Natzweiler in Alsace), Dachau and finally, Feldafing, a displaced persons camp south of Munich. Wdowinski started decipherment but he died before finishing.

23 Amos Goldberg, *Trauma in First Person , Diary Writing during the Holocaust*, Israel: Kinneret Zmora-Bitan Dvir, 2012, (Hebrew), p. 41.

24 Ibid., p. 32. Perechodnik started writing in hiding, August 1942. He died sometime after the Polish uprising began in August 1944. The first part of his diary was saved by Władysław Błażewski, a lawyer who had befriended him but the other part was lost. At the end of the war, Pajsach Perechodnik, Salek's brother, received the diary from Błażewski.
For more details see: Salek Perehodnik, *The Sad Task of Documentation, A Diary in Hiding*, Jerusalem: Keter Publishing House, 1999, (Hebrew), p. II-III.

25 Alexandra Garbarini 'Holocaust Diaries', *YIVO Encyclopedia*, https://yivoencyclopedia.org/article.aspx/Holocaust/Holocaust_Diaries, accessed: 1.1.2020. According to Garbarini, Jews like Klemperer and Kaplan who began his diary in 1933, were connected to '… broader European cultural practices of the nineteenth and twentieth centuries, in which diary writing figured prominently as a means of self-exploration, intellectual development, and historical documentation...'

26 Guy Miron, "The "Lived Time" of German Jews under the Nazi Regime', *The Journal of Modern History* 90, The University of Chicago, March 2018, p. 125. Miron showed how bans imposed on the Jewish community had a direct impact on Jews' conceptual dimensions of time and space. It appears that just as the ban defined the Nazi space, it simultaneously enlarged it for Germans while downsizing Jewish space more and more until it penetrated their own bodies.

27 Helen Berr, *Journal, The Diary of a Young Jewish Woman in Occupied Paris*, London : MacLehose Press, 2008, p. 155.

Endnotes

237

28 Ibid., p. 157
    See also: Aliza Vitis-Shomron, *Youth in Flames, a Teenage Resistance and her Fight for Survival in the Warsaw Ghetto*, Omaha, Nebraska: Tell the Story Publishing, 2015 p. 182. Vitis-Shomron who was also keeping a diary, explained that when she wanted to join the fighting, *Hashomer Hatzair* had refused because '... some people should survive to tell what they had seen. There must be witnesses left, particularly among the young.'

29 Chaim Aron Kaplan, *Scroll of Agony: Hebrew Diary of Ch. A. Kaplan Written in the Warsaw Ghetto 1st September 1939 – 4th August 1942*, Tel-Aviv: Am Oved Publishers LTD, and Yad-Vashem, Davar Edition, 1966, (Hebrew), p. 212.

30 Havi Ben-Sasson and Lea Preiss, 'Twilight Days: Missing Pages from Avraham Lewin's Warsaw Ghetto Diary, May-July 1942', *Yad-Vashem Studies 33*, Jerusalem: Yad-Vashem, 2005, p. 8, 11. Lewin's diary had gaps that were thought to be missing parts until researchers Lea Preiss and Havi Ben-Sasson came across a diary in the Hersh Wasser Collection which was considered anonymous. After careful examination of contents, style, linguistic patterns and tone, the two researchers concluded that the author of these pages was none other than Avraham Lewin.

31 Amos Goldberg, *Trauma in First Person , Diary Writing during the Holocaust*, (Hebrew), p. 32.
    See also: Kata Bohus, 'Anne and Eva: Two Diaries, Two Holocaust Memories in Communist Hungary', *Remembrance and Solidarity Studies in 20th Century European History*, issue 5, December 2016, p. 102-103. Interestingly, in Hungary, for example, the documentary aspects in Anne Frank's diary were treated as representation of the struggle between fascism to anti-fascism in the course of which Jews formed only one group among the targeted anti-fascist population. This approach was not shared by the Jewish community in Hungary who viewed Anne Frank's experiences as representing a particularly Jewish experience.

32 Ester Farbstein, 'Young Moshe's Ark; Reappraisal of the Diary of Moshe Flinker', in '*So spricht der Ewige: ... Und die Straßen der Stadt Jerusalem werden voll sein mit Knaben und Mädchen, die in ihren Straßen spielen*' (gemäß Sacharjah 8,4-5) (Thus saith the LORD of hosts: ... And the broad places of the city shall be full of boys and girls playing ...), die Siebte Joseph Carlebach-Konferenz ; das jüdische Kind zwischen hoffnungsloser Vergangenheit und hoffnungsvoller Zukunft, (the Seventh Joseph Carlebach Conference: the Jewish Child, Between a Lost Past to a Promising Future), Miriam Gillis - Carlebach and Barbara Vogel (editors), München Hamburg: Dölling und Galitz Verlag, 2008 p. 211-212.

33 Laurel Holliday, *Children in the Holocaust and World War II : Their Secret Diaries*, New York: Pocket Books (a Division of Simon & Schuster), 1995, p. xiv,

34 Nicholas Chare and Dominic Williams, *The Auschwitz Sonderkommando: Testimonies, Histories, Representations*, Cham, Switzerland: Palgrave Macmillan, 2019, p. 13.
See also: Zoë Vania Waxman, locations 561, 888. Waxman also stressed the historical intent of these texts.

35 Nicholas Chare and Dominic Williams, p. 9.

36 Leila Zenderland, 'Social Science as a "Weapon of the Weak",: Max Weinreich, the Yiddish Scientific Institute, and the Study of Culture, Personality, and Prejudice', *Isis*, Vol. 104, No. 4, The University of Chicago Press on behalf of The History of Science Society, December 2013, p. 756.

37 Reuven Feldschuh (Ben-Shem), *Deciphered Diary*, pic. 507. Ben-Shem reported Mr. Platt's journey to Treblinka and back.

38 Alexandra Garbarini, 'Document Volumes and the Status of Victim Testimony in the Era of the First World War and Its Aftermath', in *Études arméniennes contemporaines, Le témoignage des victimes dans la connaissance des violences de masse, Études*, 5, 2015, paragraph 8. https://doi.org/10.4000/eac.782, accessed: 18.7.2020.
See also: David G. Roskies and Naomi Diamant, *Reading in Time [A Curriculum for Holocaust Literature], A Companion to Holocaust Literature, a History and Guide*, Waltham Massachusetts: Brandeis University Press, 2013, p. 4-5. The writers attribute the inspiration for how *Black Books* were assembled to World War I models of *Black Books*.

39 Ibid., paragraph 14. Garbarini analysis of the introduction to this book showed that the editor vouched for the validity of these testimonies based on the ethnicity of witnesses, insinuating that because they were not Armenians, their testimonies were credible.

40 Ibid., paragraph 29.

41 André Kaspi, 'Le Centre de Documentation Juive Contemporaine', (Center of Contemporary Jewish Documentation), *Revue d'histoire moderne et contemporaine (1954-)*, T. 23e, No. 2, Société d'Histoire Moderne et Contemporaine Stable, Apr. - Jun., 1976, (French), p. 305.

42 Jonathan Judaken, 'Léon Poliakov, the Origins of Holocaust Studies, and Theories of Anti-Semitism: Rereading *'Bréviaire de la haine'*, in Seán Hand and Steven T. Katz (editors), *Post-Holocaust France and the Jews, 1945-1955*, USA: New York University Press, 2015, p. 185. Count François de Menthon (1900 -1984), who was appointed lead prosecutor at the Nuremberg War Crimes Tribunal, had little material to present in court and therefore he turned to Leon Poliakov (1910-1997), a historian, who was appointed by Schneersohn as the general manager of the CDJC, to receive copies of documents the Gestapo had left behind at police headquarters in Paris.
See also: George Bensoussan, 'The Jewish Contemporary Documentation Center (CDJC) and Holocaust Research in France, 1945-1970, in, David Bankier and Dan Michman (editors), *Holocaust Historiography in Context:*

Endnotes

239

Emergence, Challenges, Polemics and Achievements, Jerusalem : Yad-Vashem in association with Berghahn Books, 2008, p. 246. The CDJC provided documents against Nazi perpetrators, most notably, Maurice Papon and Klaus Barbie.

43 Peter Stupples, 'Il'ya Erenburg and the Jewish Anti-Fascist Committee', *New Zealand Slavonic Journal*, No. 2, Australia and New Zealand Slavists' Association, 1977, p. 17-18.

44 Ilya Ehrenburg and Vasily Grossman, p. xiv. Irena, Ehrenburg's daughter, found in her father's papers, a folder containing parts of the book and smuggled them to Israel through a foreign diplomat.

45 David G. Roskies and Naomi Diamant, *Holocaust Literature, A History and Guide*, location 1026. Avraham Tory's diary, (formerly: Golub) (1909-2002), the secretary of the Jewish council in the Kovno Ghetto, stands out as both personal and official, which also contained copies of written and oral German orders.

46 Samuel D. Kassow, 'Vilna and Warsaw, Two Ghetto Diaries: Herman Kruk and Emanuel Ringelblum', in Robert Moses Shapiro (editor), *Holocaust Chronicles Individualizing the Holocaust Through Diaries and other Contemporaneous Personal Accounts*, Hoboken, New-Jersey: KTAV Publishing House, 1999, p. 172-3, 176.

47 See also: Aba Kovner, *Fareynegte Partizaner Organizatsye – FPO in the Camps, From Herman Kruk's Estate*, in Reizl Korchak (Ruz'ka), *Flames in Ash*, Israel: Moreshet and Sifriat Poalim Worker's Book-Guild (*Hashomer Hatzair*), 1965 (Hebrew), p. 375, 384. Kovner's text precedes Kruk's Recovered Klooga Camp Diary.

48 Samuel D. Kassow, *Who Will Write Our History?* p. 210-211.

49 Michal Unger, 'About the Author', in Yosef Zelkovich, *In Those Terrible Days: Writings from the Łódź Ghetto*, Jerusalem: Yad-Vashem, 2002, p. 14.

50 Isaiah Trunk, *Łódź Ghetto: A History*, Bloomington, USA: Indiana University Press, 2006, p. 4.
    See also: 'The Zonabend Collection: Documentation From the Łódź Ghetto', EHRI, Holocaust Research Infrastructure, https://portal.ehri-project.eu/units/il-002798-4019640, accessed 19.5.2020.

51' Discovery of one section of the Łódź Ghetto Archive, November 1946', Yad-Vashem.
    https://www.yadvashem.org/holocaust/this-month/november/discovering-lodz-ghetto-archive.html, accessed 19.5.2020.

52 Daniel Grinberg, 'Unpublished Diaries and Memoires in the Archives of the Jewish Historical Institute in Poland', in Robert Moses Shapiro (editor), *Holocaust Chronicles Individualizing the Holocaust Through Diaries and other Contemporaneous Personal Accounts*, Hoboken, New-Jersey: KTAV Publishing House, 1999, p. 257.

53 Boaz Cohen, 'Bound To Remember – Bound To Remind, Holocaust Survivors and the Genesis of Holocaust Research', in, Johannes-Dieter Steiner and Inge

Weber-Newth (editors), *Beyond Camps and Forced Labor: Current international research on survivors*, Osnabruck: Secolo Verlag, 2004, p. 291. Cohen stressed that it was east European Jews who were most prominent in these initiatives of collecting testimonies, and that they were part of the pre-war Jewish intelligentsia although the majority were not historians.

54 Laura Jockusch, 'Historiography in Transit: Survivor Historians and the Writing of Holocaust History in the late 1940s', *Leo Baeck Institute Yearbook*, Vol. 58 Issue 1, Published by Oxford University Press on behalf of The Leo Baeck Institute, 2013, p. 75. Jockusch argued that the urge to document was not only in east Europe but engulfed the whole Jewish community. This was manifested through fourteen different historical commissions established all over Europe.

55 Natalia Aleksiun, 'The Central Jewish Historical Commission in Poland', p. 74, 94.

56 Feliks Tych, The Emergence of Holocaust Research in Poland: The Jewish Historical Commission and The Jewish Historical Institute (ŻIH), 1944-1989, in David Bankier and Dan Michman (editors), *Holocaust Historiography in Context: Emergence, Challenges, Polemics and Achievements*, Jerusalem: Yad-Vashem in association with Berghahn Books, 2008, p. 229, 227

57 Ibid., p. 229, 228. It is plausible to presume that at least Reuven Ben-Shem was aware of the existence of the archive because Rachel Auerbach, a prolific worker of at the archive, was Ben-Shem's cousin, and had resided with the family in the ghetto for more than two years. Furthermore, Ben-Shem was well associated with the elite and also in frequent contact with members of the *Oneg Shabbat* archive. Lastly, after the destruction of the ghetto and Ringelblum's murder, it is possible that confidentiality as far as the existence of the archive was less observed if only because it was assumed lost under the rubble of the ghetto. Regardless, *Oneg Shabbat's* methodology, was not strange to the majority of east European Jews. It was a familiar practice and consequently, it is likely that people willingly cooperated even though the exact purpose remained confidential.

58 Ibid., p. 229.

59 Andrzej Żbikowski, 'Central Committee of Polish Jews (CKŻP), The Main and Basic Political and Social Organization of the Jewish Community', November 25, 2013, Jewish Historical Institute, from: https://www.jhi.pl/en/articles/central-committee-of-polish-jews,57, accessed: 5.1.2020. Żbikowski wrote that apparently, because in some cases people registered twice, the accurate number of survivors was much lower.

60 Boaz Cohen, 'Bound To Remember – Bound To Remind, Holocaust Survivors and the Genesis of Holocaust Research', p. 292.

61 Ibid., p. 291.

62 Laura Jockusch, 'Historiography in Transit: Survivor Historians and the Writing of Holocaust History in the late 1940s', p. 85.

Endnotes 241

63 Alan Rosen, David Boder, Early Postwar Voices: David Boder's Life and Work, The Voices Project, Illinois Institute of Technology, Chicago. https://iit. aviaryplatform.com/catalog?utf8=%E2%9C%93&search_field=advanced&f[c ollection_id_is][]=231&search_type=simple&title_text[]=&resource_descript ion[]=&indexes[]=&transcript[]=&op[]=&type_of_search[]=simple&type_of _field_selector[]=simple&keywords[]= accessed: 13.7.2020.

64 Jockusch Laura, *Collect and Record!*, locations 2341-2349.

65 Maria Hochberg-Marianska and Noe Grüss, (editors), *The Children Accuse*, UK: Vallentine Mitchell, 2005, p. xxxi.

66 Lena Küchler (later, Küchler-Silberman), *My Children*, Paris: Editions Poly-glottes, October 12, 1948, (Yiddish).

67 The Benjamin Tenenbaum (Tene) Collection: Testimonies of Child Survivors of the Holocaust, EHRI, Holocaust Research Infrastructure, from: https:// portal.ehri-project.eu/units/il-002806-tenenbaum_coll, accessed: 15.5.2020. See also: Benjamin Tenenbaum (compiler and editor), *One of a City and Two of a Family, a selection from amongst one thousand autobiographies of Jewish children in Poland)*, Palestine: Sifriyat Poalim – Workers' Book-Guild (*Hashomer Hatzair*), 1947, (Hebrew).

68 Laura Jockusch, *Collect and Record!*, locations 2628-2633. See also: Fela Drewniak, a letter from Moscow addressed to the Central Jewish Commission in Lublin, 29.1.1945. Ghetto Fighters' House, Kibbutz Lohamei HaGeta'ot, The Berman Collection, file 19972. Fela Drewniak asked the Commission to help her find her father and brother, both tailors who resided in Lublin and from whom she had not heard for a very long time.

69 Witold Medykowski, To Record and Save from Oblivion: Collecting Testimo-nies About the Holocaust in Poland After the War, *Arkhion*, Vol. 14-15, 2007, (Hebrew), p. 52.

70 Ibid., p. 50-51.

71 Israel Gutman, *Issues in Holocaust Scholarship, Research and Reassessment*, Jerusalem: The Zalman Shazar Center for Jewish History and Yad-Vashem, 2008, (Hebrew), p. 23-24.

72 Rita Horváth, p. 475. See also: Michlean J. Amir and Rosemary Horowitz, 'Yizkor Books in the Twenty-First Century: A History and Guide to the Genre', *Judaica Librarianship*, Volume 14, 2008, DOI: 10.14263/2330-2976.1073, p. 40. Michlean and Horowitz maintained that *Yizkor Books* were considered tombstones in cases where actual memorials were not accessible, a practice that was not strange in Jewish tradition.

73 Rita Horváth, p. 473.

74 Jack Kugelmass and Jonathan Boyarin (editors), *From a Ruined Garden: The Memorial Books of Polish Jewry*, Bloomington: Indiana University Press, 1998, p. 25. The editors stated that the very name given to these books, *Yizkor Books*,

242   *Emanuel Ringelblum and Reuven Ben-Shem's War Writings*

suggested that their main purpose was commemoration rather than providing historical accounts. This aspect was typically marked by adding lists of names of the murdered members of the community.

75   Eliyahu Eisenberg (editor), *Płock Memorial Book, A History of an Ancient Jewish Community in Poland,* Tel Aviv: Hamenora Publishing House, 1967, (Hebrew & Yiddish), p. 70-74.

76   Dr. Nathan Eck, 'Emanuel Ringelblum', in Israel Cohen (editor), *Buczacz Memorial Book,* Tel-Aviv: by The Committee to Commemorate Buczacz, Am Oved Publishers, 1956, p. 225. Natan Eck wrote a tribute to Emanuel Ringelblum and so did Melech Rawitz, an article also titled 'Emanuel Ringelblum', p. 227.

77   Nachman Meisel, 'Dr. Emanuel Ringelblum', in Pinye Kats (editor), *Warsaw Memorial Book,* Tomb I, Former Residents of Warsaw and surroundings in Argentina, Buenos Aires: Graficon Publishers, 1955 (Yiddish), columns 1173-1188.

CHAPTER III

1   Alexandra Garbarini, *Numbered Days, Diaries and the Holocaust,* USA: Yale University Press, 2006, p. 2.

2   Amos Goldberg, *Trauma in First Person , Diary Writing during the Holocaust,* Bloomington, Indiana, USA: Indiana University Press, 2017, p. 6. Goldberg also includes these in one category.
See also: Alexandra Zapruder (compiler and editor), *Salvaged Pages, Young Writer's Diaries of the Holocaust,* USA: Yale University Press, 2015, p. 447-449. Zapruder addressed the issue of genre, namely, that in relation to Holocaust literature, it was difficult to distinguish between a diary and memoire. One explicit example is Mary Berg's diary which was written in the Warsaw Ghetto, but when it was released, she added more entries to the original. In that respect, the text may be classified as a diary but also a memoire.

3   Daniel R. Woolf, 'Genre into Artifact: The Decline of the English Chronicle in the Sixteenth Century' *The Sixteenth Century Journal,* published by The Sixteenth Century Journal, Vol. 19, No. 3, Autumn 1988, p. 323

4   Amos Goldberg, *Trauma in First Person , Diary Writing during the Holocaust,* (Hebrew), p. 35.

5   Ibid., p. 35.

6   Ibid., p. 35-36.

7   Zoë Vania Waxman, location 193. According to Waxman, only after the London radio broadcast, June 26, 1942, did Ringelblum react by gathering all types of evidence. This is not entirely accurate as compilation of materials and information started from the beginning of the war and was designed to create a body of knowledge for future research. In fact, it is from these materials that the report to the Allied Forces was prepared. When nothing significant

Endnotes

243

happened after that radio broadcast, efforts were directed at gathering more evidence but also making sure materials would survive the war.

8   Batia Temkin-Berman, *City Within a City, Underground Warsaw Diary 1944-1945*, Tel-Aviv: Am Oved Publishing Ltd, Yad-Vashem, 2008, (Hebrew), p. 108. In her diary she stated that even while Ringelblum was in Trawniki, he documented life in the camp and when he was smuggled out of the camp, Shimon Malinowski, a member of the Bund, kept documenting but eventually the diary was lost.

9   Rachel L. Einwohner, 'The Need to Know: Cultured Ignorance and Jewish Resistance in the Ghettos of Warsaw, Vilna, and Łódź', *The Sociological Quarterly*, Vol. 50, No. 3, Taylor & Francis, Ltd., Summer, 2009, p. 415. Einwohner wrote that despite the news of organized murder in Vilnius, the older generation, in particular, were against active resistance because they believed that it would bring more harm than benefits and that if they did not rebel, there was a greater chance the majority of the community would be saved.

10   Dr. Hillel Seidman, *Diary of the Warsaw Ghetto*, New York: The Jewish Week, 1957, (Hebrew), p. 11.

11   Ibid., p. 11.

12   Primo Levi, *If This Is A Man*, Tel Aviv: Am-Oved Publishing, 2011, (Hebrew), p. 7-8.

13   Alexander Donat, *The Holocaust Kingdom, A Memoire*, UAS: Holocaust Library New York, 1978, p. 211.

14   Samuel D. Kassow, 'Documenting Catastrophe, the Ringelblum Archive and the Warsaw Ghetto', in Norman J. W. Goda (editor), *Jewish Histories of the Holocaust, New Transitional Approaches*, Berghahn New-York, 2014, p. 173.

15   Emmanuel Ringelblum, *Last Writings, January 1943-April 1944*, p. 9.

16   Maria Delaperrière, 'Testimony as a Literary Problem', *Teksty Drugie, English Edition, Theory of Literature, Critique, Interpretation: Nonfiction, Reportage and Testimony*, Special Issue, 2, Publishing House of the Institute of Literary Research, 2014, p. 44. According to Delaperrière, an intrinsic characteristic of testifying always involved tension between narration and accepting the testimony as credible.

17   Samuel D. Kassow, 'Documenting Catastrophe, the Ringelblum Archive and the Warsaw Ghetto', 173.

18   Ibid., p. 186.

19   Zygmunt Bauman, *Modernity and the Holocaust*, Bodmin, Cornwall: Polity Press, 2008, p. ix-x.

20   Ibid., p. ix.

21   Samuel D. Kassow, 'Documenting Catastrophe, the Ringelblum Archive and the Warsaw Ghetto', p. 183. There is no doubt that Kassow's approach that stressed Ringelblum's intuitive insight about the importance of chronicling

the present was confirmed quickly as the scale of changes in space, introduced by the Nazis, along with extreme brutality, indicated a pattern rather than random and local savagery.

22 Rachel Auerbach, *Warsaw Testaments Encounters, Actions, Fate 1933–1943*, p. 22.

23 Marian Turski, p. 118.

24 Alexandra Garbarini, 'Diaries, Testimonies, and Jewish Histories of the Holocaust', *Histories of the Holocaust, New Transitional Approaches*, p. 92.

25 Michael Bernard-Donals, *An Introduction to Holocaust Studies*, New Jersey: Upper Saddle River: Pearson Education, 2006. p. 71-73.

26 Henri Lefebvre, p. 110.

27 Ibid., p. 110.

28 Zoë Vania Waxman, locations 345-358. Waxman brings the story of Israel Lichtenstein, a member of *Oneg Shabbat* staff, who had written his last will seven days after deportations from Warsaw started. In this testament he expressed his wish that he and his family be remembered.

29 Chaim Aron Kaplan, *Scroll of Agony: Hebrew Diary of Ch. A. Kaplan Written in the Warsaw Ghetto 1st September 1939 – 4th August 1942*, p. 144.

30 Ibid., p. 144.

31 Ibid., p. 144.

32 Alexandra Garbarini with Emil Kerenji, Jan Lambertz, Avinoam Patt, *Jewish Responses to Persecution: 1938–1940, Documenting Life and Destruction, Holocaust Sources in Context*, Vol. 2, Lanham, USA: AltaMira Press, 2011, p. 438.

33 Alexandra Garbarini, *Numbered Days*, p. 3.

34 Amos Goldberg, *Trauma in First Person, Diary Writing During the Holocaust*, p. 33.

35 David Patterson, *Along the Edge of Annihilation: the collapse and recovery of life in the Holocaust diary*, USA: University of Washington Press, 1999. p. 39. Patterson wrote that '... for the diarist the word is a refuge...' but he denotes that it is not only a space where one can flee but it is '... a realm in which he seeks a life.'

36 Alexandra Garbarini, *Numbered Days*, p. 115-116.

37 Ibid., p. 117.

38 Boaz Neumann, p. 232.

39 Ibid., p. 235, 237.

40 Ibid., p. 243.

41 Alexandra Garbarini, *Numbered Days*, p. 117. Garbarini's example of what Ehrlich did in his diary, illustrates that not only had he become sensitive to changes in the language but he used old 'cultural building blocks' in order to parallelly place the universe of Theresienstadt in the diary, in a deciphered manner. Yet, this achieved the opposite as it exposed the abnormality of Theresienstadt by using language in its old cultural order.

42 Rachel L. Einwohner, p. 424. Without going into the question of intentionalism versus functionalism, Einwohner explained that Jews had drawn their conclusions mostly from what they experienced locally. That is the reason why Jews in Vilnius could understand more quickly that murderous German intents against Jews were global and not local. In contrast, in Warsaw as well as Łódź, things did not automatically suggest that there was going to be categorical annihilation of Jews.

43 David Wdowinski, p. 76-77.

44 Zoë Vania Waxman, location 96.

45 Zivia Lubetkin, the Eichmann Trial, Minutes of Session 25, Wednesday, May 3,1961, District Court Jerusalem, ŻZW - Żydowski Związek Wojskowy, Jewish Military Union, The Warsaw Ghetto Uprising, Biographies, Questionnaires, Testimonies, 1961-2001, file 70 (9/7 - B), Criminal Record 40/61, (Hebrew), Jabotinsky Institute, p. 96.

46 Alexandra Garbarini, *Numbered Days*, p. 7-8. Garbarini relied on her evaluation based on the English version of Yisrael Gutman's book, *The Jews of Warsaw 1939-1943, Ghetto – Underground – Uprising*, Indiana University Press, 1989.
    See Auerbach's remarks earlier, *Warsaw Testaments Encounters, Actions, Fate 1933–1943*, p. 22, where she emphasized that only in retrospect could cultural activism be regarded as standing up to the Nazis.

47 Esther Farbstein 'Diaries and Memoirs as a Historical Source - The Diary and Memoir of a Rabbi at the 'Konin House of Bondage', Shoah Resource Center, The International School for Holocaust Studies, p. 8. https://www.yadvashem.org/odot_pdf/Microsoft%20Word%20-%203134.pdf accessed 6.7.2019. Their testimony was given to the Ringelblum archive team and was included in a report sent to the Polish government in exile in London. Michael Podchlebnik survived the war, testified at the Eichmann trial and was interviewed for Claude Lanzman's movie, *Shoah*. See: Claude Lanzman, *Shoah, The Complete Text of the Acclaimed Holocaust Film*, USA : Da Capo Press, 1995, p. 67-68.

48 Zivia Lubetkin, p. 31.

49 Amos Goldberg, *Trauma in First Person, Diary Writing During the Holocaust*, p. 57.

50 Amos Goldberg, *Trauma in First Person, Diary Writing during the Holocaust*, (Hebrew), p. 119.

51 Reuven Feldschuh (Ben-Shem), *Deciphered Diary*, pic. 493-4.

52 Amos Goldberg, *Trauma in First Person, Diary Writing During the Holocaust*, p. 119.

53 Ibid., p. 131.

54 David Patterson, p. 40.

55 Colin Davis, *Traces of War: Interpreting Ethics and Trauma in Twentieth-century French Writing*, Liverpool: Liverpool University Press, 2018, p. 198.

246   *Emanuel Ringelblum and Reuven Ben-Shem's War Writings*

56   Amos Goldberg, *Trauma in First Person, Diary Writing during the Holocaust*, (Hebrew), p. 43

57   Ibid., p. 42-43.

58   Salek (Calel) Perehodnik, p. 11.

59   Alexandra Garbarini, *Numbered Days*, p. 143.

60   David G. Roskies, 'Wartime Victim Writing in Eastern Europe', in Alan Rosen (editor), *Literature of the Holocaust*, USA: Cambridge University Press, 2013, p. 27.

61   Avraham Lewin, *From the Notebook of the Yehudiya Teacher: The Warsaw Ghetto, April 1942-January 1943*, Tel-Aviv: Ghetto Fighter's House and Hakibbutz Hameuchad Publishing House Ltd., (Hebrew), 1969, p. 102.

62   Maria Delaperrière, p. 51-2. Like Goldberg, Delaperrière denotes the different uses of pronouns such as 'I', 'we', etc., to signify the writer. Her study of Gustaw Herling-Grudzinski, written after he was released from a Soviet work camp could correspond to Holocaust narratives as they too expose human mechanisms of coping with experiences through writing. Delaperrière writes that the use of third person pronouns in those texts could be regarded as the writer's attempt to distance himself from the event he was writing about and regain dignity.

63   Avraham Lewin, p. 122. Between September 6 -12, 1942, the last phase of the Displacement Action also known as the 'the cauldron' took place.

64   Ibid., p. 51. This entry from May 25 1942 discusses an event in Łódź when children who were sick and had intellectual disabilities were hunted down and murdered.

65   Reuven Feldschuh (Ben-Shem), *Deciphered Diary*, pic. 247.

66   Ibid., pic. 247

67   Ibid., pic. 247

68   Ibid., pic. 247

69   Elie Wiesel, *Night*, Preface to the New Translation by Elie Wiesel, New York: Hill and Wang, a Division of Farrar, Straus and Giroux, 2006, p. II.

70   Chajka Klinger, *I am Writing These Words to You, The Original Diaries, Będzin 1943*, Israel: Yad-Vashem and Moreshet, 2016, (Hebrew), p. 26-27.

71   Ibid., p. 28.

72   David Welch, Introduction, in Nicholas J. Cull, David Culbert, and David Welch (editors), *Propaganda and Mass Persuasion: A Historical Encyclopedia, 1500 to the Present*, Santa Barbara, Calif.: ABC-CLIO, 2003, p. xvii, 25. The Nazis clung to this genre for their purposes while the Allied Forces refrained from using 'atrocity propaganda' because it was considered unreliable.
See also: Nicholas J. Cull, 'Poland', p. 303. Cull discussed the link between public mistrust in information created after the First World War and how it affected the first news of systematic murder during the Second World War.
See also: Philip M. Taylor, 'Psychological Warfare', in Cull J. Nicholas, Culbert David, and Welch David (editors), *Propaganda and Mass Persuasion: A*

Historical Encyclopedia, 1500 to the Present, Santa Barbara, Calif.: ABC-CLIO, 2003, p. 326.

73 Alexandra Garbarini, 'Document Volumes and the Status of Victim Testimony in the Era of the First World War and Its Aftermath', paragraph 4. Garbarini, concluded that Holocaust testimonial literature was not in fact that unusual and particularly Jewish. Rather it was part of the legacy of efforts to document mass violence similar to what has been done in document volumes which sought to record atrocities, such as James Bryce and Arnold Toynbee's *The Treatment of Armenians in the Ottoman Empire 1915-1916* and the Comité des Délégations Juives, *Les Pogromes en Ukraine sous les gouvernements ukrainiens (1917-1920)*.

74 Ibid., paragraphs 27.

75 Boaz Cohen, 'Holocaust Testimonies and Historical Writing, Debates, Innovations, and Problems in the Early Postwar Period', *Yad-Vashem Studies*, Vol. 45:2 (2017) pp. 159-183, p. 159-160.
    See also: David Engel, *Historians of the Jews and the Holocaust*, p. 127.

76 Sybille Krämer, 'Epistemic Dependence and Trust, On Witnessing in the Third-Second- and First-Person Perspectives', in Sybille Krämer and Sigrid Weigel (editors), *Testimony/Bearing Witness, Epistemology, Ethics, History and Culture*, USA: Rowman & Littlefield, 2017, p. 249. According to Krämer, Coady's research, *'Testimony, a Philosophical Study'*, which proposed regarding testimonies as epistemic sources 'sui generis', changed the approach to testimonies from inferior sources provided that both the person and the contents of his testimony were reliable.

77 Anna Bikont, *The Crime and the Silence, Confronting the Massacre of Jews in Wartime Jedwabne*, USA: Farrar, Straus and Giroux, 2004, p. 241. Prof. Gutman was head of The International Institute for Holocaust Research, and himself a Holocaust survivor. Gutman was referring to testimonies of survivors from Jedwabne who claimed that in one day, July 10, 1941, all the Jews of the city were burned alive in a barn by their Polish neighbors.

78 Ibid., p. 56-58. In a discussion with Helena Datner, Szymon Datner's daughter, Bikont asked her about that publication and the discrepancy between the text in Polish and a different report published in Yiddish by Datner himself in 1946 when he specifically noted that Jedwabne's Jewish population was indeed murdered by their neighbors. Helena asserted that she had known about the murder for years but did not realize the scale of it until Jan Gross's book, *Neighbors* was published. She also mentioned the serious clashes her father had had with the Polish communist authorities.

79 Boaz Cohen, 'Rachel Auerbach, Yad-Vashem and Israeli Holocaust Memory', *Polin: Studies in Polish Jewry, Vol. 20, Making Holocaust Memory*, Gabriel N. Finder, Natalia Aleksuin, Antony Polonsky and Jan Schwarz (editors), Oxford; Portland, Oregon: The Littman Library of Jewish Civilization, 2008, .p. 204-206.

80 David Engel, *Historians of the Jews and the Holocaust*, p. 135.

81 Hannah Arendt, *Eichmann in Jerusalem: A Report on the Banality of Evil*, USA: Penguin Classics, 2006, p. 117-118.

82 Norman Podhoretz, 'Hannah Arendt on Eichmann: A Study in the Perversity of Brilliance', *Commentary*, Vol. 36, No. 3, September 1963, p. 202.

83 Ibid., p. 206.

84 Guy Miron, *From Memorial Community to Research Center, The Leo Baeck Institute, Jerusalem*, Israel: The Leo Baeck Institute, (Hebrew), 2005, p. 54-55. See also: Bruno Bettelheim: 'Eichmann; The System; The Victims', *The New Republic*, June 15, 1963, Vol 148, no, 24, pp. 23-33.

85 Guy Miron, *From Memorial Community to Research Center*, p. 56.

86 Hannah Arendt, *Eichmann in Jerusalem: A Report on the Banality of Evil*, p. 18, 218. Arendt was particularly critical of Gideon Hausner, the prosecutor in the Eichmann trial, because he based his case on testimonies of witnesses who spoke about what happened to them yet the occurrences, according to Arendt, were not connected to Eichmann. On p. 218, Arendt wrote that '... documents clearly showed he (Eichmann) had next to nothing to do with what happened in the east.' Arendt's approach in the book aligns with the attitude prevalent until the 1980s in historical research and was characterized by separating the history of the third Reich from that of its victims.

87 Ibid., p. 209

88 Kasper Risbjerg Eskildsen, 'Inventing the archive: Testimony and virtue in modern historiography', *History of the Human Sciences*, 26 (4), Sage, 2013, p. 12.
See also: Amos Goldberg, 'The Holocaust and History in the Post-Modern Era', *Theory and Criticism*, 40, The Van Leer Jerusalem Institute, 2013, (Hebrew), p. 126. Goldberg cited the historian Dan Stone who claimed that research of the Holocaust was one of the most traditional and followed in the guidelines set by Leopold von Ranke in order to recreate the history as it really was.

89 Annette Wieviorka, *The Era of the Witness*, USA: Cornell University Press, 2006, p. 96-99.

90 Shoshana Felman, 'Education and Crisis, Or the Vicissitudes of Teaching' in Dori Laub M.D and Shoshana Felman, *Testimony, Crises of Witnessing in Literature, Psychoanalysis and History*, USA: Routledge, 1992, p. 5-6.

91 Dori Laub M.D, 'An Event Without A Witness', in Laub Dori M.D & Felman Shoshana, *Testimony, Crises of Witnessing in Literature, Psychoanalysis and History*, USA: Routledge, 1992, p. 82.

92 Dori Laub M.D., 'Bearing Witness, or the Vicissitudes of Listening', in Dori Laub M.D and Shoshana Felman, *Testimony, Crises of Witnessing in Literature, Psychoanalysis and History*, USA: Routledge, 1992, p. 59-63.

93 Saul Friedländer, 'An Integrated History of the Holocaust: Some Methodological Challenges', in Dan Stone (ed), *The Holocaust and Historical*

Methodology, (New York: Berghahn, 2015), especially p. 181-2, 186. Friedländer wrote that, he implemented for the first time a methodology integrating German and Jewish individual testimonies as the foundation of his research in his book *Nazi Germany and the Jews.* Thus, a broader picture was created and one which enabled a better understanding of Nazism and its irrational persecution of Jews.

See also: Wulf Kansteiner, 'Modernist Holocaust Historiography: A dialogue between Saul Friedländer and Hayden White', in Dan Stone (ed), *The Holocaust and Historical Methodology,* p. 22-23.

94 Martin Broszat and Saul Friedländer, 'A Controversy about the Historicization of National Socialism', *New German Critique,* No. 44, *Special Issue on the Historikerstreit* (Spring - Summer, 1988), p. 95. Friedländer asked Broszat further if reservations about Jews were also made about others involved in the war, such as the French for example.

See also: Wulf Kansteiner, p. 223.

95 Saul Friedländer, 'An Integrated History of the Holocaust: Some Methodological Challenges', p. 184.

96 Saul Friedländer, 'Introduction' in Saul Friedländer (editor), *Probing the Limits of Representation : Nazism and the 'Final Solution',* USA: Harvard University Press, 1992, p. 2.

97 Penelope J. Corfield, 'Time and the Historians in the Age of Relativity', *Geschichte und Gesellschaft. Sonderheft,* Vol. 25, Vandenhoeck & Ruprecht (GmbH & Co. KG), 2015, p. 87. Interestingly, the writer of this article created a link between the theory of relativity introduced by Albert Einstein to such development in the field of the humanities.

98 Dan Stone, 'Introduction' in Dan Stone (editor), *The Holocaust and Historical Methodology,* p. 2.

See also: Amos Goldberg, *Trauma in First Person, Diary Writing During the Holocaust,* p. 127, 130. Goldberg argued that Friedlander may be the only historian who tried to bridge the gap between the theoretical and the historical.

99 Emmanuel Ringelblum, *Last Writings, January 1943-April 1944,* p. 19-21. Ringelblum gave a short review of the diaries with which he was familiar and those that, as he said, were sadly out of his reach for various reasons.

100 Omer Bartov, 'Wartime Lies and Other Testimonies Jewish-Christian Relations in Buczacz, 1939–1944', *East European Politics and Societies,* Vol 25, no. 3, Sage, August 2011, p. 489-490.

101 Ibid., p. 489

102 Ibid., p. 487

103 Alexandra Garbarini, 'Diaries, Testimonies, and Jewish Histories of the Holocaust', p. 92.

104 Emmanuel Ringelblum, *Diary and Notes from the Warsaw Ghetto, September 1939 - December 1942,* p. 371.

105 Rachel Auerbach, *Warsaw Testaments: Encounters, Actions, Fate 1933–1943*, p. 70.

106 Ibid., p. 76.

107 Emmanuel Ringelblum, *Diary and Notes from the Warsaw Ghetto*, p. 371. Ringelblum's reflection concerning the role of the *Self-Help* in the ghetto went beyond a recognition of its failure as he wrote that it might be better to invest in saving the elite, a suggestion totally opposing his personal sentiments and beliefs. Rationally, Ringelblum understood that it was not possible to save everyone, but emotionally it went against any humane standards as well as Ringelblum's strong social convictions that each human was valuable in his own right.
See also: Samuel D. Kassow, *Who Will Write Our History?*, p. 142-3.

108 Ibid., p. 143. Kassow ended the discussion on this issue by stating that Ringelblum found comfort in the fact that although most Polish Jews would not survive, the archive would be there to tell their story.

109 Reuven Feldschuh (Ben-Shem), *Deciphered Diary*, pic. 26

110 Ibid., pic. 26.

111 Ibid., pic. 27. Ben-Shem wrote that they remained speechless. After this, the woman called the children, hugged them, and asked for their forgiveness. Ben-Shem's party left placing by the door the parcel of food. Later he heard that the mother and one of the children had died. The other child was cared for by the committee.

112 Victoria Nizan, 'The Role and Value of Diaries in Teaching History – Case Study', *ERD 2017 Education, Reflection, Development*, Fifth Edition, www.FutureAcademy.org.UK, 2018, p. 784.
http://dx.doi.org/10.15405/epsbs.2018.06.93, accessed 1.7.2021.

113 Saul Friedländer, 'An Integrated History of the Holocaust: Some Methodological Challenges', p. 187-8. Friedländer's article relates to adopting such an approach to studies of the Holocaust alone. I wish to broaden this approach to other periods and events because of the additional insights offered by personal accounts.

114 David Engel, *Historians of the Jews and the Holocaust*, p. 26-27. In his book, David Engel discussed the separation of the field of Holocaust research from that of Jewish history, which he opposed. According to Engel, historians of our era should adopt the same attitude implemented by earlier Jewish historians when discussing other disasters. For example, the expulsion from Spain in 1492 was indeed placed in a central position, but it did not become an obstacle in researching Jewish history in contrast to the manner the Holocaust has become. In other words, after the expulsion, historians relating to previous events refrained from weighing them in light of the expulsion. Engel believes that historians of our era should do the same with the Holocaust and it must not cast its shadow backwards.

Endnotes

251

115 Alexandra Garbarini, *Numbered Days*, p. 92.

116 Victoria Nizan, 'The Role and Value of Diaries in Teaching History – Case Study', p. 786.

117 Marian Turski, p. 118.

118 Amos Goldberg, *Trauma in First Person , Diary Writing during the Holocaust*, p. 33.

119 David Engel, *Historians of the Jews and the Holocaust*, p. 112.

120 David Roskies and Naomi Diamant, locations 394-444. Roskies held a discussion about the different approaches to classifying Holocaust literature in libraries as mirroring the changes in attitude to conceptualizing the topic and what might be included in that category. One such example is classification changes introduced by the Library of Congress following the surge in publications concerning the Holocaust.
See also: Beate Müller, 'Trauma, Historiography and Polyphony: Adult Voices in the CJHC's Early Postwar Child Holocaust Testimonies', History and Memory, Vol. 24, No. 2, Indiana University Press, (Fall/Winter 2012), p. 175. As interest in communal and private records grew, it led to democratization of written expression, with a growing appreciation for records produced by ordinary people. This trend of democratization was not unique only to Jews but followed a tradition in Polish social sciences.

121 Alexandra Garbarini, *Numbered Days*, p. 11. Garbarini gave the example of Etty Hillesum, whose writing style changed from an intimate portrait of her life, probably influenced by *Augustine's confessions* into what is referred to as 'journalistic' because her focus was on the external events. Conversely, Goldberg explained the transition from the personal to communal occurred because of the invasive nature of external events into one's life.

122 Ibid., p. xi-xii. It is worthwhile addressing Garbarini's book where she provided an extensive analysis of motives which have driven people to write.

123 Adolf – Abraham Berman, *Where Fate Destined Me to Be, with the Jews of Warsaw, 1939-1942*, Israel: Hakibbutz Hameuhad and Lohamei Haghetaot (Ghetto Fighters' House), 1977, p. 9-10. Berman's wife, Batia, is an interesting case as she kept a diary before the war but in the ghetto she stopped. She resumed writing only on May 5, 1944 and she focused of describing their clandestine activities on the Aryan side.

124 Omer Bartov, *The Ringelblum Archive as the Earliest Historiography of the Holocaust and its Impact on Research*, November 5, 2020, hosted by European Network Remembrance and Solidarity, https://www.youtube.com/watch?v=_PEG7QII2cw&t=2287s, accessed: 5.11.2020.

125 Nora Strejilevich, 'Beyond the Language of Truth', *Human Rights Quarterly*, Vol. 28, No. 3, The Johns Hopkins University Press, August 2006, p .707. Strejilevich's discussion focuses on the inherent incapacity of testimonials to represent a truth in the sense that historians expect. This is due to their narrative characteristics, which automatically render them into a form of interpretation.

126 Wulf Kansteiner, 'Success, Truth, and Modernism in Holocaust Historio-graphy: Reading Saul Friedländer Thirty-Five Years after the Publication of 'Metahistory", *History and Theory*, Vol. 48, No. 2, Theme Issue 47: Historical Representation and Historical Truth, Wiley for Wesleyan University, May, 2009 p. 52.

127 Omer Bartov, *Genocide from Below: Rewriting the Holocaust as First-Person Local History*, Discussion with Jan Burzlaff, December 9, 2020, The Holocaust Studies Program at Western Galilee College.

128 Omer Bartov, *Anatomy of a Genocide: The Life and Death of a Town Called Buczacz*, New York: Simon & Schuster, January 23, 2018, Kindle edition, p. 259.

CHAPTER IV

1 Reinhard Heydrich, Yad-Vashem. https://www.yadvashem.org/odot_pdf/ Microsoft%20Word%20-%206366.pdf, accessed 8.5.2019. Heydrich was head of the Nazi Security Police (SIPO), the Security Service (SD), and the Reich Security Main Office (Reichssicherheitshauptamt, RSHA), p. 2.

2 Jacek Leociak, 'Topography and Communication', p. 55. In the General Government, Jews were ordered to wear an armband while in the territories officially annexed to Germany, the Reichsgau Wartheland (also: Warthegau), Jews were required to wear a yellow badge that was sewn on their clothes.

3 Yisrael Gutman, *The Jews of Warsaw 1939-1943, Ghetto – Underground - Uprising*, Jerusalem: Yad-Vashem, (Hebrew), 2011, p. 75-77. According to Gutman, when Czerniaków and other representatives from the Jewish Council of Warsaw visited Dr. Arlt in Krakow, the latter stated that marking the Jews was meant to warn German soldiers off fancying Jewish girls and thus jeopardizing German racial laws.

4 Emmanuel Ringelblum, *Diary and Notes from the Warsaw Ghetto*, p. 80. Ringelblum gave an example of attempted negotiations conducted by Dr. Alten, head of the Jewish Council in Lublin. He tried to convince the Germans to sew the badge only in the front instead of also in the back (these requirements were unique to this area). Ringelblum reported that when the Germans referred to the badge as the badge of shame, Dr. Alten said it was the badge of honor. As a result, he was imprisoned for three days.

5 Victor Klemperer, *I Shall Bear Witness, The Diaries of Victor Klemperer, 1933-1941*, London: Phoenix Paperback, Orion House, 1999, p. 11. Klemperer, who wrote a diary during most of his adulthood, mentioned the Middle Ages on March 30, 1933, two days before the Nazi boycotted Jewish businesses. He wrote that the atmosphere in Germany resembled a pogrom in the heart of the Middle Ages or Tsarist Russia. A day later, he noted that the streets were full of yellow notices and guards. All these evoked memories of a past that he had never experienced personally, yet it was part of Jewish collective memory

which functioned as fulcrum, a reference which was supposed to prepare the individual and the entire community for a 'familiar' pattern of events. Thus, the words 'pogrom' and 'Middle Ages' conveyed the idea that the events had chaotic characteristics. Still, because pogroms were incited by the government, it was assumed that Germany being a state of law, would not continue to spur riots of this sort. The notion of the Middle Ages was frightening but it also contained the hope that such deterioration would be stopped.

6   Jacek Leociak, 'Topography and Communication', p. 55. According to Leociak, in the Middle Ages, the marking of Jews usually preceded the decree to confine Jew to ghettoes.

7   Hannah Johnson and Nina Caputo, 'The Middle Ages and The Holocaust: Medieval Anti-Judaism in The Crucible of Modern Thought', *Postmedieval: A Journal of Medieval Cultural Studies*, Volume 5, Issue 3, Macmillan Publishers, September 2014, p. 270. According to the researchers, comparisons between Nazi Germany and the Middle Ages and the use of the term 'medieval' signified mainly a psychological and emotional condition unrelated to time and space. In the Middle Ages Jews could find references to historical and ideological processes that they felt were unprecedented.
See also: Max Weinreich, p. 93. Weinreich claimed that the Nazis had deliberately used old terminology such as the word 'ghetto' to convey the message to the outside world that the ghettos of the present were reinstating the ghetto of the Middle Ages whereas in reality the new ones were utterly different.

8   Zygmunt Bauman, p. 72. As stated by Bauman, it was the scientific approach to race that allowed rendering traditional antipathies towards Jews into 'an exercise in sanitation.' That meant, that Jews were the bearers of an 'ineradicable vice', something that was inseparable as well as incurable.

9   Emmanuel Levinas, *Difficult Freedom, Essays on Judaism*, Baltimore: The Johns Hopkins University Press, 1990, p. 153. French Jewish prisoners were separated from their French comrades because they were Jewish, but they were kept alive, because they were French soldiers. In his book, Levinas discussed his experiences in the Jewish prisoner of war camp in Germany and alluded to the sensation of being stripped off his human nature by the look of the other, the German guards as well as the women and children who used to pass near the camp and stare at them.

10   Emmanuel Ringelblum, *Diary and Notes from the Warsaw Ghetto*, p. 44. Here Ringelblum reported about one in numerous cases of sheer abuse. On December 28, a Thursday, tram No. 4 travelling to Praga was stopped, twenty-five Jews were taken out, brought to the castle, ordered to undress and lie on the ground like dogs.

11   Ibid., p. 76.

12   Barbara Engelking and Jacek Leociak, 'Chronology: September 1939-May 1943', p. 37.

13 Jacek Leociak , 'Boundaries of the Warsaw Ghetto', p. 53-54. Leociak brought Apolinary Hartglas's (1883 – 1953) testimony who was present at the meeting. Hartglas wrote that Neumann-Neurode seemed surprised and said he did not give such an order. However, after speaking to the gestapo, he retracted and said it was a misunderstanding yet claimed there was nothing to worry about for now.

14 Ibid., p. 56-57. Plans to erect a ghetto began officially on January 18, 1940, when Waldemar Schön was appointed head of the Resettlement Division of the Warsaw District. This venture stopped in March 1940, apparently, because of the plan to set up a Jewish reserve in the area of Lublin. Yet, some streets in Warsaw were barbed wired while Czerniaków received orders to build walls around an area to which the German referred as the region 'threatened by epidemic' (Seuchensperrgebiet).
See also: Diana Plotkin, 'Smuggling in the Ghetto, Survivors accounts from Warsaw, Łódź and Kraków Ghettoes', in Eric J. Sterling (editor), *Life in the Ghettos During the Holocaust*, USA: Syracuse University Press, 2005, p. 85-86. Plotkin quoted Gutman on this issue. This information is based on the report presented by Jürgen Stroop (1895–1952), SS-Gruppenführer and Generalleutnant (head of police) in Warsaw and the man who suppressed the Warsaw ghetto uprising in 1943.

15 Emmanuel Ringelblum, *Diary and Notes from the Warsaw Ghetto*, p. 93.
See also: Barbara Engelking and Jacek Leociak, 'Chronology: September 1939-May 1943', p. 38.

16 Emmanuel Ringelblum, *Diary and Notes from the Warsaw Ghetto*, p. 125

17 Ibid., p. 127. Such remarks show that even for people like Ringelblum, it was hard to understand what was going on.

18 Adam Czerniaków, *The Warsaw Diary of Adam Czerniaków, Prelude to Doom*, Chicago: Ivan R. Dee, Publisher, 1999, p. 135-136. Czerniaków noted in 2.4.1940, that he had to ask for permission to get a loan from the bank, 160,000 zlotys in order to pay for the wall.

19 Andrew Charlesworth, 'The Topography of Genocide', in Dan Stone (editor), *The Historiography of the Holocaust*, USA: Palgrave Macmillan, 2004, p. 241.

20 Yisrael Gutman, *The Jews of Warsaw 1939-1943, Ghetto – Underground – Uprising*, (Hebrew), p. 106.

21 Agnieszka Kajczyk, "Bridge of Sighs' of the biggest Ghetto in Europe', Jewish Historical Institute, https://www.jhi.pl/en/articles/bridge-of-sighs-of-the-biggest-ghetto-in-europe,249, accessed 8.3.2021.

22 Emmanuel Ringelblum, *Diary and Notes from the Warsaw Ghetto*, p. 164.

23 Volksdeutsche, Yad-Vashem, https://www.yadvashem.org/odot_pdf/Microsoft%20Word%20-%206345.pdf. Accessed 9.2.2021. Volksdeutsche is a Nazi term, literally meaning 'German-folk,' used to refer to ethnic Germans, living outside of Germany.

Endnotes

24   Emmanuel Ringelblum, *Diary and Notes from the Warsaw Ghetto*, p. 166.

25   Ibid., p. 167.

26   Ibid., p. 169.

27   Sebastian Rejak and Elżbieta Frister (editors), *Inferno of Choices, Poles and the Holocaust*, Warsaw: Oficyna Wydawnicza RYTM, 2012, p. 20.

28   Nachman Blumental and Josef Kermish, *Resistance and Revolt in the Warsaw Ghetto, A Documentary History*, Vol. 5, Jerusalem: Yad-Vashem, 1965, p. 355. The writers added that the number of refugees was so high that in some of the "points", like on Muranowska 5 for example, there were 300 people living in one hall.

29   Reuven Feldschuh (Ben-Shem), *Deciphered* Diary, pic. 33.

30   Emmanuel Ringelblum, *Diary and Notes from the Warsaw Ghetto*, p. 155, 164. The streets were inundated with messages for exchanging flats.

31   Ibid., p. 166.

32   Ibid., p. 164.

33   Noemi Szac Wajnkranc, *Gone with The Fire, Notes about the Warsaw Ghetto written in Hiding by Noemi Szac Wajnkranc*, Jerusalem, Yad-Vashem, 2003, p. 25.

34   Emmanuel Ringelblum, *Diary and Notes from the Warsaw Ghetto*, p. 179.

35   Ibid., p. 186-187.

36   Ibid., p. 186-190. Ringelblum wrote about other phenomena such as sheer abuse, but I have chosen not to relate to these here as they do not automatically belong to the current discussion.

37   Raul Hilberg, 'The Ghetto as A Form of Government', *The Annals of the American Academy of Political and Social Science*, Vol. 450 ,Reflections on the Holocaust: Historical, Philosophical, and Educational Dimensions, Sage, Jul., 1980, p. 101-102. Hilberg addressed the difficult position of the *Judenrat* who were expected to carry out different tasks required of them and yet, each of these needed the approval of the Nazis.

38   Chaim Aron Kaplan, *Scroll of Agony: Hebrew Diary of Ch. A. Kaplan Written in the Warsaw Ghetto 1st September 1939 – 4th August 1942*, p. 390.

39   Ibid., p. 391-392. Kaplan was alluding to the fact that indeed the Germans were very particular in referring to the Jewish ghetto by the euphemism 'a Jewish quarter' and that '... this time too they lied.'

40   Zivia Lubetkin, p. 11. Zivia Lubetkin's testimony at the Eichmann trial: one of the leaders of the Jewish Combat Organization (ŻOB) and the only woman in the High Command of the Warsaw underground, expressed the same notion of surprise in her testimony.

41   Hannah Arendt, *Essays in Understanding, 1930-1954*, p. 239-240.

42   Barbara Engelking, 'The Inhabitants of the Ghetto: Demographic Data', p. 49. Engelking pointed out that the numbers according to Tatiana Bernstein and Adam Rutkowski were higher.

43   Jacek Leociak, 'Topography and Communications', p. 96-98. Leociak presented the division of the ghetto in a different way.

44 Ibid., p. 97. Leociak specified that family members were 'illegal' and therefore hunted down.

45 Dan Michman, *The Emergence of Jewish Ghettos During The Holocaust*, USA: Cambridge University Press and Yad-Vashem, 2014, p. 87-89.

46 Ibid., p. 149.

47 Emmanuel Ringelblum, *Diary and Notes from the Warsaw Ghetto*, p. 76 (February 1940), p. 96 (March 1940), 109, 141. These references are but a few examples where Ringelblum documented broad daylight robbery from Jews.

48 Havi Dreifuss, Jewish Responses to the Holocaust, Lecture: *Warsaw Ghetto, the End, April 1942-June 1943*, The Emil A. and Jenny Fish Center for Holocaust & Genocide Studies, Yeshiva University, accessed, 18.4.2021. Dreifuss stated that as of April 18, 1942, the Germans entered the ghetto almost every night. See also: Emmanuel Ringelblum, *Diary and Notes from the Warsaw Ghetto*, p. 354-356, 358-362. Ringelblum also pointed out that as of April 18, 1942, the atmosphere in the ghetto changed and that almost every political activity that until then had been carried out relatively in the open, stopped.

49 Dan Michman, p. 79. According to Michman, the terms ghetto and 'Jewish Residential Quarter' were used as synonyms.

50 Max Weinreich, p. 90-94.
See also: Dan Michman, p. 87. Michman used the same source as Weinreich, a passage from Peter Heinz Seraphim lecture given in March 1941, which maintained that there should be no contact between Jews and non-Jews .

51 Raul Hilberg, p. 98.

52 Reuven Feldschuh (Ben-Shem), *Deciphered Diary*, pic. 11.

53 Emmanuel Ringelblum, *Diary and Notes from the Warsaw Ghetto*, p. 172.

54 Ibid., p. 258.
For a comprehensive review of the term ghetto and the reasons for its establishment during the second World War, see Dan Michman, p. 61-89.

55 Anne Kelly Knowles; Tim Cole; Alberto Giordano (eds.), *Geographies of the Holocaust* (The Spatial Humanities),), Indiana University Press, 2014, location 67.

56 Ibid., location 155.

57 Emmanuel *Diary and Notes from the Warsaw Ghetto*, p. 199.

58 Ibid., p. 258, 296.

59 Max Weinreich, p. 76. According to Weinreich, the literature linking Judaism to bolshevism '... took it for granted that bolshevism was simply another name for Judaism.'

60 Emmanuel Ringelblum, *Diary and Notes from the Warsaw Ghetto*, p. 28.

61 Reuven Feldschuh (Ben-Shem), *Deciphered Diary*, pic. 8.

62 Ibid., pic. 195-196.

63 Emmanuel Ringelblum, *Diary and Notes from the Warsaw Ghetto*, p. 25.

64 Ibid., p. 65.

65 Ibid., p. 30.

Endnotes 257

66 Lea Prais, p. 97.
67 Ibid., p. 77-79. Prais claims there was inconsistency between the reports provided by Erich Koch, the governor of eastern Prussia, and Bezirk Zichenau with regard to the reality because he was interested in banishing the Jews while this was against orders issued by Göring banning deportations to the General Government. In other words, this is one example of a personal initiative to target the Jewish population against orders from above. Yet, the rationale was not motivated by a concern about the wellbeing of the refugees but a desire to avoid the pandemonium that such displacements created in the General Government.
68 Ibid., p. 67-68.
69 Ibid., p. 71. Prais wrote that both of Himmler's plans, November-December 1939 and January-February 1940, specified that all Jews had to be expelled. In addition to them, they also included Poles who settled in those areas after 1919, as well as Polish hostile elements, particularly those from Poznań, south and east Prussia, and east upper Silesia.
70 Ibid., p. 79
71 Ibid., p. 80-81.
72 Emmanuel Ringelblum, *Diary and Notes from the Warsaw Ghetto*, p. 11, 15, 18. Ringelblum reported more information from Serock.
73 Mezdelewski Arie, testimony, images\moreshet\ (manuscript)\D.2.164-testimonies.pdf., Yad Yaari Research & Documentation Center, (Yiddish & Hebrew). https://www.infocenters.co.il/yadyaari/notebook_ext.asp?book=143593&lang=heb&site=yadyaari
74 Emmanuel Ringelblum, *Diary and Notes from the Warsaw Ghetto*, p. 14, 20, 23.
75 Ibid., p. 20.
76 Ibid., p. 97.
77 Ibid., p. 62. In 7-9 January 1940 Ringelblum wrote that in the vicinity of Mordy, Losice and Siedlce, there were also Polish refugees from Pomerania who were living under severe conditions.
See also: Ibid., p. 15. Ringelblum mentioned that there were about 50,000 Polish refugees from Poznan in Warsaw.
78 Lea Prais, p. 79, 95. According to Prais, the policy of deportations created chaos as many of those operations were uncoordinated, and in some cases, against orders.
79 Emmanuel Ringelblum, *Diary and Notes from the Warsaw Ghetto*, p. 104.
80 Lea Prais, p. 311.
81 Emmanuel Ringelblum, *Diary and Notes from the Warsaw Ghetto*, p. 229.
82 Ibid., p. 316.
83 Reuven Feldschuh (Ben-Shem), *Deciphered Diary*, pic. 127.
84 Ibid., pic. 130.
85 Ibid., pic. 131.

86 Martin Gumpert, The Physicians of Warsaw', *The American Scholar*, Vol. 18, No. 3, The Phi Beta Kappa Society, Summer 1949, p. 289.

87 Lea Prais, p. 312-330.

88 Samuel D. Kassow, *Who Will Write Our History?*, p. 340-341.

89 Ibid., p. 339. 'Wild' and 'legal' were terms referring to the status of the remaining Jews in the ghetto. The 'legal' were those who were granted a number from the German authorities that provided them with work, housing, and some food. The 'wild' - those without numbers, were denied everything. Among them were many women and children who had evaded deportations for the time being.

90 Havi Dreifuss (Ben-Sasson), *Warsaw Ghetto – The End, April 1942-June 1943*, Jerusalem: Yad-Vashem, 2017, (Hebrew), p. 143.

91 Ibid., p. 254.

92 Henryk Krzepicki, Interview by institute assistant, Luba Melchior, Polish Research Institute at Lund University, Sweden. Protocol No. 83, January 5, 1946, https://www.alvin-portal.org/alvin/attachment/document/alvin-record:101164/ATTACHMENT-0011.pdf, accessed 9.4.2021.

93 Reuven Feldschuh (Ben-Shem), *Deciphered* Diary, pic. 497.

94 Henryk Krzepicki, https://www.alvin-portal.org/alvin/attachment/document/alvin-record:101164/ATTACHMENT-0011.pdf

95 Kelvin E. Y. Low, 'Presenting the Self, the Social Body and the Olfactory: Managing Smells in Everyday Life Experiences', *Sociological Perspectives*, Vol. 49, Issue 4, pp. 607-631, Pacific Sociological Association, Sage, 2006, p. 613.

96 Reuven Feldschuh (Ben-Shem), *Deciphered* Diary, pic. 507.

97 Ibid., pic 497.

98 Havi Dreifuss (Ben-Sasson), *Warsaw Ghetto – The End, April 1942-June 1943*, p. 176. Walter Caspar Többens was a Nazi German textile manufacturer.

99 Ibid., p. 176

100 Wolf Gruner, *Jewish Forced Labor Under the Nazis: Economic Needs and Racial Aims, 1938-1944*, Cambridge University Press, 2006, p, 263. According to Gruner, replacing Jewish workers with non-Jews was impossible in certain professions as these were almost exclusively Jews' expertise.

101 Philip Friedman, 'The Jewish Ghettos of the Nazi Era', *Jewish Social Studies*, Vol. 16, No. 1, Indiana University Press, 1954, p. 76. Friedman, one of the pioneers in Holocaust research and a survivor himself, wrote that, in an address in Lwów (April 1, 1942), Ludwig Fischer, Warsaw's Governor, and Hans Frank, the Governor General, said that ghettoization was a means to exterminate Jews by starvation.

102 Yisrael Gutman, *The Jews of Warsaw 1939-1943, Ghetto – Underground - Uprising*, (Hebrew), p. 152.
See also: Havi Dreifuss (Ben-Sasson), *Warsaw Ghetto – The End, April 1942-June 1943*, p. 62. Dreifuss explained that black-market trade was much more profitable, which was why people preferred to try their luck there.

Endnotes 259

103 Yisrael Gutman, *The Jews of Warsaw 1939-1943, Ghetto – Underground – Uprising*, (Hebrew), p. 158. The numbers Gutman provided were 70,000 shop employees, 60,000 men and 10,000 women.
104 Havi Dreifuss (Ben-Sasson), *Warsaw Ghetto – The End, April 1942-June 1943*, p. 173-174.
105 Ibid., p. 177-178.
106 Ibid., p. 356-366. Dreifuss presented Többens's different strategies to convince Jews to voluntarily be evicted to camps in Lublin.
107 Wolf Gruner, p. 271.

CHAPTER V

1 Emmanuel Ringelblum, *Diary and Notes from the Warsaw Ghetto*, p. 243. According to Ringelblum, the urge to write was so intense people wrote in labor camps too.
2 Samuel D. Kassow, *Who Will Write Our History?*, p. 112. Here Kassow specifies Ringelblum's various professional contacts.
3 Emmanuel Ringelblum, *Last Writings, January 1943-April 1944*, p. 4.
4 Ibid., p. 19.
5 Ibid., p. 21. His observation is important as it sheds light on the unavailability of many people, who, at that stage, were experiencing chaos that prevented them from writing.
6 Ibid., p. 21.
7 Emmanuel Ringelblum, *Diary and Notes from the Warsaw Ghetto*, p. 37.
8 Emmanuel Ringelblum, *Last Writings, January 1943-April 1944*, p. 38.
9 Emmanuel Ringelblum, *Diary and Notes from the Warsaw Ghetto*, p. 37. See also: Samuel D. Kassow, *Who Will Write Our History?*, p. 166-167, 169. When the war broke out, Shimon Huberband, (1909-1942) lived in Piotrków Trybunalski. At first, his family escaped to the village of Sulejow where Huberband's wife and children were killed in a German bombardment. Huberband moved to Warsaw in 1940 and Ringelblum helped him to find employment at the *Aleynhilf (Self-Help)*. In addition, Huberband became one of the first to participate in *Oneg Shabbat* and according to Kassow, he was 'indispensable' especially in documenting religious life in the ghetto. When deportations began, Huberband worked at Emil Weitz's brush makers shop from where he was deported to Treblinka in August 1942.
10 Emmanuel Ringelblum, *Last Writings, January 1943-April 1944*, p.4.
11 Ibid., p. 3.
12 Nechama Tec, 'Unheralded Historian: Emmanuel Ringelblum', in *Yalkut Moreshet*, periodical 75, Israel: Moreshet, April 2003, (Hebrew), p. 71, 75. According to Tec, the reason Ringelblum tried to refrain later from using coded language had to do with reviewing his notes and realizing that a future historian may find them incomprehensible. Along with the growing sensation

that he might not survive the war and others would deal with his notes, Ringelblum avoided further codification.

13 Weichert Michael (Michał), YIVO Encyclopedia. https://yivoencyclopedia.org/article.aspx/Weichert_Micha%C5%82, accessed 19.9.2019. Michael Weichert, 1890-1967, a theater director, historian, critic, and communal activist. Between 1940-1942, he headed the Jewish Social *Self-Help* in Warsaw. In July 1942, he received permission from the Nazis to continue *self-help* activities under a new name, Jewish Aid Office, until December 1942. In March 1943 he was allowed to establish the same body in Kraków, but his activities there led to accusations of collaboration with the Nazis. In 1946, he was tried in Poland and exonerated. He immigrated to Israel in 1958.

See also: David Engel, 'Who is a Collaborator?: The Trials of Michał Weichert', in, *The Holocaust, History and Memory, Jubilee book in Honor of Israel Gutman*, Jerusalem: Yad-Vashem, 2002, p. 3, 21-22. Engel examined this case and concluded that Weichert was a borderline case in terms of cooperation. After Weichert's exoneration in a Polish court, he agreed to be tried by Jews who found him guilty in a verdict issued on December 19, 1949, in Poland. According to Engel, this discrepancy exposed the margins of how Jews and Poles interpreted collaboration. Conversely, Weichert refusal to adhere and attempt to prove that he had not cooperated with Germans suggests that his activities were in the grey zone, a tactic that may have been adopted by other Jews during the war.

14 Emmanuel Ringelblum, *Diary and Notes from the Warsaw Ghetto*, p. 54.

15 Ibid., Introduction, p. xiv (14). Gutman argued that not only did Ringelblum sense the importance of the hour, but he followed the model of other records Jews had left after disasters such as the book *Yeven Mezulah* (Venice, 1653), describing the course of the Khmelnytsky Uprising in the Polish–Lithuanian Commonwealth from a Jewish perspective.

16 Laura Jockusch, *Collect and Record!*, location, 889.

17 Israel Gutman, 'Emanuel Ringelblum: The Historian and His Era', in Gutman Israel, (editor), *Emanuel Ringelblum: The Historian and his Era*, pp. 78-108, Jerusalem: Yad-Vashem, 2006, (Hebrew), p. 84. Gutman noted that politics in the archive was manifested in the choice of issues to cover and discuss but not in the actual work of recording the whereabouts of Jews in the Warsaw Ghetto.

18 Emmanuel Ringelblum, *Diary and Notes from the Warsaw Ghetto*, p. 367.

19 Ibid., *Last Writings, January 1943-April 1944*, p. 7.

20 Ibid, *Diary and Notes from the Warsaw Ghetto, September 1939 - December 1942*, Introduction, p. xiv (14).

21 Samuel D. Kassow, *Who Will Write Our History?*, p. 214. Kassow argued that closing the ghetto had actually contributed to the creation of such a 'cultural space' because the Nazis paid little attention to Jewish political activities.

Endnotes

22 Emmanuel Ringelblum, *Last Writings, January 1943-April 1944*, p. 22. Translation is from: David G. Roskies (editor), *Voices from the Warsaw Ghetto, Writing Our History*, (translation: Elinor Ronbinson). New Haven and London: Yale University Press, 2019, Kindle edition, Location 1076-1082. The translator used the Yiddish form of the archive name, O[yneg] S[habes], whereas in this book, I chose to use the Hebrew form, *Oneg Shabbat*.

23 Laura Jockusch, *Collect and Record!*, location 924. Jockusch argued that Ringelblum was also aware of the value of documentation because he was confident Nazis would be put on trial and the materials collected serve as evidence.

24 Emmanuel Ringelblum, *Diary and Notes from the Warsaw Ghetto*, p. 393-394.

25 Samuel D. Kassow, *Who Will Write Our History?*, p. 358.

26 *Daily News Bulletin*, JTA News (Jewish Telegraphic Agency), New York: Volume IX, no. 146, Sunday, June 28, 1942, p. 2. The newspaper stated that the broadcast was addressed at Jews in Poland and was repeated on BBC in all European languages every day during the following week. Furthermore, twenty-three British parliament members submitted a resolution to the House of Commons expressing their indignation and promising retribution. The newspaper added that the Government-in-Exile confirmed that information.

27 Emmanuel Ringelblum, *Diary and Notes from the Warsaw Ghetto*, p. 386.

28 Ibid., p. 386.

29 Samuel D. Kassow, *Who Will Write Our History?*, p. 298.

30 Yisrael Gutman, *The Jews of Warsaw 1939-1943, Ghetto – Underground - Uprising*, (Hebrew), p. 429-430. Gutman added that when organized extermination started in Poland itself, the Government-in-Exile continued to withhold the information because they wanted to avoid a direct demand from Poles to help Jews.

31 Emmanuel Ringelblum, *Diary and Notes from the Warsaw Ghetto*, p. 387.

32 Ibid., p. 387.

33 Ibid., p. 387.

34 Ibid., p. 387.

35 Ibid., p. 388

36 Ibid., p. 388

37 Jan Karski, *Story of a Secret State: My Report to the World*, London, Penguin, 2011, Kindle edition, p. 444-445. Szmul Zygielbojm fled Warsaw in December 1939 because he was wanted by the Nazis. Once abroad, he relentlessly worked in order to get politicians in America and Great Britain to do something to help the Jews. In 1942, he was one of two representatives of the Jewish minority in Poland who had seats in the Polish National Council of the Polish Government-in-Exile. Reports brought by Jan Karski, the failure of the Bermuda conference and the failure of the Warsaw Uprising, had pushed him to commit suicide between 11 and 12 May 1943, in the last days of the uprising.

38 Emmanuel Ringelblum, *Diary and Notes from the Warsaw Ghetto*, p. 389.
39 Ibid., p. 389.
40 Ibid., p. 387.
41 Ibid., p. 387.
42 Shlomo Yitzchaki (1040 – 1105), known by the acronym Rashi, a notable French Rabbi who had written a comprehensive commentary on the Talmud and the Bible.
43 Reuven Feldschuh (Ben-Shem), *Manuscript 1*, pic. 2.
44 Ibid., pic. 2.
45 Ibid., pic. 2. Ben-Shem referred to the two times the land of Israel was conquered, the temple in Jerusalem destroyed, and the Jewish people exiled.
46 Ibid., pic. 2. Interestingly, he forbade publication in Yiddish but not in German.
47 Gabriela Spector-Mersel, p. 174. Flattening is the last mechanism among six of narrative selection around which a story evolves. Flattening is reducing the importance of facts, events, and periods in the life history thus reporting them while indicating their insignificance.
48 Alexandra Garbarini, *Numbered Days*, p. 95–128. Garbarini discussed family diaries whose purpose was to create a semblance of family ties in a situation when no such contact was possible. In that respect, Ben-Shem's diary may be, at least partially, considered as an apparent attempt of correspondence with his family in safety.
49 Reuven Feldschuh (Ben-Shem), *Manuscript*, pic. 2.
50 Ibid., pic 2.
51 Reuven Feldschuh (Ben-Shem), *Deciphered Diary*, pic. 698. On April 3, 1943, Ben-Shem wrote with satisfaction that Josima did not know Yiddish at all and as she was supposed to be hidden as a Polish girl at the Sobotka's house, she would be safe. The reason was that she could not be recognized as a Jew as had happened to Rachel (Auerbach) who spoke in Yiddish in her sleep thus exposing her identity to the people with whom she was hiding.
52 Wendy Zierler, 'My Own Special Corner, Sacred, Beloved': The Hebrew Diary of Hava Shapiro (1878-1943), *Hebrew Studies*, 53, National Association of Professors of Hebrew (NAPH), 2012, p. 236. Zierler wrote about the so far only known diary in Hebrew written by a woman where she explained the status of Hebrew. For centuries Hebrew was , a male elite language as it was used only by men and only for religious purposes, thus becoming known as 'father tongue' as opposed to the 'mother tongue', Yiddish. Hebrew was revived only in the nineteenth century and before it became a language for modern use, it was born through conscious and deliberate endeavors to use it in literature.
53 Reuven Feldschuh (Ben-Shem), *Deciphered* Diary, pic. 551.
See also Havi Dreifuss (Ben-Sasson), *Warsaw Ghetto – The End, April 1942-June 1943*, p. 297. Dreifuss wrote that a short period of cultural revival in the

Endnotes 263

ghetto of after the great deportation and which had begun in November 1942, was probably linked to efforts the German had invested in maintaining a seemly routine in the ghetto.

54 Ibid., pic. 29.

55 The house committees were unique to the Warsaw Ghetto, and they dealt with attempts to alleviate the growing social needs of the block residents. For a time, there were more than 2,000 committees where thousands volunteered. From: https://training.ehri-project.eu/jewish-administrations, accessed: October 15, 2020.

56 Reuven Feldschuh (Ben-Shem), *Deciphered Diary*, pic. 29.

57 Ibid., pic. 29.

58 Ibid., pic. 29.

59 Ibid., pic. 29.

60 Ibid., pic. 29.

61 Ibid., pic. 29.

62 Ibid., pic. 29.

63 Barbara Engelking, 'Culture and Entertainment', p. 627. The concert took place on March 15, 1941. Josima, then, 11 years old, played Mozart's Piano Concerto in E-flat major.

64 Reuven Feldschuh (Ben-Shem), pic. 78-79. Ben-Shem was referring to the article published in *Gazeta Żydowska*, March 21, 1941, 'Josima Feldschuh, na nadzwyczajnym koncercie symfonicznym' (Josima Feldschuh, at an extraordinary symphony concert). The newspaper can be found at The Jewish Historical Institute, Warsaw. https://cbj.jhi.pl/documents/791447/3/, accessed, 15.4.2021.

65 Reuven Feldschuh (Ben-Shem), *Deciphered Diary*, pic. 252.

66 The term refers to a week of mourning period in Judaism following the death and burial of first-degree relatives.

67 Reuven Feldschuh (Ben-Shem), *Deciphered Diary*, pic. 324.

68 Gabriela Spector-Mersel, p. 174. Inclusion refers to details one chooses to include in the story and that by their presence, they support the end point of the narrative.

69 Ibid., p. 174. When it is not obvious to begin with, sharpening is a mechanism to emphasized importance in a story.

70 Guy Miron, *To Be a Jew in Nazi Germany, Space and Time*, p. 244 250. Miron suggests that as space was literally more and more out of reach for Jews, in its physical sense as well as time related (experiencing reduced options to plan the future) the past became more significant but also creating a conscious space of awareness to compensate for the lost personal and public spaces.

71 Ruth Ben-Shem, p. 155.

72 Rachel Smitizki, a letter from March 3, 1963, addressed to Reuven Ben-Shem, Jerusalem: Yad-Vashem. Rachel Smitizki was a worker at the Yad-Vashem

archive. She sent him eighty pages which contained pages 271-350 and for which she asked Ben-Shem to confirm the receipt. She added that she thought the diary was outstanding and asked his permission to show one or two pages to Isaac Ramba to include them in texts which were intended to be read at the ceremony commemorating the Warsaw uprising. She stated that she and Dr. Joseph Kermish were working on deciphering his diary and that they needed his help.

73 Reuven Ben-Shem, letter to Joseph Kermish, October 15, 1963, Jerusalem: Yad-Vashem (Hebrew). The Letter was Ben-Shem's reply to Kermish's, September 12, 1963. Ben-Shem expressed his surprise and disappointment that although Kermish announced that the work on the diary was completed, the question of whether it would be published would have to be resolved by the Yad-Vashem board. Ben-Shem stated that he was particularly hurt 'by Kermish's vocabulary, that despite the fact the diary was already prepared,' the Yad-Vashem Board would have to determine '...if the diary was worthy of publication...'.

74 Moshe Kol, a letter from 19 October, 1979, in reply to Ben-Shem's letter, the Ben-Shem family Archive. The letter concerned the publication of his diary. Moshe Kol was the former Minister of Tourism and Ben-Shem's longtime friend. Ben-Shem addressed him with a suggestion to downsize the volume of his diary and publish it. Kol replied that it was impossible to take on such a project as huge sums of money were necessary, money that they did not have.

CHAPTER VI

1 Henri Lefebvre, p. 170.

2 Ibid., p. 170.

3 Ibid., p. 170.

4 Ibid., p. 170.

5 Jacek Leociak, 'Topography and Communications', p. 58. Leociak discussed particularly violent attacks during Easter, 22-29.3.1940, also referred to as the 'Easter Pogrom', when Poles attacked Jews including their property. According to Leociak, the events were inspired by the Germans and the latter took advantage of these events to film and show how they 'stopped' the violence. Later they used these events to justify the establishment of a ghetto claiming it was crucial to protect the Jews from the Poles.

6 Isaiah Trunk, *Judenrat: The Jewish Councils in Eastern Europe Under Nazi Occupation*, USA: University of Nebraska Press, 1996, p. 294. Hans Frank, head of the General Government in Poland, issued an order on October 15th, 1941, that anyone leaving the ghetto would be shot.

7 Chaim Aron Kaplan, *The Continuation of Our Scroll of Agony*, Unpublished Manuscript, Givat Haviva, Notebook 11, 8.10.1941-2.5.1942, (Hebrew), Moreshet, p. 182-183.

Endnotes

8   Emmanuel Ringelblum, *Diary and Notes from the Warsaw Ghetto*, p. 333-334.

9   Reuven Feldschuh (Ben-Shem), *Deciphered Diary*, pic. 211.

10   Ibid., pics. 209-212. In Ben-Shem's deciphered diary, there were a number of inaccuracies. First, he wrote that there were eleven convicted Jews, whereas there were in fact, eight. In addition, he added details that could not be verified, for instance, that one of the women had just given birth to a baby before her execution. Two years before his death, 1978, excerpts of his diary were published in Moreshet: Reuven Ben-Shem, 'Excerpts from Reuven Ben-Shem's Diary, 1941', *The Moreshet Journal* 25, Tel Aviv: Moreshet, April 1978, (Hebrew). This version stated not only that these people had been arrested for not wearing the badge, but that it was a yellow badge, whereas in Warsaw, Jews wore a white armband with a blue Star of David on it. Furthermore, Ben-Shem changed the number of those executed to nine, still inaccurate.

11   Reuven Feldschuh (Ben-Shem), *Deciphered Diary*, pic. 55.

12   Ibid, pic. 55.

13   Emmanuel Ringelblum, *Diary and Notes from the Warsaw Ghetto*, p. 87. On March 6, 1940 Ringelblum noted that Germans were reluctant to behave civilly to Jews because they were afraid of their comrades' reactions. In this entry, he wrote about a certain German who was having a polite conversation with a Jew, but when he saw another German approaching, he raised his voice yelling and cursing the Jew, telling him to get lost.

14   David Engel, 'A Problematic Tradition? Comments on the Political Tendencies and Culture of the Jews of Poland Between the Two World Wars', in Bartal Israel and Gutman Israel (editors), *The Broken Chain, Polish Jewry Through the Ages, Vol. II, Society, Culture, Nationalism)*, Jerusalem: The Zalman Shazar Center, (Hebrew), 2001, p. 649.

15   Jean-Gerard Bursztein, *La Psychanalyse des Nazis -Essai Sur la Destruction de la Civilisation*, Tel-Aviv: Resling Publishers, 2004, (Hebrew), p. 90, 93-94. Bursztein claimed that the process of naming the Jews differently, which preceded labelling them physically, represented what the Nazis themselves may not have conceived then, namely, that the end of Jews must be death. According to Bursztein, the otherness of Jews was expressed in the symbolic order that they represented, the law, since Jews defined themselves in relation to their laws. Because a Jew was the signifier of the law, Jews were attacked. This psychoanalytical approach suggests that in the same manner that the psychotic wanted to get rid of the object of pleasure, social psychosis wanted to get rid of the object that represented restraint and ultimate law.

16   Amos Goldberg, *Trauma in First Person, Diary Writing during the Holocaust*, (Hebrew), p. 142. According to Goldberg, that space would later disappear (in Auschwitz) once the tattooed number became an eternal mark, an integral part of one's body.

17 Ibid., p. 147-148. Goldberg cited the sociologist Erving Goffman who claimed that the act of labeling functions like an invading force into one's intimate private individuality. Goldberg added that according to Lacan, the idea of marking someone disrupts the perpetual movement from signifier to signified thus imposing one classification which prevents desire and action. In other words, the absence of the gap between the signified and the signifier prevents life.

18 Amos Goldberg, 'A Fool or a Prophet: Rubinstein the Warsaw Ghetto Jester', The 2019 J. B. and Maurice C. Shapiro Annual Lecture at the United States Holocaust Memorial Museum 13.3.2019, United States Holocaust Memorial Museum, p. 11. https://www.academia.edu/38809091/A_Fool_or_a_Prophet_Rubinstein_the _Warsaw_Ghetto_Jester, accessed: 7.4.2019.

19 Ibid., p. 14-15.

20 Reuven Feldschuh (Ben-Shem), *Deciphered Diary*, pic. 17.

21 Bernard Goldstein, *Five Years in the Warsaw Ghetto (The Stars Bear Witness)*, Canada: AK Press / Nabat, 2005, p. 77.

22 Havi Dreifuss (Ben-Sasson), *Warsaw Ghetto – The End, April 1942-June 1943*, p. 62.

23 Reuven Feldschuh (Ben-Shem), *Deciphered Diary*, pics. 106-107.

24 Yisrael Gutman, *The Jews of Warsaw 1939-1943, Ghetto – Underground – Uprising*, (Hebrew), p. 211.

25 Emmanuel Ringelblum, *Diary and Notes from the Warsaw Ghetto*, p. 64.

26 Ibid., p. 191.

27 Ibid., p. 197.

28 Yisrael Gutman, *The Jews of Warsaw 1939-1943, Ghetto – Underground – Uprising*, (Hebrew), p. 76.

29 Lena Kuchler - Zilberman, *We Accuse, Children's Testimonies from the Holocaust*, Israel: Sifriat Poalim, 1969, (Hebrew), p. 13. The term 'good looks' or 'Arian' refers to people who looked more Polish than Jewish. For example, Victor, a child from Lena Kuchler's orphanage, testified that his father and many other Jews who looked Polish refrained from wearing the armband despite the risks involved.

30 Katarzyna Person, *Assimilated Jews in the Warsaw Ghetto, 1940-1943*, USA: Syracuse University Press, 2014, p. 26-27. Here Person cited Ludwik Landau's diary, where he noted that on top of other problems created with the armband, Nazi authorities had not finalized legally the question of who was considered a Jew.

31 Adam Czerniaków, p. 114. In his diary, Czerniaków wrote that a whole industry emerged around the armbands and that varied materials, such as rubber, cellulose, etc., were used to meet the demand.

32 Amos Goldberg, 'A Fool or a Prophet: Rubinstein the Warsaw Ghetto Jester', p. 16.

33	Emmanuel Ringelblum, *Diary and Notes from the Warsaw Ghetto*, p. 282. See also: Barbara Engelking, 'Culture and Entertainment', p. 573. Engelking wrote she found no evidence to assert Ringelblum's claim that the theater staged the play 'Ale glajch' based on Rubinstein's character.
34	Amos Goldberg, 'A Fool or a Prophet: Rubinstein the Warsaw Ghetto Jester', p. 17
35	Yisrael Gutman, *The Jews of Warsaw 1939-1943, Ghetto – Underground – Uprising*, (Hebrew), p. 128
36	Genesis, chapter 3, verse 19. http://www.vatican.va/archive/bible/genesis/documents/bible_genesis_en.html accessed 24.5.2019.
37	Zygmunt Bauman, p. 91. According to Bauman, the mere attempt to define a group, suggests that it is targeted for special treatment.
38	Emmanuel Ringelblum, *Diary and Notes from the Warsaw Ghetto*, p. 407.
39	Barbara Engelking, 'The Judenrat', p. 141. The Germans came up with a variety of 'exceptions', mostly translated into creating another form of armband, generally to signify that those wearing them were in a higher position than the rest of those marked by the regular armband. See also: Henryk Bryskier, *The Jews of Warsaw Under The Swastika, A Testimony from The Ghetto Days*, Jerusalem: Yad-Vashem, 2018, (Hebrew), p. 141-145. Bryskier specified twenty different types of armbands that the Nazis in the Warsaw Ghetto invented. These were precious to their owners as they protected them from being kidnapped. Bryskier wrote that at some point, there were so many kinds of armbands that there were not enough colors. See also: Władysław Szlengel, 'Opaski' ('Badges'), a poem, Central Jewish Library, Collection of satiric compositions, The Jewish Historical Institute, Warsaw, ARG I 1240 (Ring. I/526), September, 1941, (Polish). https://cbj.jhi.pl/documents/967862/9/, accessed: 30.5.2019. In this, the author claimed that everybody in the ghetto had a different badge and that people competed over the best badge such as: the deaf, the blind, the midwives, the policemen, etc.
40	Andrzej Żbikowski, Opaski z gwiazdą Dawida - wstęp do Holokaustu, *Najnowsze* 1.12.2016, (Polish). https://opinie.wp.pl/opaski-z-gwiazda-dawida-wstep-do-holokaustu-6126041529271937a, accessed, 3.6.2019. According to Professor Żbikowski, even if Jews did not obey orders, it would be difficult to hide one's identity as neighbors knew who was Jewish and who was not. He added that attempts to hide identity led to extortions (szmalcownictwo) and therefore, were rather unsuccessful.
41	Yisrael Gutman, *The Jews of Warsaw 1939-1943, Ghetto – Underground – Uprising*, (Hebrew), p. 39-41. See also: Jonas Turkow, *There Once Was A Jewish Warsaw*, Tel Aviv: Mifaley Tarbut Vechinuch LTD., 1969, (Hebrew), p. 14. Turkow wrote that there were cases of rape of women in front of their husbands, children and parents.

42 Chaim Aron Kaplan, *Scroll of Agony: Hebrew Diary of Ch. A. Kaplan Written in the Warsaw Ghetto 1st September 1939 – 4th August 1942*, p. 43.
See also: Emmanuel Ringelblum, *Diary and Notes from the Warsaw Ghetto*, p. 10.

43 Yisrael Gutman, *The Jews of Warsaw 1939-1943, Ghetto – Underground – Uprising*, (Hebrew), p. 75

44 Chaim Aron Kaplan, *Scroll of Agony: Hebrew Diary of Ch. A. Kaplan Written in the Warsaw Ghetto 1st September 1939 – 4th August 1942*, p. 40. On October 1, 1939, Kaplan described the ruined city: 'There are streets which are hardly recognizable: they changed completely after the destruction and fires.'

45 Barbara Engelking, 'The Inhabitants of the Ghetto: Demographic Data', p. 48.

46 Chaim Aron Kaplan, *Scroll of Agony: Hebrew Diary of Ch. A. Kaplan Written in the Warsaw Ghetto 1st September 1939 – 4th August 1942*, p. 269.

47 Havi Dreifuss (Ben-Sasson), *'We Polish Jews'?, The Relations between Jews and Poles during the Holocaust – The Jewish Perspective*, Jerusalem: Yad-Vashem, (Hebrew), 2009, p. 165.

48 Havi Dreifuss (Ben-Sasson), *'We Polish Jews?'*, p. 79. Dreifuss discussed the Jewish reactions to Polish violence provoked by the armband. At this stage of the war, she claimed, Jews were careful not to blame the entire Polish society for violence against them.

49 Adolf – Abraham Berman, p. 62.
See also: Chaim Aron Kaplan, *Scroll of Agony: Hebrew Diary of Ch. A. Kaplan Written in the Warsaw Ghetto 1st September 1939 – 4th August 1942*, p. 211. In March 30, 1940, Kaplan wrote that for three days the streets of Warsaw turned into chaos and that Poles (whose identity was not specifically stated) attacked innocent passersby while the so called 'civilized' occupant was watching without interfering.

50 Emmanuel Ringelblum, *Diary and Notes from the Warsaw Ghetto*, p. 19.

51 Ibid., p. 19.

52 Ibid., p. 34. This situation of ignoring German orders changed quite rapidly in the coming months, and punishment for not wearing the armbands became harsher as time passed.

53 Barbara Engelking and Jacek Leociak, 'Chronology', p. 37. This decree was enforced as of 1.12.1939.

54 Emmanuel Ringelblum, *Diary and Notes from the Warsaw Ghetto*, p. 34.

55 Ibid., p. 42.

56 Ibid., p. 42.

57 Ibid., p. 54.

58 Ibid., p. 64

59 Ibid., p. 201. Ringelblum wrote that a man called Baruch was arrested because he was not wearing the armband, and sent to Auschwitz where he died.

60 Ibid. p. 197. The comparison between the behavior of the Polish population to that of the Belgians and French was written on November 29-December

Endnotes

269

2, 1940. According to information Ringelblum had, the yellow badge had already been introduced there, but the decree was cancelled because of pressure introduced by the local populations. As mentioned before, this information was false as the edict to don the Jewish badge was introduced in France and Belgium only in mid-1942, and the local populations did not react against it.

61 Ibid., p. 86. Jews were also kidnapped for forced labor, but in general, they were not sent to Germany but to other parts of Poland.
See also: Chaim Aron Kaplan, *Scroll of Agony: Hebrew Diary of Ch. A. Kaplan Written in the Warsaw Ghetto 1st September 1939 – 4th August 1942*, p. 239.

62 Emmanuel Ringelblum, *Diary and Notes from the Warsaw Ghetto*, p. 212.

63 Blösche Josef, *Holocaust Historical Society.* https://www.holocausthistorical society.org.uk/contents/germanbiographies/josefblosche.html 12.4.2019. Josef Blösche, or 'Frankenstein', was put on trial in Erfurt in April 1969, found guilty and sentenced to death for shooting of about 1,000 Jews in 1943, raping and then killing women in the ghetto and shooting randomly at Jews in the ghetto. From: https://www.Jewishvirtuallibrary.org/josef-bl-ouml-sche, accessed 12.4.2019.

64 Emmanuel Ringelblum, *Diary and Notes from the Warsaw Ghetto*, p. 374, 380.

65 Ibid., p. 374, 380.

66 Reuven Feldschuh (Ben-Shem), *Deciphered Diary*, pic. 181.

67 Adam Czerniaków, p. 365. On 10.6.1942. Czerniaków wrote that he had discussed the issue of 'Frankenstein' with the Gestapo. He did not note how the Gestapo reacted.

68 Emmanuel Ringelblum, *Diary and Notes from the Warsaw Ghetto*, p. 83.

69 Ibid., p. 375.

70 Samuel D. Kassow, *Who Will Write Our History?*, p. 148.

71 Emmanuel Ringelblum, *Diary and Notes from the Warsaw Ghetto*, p. 70.

72 Ibid., p. 70. The numbers Ringelblum wrote were not accurate, 120 prisoners of war were murdered.

73 Ibid., p. 70.

74 Adam Czerniaków, p. 112. On January 28, two days before Ringelblum was attacked, Czerniaków wrote in his diary that teenagers, whom he also called hooligans, had beaten up Jews around the city and that on that day they came to the Community building and broke windows, etc.

75 Yisrael Gutman, *The Jews of Warsaw 1939-1943, Ghetto – Underground – Uprising*, (Hebrew), p. 70. Gutman claimed she was an old Polish woman.
See also: Adam Czerniaków, p. 115. From his diary, it seems that he had already complained about this woman before and that the answer he received did not really indicate that something would be done about her.

76 Emmanuel Ringelblum, *Diary and Notes from the Warsaw Ghetto*, p. 71.

77 Kusociński, Janusz Tadeusz 1907 – 1940, *Polskie radio.* https://www. polskieradio.pl/39/156/Artykul/1023044,Janusz-Kusocinski-nieugiety-na-biezni-i-na-polu-walki, accessed: 24.3.2019. Janusz Tadeusz Kusociński, 1907 – 1940, was a famous Polish athlete. Only a few months after the event Ringelblum described, Kusociński was arrested and on June 21, 1940, executed by the Germans at Mokotów Prison, Warsaw.

78 Emmanuel Ringelblum, *Diary and Notes from the Warsaw Ghetto,* p. 13. See also: Katarzyna Person, p. 26-27. Person wrote that the armband decree was enforced on converts too although, legally, the definition of who could be considered a Jew was accepted in the General Government only in August 1940.

79 Havi Ben-Sasson (Dreifuss), 'Christians in The Ghetto: All Saints' Church, Birth of the Holy Virgin Mary Church, and the Jews of the Warsaw Ghetto', *Yad-Vashem Studies* 31, Jerusalem: Yad-Vashem, 2003, p. 157. The community of converts in Warsaw consisted of about 2,000 people. However, the All Saints Church community adopted a double un-Jewish identity to set themselves apart: a Christian and a Polish national identity.

80 Dr. Israel Milejkowski was a Jewish physician on the staff of the Czyste hospital, and a Zionist activist. He was part of the *Judenrat* ghetto's health department and active in *Jewish Self-Help.*

81 Emmanuel Ringelblum, *Diary and Notes from the Warsaw Ghetto,* p. 206.

82 Ibid., p. 21, 172. These two entries are examples of converts' suicide mentioned by Ringelblum.

83 Ibid., p. 185.

84 Havi Ben-Sasson (Dreifuss), 'Christians in The Ghetto: All Saints' Church, Birth of the Holy Virgin Mary Church, and the Jews of the Warsaw Ghetto', p. 167-172. The overall attitude to converts among Jews was not positive, especially because they set themselves apart from the Jews in the ghetto, and some, including priests, made occasional antisemitic remarks.

85 Dariusz Libionka, 'Antisemitism, Anti-Judaism and the Polish Catholic Clergy during the Second World War, 1939-1945', in Robert Blobaum (editor), *Antisemitism and Its Opponents in Modern Poland,* USA: Cornell University Press, 2005, p. 238. Libionka described efforts made by archbishop Adam Sapieha and Count Adam Roniker, president of the Central Welfare Council (Rada Główna Opiekuńcza) to exempt converts from edicts aimed at Jews. Their attempts were not successful.

86 Emmanuel Ringelblum, *Diary and Notes from the Warsaw Ghetto,* p. 238. Ringelblum wrote that the community prepared armbands for them.

87 Ludwik Hirszfeld, *The Story of One Life: (Rochester Studies in Medical History, 16),* Rochester, USA: University of Rochester Press, 2010, p. 186.

88 Henri Lefebvre, p. 184.

89 Ibid., p. 184.

Mary Douglas, *Purity and Danger, An Analysis of Concepts of Pollution and Taboo*, UK: Taylor & Francis e-Library, 2001, p. 116. Mary Douglas wrote that the body, being complex, could represent any other multifaceted structures. Indeed, marking the body signified that its boundaries could be traversed. In other words, the Jewish symbol altered interactional relationships and transgressed the body's boundaries enabling the destruction of the entire Jewish society.

90   Yisrael Gutman, *The Jews of Warsaw 1939-1943, Ghetto – Underground – Uprising*, (Hebrew), p. 73.

91   Helene Berr, p. 71. Berr wrote that her father had been arrested because his badge was not properly stitched.

92   David Seamon, 'Physical Comminglings: Body, Habit, and Space Transformed Into Place', *The Occupational Therapy Journal of Research*, Volume 22, Sage, Supplement, Winter 2002, DOI: 10.1177/153944920202220S106, p. 43s-44s. Seamon claimed that there was great importance to habits of movement, he referred to them as 'body-subject', because they alleviated uncertainty while allowing the mind to be free enough to continue developing while ordinary actions were conducted almost automatically.

93   Guy Miron, 'Lately, Almost Constantly, Everything Seems Small to Me': The Lived Space of German Jews under the Nazi Regime, *Jewish Social Studies: History, Culture, Society* n.s. 20, no. 1, Fall 2013, p. 142. Miron claimed that in the experience of German Jews, Nazification of spaces created '... an experience of a 'shrinking world,' ... the shrinking of physical lived space yielded parallel mental processes.' I argue that this was only partially accurate about Warsaw because although Jews indeed drew inward, this retreat offered little refuge as both private spaces and the stigmatized personal body were constantly violated. In this respect, rather than excluding Jews from the public arena, Nazification in Poland meant abstraction of boundaries, penetration of Jewish spaces as well as bodies. If the signifier intended to exclude Jews, it simultaneously made them apparent. If armbands were intended to deter people from communicating with Jews, the signifier 'announced' that abusing these bodies was not only permitted, but also encouraged. Alternatively, the visible characteristics of banishment introduced in Poland from the beginning, prevented many Jews from withdrawing inward because of their visibility.

94   Boaz Neumann, p. 226-227. Neumann's examples discuss sensations of estrangement among German Jews, feelings often expressed by Jews from other countries as well.

95   Helene Berr, p. 56.

96   Yitskhok Rudashevski, 'Vilna Ghetto', 8.7.1941, in Alexandra Zapruder (ed), *Salvaged Pages, Young Writers' Diaries of the Holocaust*, USA: Yale University Press, 2015, p. 199.

97 Ruth Kluger, *Still Alive, A Holocaust Girlhood Remembered*, New York,: The Feminist Press of the City University of New York, 2003, p. 21.

98 Thania Acarón, 'Shape-in(g) Space: Body, Boundaries, and Violence', *Space and Culture*, Vol. 19 (2), Sage, 2016, DOI: 10.1177/1206331215623208, p. 143. Acarón argued that proprioception, the ability to feel movements without looking at one's body, is linked to self-appreciation that derives from the way the body is perceived by others. This model of reciprocal movement implies that spatiality is also related to how we regard ourselves. Employing this theory to analyze effects of donning Jewish symbols suggests that exposing Jewishness publicly shaped not only reactions of the surroundings but involved alteration in the victims' self-assessment.

99 Setha Low, 'Anthropological Theories of Body, Space, and Culture', *Space & Culture*, vol. 6 no. 1, City University of New York, Sage, February 2003, DOI: 10.1177/1206331202238959, p. 13.

100 Rene Descartes, *Discours de la méthode, Pour bien conduire sa raison, et chercher la vérité dans les sciences, (Discourse on the method of rightly conducting the reason, and seeking the truth in the sciences)*, (1637), La Gaya Scienza, June, 2012, (French), p. 34. This sentence means 'I think, therefore I am'.

101 Levinas Emmanuel, *Difficult Freedom, Essays on Judaism*, Baltimore: The Johns Hopkins University Press, 1990, p. 153.

102 Ibid., p. 153.

103 Katarzyna Person, *The Easter Pogrom, 1940*, The Jewish Historical Institute, 21.03.2018. From: https://www.jhi.pl/en/articles/the-easter-pogrom-1940,354, accessed 3.5 2021. Like Havi Ben-Sasson (Dreifuss), Katarzyna Person suggested that the experience of violence against Jews on the part of Poles in the first year of the war, including the Easter pogrom (March 1940), diminished and sometimes disappeared from the collective memory of Warsaw Jews. The reason for this appears to be the relative insignificance of these attacks in view of the following much worse experiences of ghettoization and eventually, total annihilation.

104 Elie Wiesel, p. 11.

105 Jean-Gerard Bursztein, p. 94.

106 Ibid., p. 97.

107 Jean-Gerard Bursztein, p. 97-8. Bursztein claimed Jews were annihilated before they had the time to comprehend what was happening. This seems accurate about western Europe and some of the former Soviet Union territories where badges were introduced close to deportations. In Germany, for example, marking was enforced as of September 1941, and massive deportations began in October. In Poland, however, badges were introduced right from the beginning, about two years before deportations. Yet, the decree

Endnotes 273

lost its poignancy because of the huge number of other decrees, and when the ghetto closed, it became a minor problem.

CHAPTER VII

1   Emmanuel Ringelblum, *Diary and Notes from the Warsaw Ghetto*, p. 197.
2   Roland Barthes, 'Textual Analysis: Poe's 'Valdemar'', in Martin McQuillan (editor), *The Narrative Reader*, UK: e-Library by Taylor and Francis, 2002, p. 134. Barthes claimed that all codes were cultural and forms of '... 'Déjà' (already), a constitutive of all the writings in the world.'
3   Lea Prais, p. 416-419. Praise shows how the deteriorating conditions in the ghetto affected family ties, especially within the extended family.
4   Berl Lang, 'Oskar Rosenfeld and The Realism of Holocaust-History: 'On Sex, Shit, and Status', *History and Theory*, 43, USA: Wesleyan University, May 2004, p. 285.
5   Emmanuel Ringelblum, *Diary and Notes from the Warsaw Ghetto*, p. 144
6   Emmanuel Ringelblum, *Last Writings, January 1943-April 1944*, p. 12
7   Ibid., p. 12.
8   Emmanuel Ringelblum, *Diary and Notes from the Warsaw Ghetto*, p 306.
9   Mark Celinscak, A Procession of Shadows: Examining Warsaw Ghetto Testimony', *The New School Psychology Bulletin*, Vol. 6 No. 2, The New School for Social Research, 2009, p. 41. Celinscak argued that diarists wrote for lost communities, and in this respect, the personal and collective overlapped.
10 Berl Lang, p. 285.
11 Amos Goldberg, *Trauma in First Person, Diary Writing during the Holocaust*, (Hebrew), p. 147. Goldberg claimed that this type of diary was intended to create a bridge between the present and future. It is documentary writing and not an autobiographical diary.
12 Noemi Szac Wajnkranc, p. 23.
    Emmanuel Ringelblum, *Diary and Notes from the Warsaw Ghetto*, p. 167.
13 Adam Czerniaków, p. 210-211. In his diary, Czerniaków, wrote on October 27, 1940, barely two weeks before the ghetto was closed, there were 55,000 people without a roof over their heads.
14 Chaim Aron Kaplan, *The Continuation of Our Scroll of Agony*, Unpublished Manuscript, Givat Haviva, Notebook 10, p. 43. In an entry dated 22.5.1941, Kaplan described the bitter reality of homeowners whose private property was constantly invaded by *Kehilla* officials to find accommodation for refugees. Here, Kaplan alluded to corrupt officials who took advantage of the situation to fill their pockets with money.
15 Janina Bauman, *Winter in the Morning, a Young Girl's Life in the Ghetto and Beyond 1939-1945*, New-York: the Free Press, Macmillan Inc. 1986, p. 38.
16 Noemi Szac Wajnkranc, p. 23.

17 Reuven Feldschuh (Ben-Shem), *Deciphered Diary*, pic. 237. Hanna Dickstein was a famous pianist, who tutored Ben Shem's daughter, Josima. Moving to the kitchen should not be taken lightly, as it meant that the Dicksteins would constantly have people coming in and out of their room since there usually was one communal kitchen.

For more about Hanna Dickstein, go to *Internetowej Bazie danych getta warszawskiego (The Internet Database of the Warsaw Ghetto)* https://new.getto.pl/en/People/D/Dickstein-Hanna-Unknown, accessed, 11.12.2020.

18 Emmanuel Ringelblum, *Diary and Notes from the Warsaw Ghetto*, p. 239.

19 Ibid., p. 331.

20 Reuven Feldschuh (Ben-Shem), *Deciphered Diary*, pic. 245.

21 Ibid., pic. 245.

22 Ibid., pic. 245. In January 1941, Ben-Shem alluded to the fact that there was no glass on Lipman's windows and that wall maps separated the inside from the outside. Apparently, Lipman lived in Switzerland before the war and had an agency selling maps, which in the ghetto, served to cover draughts from the outside.

23 Bernard Goldstein, p. 34.

24 Reuven Feldschuh (Ben-Shem), *Deciphered Diary*, pic. 34.

25 Emmanuel Ringelblum, *Diary and Notes from the Warsaw Ghetto*, p. 231.

26 Noemi Szac Wajnkranc, p. 24.

27 Henri Lefebvre, p. 162

28 Emmanuel Ringelblum, *Diary and Notes from the Warsaw Ghetto* p. 269.

29 Lea Prais, p. 307.

30 Ibid., p. 313.

31 Joshua Perle, 'Churban Varshe', Yad-Vashem Archive, M.10/AR.2-199, quoted in Lea Prais, p. 314.

32 Reuven Feldschuh (Ben-Shem), *Deciphered Diary*, pic. 127.

33 Ibid., pic. 127.

34 Lea Prais, p. 419.

35 Charles G. Roland, *Courage Under Siege, Starvation, Disease, and Death in the Warsaw Ghetto*, USA: Oxford University Press, 1992, p. 120. Roland specified that typhus was the disease that ravaged the ghetto, not typhoid fever, often confused with typhus.

36 Emmanuel Ringelblum, *Diary and Notes from the Warsaw Ghetto*, p. 304.

37 Charles G. Roland, p. 104.

38 Emmanuel Ringelblum, *Diary and Notes from the Warsaw Ghetto*, p. 205.

39 Ibid., p. 215.

40 Charles G. Roland, p. 102. Roland drew attention to social gaps in the ghetto, a familiar phenomenon related to the Warsaw Ghetto. Initially, regardless of built-in class differences of the Jews of Warsaw, refugees constituted about one-fifth of the ghetto residents but their economic situation was meager from the beginning, as they were robbed of all their possessions.

Endnotes

41 Emmanuel Ringelblum, *Diary and Notes from the Warsaw Ghetto*, p. 247

42 Ibid., p. 306.

43 Ibid., p. 306.

44 Dr. Med. Emil Apfelbaum (Chief editor), *Maladie de Famine: Recherches cliniques sur la famine exécutées dans le ghetto de Varsovie en 1942, (Clinical Research about Hunger Related Diseases in the Warsaw Ghetto in 1942)*, Warsaw : American Joint Distribution Committee, 1946, *(French)*, p. 34-35. The research conducted by doctors in the ghetto concluded that there was no difference between mortality levels of men and women. The research was based on 492 autopsies conducted on hunger victims between 1.1.1940 - 22.7.1942, and analysis of the data suggested significant differences in certain age groups. For example, among children under 10, the number of boys who died was five times higher than that of girls. In the 10-19 age group, the numbers were higher by a third. However, the difference stabilized to almost identical in the 20-40 age groups. This changed drastically in the 40-49 age group with 13% more dead women. However, in the 50-59 age group, this trend reversed and the number of dead men was 10% higher.

45 Emmanuel Ringelblum, *Diary and Notes from the Warsaw Ghetto*, p. 380.

46 Henri Lefebvre, p. 170.

47 Alan Adelson and Robert Lapides (editors), *Lodz Ghetto*, New York: Viking Penguin, 1989, from Oskar Rosenfeld, notebook B, p. 273-4.

48 Ibid., p. 273-4.

49 Mary Douglas, 'The Idea of a Home: A Kind of Space', *Social Research*, 58:1, The Johns Hopkins University Press, Spring 1991, p. 305

50 Henri Lefebvre, p. 197.

51 Janina Bauman, *Beyond These Walls, Escaping the Warsaw Ghetto, A Young Girl's Story*, UK: Virago Press, 2006, p. 128.

52 Julia Kristeva, *Powers of Horror, An Essay on Abjection*, USA: Colombia University Press, 1982, p. 1.

53 Reuven Feldschuh (Ben-Shem), *Deciphered Diary*, pic. 34.

54 Ibid., pic. 34.

55 Ibid., pic. 34.

56 Abraham Lipman, record no. 288940, Yad-Vashem, Hall of Names. This record was filled out in memory of Abraham Lipman. It stated that his son was ten years old and his name was Gavriel. In a file filled out for Gavriel, no. 1124260, the person filling out the form wrote that the boy was five years old. Ben-Shem wrote that Gavriel was about nine.

57 Reuven Feldschuh (Ben-Shem), pic. 33.

58 Ibid., pic. 33.

59 Emmanuel Ringelblum, *Diary and Notes from the Warsaw Ghetto*, p. 307.

60 Reuven Feldschuh (Ben-Shem), *Deciphered Diary*, pic. 248-9.

61 Ibid., pic., 251. Lustman's son was Ben-Shem's former youth movement student.

62 Ibid., pic. 250. Ben-Shem wrote that Lustman tried to save Pnina the trip by convincing her to give him the fur promising he would arrange to sell it for her. She refused and went with him.

63 Anne Kelly Knowles; Tim Cole; Alberto Giordano (eds.), locations 117-127. The writers adopted the view that spatial analysis could pinpoint the reciprocal relationships between things and people. Since the Holocaust affected not only the meaning of places but also their materiality, in this case, dwellings, changes in materiality forcibly imposed alteration of meaning.

64 Bernard Goldstein, p. 82-83.

65 Henri Lefebvre, p. 162.

66 Ibid., p. 200.

67 Ludwik Hirszfeld, p. 244.
See also: Antony Polonsky, 'Hirszfeld, Ludwik', *YIVO Encyclopedia*, https://yivoencyclopedia.org/article.aspx/Hirszfeld_Ludwik, accessed 22.5.2021. In the ghetto, Hirszfeld lived with his wife and daughter in the presbytery of All Saints' Church on Grzybowski Square in Warsaw.

68 Emmanuel Ringelblum, *Diary and Notes from the Warsaw Ghetto*, p. 330.

69 Agnieszka Witkowska-Krych, 'Our Children Must Live Because the Child Is the Most Sacred Thing We Have.' The Portrayal in Gazeta Żydowska of the Children's Month Campaign in the Warsaw Ghetto', Museum of Warsaw, 2020, p. 203. https://muzeumwarszawy.pl/wp-content/uploads/2020/01/6B.-Nasze-dzieci-ang-K1.pdf, accessed: 13.12.2020. Witkowska-Krych wrote that the event was organized by Centos, Centrala Związku Towarzystw Opieki nad Sierotami i Dziećmi Opuszczonymi (Central Office of the Union of Societies for the Care of Orphans and Abandoned Children), and Ringelblum, Czerniaków and Korczak criticized the campaign. Indeed, Ringelblum wrote that the campaign expenses exceeded the revenues and therefore, did not achieve its purpose.

70 Emmanuel Ringelblum, *Diary and Notes from the Warsaw Ghetto*, p. 299. At nine o'clock curfew was enforced in the ghetto.

71 Seymour Chatman, 'Point of View', in Martin McQuillan (editor), *The Narrative Reader*, UK: e-Library by Taylor and Francis, 2002, pp. 96-98. This article deals with the roles of a narrator in literature and ways of introducing points of view, his own as well as others. Regarding Ringelblum's narratology, I propose that despite the tenacity to be objective, this passage hints that he may have been unaware that through the frustration he experienced, he unintentionally introduced the viewer's perspective, his own. Although this form of narrative may be regarded as somewhat biased, it is this ambiguity of the text that produced a more coherent and comprehensive image of a reality that consisted of not only the writer's point of view but also the reciprocal relationships between what was witnessed and the effect it produced.

72 Reuven Feldschuh (Ben-Shem), *Deciphered Diary*, pic. 2.

Endnotes

73 Bernard Goldstein, p. 34.

74 Reuven Feldschuh (Ben-Shem), *Deciphered Diary*, pic. 202.

75 Ibid., pic. 202.

76 Emmanuel Ringelblum, *Diary and Notes from the Warsaw Ghetto*, p. 343.

77 Shoshana Felman, 'Camus' The Plague, or a Monument to Witnessing', in Dori Laub M.D & Shoshana Felman, *Testimony, Crises of Witnessing in Literature, Psychoanalysis and History*, USA: Routledge, 1992, p. 111. Felman claimed that the main purpose of testimony was to impart '... carnal knowledge of victimization...'

78 Reuven Feldschuh (Ben-Shem), *Deciphered Diary*, pic. 98.

79 Ibid., pic. 97.

80 Ibid., pic. 97.

81 Ibid., pic. 98.

82 Ibid., pic. 98.

83 Ibid., pic. 98.

84 Ibid., pic. 98.

CHAPTER VIII

1 Henri Lefebvre, p. 97

2 Ibid., p. 97

3 Ibid., p. 97

4 Wendy Lower, *The Ravine, A Family, A Photograph, A Holocaust Massacre Revealed*, New York: Houghton Mifflin Harcourt, 2021, p. 13. Lower wrote that by 1939, 10% of Germans owned cameras.

5 Justice Robert H. Jackson, Chief of Counsel for the United States, opening statement to the International Military Tribunal, Nuremberg Trials, November 21, 1945, the Palace of Justice at Nuremberg, Germany. *The Robert H. Jackson Center.* https://www.roberthjackson.org/speech-and-writing/opening-statement-before-the-international-military-tribunal/, accessed: 13.6.2021. Apparently, the idea that photography offered proof beyond doubt was a common notion. Indeed, in his speech, Jackson stated clearly the attitude to photography saying, 'We will not ask you to convict these men on the testimony of their foes... They (Germans) arranged frequently to be photographed in action. We will show you their own films. You will see their own conduct and hear their own voices as these defendants re-enact for you, from the screen, some of the events in the course of the conspiracy.' He added that most of the evidence would be documentary and include photographs and films taken by the Nazis but also by the American Forces. 'We will show you these concentration camps in motion pictures, just as the Allied armies found them when they arrived, and the measures General Eisenhower had to take to clean them up.' Jackson's tactic was that the evidence against the Nazis

278   *Emanuel Ringelblum and Reuven Ben-Shem's War Writings*

was conclusive and therefore, the 'foes' testimony, namely, people, would not be needed to convict Nazi criminals.

6   Pierre Taminiaux, *The Paradox of Photography*, New York: Rodopi B. V., 2009, p. 164. Taminiaux spoke about the fact that the invention of photography developed the visual aspects of language, yet the poetic essence of the visual remained a perpetual effort and an unresolved issue.

7   Emmanuel Ringelblum, *Last Writings, January 1943-April 1944*, p. 10.

8   Ibid., p. 9, 11, 13.

9   Ibid., p. 10.

10   Ibid., p. 10-11. This is an indication of the developing purpose assigned to the archive to serve as a resource of evidence against Nazis.

11   Ibid., p. 10.

12   Emmanuel Ringelblum, *Diary and Notes from the Warsaw Ghetto, September 1939 - December 1942*, p. 289.

13   Ibid., p. 145.

14   Ibid., p. 298.

15   Reuven Feldschuh (Ben-Shem), *Deciphered Diary*, pic. 108. J. J. Prapus was the secretary of the 'Der Moment' newspaper and Ben-Shem's close friend. He was murdered during the great deportation. Together with Ben-Shem, they came up with, in fact, sixty-eight categories, as whoever printed this passage had, probably by mistake, skipped number thirteen.

16   Ibid., pic. 118.

17   Ibid., pic. 118.

18   Ibid., pic. 118.

19   Emmanuel Ringelblum, *Diary and Notes from the Warsaw Ghetto*, p. 298. Ringelblum also mentioned the phenomenon and said that it became 'fashionable'.

20   Robert Antelme, *The Human Race*, Tel Aviv: Am Oved, 2011, (Hebrew), p. 90. Antelme recounted an incident when someone at the camp found a piece of broken mirror that aroused great excitement among the prisoners because, for the first time after a long period, they faced their presence as individuals. This was extremely uncomfortable as survival in the camp meant that both Nazis and prisoners purposely erased their individuality. To use this anecdote, it is possible to claim that people in the ghetto used photographs as affirmation of their own existence.

21   David Welch, p. xv.

22   Nina Springer-Aharoni, Holocaust Ghetto Photography as Historical Records, 18.7.2013, p. 1. https://www.yadvashem.org/yv/he/research/ghettos_encyclopedia/shpringer.pdf, accessed: 1.1.2021. See also, Daniel Uziel ,'Wehrmacht Propaganda Troops and the Jews', Jerusalem: *Yad-Vashem Studies*, Vol. 29, 2001, p. 5-6. https://www.yadvashem.org/odot_pdf/Microsoft%20Word%20-%202021.pdf, accessed: 20.9.2020.

Endnotes

23 Person, Katarzyna, *The Easter Pogrom, 1940*, The Jewish Historical Institute, 21.03.2018. From: https://www.jhi.pl/en/articles/the-easter-pogrom-1940,354, accessed 3.5 2021.

24 Emmanuel Ringelblum, *Diary and Notes from the Warsaw Ghetto*, p. 104, 28. As early as December 1939, Ringelblum reported that Germans were filming and photographing everything, not only in Warsaw but all over Poland.

25 Ibid., p. 119. Jewish policemen were asked to arrest a German officer for not crossing the road according to the law, all of which was conducted in front of rolling cameras.

26 Jonas Turkow, p. 48.

27 Emmanuel Ringelblum, *Diary and Notes from the Warsaw Ghetto*, p. 360. Despite what Ringelblum wrote, some of the filming consisted of street scenes that were not staged. Concerning the problem of motive, see also: Laliv Melamed, 'A Film Unraveled: An Interview with Yael Hersonski', *Int J Polit Cult Soc*, 26, New York: Springer Science + Business Media, 2013, DOI 10.1007/s10767-013-9136-9, Laliv Melamed, p. 11-13.

28 Avraham Lewin, p. 46.

29 Ibid., p. 38.

30 Henri Lefebvre, p. 97

31 Susan Sontag, *On Photography*, New York: RosettaBooks, LLC, electronic book, 2005, p. 84. Sontag quoted Godard and Gorin that a photograph was 'mute' and it was the words that gave it its meaning. In other words, without language, what we see can only be interpreted through the eyes.
See also: Georges Didi-Huberman, *Images in Spite of All, Four Photographs from Auschwitz*, USA: University of Chicago Press, 2012, p. 66-67. Didi-Huberman pointed out that Raul Hilberg complained about the difficulty to decipher documents, in particular visual materials. The problem was fundamental as from the beginning, interpretations were wrong. For example, pictures of the execution of children and women from the ghetto of Mizocz are still used to describe the death chambers of Treblinka.

32 Emmanuel Ringelblum, *Diary and Notes from the Warsaw Ghetto*, p. 360.

33 Reuven Feldschuh (Ben-Shem), *Deciphered Diary*, pic. 307.

34 Ibid., pic. 293.

35 Ibid., pic. 305-308. Ben-Shem elaborated on the kind of scenes that Jews were ordered to play in the ghetto and how the German crew was filming it relentlessly.

36 Ibid., pic. 308 and Emmanuel Ringelblum, *Diary and Notes from the Warsaw Ghetto*, p. 381. He recounted about a woman who was dragged from prison to be filmed in the *mikvah* on Żelazn Street (June 10, 1942).

37 Rachel Auerbach, *In the Outskirts of Warsaw*, p. 31, 33.

38 Chaim Aron Kaplan, *Scroll of Agony: Hebrew Diary of Ch. A. Kaplan Written in the Warsaw Ghetto 1st September 1939 – 4th August 1942*, p. 491.

39 Bernard Goldstein, p. 78.

Avraham Lewin, p. 30. Avraham Lewin traced the event to Wednesday, May 13, 1942, between 15:00-18:00.

See also: Emmanuel Ringelblum, *Diary and Notes from the Warsaw Ghetto*, p. 381.

40 Nina Springer-Aharoni, p. 2. Springer-Aharoni provided another example of wrongly used films when footage of the Polish Uprising were used as if they were authentic films documenting the Jewish uprising.

41 Laliv Melamed, p. 11, 16-17.

42 Ursula Böser, 'Yael Hersonski's Re-representation of Archival Footage from the Warsaw Ghetto', *Film Criticism*, Vol 37, No. 2, Allegheny College, Winter 2012-2013, p. 41.

43 Bob Fisher, Ghetto Life, *ICG, International Cinematographer Guild Magazine*, November 8, 2010, from: https://www.icgmagazine.com/web/ghetto-life/, accessed 24.12.2020.

44 Laliv Melamed, p. 13-14.

45 Walter Benjamin, *A Short History of Photography*, p. 25. https://monoskop.org/images/7/79/Benjamin_Walter_1931_1972_A_Short_History_of_Photography.pdf, accessed 7.6.2021. In his iconic essay published originally in *The Literarische Welt* on September 18, 25 and 2.10.1931, Benjamin foresaw such a situation when he wrote that as cameras become smaller and their capacities to '... capture transitory and secret pictures...' would increase, words would have to be added to the footage because without it photographic construction would remain speculative. Although cameras in 1939 were not small, they were portable enough which put German photographers in a position to take pictures easily.

46 Laliv Melamed, p. 14.

47 Adam Czerniaków, p. 349.

48 Yehudit Levin and Daniel Uziel, 'Normal People and Unusual Photographs', Yad-Vashem, 'LEKKET', no. 26, 1997-8, (Hebrew), p. 202. The writers proposed viewing the action of photographing as part of the crime. https://www.yadvashem.org/yv/he/holocaust/about/related/articles/002026009Levin_Uziel.pdf.

49 Ursula Böser, p. 45. In her article, Böser quoted Hersonski who related to Willy Wist, one of the cameramen of that film who was interrogated in preparation for the trial of Heinz Auerswald, Commissioner of the Warsaw Ghetto. Wist pointed to the many technical difficulties the team encountered during filming.

50 Nina Springer-Aharoni, p. 8.

51 Emmanuel Ringelblum, *Diary and Notes from the Warsaw Ghetto*, p. 381, 358. See also: Wendy Lower, *The Ravine, A Family, A Photograph, A Holocaust Massacre Revealed*, p. 15-16. Lower wrote that once the invasion of the USSR began, bans were issued forbidding soldiers in the area of Zhytomyr to take pictures of the massacres. According to Lower, there is information only about

Endnotes

one case of a soldier who was put on trial, not for killing Jews, but for taking pictures of the act.

52 Nina Springer-Aharoni, p. 9-13

53 Reuven Feldschuh (Ben-Shem), *Deciphered Diary*, pic. 144.

54 Emmanuel Ringelblum, *Diary and Notes from the Warsaw Ghetto*, p. 285.

55 Ibid., p. 242.

56 Ibid., p. 305.

57 Reuven Feldschuh (Ben-Shem), *Deciphered Diary*, pic. 226.

58 Ibid., pic. 142.

59 Ibid., pic. 287-288.

Chaba Efrat, *My Portion in the Land of the Living, Avraham Carmi's Story*, Tel Aviv: Miskal -Yedioth Ahronoth Books and Chemed Books, (Hebrew), 2013, p. 51, 309, 333. In his book, Carmi mentioned several times the photographs that his uncle, Avraham-Moshe Posner made sure to take. He specified that men were photographed and that the reason was to prevent a situation where women would not be in the dark regarding their husbands' fate. In a phone call to Carmi, he asserted that the one photo album that was in his possession was handed to Yad-Vashem but according to him, there were several more albums which were left in the cemetery in Warsaw and were probably buried under the building rubble where they used to live.

60 Suzan Sontag, p. 7.

61 Judith Keilbach, 'Photographs, Symbolic Images, and the Holocaust: On the (Im)Possibility of Depicting Historical Truth', *History and Theory, Theme Issue* 47, Wesleyan University, May 2009, p. 64. Keilbach wrote that many of these photographs were found in pockets of dead soldiers, often side by side with pictures of their mothers, fiancées, etc.

62 Helmut Gernsheim, *Creative Photography: Aesthetic Trends, 1839-1960*, New-York: Dover Publications, INC., 1991, p. 229.

63 Reuven Feldschuh (Ben-Shem), *Deciphered Diary*, pic. 217. Ben-Shem referred to the ghetto as hell numerous times.

64 According to Yad-Vashem, photographs in Warsaw came from four sources: the ZSS - Zydowska Samapomoc Spolczna (*Jewish Social Self-Help*) which was funded by the JDC (American Jewish Joint Distribution Committee) and whose photos stressed the different welfare activities.

The second source came from Jüdische Produktionsgesellschaft GMBH, the Jewish corporation of shops or small factories operating in the ghetto. Photos were taken probably at the end of 1941, and they were the initiative of the Jewish management of the shops, probably in order to prove to Germans that Jews were valuable workers.

The third source comes from private initiatives of soldiers who visited the ghetto. The most famous were albums created by a soldier called Heinz Jost whose photos were handed to Yad-Vashem by his relative after his death. The other notable album was prepared by a soldier from the supply corps who arranged the picture in an album given the title 'Das Warschauer Ghetto. Ein Kulturdokument für Adolf Hitler' (The Warsaw Ghetto. A cultural document for Adolf Hitler). https://www.yadvashem.org/yv/he/exhibitions/warsaw_ ghetto/introduction.asp. Accessed, 20.9.20202.

See also: Yehudit Levin and Daniel Uziel, p. 211. https://www.yadvashem.org/ yv/he/holocaust/about/related/articles/002026009Levin_Uziel.pdf. Accessed, 20.9.20202. Levin and Uziel examined the album and pointed out a dissonance between the title dedicating the album to Hitler and the contents of the photographs, which do not seem to suggest necessarily an antisemitic point of view. However, the antisemitic context of the album is created by the fact the soldier had dedicated the album to Hitler and that its content included sixty-five photographs the soldier had taken himself in the ghetto.

The fourth is the Jürgen Stroop collection, documenting the Jewish uprising which started on April 19, 1943. Stroop entitled the album which contained about 50 photographs, 'Es gibt keinen jüdischen Wohnbezirk in Warschau mehr' (the Jewish quarter in Warsaw exists no longer). https://www. yadvashem.org/yv/en/exhibitions/warsaw_ghetto/introduction.asp, accessed: 20.9.20202.

65   Rachel Auerbach, *In the Outskirts of Warsaw*, p. 33.

66   Reuven Feldschuh (Ben-Shem), *Deciphered Diary*, pic. 141.

67   Emmanuel Ringelblum, *Diary and Notes from the Warsaw Ghetto*, p. 290. Ringelblum reported this phenomenon too, and wrote, 'Often there are trips to the cemetery. They constantly take pictures of the dead and meanwhile they laugh heartedly.'

68   Bernd Hüppauf, 'Emptying the Gaze: Framing Violence through the Viewfinder', *New German Critique*, No. 72, published by: Duke University Press, Autumn, 1997, p. 43.

69   Reuven Feldschuh (Ben-Shem), *Deciphered Diary*, pic. 36.

70   Susan Sontag, p. 84. Sontag debated the relationship between captions and pictures and suggested that a photo cannot really be interpreted if a caption is missing but its presence could not guarantee a picture's meaning permanently.

See also: Georges Didi-Huberman, p. 68-69. Interestingly, Didi-Huberman reacted to Jacques Mandelbaum's argument claiming that images were not 'adequate' to embody the Holocaust and therefore, should be abandoned. He claimed that all signs, words or images were to begin with insufficient to represent the world, but that this did not mean one should throw them all away because they do not manage to mirror everything.

71   Emmanuel Ringelblum, *Diary and Notes from the Warsaw Ghetto*, p. 205, 215, 232.

72   Katarzyna Person, *Assimilated Jews in the Warsaw Ghetto, 1940-1943*, pp. 109-110. Person reviewed a large variety of entertainment in the ghetto including the club at hotel Britania.

See also: Emmanuel Ringelblum, *Diary and Notes from the Warsaw Ghetto*, p. 232.

73 Ibid., p. 232.

74 Nicholas Chare, *Auschwitz and Afterimages: Abjection, Witnessing and Representation*, USA: I.B. Tauris, 2011, p. 134. Following Lyotard, Chare explained that the 'differend' described conflicting choices of representation through language. Ringelblum's text arrangement, apparently exemplifies how with lean language, the internal arrangement in the text echoed not only the conflict of how to portray events but also imbedded and unspoken messages.

75 Emmanuel Ringelblum, *Diary and Notes from the Warsaw Ghetto*, p. 232.

76 Ibid., p. 232.

77 Reuven Feldschuh (Ben-Shem), *Deciphered Diary*, pic. 43.
See also: Emmanuel Ringelblum, *Diary and Notes from the Warsaw Ghetto*, p. 250, 269.

78 Reuven Feldschuh (Ben-Shem), *Deciphered Diary*, pic. 43- 44.

79 Teresa Bridgeman, 'Time and Space', in David Herman (editor), *The Cambridge Companion to Narrative*, UK: Cambridge University Press, 2007, p. 52-54. Bridgeman explained the link between the time of reading and space of text where a story was written, which accordingly tied narratives and time together.

80 Uri Margolin, 'Character', David Herman (editor), *The Cambridge Companion to Narrative*, UK: Cambridge University Press, 2007, p. 78. Margolin suggested that the combination of information with a category leads to categorization, which in turn, leads the reader to formulating more connections within a text.

81 Reuven Feldschuh (Ben-Shem), *Deciphered Diary*, pic. 43.
Emmanuel Ringelblum, *Diary and Notes from the Warsaw Ghetto*, p. 250, 269.
On p. 269 Ringelblum reported that snatching food had become a profession.

82 Emmanuel Ringelblum, *Diary and Notes from the Warsaw Ghetto*, p. 282.

83 Viktor E. Frankl, *Man's Search for Meaning*, UK: Rider, 2008, p. 44.

84 Bernard Goldstein, p. 69.

85 Judith Keilbach, p. 69. Keilbach used the phrase 'generic abstractions' to explain how photographs lose their contexts and become symbols.

86 Julia Kristeva, p. 16. Kristeva theorized that writing means possessing the dual ability to put oneself in others' shoes yet be able to shove abjection aside merely by writing.

87 Henri Lefebvre, p. 185.

88 Maurice Blanchot, *The Writing of A Disaster*, USA: University of Nebraska Press, 1995, p. 64.

89 Marie Laure Ryan, 'Towards a Definition of Narrative', in David Herman (editor), *The Cambridge Companion to Narrative*, UK: Cambridge University Press, 2007, p. 25. In her discussion about what could be considered basic units of narratives, Laure Ryan proposed relying on semantics only if it manages to evoke a type of mental image. In the context of the diaries,

although a mental image was created, it needed to be explained, as the language covered several aspects, for instance, the relationship between what was written and its influence on the writer.

90   Emmanuel Ringelblum, *Diary and Notes from the Warsaw Ghetto*, p. 243. This prayer is used for the dead.

91   A Bimah in a synagogue is a raised platform from which the *Torah* is read.

92   Emmanuel Ringelblum, *Diary and Notes from the Warsaw Ghetto*, p. 243

93   Hayden White, *The Practical Past*, USA: Northwestern University Press, 2014, p. 94. White lent significance to emplotment, text arrangement, as a means of generating meanings in texts by the effect they produced in an orderly narrative.

94   Emmanuel Ringelblum, *Diary and Notes from the Warsaw Ghetto*, p. 243

95   Ibid., p. 243.

96   Reuven Feldschuh (Ben-Shem), *Deciphered Diary*, pic. 106-121.

97   Ibid., pic. 112

98   Ibid., pic. 112.

99   Eryk Emil Tahvonen, *The Crisis of Imagination, Representation and Resistance in Holocaust Diaries*, Saarbrücken: VDM Verlag Dr. Müller Aktiengesellschaft & Co. KG, 2008, p. 46. Tahvonen argues that like Dawid Sierakowiak (1924-1943), Ringelblum conflated the victims with their oppressors. According to Tahvonen there were several reasons for this, one of which was that perpetrators became so integrated in the victim's world that they were no longer regarded as the sole cause of the deteriorating conditions in the ghetto.

100 Mary Douglas, 'The Idea of a Home: A Kind of Space', p. 305.

101 Reuven Feldschuh (Ben-Shem), *Deciphered Diary*, pic. 202. Ben-Shem also discussed the phenomenon of multitudes seeking help on the outside, many of whom were too weak to return to their homes at night, and therefore, died in the street.

102 Ibid., pic. 217. This is one of many occasions that Ben-Shem compared his situation to that of others. He wrote that he was relatively lucky as he still had a door to his room, even a lock, as well as a window and a stove, luxury in comparison to others in his block who had no doors to their houses as they burnt them to keep themselves warm.

103 Chaim Aron Kaplan, *Scroll of Agony: Hebrew Diary of Ch. A. Kaplan Written in the Warsaw Ghetto 1st September 1939 – 4th August 1942*, p. 452. On February 27, 1941, Kaplan wrote '… everyone is looking for prey for his soul and his family's, who are hungry and thirsty. … Thousands of people prowl and everybody go outside to 'swim with the current'. It isn't anything but an incessant 'fair'… Congestion is so huge that there is no room even in the middle of the street.'

104 Emmanuel Ringelblum, *Diary and Notes from the Warsaw Ghetto*, p. 280.

105 Reuven Feldschuh (Ben-Shem), *Deciphered Diary*, pic. 94.

Endnotes

106 Ibid., pic. 94.

107 Ibid., p. 125.

108 Victoria Nizan, 'Smelling the Ghetto. Smells in the Warsaw Ghetto According to Ruben Ben-Shem's (Feldschu) Diary', *Journal of Global Politics and Current Diplomacy (JGPCD)*, no. 5, Issue 1, Centrul pentru Dialog European și Diplomație Culturală (Center for European Dialogue and Cultural Diplomacy) (DEDIC), April 2017, p. 12-13.

109 Barbara Engelking, 'Possibilities of Escape', p. 737.

110 Ibid., p. 740-745. Engelking specified dangers awaiting Jews on the Aryan Side. Men constituted a particular risk as their Jewish origin could be more easily detected.

111 Havi Dreifuss (Ben-Sasson), *Warsaw Ghetto – The End, April 1942-June 1943*, p. 191. Dreifuss wrote that because of deportations, there were substantial demographic changes in the ghetto. This resulted in a drastic decline in the numbers of women who were unable to receive work permits.

112 Barbara Engelking, 'Possibilities of Escape', pp. 730-737. Engelking elaborated on the upheaval of shop life contrasting its huge surge of hope versus the incredulous ordeals involved in being a shop worker.

113 Havi Dreifuss (Ben-Sasson), *Warsaw Ghetto – The End, April 1942-June 1943*, p. 182.

114 Emmanuel Ringelblum, *Diary and Notes from the Warsaw Ghetto*, p. 394.

115 Laurence L. Langer, *Holocaust Testimonies: The Ruins of Memory*, USA: Yale University Press, 1991. p. 19. Langer characterized written testimonies as being more conscious of making narratives clear to readers who were not part of that unfamiliar world. He contrasted this to testimonies collected orally by filming, taping, or even speaking live before an audience. Silence in oral history, pauses or other forms expose gaps in a different way yet create the same notion of speculation that lies behind the words.

116 Samuel D. Kassow, *Who Will Write Our History?*, p. 305.

117 Havi Dreifuss (Ben-Sasson), *Warsaw Ghetto – The End, April 1942-June 1943*, p. 200. When Dreifuss's book was written, it was assumed that Ben-Shem's writings were contemporaneous.

118 Elaine Scarry, *The Body in Pain: The Making and Unmaking of the World*, USA: Oxford University Press, 1985, p. 6. Scarry wrote that people in great pain were deprived of speech, and therefore sometimes speech about pain was brought up by others who spoke for those in pain. In this sense, it may be reasonable to assume that Ben-Shem, whose deciphered diary was edited in safety, could be regarded as the other, the one who spoke on behalf of victims and also the one articulating their pain for them.

119 Reuven Feldschuh (Ben-Shem), *Deciphered Diary*, pic. 416. The date, 18.9.1942, was a few days after the cauldron action, which took place on September 6-12, 1942.

See also: Havi Dreifuss (Ben-Sasson), *Warsaw Ghetto – The End, April 1942-June 1943*, p. 228. According to Dreifuss, most shop owners cooperated in that action.

120 Alexandra Garbarini, *Numbered Days*, p. 163. Garbarini argued that one common feature which characterized the Jewish experience during the war was individuals' continual '... struggle to believe and conceptualize the horror of genocide.'

121 Avraham Lewin, p. 92.

122 Emmanuel Ringelblum, *Diary and Notes from the Warsaw Ghetto*, p. 378.

123 Perez Opochinsky, *Sketches from The Warsaw Ghetto*, Tel Aviv: Ghetto Fighters' House & Hakkibutz Hameuchad, 1970, (Hebrew), p. 181, 185.

124 Yisrael Gutman, *The Jews of Warsaw 1939-1943, Ghetto – Underground – Uprising*, (Hebrew), p. 338. Gutman wrote that people who owned working tools were more likely to be accepted as shop workers.

125 Reuven Feldschuh (Ben-Shem), *Deciphered Diary*, pic. 304.

126 Ibid., pic. 304.

127 Ibid., pic. 305.

128 Ibid., pic. 305.

129 Ibid., pic. 329.

130 Ibid., pic. 329.

131 Ibid., pic. 329.

132 Ibid., pic. 329

133 Ibid., pic. 329.

134 Ibid., pic. 329.

135 Ibid., pic. 336.

136 Ibid., pic. 329.

See also: Henry Abramson, *Torah from the Years of Wrath 1939-1943: The Historical Context of the Aish Kodesh* (Holy Fire), USA: Henri Abramson, October 2017, p. 123. chrome-extension://efaidnbmnnnibpcajpcglclefind mkaj/https://touroscholar.touro.edu/cgi/viewcontent.cgi?article=1004&conte xt=lcas_books, accessed 4.7.2021.

Abramson quoted Rabi Kalonymus Kalmish (Kalman) Shapira, who said that the virtue of a Jew was believing in God no matter what.

137 Saul Friedländer, *The Years of Extermination: Nazi Germany and the Jews, 1939–1945*, New York: HarperCollins e-books, 2007, p. 432.

138 Simone Gigliotti, *The Train Journey, Transit, Captivity, and Witnessing in the Holocaust*, UK: Berghahn Books (eBook), 2010, p. 73-74. Gigliotti quoted from Isabella Leitner's book, *Fragments of Isabella: A Memoir of Auschwitz*, USA: Thomas Y. Crowell Publishers, 1978.

139 Reuven Feldschuh (Ben-Shem), *Deciphered Diary*, pic. 329.

140 Ibid., pic. 329.

141 Ibid., pic. 329.

142 Guy Miron, "The Lived Time": of German Jews under the Nazi Regime', p. 136-138. Miron discussed time subjectivity as a phenomenon linked to a capability to respond and predict the future. Ben-Shem's arrest provoked a similar reaction, that is, a sensation of disorientation linked to time and space. While moments seem eternal, his imagination raced with scenes involving his and his family's death. This time capsule evaporated as soon as he was set free and was able to resume his plans designed to secure a future.

143 Isabella Leitner, *Fragments of Isabella: A Memoir of Auschwitz*, USA: Thomas Y. Crowell Publishers, 1978, p. 46-47. One example of twisted values was provided by Leitner as she recounted the urgency to make her fifteen year old sister look older and healthier for the selection conducted by Mengele in Auschwitz. Her description highlighted how assuming responsibility over her sister's life exempted Mengele from accountability as if he was only selecting, whereas his choices depended on her capacity to make her sister seem older and healthier.

144 Emmanuel Ringelblum, *Diary and Notes from the Warsaw Ghetto*, p. 418.

145 Simone Gigliotti, p. 63-64. Gigliotti asked what Ringelblum might have asked himself: 'How could language capture scenes, migrations, emotions, and experiences that were, above all, embodied? How did extremity create frustrated witnesses and testifiers?' Gigliotti wrote that an array of emotions such as anxiety and fear, were involved in the process of roundups. Ringelblum did not mention them; instead, he discussed actions and their implications remained the task of the reader.

146 Reuven Feldschuh (Ben-Shem), *Deciphered Diary*, pic. 395.

147 Ibid., pic. 395.

148 Julia Hell, 'Modernity and the Holocaust, or, Listening to Eurydice', *Theory, Culture & Society* Vol. 27(6), Sage, 2010, DOI: 10.1177/0263276410382026, p. 140-142. Hell discussed echoes of Orpheus and Eurydice typography in Holocaust literature. Hell showed how the story of Orpheus and Eurydice is a recurring theme in Holocaust literature but it is how the Orphic gaze is interpreted that makes a difference. One interesting interpretation relates to Janina Bauman's preface to *A Dream of Belonging* (1987), when she wrote, 'I look back puzzled, trying to understand'. Hell interpreted this as Bauman's attempt to decipher her life. She cited Bauman's words: 'She is a puzzle, that woman, to me. She has brought me here. Let her account for that'. Hell suggested that Bauman was trying to understand her life, past and present, as if in the present, she were Orpheus who was looking at who she had been in the past, that is, Eurydice while the product of this meeting, gazes, was the text.
      On the frequent allusions to hell in Holocaust literature, see: Robert Jan Van Pelt, 'Paradise/Hades, Purgatory, Hell/ Gehenna: A Political Typology of the Camps', in Jonathan C. Friedman (editor), *The Routledge History of the Holocaust*, New York & Canada: Routledge, 2011.

See also: Otto Dov Kulka, *Landscapes of the Metropolis of Death*, Tel-Aviv: Proza, Yediot Ahronot and Chemed Books, 2013, (Hebrew), p. 88. In his recollection, Kulka referred to Auschwitz as Hades, telling about the last time he saw his mother 'It is not clear to me who was Orpheus and who Eurydice but mother never turned her head back, she left and disappeared.'

149 Havi Dreifuss (Ben-Sasson), *Warsaw Ghetto – The End, April 1942-June 1943*, p. 269. Dreifuss explained the housing conditions were much worse than before with lacking sanitary infrastructure, water, electricity, or gas. Some apartments had doors and windows removed.

150 Emmanuel Ringelblum, *Diary and Notes from the Warsaw Ghetto*, p. 406.

151 Reuven Feldschuh (Ben-Shem), *Deciphered Diary*, pic. 389.
Havi Dreifuss (Ben-Sasson), *Warsaw Ghetto – The End, April 1942-June 1943*, p. 178. Dreifuss also used this passage from Ben-Shem's diary. She wrote that the more the ghetto population diminished, the more often shop workers encountered apartments that testified to the fate of their previous residents.

152 Reuven Feldschuh (Ben-Shem), Deciphered Diary, pic. 390.

153 Ibid., pic. 390.

154 Ibid., pic. 390.

155 Emmanuel Ringelblum, *Diary and Notes from the Warsaw Ghetto*, p. 409.

156 Ibid., p. 405.

157 Ibid., p. 409

158 Ibid., p. 406.

159 Havi Dreifuss (Ben-Sasson), *Warsaw Ghetto – The End, April 1942-June 1943*, p. 164-165.

160 Emmanuel Ringelblum, *Diary and Notes from the Warsaw Ghetto*, p. 404.

161 Havi Dreifuss (Ben-Sasson), *Warsaw Ghetto – The End, April 1942-June 1943*, p. 335.

162 Reuven Feldschuh (Ben-Shem), *Deciphered Diary*, pic. 404.
See also: Dominick LaCapra, *Writing History, Writing Trauma*, USA: John Hopkins University Press, 2014, p. 167-168. In this interview, LaCapra addressed the question of intent in the motivation to murder Jews also relating to the notion of 'glee', which too often characterized murder acts. Ben-Shem's writings repeatedly brought up this disturbing attitude in discussing the conduct of perpetrators. Here it is manifested by the phrase 'a hunter's smile'. According to LaCapra, in *Hitler's Willing Executioners* (1996), Daniel Jonah Goldhagen tried to explain this but was unsuccessful ending up with repeating the term 'eliminationist antisemitism'.

163 Ibid., pic. 406.

164 Ibid., pic. 405.

165 Katya Mandoki, 'Terror and aesthetics: Nazi Strategies for Mass Organization', *Culture, Theory and Critique* 42:1, 64-81, Routledge, 5 June 2009, DOI: 10.1080/14735789909391490, p. 78-79. According to Mandoki, in extreme situations, terror leaves no space between people or things. It is a situation

when 'psychological and perceptive distance' disappear, fear takes hold of people, and they stop seeing one another. Mandoki's observation may explain how during selections, personal hardship obliterated sensitivity to others.

166 Reuven Feldschuh (Ben-Shem), *Deciphered Diary*, pic. 407. Black Friday refers to August 21, 1942, when many women and children were captured and deported, leaving the men to mourn them.

167 Helene Berr, p. 56. Berr writes about realizing how others felt uncomfortable because she donned the badge, whereas she said about herself that it was a crucifixion, 'no longer myself... I had become a foreigner ... ... as if my forehead has been seared by a branding iron.'

168 Amos Goldberg, *Trauma in First Person, Diary Writing during the Holocaust*, (Hebrew) p. 99-101.
See also: Henri Lefebvre, p. 193. Lefebvre introduced parallels between the production of space and the body, suggesting that the production of space was extensions of the body. Therefore, each 'demarcated and oriented' space unfolded the relationships within the space. In that sense, the erection of the Warsaw Ghetto had simultaneously disrupted the order of the city of Warsaw while introducing a new place, the ghetto, with its own order wholly detached from the city in which it was established yet forming an obstacle, effectively and conceptually on both sides of the wall.

169 Dalia Ofer, 'Cohesion and Rupture: The Jewish Family in the east European Ghettos during the Holocaust', Max and Rita Haber professor Emeritus, Avraham Harman Institute of Contemporary Jewry, from: https://www.academia.edu/17734363/Cohesion_and_Rupture_The_Jewish_Family_in_th e_East_European_Ghettos_during_the_Holocaust, accessed 15.2.2021, p. 6. Ofer discussed various ways of earning money including one common way, selling one's belongings.

170 Wendy Lower, *The Ravine, A Family, A Photograph, A Holocaust Massacre Revealed*, p. 112-116. Lower addressed the lack of focused attention on the destruction of the family unit during the war. She quoted Ben Ferencz's, the leading American prosecutor during the Nuremberg trials, who was among the few whose speech had centered on imagining what was behind the numbers of the dead, men, women, and children, many times members of one family who were murdered at the same time. Indeed, one of the harshest realities of life in the shops was what happened to the family especially, the women and children who were forced to witness each other's torture and death.

171 Martin Jay, 'In The Realm of the Senses: An Introduction', *The American Historical Review*, Vol. 116, No. 2, Oxford University Press on behalf of the American Historical Association, April 2011, p. 309. Jay pointed out that senses serve to protect humans by providing them with information about the world, warnings, but also pleasure and pain. In the ghetto, senses were constantly stimulated and challenged one's integrity.

290 *Emanuel Ringelblum and Reuven Ben-Shem's War Writings*

172 Yitzhak Zuckerman ('Antek'), *A Surplus of Memory Chronicle of the Warsaw Ghetto Uprising*, USA: University of California Press, 1993, p. 265-6. Zuckerman wrote that he agreed with Auerbach that all survivors felt guilty but he dismissed this approach saying that the only ones to blame were the Germans.

173 Christian Schmid, 'Henri Lefebvre's theory of the production of space: towards a three-dimensional dialectic', in Kanishka Goonewardena, Stefan Kipfer, Richard Milgrom, Christian Schmid (editors), *Space, Difference, Everyday Life: Reading Henri Lefebvre*, Taylor & Francis e-Library, 2008, p. 29. Drawing on Lefebvre's theory, Schmid posited that because space and time were socially produced, they could be understood in relation to a specific society. This defined the shops as first, relational but also a fundamentally historical phenomenon.

174 Amos Goldberg, *Trauma in First Person, Diary Writing during the Holocaust*, (Hebrew), p. 21. In his book, Goldberg discusses the idea that the torture Nazis inflicted on their victims actually altered the nature of the human species. The pressure killed a man before he physically died.

175 Zygmunt Bauman, p. 129-130, 138. According to Bauman, Jews were encouraged to maintain traditional patterns of logical reasoning, which was why they believed that working for the Germans would save their lives. In other words, because Jews could not conceive their death sentence to be final and senseless, it was easier to decipher the situation in logical terms, which assumed that 'productivity' was a solid basis on which to rely as a means of saving one's life.
On p. 138, Bauman discussed Chaim Mordechaj Rumkowski (1877–1944), head of the Jewish Council in Łódź and others who, regardless of incriminating evidence against the Germans, persisted that the only way to avoid death was to prove to the Germans that Jews were necessary.

176 Boaz Neumann, p. 214-216, 243-244. Neumann discussed the change in the German language from metaphorical to literal. One of the difficulties Jews faced was to internalize this change. Time and again they were exposed to the existence of such places as Treblinka, but the information was too difficult to digest.

177 Ibid., p. 97. Here Neumann discussed the incapacity of victims to understand Auschwitz because the process of figuring out what was going on proved futile as it involved trying to understand a new world using the concepts of the old world.

CONCLUSIONS

1 Henri Lefebvre, p. 38-39.

2 Samuel D. Kassow, 'Vilna and Warsaw, Two Ghetto Diaries: Herman Kruk and Emanuel Ringelblum', p. 172-3, 176. This source was mentioned before

to draw the attention to the background of the research of Jewish history, which was until the mid-1920s, largely individual which was the reason information and insights were commonly organized through writing diaries.

3   Boaz Neumann, p. 97. Neumann discussed here the incapacity of victims to understand Auschwitz because the process of figuring out what was going on proved futile as it involved trying to grasp a new world using old world concepts.

4   Berber Bevernage, *History, Memory, and State-Sponsored Violence, Time and Justice*, UK: Taylor & Francis, 2012, p. 15-16. Bevernage's interesting theory suggests that too much memory invades the present thus makes the past irrevocable preventing what one might call, moving on. Bevernage suggests that events should be remembered collectively but as a separate form so as not to disrupt the present.

List of Illustrations

Cover. The historian Dr . Emanuel Ringelblum
Ghetto Fighters' House Museum,Israel/Photo Archive, Catalog No.19189

1. Notes on the ghetto underground women couriers, handwritten by Dr. Emanuel Ringelblum. This image is also featured on the background of the cover.
Ghetto Fighters' House Museum, Israel/ Photo Archive, Catalog No. 19214

2. The historian Dr. Emanuel Ringelblum with his son Uri.
Ghetto Fighters' House Museum, Israel/ Photo Archive, Catalog No. 19212.

3. Yehudit Ringelblum (Józia), nee Herman, Dr. Emanuel Ringelblum's wife.
Ghetto Fighters' House Museum, Israel/ Photo Archive, Catalog No. 2742.

4. A conference of Jewish historians in Vilnius organized by YIVO.
Right and standing: Shmuel Lehman (second), Daniel Lerner, Rafael Mahler.
Left standing: Pinchas Kon (fifth), Rudolf Glanc, Yosef - David Derewianski, Eliahu Szulman and Emanuel Ringelblum.
Seated, fifth from right – Prof. Simon Dubnow, August 1935.
Ghetto Fighters' House Museum, Israel/ Photo Archive, Catalog No. 19197.

5. Josima Feldschuh – Pnina (Perła) and Dr. Reuven Ben-Shem's (Feldschuh) daughter.
Yad-Vashem, Photo Archive, sig. 3384/85.

6. Ruth and Reuven Ben-Shem, Givat Shmuel, Israel, circa 1946.

List of Illustrations

The Ben-Shem Family Photo Archive

7. Hugging the dog, Ben-Shem's son Kami (Nekamia), Gad Feldschuh, his brother, Rachel Auerbach, Reuven Ben-Shem, Ruth his wife and Yuli (Yoa), his daughter.
The Ben-Shem Family Photo Archive

8. Dr. Reuven Ben-Shem (Feldschuh), Kowel, *Hashomer Hatzair*, 1926.
Ghetto Fighters' House Museum, Israel/ Photo Archive, Catalog No. 30011 This image also appears on the cover.

9. Farewell party in honor of Dr. Feldschuh (Ben-Shem) (second row fifth from the right and sitting) Krakow, 13.8.1927.
Massuah, Photo Archive, The Hannah Shlomi Collection, Item ID: 84271.

10. Rachel Auerbach and Hersch Wasser, upon the discovery of part of the buried "*Oneg Shabbat*" archives.
Yad-Vashem, Photo Archive, sig. 3380/745

11. Warsaw, Crowds at the corner of Zelazna and Leszno streets.
Yad-Vashem, Photo Archive, sig.503/1548.

12. Warsaw, Boxes and jars containing the buried "Ringelblum Archives". They were found in the ghetto ruins after the war.
Yad-Vashem, Photo Archive, sig. 1605/17.

13. Announcement of the concert Josima Feldschuh gave in the Melody Palace theatre in the Warsaw Ghetto, 15.3.1941.
The Ben-Shem Family Photo Archive.

14. At their home in Givat Shmuel: Sitting: Reuven Ben-Shem and Rachel Auerbach, behind and standing: Ruth, Ben-Shem's wife.
The Ben-Shem Family Photo Archive.

15. Warsaw, a Jewish policeman directing the traffic between Leszno and Karmelicka Streets, 1941. The photograph was developed by Herbert Paetz. Avraham Haim Topas with his son are standing on the terrace.
Yad-Vashem, Photo Archive, sig. 503/1545.

16. Warsaw, children begging in the ghetto, 1940-1943.
Yad-Vashem, Photo Archive, sig. 933/140.

17. Warsaw, a starving child in a ghetto street, 1941.

Yad-Vashem, Photo Archive, sig. 3186/40.

18. A workshop in the Warsaw Ghetto, October 1940–May 1943.
United States Holocaust Memorial Museum, Leopold Page Photographic Collection, Photograph Number 05540.

19. The historian Dr. Emanuel Ringelblum.
Ghetto Fighters' House Museum, Israel/Photo Archive, Catalog No. 19190.

20. Dr Reuven Ben-Shem after the war.
The Ben-Shem Family Photo Archive.

21. A page from Dr. Reuven Ben-Shem (Feldschuh)'s handwritten original diary. This image is also featured on the background of the cover.
The Ben-Shem Family Photo Archive.

22. Warsaw, Dr Emanuel Ringelblum, his wife Yehudit with their son, Uri, circa 1930.
Yad-Vashem, Photo Archive, sig. 503/7341.

23. Dr Herzl Rosenblum (Chief Editor of Yedioth Ahronoth), Dr Reuven Ben-Shem, Moshe Gold and Elie Wiesel at Be'er Yaacov, Israel, circa 1948.
The Ben-Shem Family Photo Archive.

Bibliography

Primary Sources

Feldschuh (Ben-Shem) Reuven, *Testimonies, Diaries and Memoirs Collection*, Record Group 0.33, File Number 959, Jerusalem: Yad-Vashem Archive, (Hebrew).

Ringelblum Emmanuel, *Diary and Notes from the Warsaw Ghetto, September 1939 - December 1942*, Vol 1, Jerusalem: Yad-Vashem, Ghetto Fighters' House, 1994, (Hebrew).

Ringelblum Emmanuel, *Last Writings, Polish-Jewish Relations, January 1943-April 1944*, Jerusalem: Yad-Vashem, Ghetto Fighters' House, 1994, (Hebrew).

Ringelblum Emanuel, *Writings from the Warsaw Ghetto, Volume 1, 1939 -1942*, Tel-Aviv: I.L. Peretz Publishing House, 1985, (Yiddish).

Ringelblum Emanuel, *Writings from the Warsaw Ghetto, Volume II*, Tel-Aviv: I.L. Peretz Publishing House, 1985, (Yiddish).

Archives

Ben-Shem Reuven, letter to Joseph Kermish, 15, October, 1963, Yad Vashem Jerusalem, (Hebrew).

Ben-Shem Reuven, interview, Massuah, International Institute for Holocaust Studies, Tel Yitzhak, file 7442 , AR-T-002-17, archive 2/17/,ע tape 3, 27.10.1971.

Ben-Shem Reuven (the Board), Guidelines of *Hashomer*, Warsaw: Hashomer Hataha Haleumi in Poland Publications, Bulletin no. 1, December 1927.

Ben-Shem Reuven, 'The Principles of *Hashomer Haleumi*, Warsaw, Iyar (May-June), 1929, Circular number 23/89. File: AR-A-019-29, computerized: 17396, Moshe Kol's Collection, Massuah, Tel Yitzhak.

Drewniak Fela, a letter from Moscow addressed to the Central Jewish Commission in Lublin, 29.1.1945. Ghetto Fighters' House, Kibbutz Lohamei HaGetaot, the Berman Collection, file 19972.

Gazeta Żydowska, March 21, 1941, 'Josima Feldschuh, na nadzwyczajnym koncercie symfonicznym' (Josima Feldschuh, at an extraordinary symphony concert), (Polish). The Jewish Historical Institute, Warsaw. https://cbj.jhi.pl/documents/791447/3/, accessed, 15.4.2021.

Kaplan, Chaim Aron, *The Continuation of Our Scroll of Agony*, Unpublished Manuscript, Notebook 10,11, (14.4.1941-2.5.1942), (Hebrew). Moreshet, Givat Haviva.

Krzepicki Henryk, interview by institute assistant, Luba Melchior, Polish Research Institute at Lund University, Sweden. Protocol No. 83, January 5, 1946. https://www.alvin-portal.org/alvin/attachment/document/alvin-record:101164/ATTACHMENT-0011.pdf, accessed 9.4.2021 .

Lipman Abraham, record no. 288940, Yad-Vashem, Hall of Names, Yad-Vashem, Jerusalem.

Lipman Gavriel, record no. 1124260, Yad-Vashem, Hall of Names, Yad-Vashem, Jerusalem.

Lubetkin Zivia, The Eichmann Trial, Minutes of Session 25, Wednesday, May 3,1961, District Court Jerusalem, in ŻOB (Żydowska Organizacja Bojowa, or the Jewish Fighting Organization) 1961-2001' (ŻZW - Żydowski Związek Wojskowy, Jewish Military Union, The Warsaw Ghetto Uprising, Biographies, Questionnaires, Testimonies, 1961-2001), file 70 (9/7 - B), Criminal Record 40/61, (Hebrew), Jabotinsky Institute, Tel-Aviv.

Kol Moshe, letter to Ben-Shem, the Ben-Shem family Archive, 19 October, 1979, (Hebrew).

Mezdelewski Arie, testimony, Yad Yaari, Givat Haviva, images\moreshet\ (manuscripts)\D.2.164-testimonies.pdf., Yad Yaari Research & Documentation Center, (Yiddish & Hebrew). https://www.infocenters.co.il/yadyaari/note book_ext.asp?book=143593&lang=heb&site=yadyaari, accessed 30.5.2019.

Rosen Alan, David Boder, Early Postwar Voices: David Boder's Life and Work, The Voices Project, Illinois Institute of Technology, Chicago. https://iit.aviary platform.com/catalog?utf8=%E2%9C%93&search_field=advanced&f[collectio n_id_is][]=231&search_type=simple&title_text[]=&resource_description[]= &indexes[]=&transcript[]=&op[]=&type_of_search[]=simple&type_of_field_ selector[]=simple&keywords[]= accessed: 13.7.2020.

Szlengel Władysław, 'Opaski' ('Badges'), a poem, Central Jewish Library, Collection of satiric compositions, The Jewish Historical Institute, Warsaw, ARG I 1240 (Ring. I/526), September, 1941, (Polish). https://cbj.jhi.pl/documents/967862/ 9/, accessed: 30.5.2019.

Smitizki Rachel, a letter addressed to Reuven Ben-Shem, March 3, 1963, Yad-Vashem, Jerusalem, (Hebrew).

The Benjamin Tenenbaum (Tene) Collection: Testimonies of Child Survivors of the Holocaust, EHRI, Holocaust Research Infrastructure, https://portal.ehri-project.eu/units/il-002806-tenenbaum_coll, accessed: 15.5.2020.

Jabotinsky Zeev, a letter addressed to Reuven Ben-Shem (Feldschuh) and Mr. Rosenblum in London, 11.2.1931, file 1118, Jabotinsky Institute, Tel-Aviv.

Articles in English

Acarón Thania, 'Shape-in(g) Space: Body, Boundaries, and Violence', *Space and Culture*, Vol. 19 (2), Sage, 2016, DOI: 10.1177/1206331215623208, pp. 139-149.

Żbikowski Andrzej, 'Central Committee of Polish Jews (CKŻP), The Main and Basic Political and Social Organization of the Jewish Community', November

25, 2013, Jewish Historical Institute, https://www.jhi.pl/en/articles/central-committee-of-polish-jews,57, accessed: 5.1.2020.

Bartov Omer, 'Wartime Lies and Other Testimonies Jewish-Christian Relations in Buczacz, 1939–1944', *East European Politics and Societies*, Vol 25, no. 3, Sage, August 2011, pp. 486-511.

Ben-Sasson (Dreifuss) Havi, 'Christians in The Ghetto: All Saints' Church, Birth of the Holy Virgin Mary Church, and the Jews of the Warsaw Ghetto', *Yad-Vashem Studies* 31, Jerusalem: Yad-Vashem, 2003, pp. 153-173.

Ben-Sasson Havi, and Lea Preiss, 'Twilight Days: Missing Pages from Avraham Lewin's Warsaw Ghetto Diary, May-July 1942', *Yad-Vashem Studies 33*, Jerusalem: Yad-Vashem, 2005, pp. 7-60.

Bohus Kata, 'Anne and Eva: 'Two Diaries, Two Holocaust Memories in Communist Hungary', *Remembrance and Solidarity Studies in 20th Century European History*, issue 5, December 2016, pp. 97-114.

Böser Ursula, 'Yael Hersonski's Re-representation of Archival Footage from the Warsaw Ghetto', *Film Criticism*, Vol 37, No. 2, Allegheny College, Winter 2012-2013, pp. 38-56.

Broszat Martin and Friedländer Saul, 'A Controversy about the Historicization of National Socialism', *New German Critique*, No. 44, Special Issue on the Historikerstreit, Spring - Summer, 1988, pp. 85-126.

Celinscak Mark, 'A Procession of Shadows: Examining Warsaw Ghetto Testimony', *The New School Psychology Bulletin*, Vol. 6 No. 2, The New School for Social Research, 2009, pp. 38-50.

Cohen Boaz, 'Rachel Auerbach, Yad-Vashem and Israeli Holocaust Memory', *Polin: Studies in Polish Jewry*, Vol. 20, Making Holocaust Memory, Gabriel N. Finder, Natalia Aleksuin, Antony Polonsky and Jan Schwarz (editors), Oxford; Portland, Oregon: The Littman Library of Jewish Civilization, 2008, pp. 197-221.

Cohen Boaz, 'Holocaust Testimonies and Historical Writing, Debates, Innovations, and Problems in the Early Postwar Period', *Yad-Vashem Studies*, Vol. 45:2 (2017) pp. 159-183.

Corfield J. Penelope, 'Time and the Historians in the Age of Relativity', *Geschichte und Gesellschaft. Sonderheft*, Vol. 25, Vandenhoeck & Ruprecht (GmbH & Co. KG), 2015, pp. 71-91.

Delaperrière Maria, 'Testimony as a Literary Problem', *Teksty Drugie, English Edition, Theory of Literature, Critique, Interpretation: Nonfiction, Reportage and Testimony*, Special Issue, 2, Publishing House of the Institute of Literary Research, 2014, pp. 42-54.

Deutsch Nathaniel, 'When Culture Became the New Torah: Late Imperial Russia and the Discovery of Jewish Culture', *The Jewish Quarterly Review*, Vol. 102, No. 3, Summer 2012, pp. 455-473.

Douglas Mary, 'The Idea of a Home: A Kind of Space', *Social Research*, 58:1, The Johns Hopkins University Press, Spring 1991, pp. 287-307.

Einwohner L. Rachel, 'The Need to Know: Cultured Ignorance and Jewish Resistance in the Ghettos of Warsaw, Vilna, and Łódź', *The Sociological Quarterly*, Vol. 50, No. 3, Taylor & Francis, Ltd., Summer, 2009, pp. 407-430.

Eskildsen Kasper Risbjerg, 'Inventing the archive: Testimony and virtue in modern historiography', *History of the Human Sciences*, 26 (4), Sage, 2013, pp. 8–26.

Farbstein Esther, 'Diaries and Memoirs as a Historical Source - The Diary and Memoir of a Rabbi at the 'Konin House of Bondage', Shoah Resource Center, The International School for Holocaust Studies. https://www.yadvashem.org/odot_pdf/Microsoft%20Word%20-%203134.pdf accessed 6.7.2019.

Fisher Bob, Ghetto Life, *ICG, International Cinematographer Guild Magazine*, November 8, 2010, from: https://www.icgmagazine.com/web/ghetto-life/, accessed 24.12.2020.

Friedman Philip, 'The Jewish Ghettos of the Nazi Era', *Jewish Social Studies*, Vol. 16, No. 1, Indiana University Press, 1954, pp. 61-88.

Garbarini Alexandra, 'Document Volumes and the Status of Victim Testimony in the Era of the First World War and Its Aftermath', in *Études arméniennes contemporaines, Le témoignage des victimes dans la connaissance des violences de masse, Études*, 5, 2015, from: https://doi.org/10.4000/eac.782, accessed: 18.7.2020.

Gareth Williams, 'The genesis of chronic illness: narrative re-construction', *Sociology of Health and Illness*, Vol. 6 No. 2, 1984, pp. 175-200.

Goldberg Amos, 'A Fool or a Prophet: Rubinstein the Warsaw Ghetto Jester', The 2019 J. B. and Maurice C. Shapiro Annual Lecture at the United States Holocaust Memorial Museum 13.3.2019, United States Holocaust Memorial Museum. https://www.academia.edu/38809091/A_Fool_or_a_Prophet_Rubinstein_the_Warsaw_Ghetto_Jester, pp. 1-25, accessed: 7.4.2019.

Goldberg Amos, 'The Victim's Voice and Melodramatic Aesthetics in History', *History and Theory*, Vol. 48, No. 3, Wiley, Wesleyan University, Oct. 2009, pp. 220-237.

Groberg A. Kristi, 'The Life and Influence of Simon Dubnov (1860-1941): An Appreciation', *Modern Judaism*, Vol. 13, No. 1, Oxford University Press, Feb., 1993, pp. 71-93.

Gumpert Martin, 'The Physicians of Warsaw', *The American Scholar*, Vol. 18, No. 3, The Phi Beta Kappa Society, Summer 1949, pp. 285-290.

Hell Julia, 'Modernity and the Holocaust, or, Listening to Eurydice', *Theory, Culture & Society* Vol. 27(6), Sage, 2010, DOI: 10.1177/0263276410382026, pp. 125-154.

Hilberg Raul, 'The Ghetto as A Form of Government', *The Annals of the American Academy of Political and Social Science*, Vol. 450 ,Reflections on the Holocaust: Historical, Philosophical, and Educational Dimensions, Sage, Jul., 1980, pp. 98-112.

Horváth, Rita, 'The Role of the Survivors in the Remembrance of the Holocaust, Memorial Monuments and *Yizkor Books*', in Friedman C. Jonathan (editor), *The Routledge History of the Holocaust*, USA: Routledge, 2011, pp. 472-483.

Hüppauf Bernd, 'Emptying the Gaze: Framing Violence through the Viewfinder', *New German Critique*, No. 72, published by: Duke University Press, Autumn, 1997, pp. 3-44.

Jay Martin, 'In the Realm of the Senses: An Introduction', *The American Historical Review*, Vol. 116, No. 2, Oxford University Press on behalf of the American Historical Association, April 2011, pp. 307-315.

Jockusch Laura, 'Historiography in Transit: Survivor Historians and the Writing of Holocaust History in the late 1940s', *Leo Baeck Institute Yearbook*, Vol. 58 Issue 1, Published by Oxford University Press on behalf of The Leo Baeck Institute, 2013, pp. 75-94.

Johnson Hannah & and Nina Caputo, 'The Middle Ages and The Holocaust: Medieval Anti-Judaism in The Crucible of Modern Thought', *Postmedieval: A Journal of Medieval Cultural Studies*, Volume 5, Issue 3, Macmillan Publishers, September 2014, pp. 270-277.

Kajczyk Agnieszka, "Bridge of Sighs' of the biggest Ghetto in Europe', *Jewish Historical Institute*. https://www.jhi.pl/en/articles/bridge-of-sighs-of-the-biggest-ghetto-in-europe,249, accessed 8.3.2021.

Kansteiner Wulf, 'Success, Truth, and Modernism in Holocaust Historiography: Reading Saul Friedländer Thirty-Five Years after the Publication of 'Metahistory'', *History and Theory*, Vol. 48, No. 2, Theme Issue 47: Historical Representation and Historical Truth, pp. 25-53, Wiley for Wesleyan University, May, 2009.

Karlip M. Joshua, 'Between Martyrology and Historiography: Elias Tcherikower and the Making of a Pogrom Historian', *East European Jewish Affairs*, 38:3, Routledge, 16 Dec 2008, pp. 257-280.

Kaspi André, 'Le Centre de Documentation Juive Contemporaine', (Center of Contemporary Jewish Documentation), *Revue d'histoire moderne et contemporaine (1954-)*, T. 23e, No. 2, Société d'Histoire Moderne et Contemporaine Stable, Apr. - Jun., 1976, (French), pp. 305-311.

Keilbach Judith, 'Photographs, Symbolic Images, and the Holocaust: On the (Im)Possibility of Depicting Historical Truth', *History and Theory, Theme Issue* 47, Wesleyan University, May 2009, pp. 54-76.

Kuznitz E. Cecile, 'YIVO's "Old Friend and Teacher": Simon Dubnow and his Relationship to the Yiddish Scientific Institute', *Jahrbuch des Simon-Dubnow-Instituts (Simon Dubnow Institute Yearbook)*, Vol. xv, Leipzig: Vandenhoeck & Ruprecht, 2016, pp. 477-507.

Lang Berl, 'Oskar Rosenfeld and The Realism of Holocaust-History: On Sex, Shit, and Status', *History and Theory*, 43, USA: Wesleyan University, May 2004, pp. 278-288.

Low E. Y. Kelvin, 'Presenting the Self, the Social Body and the Olfactory: Managing Smells in Everyday Life Experiences', *Sociological Perspectives*, Vol. 49, Issue 4, Pacific Sociological Association, Sage, 2006, pp. 607-631.

Low Setha, 'Anthropological Theories of Body, Space, and Culture', *Space & Culture*, vol. 6 no. 1, City University of New York, Sage, February 2003, DOI: 10.1177/1206331202238959, pp. 9-18.

Mandoki Katya, 'Terror and aesthetics: Nazi Strategies for Mass Organization', *Culture, Theory and Critique* 42:1, Routledge, 5 June 2009, DOI: 10.1080/14735789909391490, pp. 64-81.

Margalit Elkana, 'Social and Intellectual Origins of the *Hashomer Hatzair* Youth Movement, 1913-20', *Journal of Contemporary History*, Vol. 4, No. 2, Sage, Apr. 1969, pp. 25-46.

Melamed Laliv, 'A Film Unraveled: An Interview with Yael Hersonski', pp. 9-19, *Int J Polit Cult Soc*, 26, New York: Springer Science+Business Media, 2013, DOI 10.1007/s10767-013-9136-9, pp. 9-19.

Michlean J. Amir and Rosemary Horowitz, '*Yizkor Books* in the Twenty-First Century: A History and Guide to the Genre', *Judaica Librarianship*, Vol 14, 2008, DOI: 10.14263/2330-2976.1073, pp. 39-56.

Miron Guy, "'Lately, Almost Constantly, Everything Seems Small to Me': The Lived Space of German Jews under the Nazi Regime', *Jewish Social Studies: History, Culture, Society* n.s. 20, no. 1, Fall 2013, pp. 121–149.

Miron Guy, 'The "Lived Time" of German Jews under the Nazi Regime', *The Journal of Modern History 90*, The University of Chicago, March 2018, pp. 116-153.

Müller Beate, 'Trauma, Historiography and Polyphony: Adult Voices in the CJHC's Early Postwar Child Holocaust Testimonies', *History and Memory*, Vol. 24, No. 2, Indiana University Press, (Fall/Winter 2012), pp. 157-195.

Narrowe H. Morton, 'Jabotinsky and the Zionists in Stockholm (1915)', *Jewish Social Studies*, Vol. 46, No. 1, Indiana University Press, Winter 1984, pp. 9-20.

Nizan Victoria, 'The Role and Value of Diaries in Teaching History – Case Study', *ERD 2017 Education, Reflection, Development*, Fifth Edition, www.Future Academy.org.UK, 2018, pp. 779-787. http://dx.doi.org/10.15405/epsbs.2018. 06.93, accessed 1.7.2021.

Nizan Victoria, 'Politics and History in Emanuel Ringelblum's War Diaries. Emanuel Ringelblum between the Two World Wars', *Journal of Global Politics and Current Diplomacy*, no. 4, Issue 2, Centrul pentru Dialog European şi Diplomaţie Culturală (Center for European Dialogue and Cultural Diplomacy) (DEDIC), April 2016, pp. 15-31.

Nizan Victoria, 'Smelling the Ghetto. Smells in the Warsaw Ghetto According to Ruben Ben-Shem's (Feldschu) Diary', *Journal of Global Politics and Current Diplomacy (JGPCD)*, no. 5, Issue 1, Centrul pentru Dialog European şi Diplomaţie Culturală (Center for European Dialogue and Cultural Diplomacy) (DEDIC), April 2017, pp. 5-25.

Ofer Dalia, 'Cohesion and Rupture: The Jewish Family in the East European Ghettos during the Holocaust', Max and Rita Haber professor Emeritus, Avraham Harman Institute of Contemporary Jewry, pp. 1-28. https://www. academia.edu/17734363/Cohesion_and_Rupture_The_Jewish_Family_in_the _East_European_Ghettos_during_the_Holocaust, accessed 15.2.2021

Penkower Noam Monty, 'The Kishinew Pogrom of 1903: A Turning Point in Jewish History', *Modern Judaism*, Vol. 24, No. 3, Oxford University Press, Oct. 2004, pp. 187-225.

Person Katarzyna, *The Easter Pogrom, 1940*, The Jewish Historical Institute, 21.03.2018. From: https://www.jhi.pl/en/articles/the-easter-pogrom-1940,354, accessed 3.5 2021.

Plotkin Diana, 'Smuggling in the Ghetto, Survivors accounts from Warsaw, Łódź and Kraków Ghettoes', in Sterling J. Eric (editor), *Life in the Ghettos During the Holocaust*, USA: Syracuse University Press, 2005, pp. 84-119.

Rabinovitch Simon, 'The Dawn of a New Diaspora: Simon Dubnov's Autonomism, from St. Petersburg to Berlin', *The Leo Baeck Institute Yearbook*, Volume 50, Issue 1, Berghahn Books, January 2005, pp. 267–288.

Schrøder Simonsen S. Cecilie, 'A Spatial Expansion of a Pocket-Size Homeland: Heinrich Heine's Construction of Jewish Space', *Partial Answers, Journal of Literature and the History of Ideas*, Vol. 14, no. 2, Baltimore: John Hopkins University Press, Jun 2016, pp. 303-321.

Seamon David, 'Physical Comminglings: Body, Habit, and Space Transformed Into Place', *The Occupational Therapy Journal of Research*, Volume 22, Sage, Supplement, Winter 2002, DOI: 10.1177/153944920202220S106, pp. 42s-51s.

Spector-Mersel Gabriela, 'Mechanisms of Selection in Claiming Narrative Identities: A Model for Interpreting Narratives', *Qualitative Inquiry*, 17(2), Sage, 2011, DOI: 10.1177/1077800410393885, pp. 172-185.

Strejilevich Nora, 'Beyond the Language of Truth', *Human Rights Quarterly*, Vol. 28, No. 3, The Johns Hopkins University Press, August 2006, pp. 701-713.

Stupples Peter, 'Il'ya Erenburg and the Jewish Anti-Fascist Committee', *New Zealand Slavonic Journal*, No. 2, Australia and New Zealand Slavists' Association, 1977, pp. 13-28.

Uziel Daniel, 'Wehrmacht Propaganda Troops and the Jews', Jerusalem: *Yad-Vashem Studies*, Vol. 29, 2001, pp. 27- 65. https://www.yadvashem.org/odot_pdf/Microsoft%20Word%20-%202021.pdf accessed: 202020.

Van Pelt Robert Jan, 'Paradise/Hades, Purgatory, Hell/ Gehenna: A Political Typology of the Camps', in Friedman C. Jonathan (editor), *The Routledge History of the Holocaust*, New York & Canada: Routledge, 2011, pp. 191-202.

Weinbaum Laurence, 'Shaking the Dust off, The Story of the Warsaw Ghetto's Forgotten Chronicler, Ruben Feldschu (Ben-Shem)', *Jewish Political Studies Review*, Vol. 22, No. 3/4, pp. 7-44, Fall 2010.

Witkowska-Krych Agnieszka, "Our Children Must Live Because the Child Is the Most Sacred Thing We Have." The Portrayal in Gazeta Żydowska of the Children's Month Campaign in the Warsaw Ghetto', Museum of Warsaw, 2020, pp. 185-205. https://muzeumwarszawy.pl/wp-content/uploads/2020/01/6B.-Nasze-dzieci-ang-K1.pdf, accessed: 13.12.2020.

Woolf R. Daniel, 'Genre into Artifact: The Decline of the English Chronicle in the Sixteenth Century' *The Sixteenth Century Journal*, published by The Sixteenth Century Journal, Vol. 19, No. 3, Autumn 1988, pp. 321-354.

Zenderland Leila, 'Social Science as a "Weapon of the Weak": Max Weinreich, the Yiddish Scientific Institute, and the Study of Culture, Personality, and Prejudice', *Isis*, Vol. 104, No. 4, The University of Chicago Press on behalf of The History of Science Society, December 2013, pp. 742-772.

Zierler Wendy, "My Own Special Corner, Sacred, Beloved': The Hebrew Diary of Hava Shapiro (1878-1943), *Hebrew Studies*, 53, National Association of Professors of Hebrew (NAPH), 2012, pp. 231-255.

Books in English

Abramson Glenda, *Drama and Ideology in Modern Israel*, Cambridge: Cambridge University Press, 1998.

Abramson Henry, *Torah from the Years of Wrath 1939-1943: The Historical Context of the Aish Kodesh* (Holy Fire), USA: Henri Abramson, October 2017. https://touroscholar.touro.edu/lcas_books/5/?utm_source=touroscholar.touro.edu%2Flcas_books%2F5&utm_medium=PDF&utm_campaign=PDFCoverPages, accessed 4.7.2021.

Adelson Alan and Lapides Robert (editors), *Lodz Ghetto*, New York: Viking Penguin, 1989.

Aleksiun Natalia, 'The Central Jewish Historical Commission in Poland', in: Finder N. Gabriel, Aleksiun Natalia, Polonsky Antony and Schwarz Jan (editors), *Making Holocaust Memory*, Vol 20, USA.: The Littman Library of Jewish Civilization in association with Liverpool University Press, 2008.

Aleksiun Natalia and Brian Horowitz, Introduction, in Aleksiun Natalia, Horowitz Brian and Polonsky Antony (editors), *Polin, Studies in Jewish Jewry, Vol. 29, Writing Jewish History in Eastern Europe*, Portland Oregon: The Littman Library of Jewish Civilization in association with Liverpool University Press, 2017.

Arad Yitzhak, *Ghetto in Flames, The Struggle and Destruction of the Jews of Vilna in the Holocaust*, Jerusalem: Yad-Vashem, 1980.

Arendt Hannah, 'Understanding and Politics, (The Difficulties of Understanding)', in *Essays in Understanding, 1930-1954, Formation, Exile, and Totalitarianism*, Kohn Jerome (editor), New York: Schocken Books, 1994, pp. 307-327.

Arendt Hannah, *Eichmann in Jerusalem: A Report on the Banality of Evil*, USA: Penguin Classics, 2006.

Barthes Roland, "Textual Analysis: Poe's 'Valdemar", in McQuillan Martin (editor), *The Narrative Reader*, UK: e-Library by Taylor and Francis, 2002, pp. 130-138.

Bartov Omer, *Anatomy of a Genocide: The Life and Death of a Town Called Buczacz*, New York: Simon & Schuster, January 23,2018, Kindle Edition.

Bauman Zygmunt, *Modernity and the Holocaust*, Bodmin, Cornwall: Polity Press, 2008.

Bauman, Janina *Beyond These Walls, Escaping the Warsaw Ghetto, A Young Girl's Story*, UK: Virago Press, 2006.

Bauman, Janina *Winter in the Morning, a Young Girl's Life in the Ghetto and Beyond 1939-1945*, New-York: the Free Press, Macmillan Inc. 1986.

Benjamin Walter, *A Short History of Photography*. https://monoskop.org/images/7/79/Benjamin_Walter_1931_1972_A_Short_History_of_Photography.pdf, accessed 7.6.2021.

Bensoussan George, 'The Jewish Contemporary Documentation Center (CDJC) and Holocaust Research in France, 1945-1970', in, Bankier David and Michman Dan (editors), *Holocaust Historiography in Context: Emergence, Challenges, Polemics and Achievements*, Jerusalem : Yad-Vashem in association with Berghahn Books, 2008, pp. 245-254.

Bernard-Donals Michael, *An Introduction to Holocaust Studies*, New Jersey: Upper Saddle River: Pearson Education, 2006.

Berr Helen, *Journal, The Diary of a Young Jewish Woman in Occupied Paris*, London: MacLehose Press, 2008.

Bevernage Berber, *History, Memory, and State-Sponsored Violence, Time and Justice*, UK: Taylor & Francis, 2012, p. 15-16.

Bikont Anna, *The Crime and the Silence, Confronting the Massacre of Jews in Wartime Jedwabne*, USA: Farrar, Straus and Giroux, 2004.

Blanchot Maurice, *The Writing of A Disaster*, USA: University of Nebraska Press, 1995.

Brenner Michael, *Prophets of the Past: Interpreters of Jewish History*, Princeton: Princeton University Press, 2010.

Bridgeman Teresa, 'Time and Space', in Herman David (editor), *The Cambridge Companion to Narrative*, UK: Cambridge University Press, 2007, pp. 52-65.

Burguière André, *The Annals School, An Intellectual History*, USA: Cornell University Press, 2009.

Chare Nicholas and Williams Dominic, *The Auschwitz Sonderkommando: Testimonies, Histories, Representations*, Cham, Switzerland: Palgrave Macmillan, 2019.

Chare Nicholas, *Auschwitz and Afterimages: Abjection, Witnessing and Representation*, USA: I.B. Tauris, 2011

Charlesworth Andrew, 'The Topography of Genocide', in Stone Dan (editor), *The Historiography of the Holocaust*, USA: Palgrave Macmillan, 2004. pp. 216-252.

Chatman Seymour, 'Point of View', in McQuillan Martin (editor), *The Narrative Reader*, UK: e-Library by Taylor and Francis, 2002, pp. 96-98.

Cohen Boaz, 'Bound to Remember – Bound To Remind, Holocaust Survivors and the Genesis of Holocaust Research', in, Steinert Johannes-Dieter and Weber-Newth Inge (editors), *Beyond camps and forced labour: current international research on survivors of Nazi persecution*, Osnabruck: Secolo Verlag, 2004, pp. 290-300.

Cull J. Nicholas, 'Poland', in Cull J. Nicholas, Culbert David, and Welch David (editors), *Propaganda and Mass Persuasion: A Historical Encyclopedia, 1500 to the Present*, Santa Barbara, Calif.: ABC-CLIO, 2003, pp. 302-305.

Czerniaków Adam, *The Warsaw Diary of Adam Czerniaków, Prelude to Doom*, Chicago: Ivan R. Dee, Publisher, 1999.

Davis Colin, *Traces of War: Interpreting Ethics and Trauma in Twentieth-century French Writing*, Liverpool: Liverpool University Press, 2018.

Didi-Huberman Georges, *Images in Spite of All, Four Photographs from Auschwitz*, USA: University of Chicago Press, 2012.

Donat Alexander, *The Holocaust Kingdom, A Memoire*, UAS: Holocaust Library New York, 1978.

Douglas Mary, *Purity and Danger, An Analysis of Concepts of Pollution and Taboo*, UK: Taylor & Francis e-Library, 2001.

Dubnow Simon, *Jewish History: An Essay in The Philosophy of History*, Philadelphia: The Jewish Publication Society of America, 1903.

Ehrenburg Ilya and Grossman Vasily, *The Complete Black Book of Russian Jewry*, New Brunswick, USA: Transaction Publishers, 2009.

Engel David, *Historians of the Jews and the Holocaust* (Stanford Studies in Jewish History and Culture), California: Stanford University Press, 2010.

Engelking Barbara & Leociak Jacek, *The Warsaw Ghetto, A Guide to the Perished City*, New Haven: Yale University Press, 2009.

Farbstein Ester, 'Young Moshe's Ark; Reappraisal of the Diary of Moshe Flinker, in *"So spricht der Ewige: ... Und die Straßen der Stadt Jerusalem werden voll sein mit Knaben und Mädchen, die in ihren Straßen spielen'* (gemäß Sacharjah 8,4-5) (Thus saith the LORD of hosts: ... And the broad places of the city shall be full of boys and girls playing ...), die Siebte Joseph Carlebach-Konferenz ; das jüdische Kind zwischen hoffnungsloser Vergangenheit und hoffnungsvoller Zukunft, (the Seventh Joseph Carlebach Conference: the Jewish Child, Between a Lost Past to a Promising Future), Gillis-Carlebach Miriam and Vogel Barbara (editors), München Hamburg: Dölling und Galitz Verlag, 2008, pp. 196-215.

Frankl E. Viktor, *Man's Search for Meaning*, UK: Rider, 2008.

Friedländer Saul, 'An Integrated History of the Holocaust: Some Methodological Challenges', in Stone Dan (editor), *The Holocaust and Historical Methodology*, New York: Berghahn, 2015, pp. 181-189.

Friedländer Saul, 'Introduction' in Friedländer Saul (editor), *Probing the Limits of Representation : Nazism and the 'Final Solution'*, USA: Harvard University Press, 1992, pp. 1-21.

Friedländer Saul, *The Years of Extermination: Nazi Germany and the Jews, 1939–1945*, New York: HarperCollins e-books, 2007.

Felman Shoshana, 'Camus' The Plague, or a Monument to Witnessing', in Laub Dori M.D & Felman Shoshana, *Testimony, Crises of Witnessing in Literature, Psychoanalysis and History*, USA: Routledge, 1992, pp. 93-203.

Felman Shoshana, 'Education and Crisis, Or the Vicissitudes of Teaching' in Dori Laub M.D and Shoshana Felman, *Testimony, Crises of Witnessing in Literature, Psychoanalysis and History*, USA: Routledge, 1992, pp. 1-56.

Frost Shimon, *Schooling as a Socio-Political Expression: Jewish Education in Interwar Poland*, Jerusalem: Magnes, 1998.

Garbarini Alexandra with Kerenji Emil, Lambertz Jan, Patt Avinoam, *Jewish Responses to Persecution: 1938–1940, Documenting Life and Destruction, Holocaust Sources in Context*, Vol. 2, Lanham, USA: AltaMira Press, 2011.

Garbarini Alexandra, 'Diaries, Testimonies, and Jewish Histories of the Holocaust', in Goda J. W. Norman (editor), *Jewish Histories of the Holocaust, New Transitional Approaches*, New-York, Oxford: Berghahn, 2017, pp. 91-104.

Garbarini Alexandra, *Numbered Days, Diaries and the Holocaust*, USA: Yale University Press, 2006.

Gernsheim Helmut, *Creative Photography: Aesthetic Trends, 1839-1960*, New-York: Dover Publications, INC., 1991.

Gigliotti, Simone, *The Train Journey, Transit, Captivity, and Witnessing in the Holocaust*, UK: Berghahn Books (eBook), 2010.

Giordano Alberto, Knowles Ann Kelly, Cole Tim, 'Geographies of the Holocaust', in Knowles Ann Kelly, Cole Tim, Giordano Alberto, (editors), *Geographies of the Holocaust*, Indiana University Press, 2014, kindle edition.

Goldberg Amos, 'Jews' Diaries and Chronicles', in Hayes Peter and Roth K. John (editors), *The Oxford Handbook of Holocaust Studies*, USA: Oxford University Press, 2010, pp. 397- 413.

Goldberg Amos, *Trauma in First Person, Diary Writing During the Holocaust*, Bloomington, Indiana, USA: Indiana University Press, 2017.

Goldstein Bernard, *Five Years in the Warsaw Ghetto (The Stars Bear Witness)*, Canada: AK Press / Nabat, 2005.

Grinberg Daniel, 'Unpublished Diaries and Memoires in the Archives of the Jewish Historical Institute in Poland', in Shapiro Robert Moses (editor), *Holocaust Chronicles Individualizing the Holocaust Through Diaries and other Contemporaneous Personal Accounts*, Hoboken, New-Jersey: KTAV Publishing House, 1999, pp. 257-264.

Gruner Wolf, *Jewish Forced Labor Under the Nazis: Economic Needs and Racial Aims, 1938-1944*, Cambridge University Press, 2006.

Yisrael Gutman's book, *The Jews of Warsaw 1939-1943, Ghetto – Underground – Uprising*, Indiana University Press, 1989.

Heller Kupfert Daniel, *Jabotinsky's Children: Polish Jews and the Rise of Right-Wing Zionism*, Princeton: Princeton University Press, 2017.

Ludwik Hirszfeld, *The Story of One Life* (Rochester Studies in Medical History, 16), Rochester, USA: University of Rochester Press, 2010, p. 186.

Hochberg-Marianska Maria, and Grüss Noe, (editors), *The Children Accuse*, UK: Vallentine Mitchell, 2005.

Holliday Laurel, *Children in the Holocaust and World War II : Their Secret Diaries*, New York: Pocket Books (a Division of Simon & Schuster), 1995.

Jockusch Laura, *Collect and Record! Jewish Holocaust documentation in early postwar Europe*, New York: Oxford University Press, 2012, Kindle Edition.

Judaken Jonathan, 'Léon Poliakov, the Origins of Holocaust Studies, and Theories of Anti-Semitism: Rereading *'Bréviaire de la haine''*, in Hand Seán and Katz T.

Steven (editors), *Post-Holocaust France and the Jews, 1945-1955*, USA: New York University Press, 2015, pp. 169-192.

Kansteiner Wulf, 'Modernist Holocaust Historiography: A dialogue between Saul Friedländer and Hayden White', in Stone Dan (editor), *The Holocaust and Historical Methodology*, New York: Berghahn, 2015, pp. 203-229.

Karski Jan, *Story of a Secret State: My Report to the World*, London, Penguin, 2011, Kindle Edition,.

Kassow D. Samuel, 'Documenting Catastrophe, the Ringelblum Archive and the Warsaw Ghetto', in Goda J. W. Norman (editor), *Jewish Histories of the Holocaust, New Transitional Approaches*, Berghahn New-York, 2014, pp. 173-192.

Kassow D. Samuel, 'The LPZ in Interwar Poland', in: Gitelman, Zvi (editor.), *The Emergence of Modern Jewish Politics, Bundism and Zionism in Eastern Europe*, Pittsburgh: The University of Pittsburgh Press, 2003, pp. 71-84.

Kassow D. Samuel, 'Vilna and Warsaw, Two Ghetto Diaries: Herman Kruk and Emanuel Ringelblum', in Shapiro Robert Moses (editor), *Holocaust Chronicles Individualizing the Holocaust Through Diaries and other Contemporaneous Personal Accounts*, Hoboken, New-Jersey: KTAV Publishing House, 1999, pp. 171-215.

Kassow D. Samuel, *Who Will Write Our History? Emanuel Ringelblum, the Warsaw Ghetto, and the Oyneg Shabes Archive*, Bloomington: Indiana University Press, 2007.

Kay J. Alex, *The Making of an SS Killer, The Life of Colonel Alfred Filbert, 1905-1990*, UK: Cambridge University Press, 2016.

Klemperer Victor, *I Shall Bear Witness, The Diaries of Victor Klemperer, 1933-1941*, London: Phoenix Paperback, Orion House, 1999.

Kluger Ruth, *Still Alive, A Holocaust Girlhood Remembered*, New York,: The Feminist Press of the City University of New York, 2003.

Knowles Anne Kelly; Cole Tim; Giordano Alberto (eds.), *Geographies of the Holocaust* (The Spatial Humanities), Indiana University Press, 2014, kindle edition.

Kohler Riessman Catherine, 'Narrative Analysis', in: *Narrative, Memory & Everyday Life*, Kelly Nancy, Horrocks Christine, Milnes Kate, Roberts Brian, Robinson David (editors), Huddersfield: University of Huddersfield, 2005, pp. 1-7.

Kohler Riessman Catherine, *Narrative Methods for the Human Sciences*, USA: Sage, 2008.

Krämer Sybille, 'Epistemic Dependence and Trust, On Witnessing in the Third-Second- and First-Person Perspectives', in Krämer Sybille and Weigel Sigrid (editors), *Testimony/Bearing Witness, Epistemology, Ethics, History and Culture*, USA: Rowman & Littlefield, 2017, pp. 259-274.

Kristeva Julia, *Powers of Horror, An Essay on Abjection*, USA: Colombia University Press, 1982.

Kugelmass Jack and Boyarin Jonathan (editors), *From a Ruined Garden: The Memorial Books of Polish Jewry*, Bloomington: Indiana University Press, 1998.

LaCapra Dominick, *Writing History, Writing Trauma*, USA: John Hopkins University Press, 2014.

Langer L. Laurence, *Holocaust Testimonies: The Ruins of Memory*, USA: Yale University Press, 1991.

Lanzman Claude, *Shoah, The Complete Text of the Acclaimed Holocaust Film*, USA: Da Capo Press, 1995.

Laub Dori, M.D., 'Bearing Witness, or the Vicissitudes of Listening', in Laub Dori M.D & Felman Shoshana, *Testimony, Crises of Witnessing in Literature, Psychoanalysis and History*, USA: Routledge, 1992, pp. 57-74.

Laub Dori, M.D., 'An Event Without A Witness' in Laub Dori M.D & Felman Shoshana, *Testimony, Crises of Witnessing in Literature, Psychoanalysis and History*, USA: Routledge, 1992, pp. 75-92.

Lefebvre Henri, *The Production of Space*, UK: Basil Blackwell, 1991.

Leitner Isabella, *Fragments of Isabella: A Memoir of Auschwitz*, USA: Thomas Y. Crowell Publishers, 1978.

Lejeune Philippe, *On Diary*, USA: University of Hawaii Press, 2009.

Levinas Emmanuel, *Difficult Freedom, Essays on Judaism*, Baltimore: The Johns Hopkins University Press, 1990.

Libionka Dariusz, 'Antisemitism, Anti-Judaism and the Polish Catholic Clergy during the Second World War, 1939-1945', in Blobaum Robert (editor), *Antisemitism and Its Opponents in Modern Poland*, USA: Cornell University Press, 2005, pp. 233-264.

Lower Wendy, *Nazi Empire-Building and the Holocaust in Ukraine*, Chapel Hill, USA: University of North Carolina Press, 2005.

Lower Wendy, *The Ravine, A Family, A Photograph, A Holocaust Massacre Revealed*, New York: Houghton Mifflin Harcourt, 2021.

Magnússon Sigurður Gylfi, 'A West Side story and the one who gets to write it', in Magnússon Sigurður Gylfi and Szijártó M. István, *What is Microhistory? Theory and Practice*, New York: Routledge, 2013, pp. 134-146.

Magnússon Sigurður Gylfi, 'Postscript: to step into the same stream twice' in Magnússon Sigurður Gylfi and Szijártó M. István, *What is Microhistory? Theory and Practice*, New York: Routledge, 2013, pp. 147-157.

Margolin Uri, 'Character', Herman David (editor), *The Cambridge Companion to Narrative*, UK: Cambridge University Press, 2007, pp. 66-79.

Mayer A. Michael, *Judaism Within Modernity: Essays on Jewish History and Religion*, Detroit: Wayne State University Press, 2001.

Medoff Rafael, *Militant Zionism in America: The Rise and Impact of the Jabotinsky Movement*, Tuscaloosa Alabama: The University of Alabama Press, 2002.

Mendelsohn Ezra, *Zionism in Poland: The Formative Years, 1915-1926*, Jerusalem: The Zionist Library, 1982.

Michman Dan, *The Emergence of Jewish Ghettos During The Holocaust*, USA: Cambridge University Press and Yad-Vashem, 2014.

Patterson David, *Along the Edge of Annihilation: the collapse and recovery of life in the Holocaust diary*, USA: University of Washington Press, 1999.

Person Katarzyna, *Assimilated Jews in the Warsaw Ghetto*, 1940-1943, USA: Syracuse university press, 2014.

Porat Dina, 'The Vilna Ghetto Diaries', in Shapiro Robert Moses (editor), *Holocaust Chronicles Individualizing the Holocaust Through Diaries and other Contemporaneous Personal Accounts*, Hoboken, New-Jersey: KTAV Publishing House, 1999, pp. 157-169.

Prais Lea, *Displaced Persons, Refugees in the Fabric of Jewish Life in Warsaw September 1939-July 1942*, Jerusalem: Yad-Vashem, 2015.

Rejak Sebastian & Frister Elżbieta (editors), *Inferno of Choices, Poles and the Holocaust*, Warsaw: Oficyna Wydawnicza RYTM, 2012.

Ringelblum Emanuel, letter to Raphael Mahler, Śródborów, December 6, 1938, in Arad Yitzhak, Gutman Yisrael, Margaliot Abraham (editors), *Documents on the Holocaust - Selected sources on the destruction of the Jews of Germany and Austria, Poland, and the Soviet Union*, Jerusalem: Yad-Vashem, 1981, p. 123-124.

Roland G. Charles, *Courage Under Siege, Starvation, Disease, and Death in the Warsaw Ghetto*, USA: Oxford University Press, 1992.

Roskies G. David, 'What is Holocaust Literature', in Lederhendler Eli, (editor), *Jews, Catholics, and the Burden of History, Studies in Contemporary Jewry*, An Annual XXI, New York: Oxford University Press, 2005, pp. 157-212.

Roskies G. David, and Naomi Diamant, *Holocaust Literature, A History and Guide*, Waltham, Mass: Brandeis University Press, 2012, Kindle Edition.

Roskies G. David, and Naomi Diamant, *Reading in Time [A Curriculum for Holocaust Literature]*, *A Companion to Holocaust Literature, a History and Guide*, Waltham Massachusetts: Brandeis University Press, 2013.

Roskies G. David, 'Wartime victim writing in Eastern Europe', in Rosen Alan (editor), *Literature of the Holocaust*, USA: Cambridge University Press, 2013.

Roskies David G., *The Jewish Search for a Usable Past*, Indiana University Press, USA: Indiana University Press, 1999.

Rudashevski Yitskhok, 'Vilna Ghetto', in Alexandra Zapruder (ed), *Salvaged Pages, Young Writers' Diaries of the Holocaust*, USA: Yale University Press, 2015.

Ryan Marie Laure, 'Towards a Definition of Narrative', in Herman David (editor), *The Cambridge Companion to Narrative*, UK: Cambridge University Press, 2007, pp. 22-38.

Scarry Elaine, *The Body in Pain: The Making and Unmaking of the World*, USA: Oxford University Press, 1985.

Schmid Christian, 'Henri Lefebvre's theory of the production of space: towards a three-dimensional dialectic', in Goonewardena Kanishka, Kipfer Stefan, Milgrom, Richard, Schmid Christian (editors), *Space, Difference, Everyday Life: Reading Henri Lefebvre*, Taylor & Francis e-Library, 2008, pp. 27-45.

Bibliography

Shandler Jeffrey, (editor), *Awakening lives, Autobiographies of Jewish Youth in Poland before the Holocaust*, New Haven and London: Yale University Press/ YIVO Institute, 2002.

Sontag Susan, *On Photography*, New York: Rosetta Books, LLC, electronic book, 2005.

Stone Dan, Introduction, in Stone Dan (editor), *The Holocaust and Historical Methodology*, New York: Berghahn, 2015, pp. 1-19.

Tahvonen Eryk Emil, *The Crisis of Imagination, Representation and Resistance in Holocaust Diaries*, Saarbrücken: VDM Verlag Dr. Müller Aktiengesellschaft & Co. KG, 2008.

Taminiaux Pierre, *The Paradox of Photography*, New York: Rodopi B. V., 2009.

Taylor M. Philip, 'Psychological Warfare', in Cull J. Nicholas, Culbert David, and Welch David (editors), *Propaganda and Mass Persuasion: A Historical Encyclopedia, 1500 to the Present*, Santa Barbara, Calif.: ABC-CLIO, 2003, pp. 323-326.

Trunk Isaiah, *Judenrat: The Jewish Councils in Eastern Europe Under Nazi Occupation*, USA: University of Nebraska Press, 1996.

Trunk Isaiah, *Łódź Ghetto: A History*, Bloomington, USA: Indiana University Press, 2006.

Turski Marian, 'Individual experience in Diaries from the Łódź Ghetto', in Shapiro Robert Moses (editor), *Holocaust Chronicles Individualizing the Holocaust Through Diaries and other Contemporaneous Personal Accounts*, Hoboken, New-Jersey: KTAV Publishing House, 1999, pp. 117-124.

Tych Feliks, 'The Emergence of Holocaust Research in Poland: The Jewish Historical Commission and The Jewish Historical Institute (ŻIH), 1944-1989', in Bankier David and Michman Dan (editors), *Holocaust Historiography in Context: Emergence, Challenges, Polemics and Achievements*, Jerusalem: Yad-Vashem in association with Berghahn Books, 2008, pp. 227-244.

Unger Michal, 'About the Author', in Yosef Zelkovich, *In Those Terrible Days: Writings from the Łódź Ghetto*, Jerusalem: Yad-Vashem, 2002.

Vitis-Shomron Aliza, *Youth in Flames, a Teenage Resistance and her Fight for Survival in the Warsaw Ghetto*, Omaha, Nebraska: Tell the Story Publishing, 2015.

Waxman Vania Zoë, *Writing the Holocaust: Identity, Testimony, Representation* Oxford: Oxford University Press, 2006, Kindle Edition.

Weinreich Max, *Hitler's Professors, the Part of Scholarship in Germany's Crimes Against the Jewish People*, USA: Yale University Press, 1999.

Welch David, Introduction, in Cull J. Nicholas, Culbert David, and Welch David (editors), *Propaganda and Mass Persuasion: A Historical Encyclopedia, 1500 to the Present*, Santa Barbara, Calif.: ABC-CLIO, 2003.

White Hayden, *The Practical Past*, USA: Northwestern University Press, 2014.

Wiesel Elie, *Night*, Preface to the New Translation by Elie Wiesel, New York: Hill and Wang, a Division of Farrar, Straus and Giroux, 2006.

Wieviorka Annette, *The Era of the Witness*, USA: Cornell University Press, 2006.

Young E. James, 'Literature' in Laqueur Walter, (editor), *The Holocaust Encyclopedia*, New Heaven and London: Yale University Press, 2001, pp. 393-398.

Young E. James, *Writing and Rewriting the Holocaust, Narrative and the Consequences of Interpretation*, USA: Indiana University Press, 1990.

Zapruder Alexandra (compiler and editor), *Salvaged Pages, Young Writer's Diaries of the Holocaust*, USA: Yale University Press, 2015.

Zuckerman Yitzhak, ('Antek'), *A Surplus of Memory, Chronicle of the Warsaw Ghetto Uprising*, USA: University of California Press, 1993.

Articles in Hebrew

Ben-Shem Reuven, 'Excerpts from Reuven Ben-Shem's Diary, 1941', *The Moreshet Journal*, 25, Tel Aviv: Moreshet, April 1978, (Hebrew), pp. 25-44.

Brunner José, 'The Eichmann Trial between History and Genealogy', *Zmanim (Epochs): A Historical Quarterly*, 98, Historical Society of Israel, 2007, pp. 70-81.

Engel David, 'Dubnow on the Particular and Universal Elements in Jewish History', *Zion*, Vol LXXVII no. 3, Jerusalem: The Historical Society of Israel and the Zalman Shazar Center, 2012, (Hebrew), pp. 303-431.

Engel David, 'Who is a Collaborator?: The Trials of Michał Weichert', in *The Holocaust, History and Memory, Jubilee book in Honor of Israel Gutman*, Jerusalem: Yad-Vashem, 2002, pp. 1-24.

Goldberg Amos, 'The Holocaust and History in the Post-Modern Era', *Theory and Criticism*, 40, The Van Leer Jerusalem Institute, 2013, pp. 121-155.

Goldin Semion, 'Letters on Old and New Jewry': Dubnow's Nationalism in the Russian and Polish Contexts', *Zion*, Vol LXXVII no. 3, Jerusalem: The Historical Society of Israel and the Zalman Shazar Center, 2012, (Hebrew), pp. 317-339.

Kermish Joseph, 'Margined-notes to Ben-Shem's 'Note-Book', *Massuah Yearbook*, Vol 10, Kibbutz Tel Yizhak: Massuah, 1982, (Hebrew), pp. 52-58.

Kol Moshe, 'Dr. Reuven Ben-Shem [Feldschuh]', *Massuah Yearbook*, no. 9, Tel Aviv: Kibbutz Tel Yizhak: Massuah, April 1981, (Hebrew), pp. 44-45.

Levin Vladimir, 'The *Folks-Partey* of Simon Dubnow – A Story of Failure?' *Zion*, Vol LXXVII no. 3, Jerusalem: The Historical Society of Israel and the Zalman Shazar Center, 2012, (Hebrew), pp. 359-368.

Levin Yehudit and Uziel Daniel, 'Normal People and Unusual Photographs', Yad-Vashem, *'LEKKET'*, no. 26, 1997-8, (Hebrew), pp. 201-220. https://www.yadvashem.org/yv/he/holocaust/about/related/articles/002026009Levin_Uziel.pdf. Accessed, 20.9.20202.

Medykowski Witold, 'To Record and Save from Oblivion: Collecting Testimonies About the Holocaust in Poland After the War', *Arkhion*, Vol. 14-15, 2007, (Hebrew), pp. 49-72.

Bibliography   311

Shlomi Hanna, 'The History of the 'Ichud' – The United Democratic Zionist in Poland on the First Year of their Existence', August 1944-1945', *Zionism Collection*, 20, 1996

Shumsky Dimitry, 'Zionism in Quotation Marks, or to What Extent was Dubnow a Non-Zionist?', *Zion*', Vol LXXVII no. 3, Jerusalem: The Historical Society of Israel and the Zalman Shazar Center, 2012, (Hebrew), pp. 369-384.

Springer-Aharoni Nina, 'Holocaust Ghetto Photography as Historical Records', 18.7.2013, pp. 1-20. https://www.yadvashem.org/yv/he/research/ghettos_encyclopedia/shpringer.pdf, accessed: 1.1.2021.

Tec Nechama, 'Unheralded Historian: Emmanuel Ringelblum', in *Yalkut Moreshet*, periodical 75, Israel: Moreshet, April 2003, (Hebrew), pp. 65-79.

Books in Hebrew and Yiddish

Antelme Robert, *The Human Race*, Tel Aviv: Am Oved, 2011, (Hebrew).

Auerbach Rachel, *Warsaw Testaments Encounters, Actions, Fate 1933–1943, (Varshever Zavoes)*, Tel Aviv: Moreshet, Mordechai Anielevich Memorial, Workers Library, 1985, (Hebrew).

Auerbach Rachel, *In the Outskirts of Warsaw*, Tel Aviv: Am-Oved, 1954, (Hebrew).

Ben-Shem Reuven, *Poland Burns (Poyln Brent)*, Buenos Aires: Tsentral-farband fun Poylishe Yidn in Argentina, 1960, (Yiddish).

Ben-Shem Reuven, *Between the Ghetto's Walls*, Tel Aviv: N. Twersky, 1946/1947, (Hebrew).

Ben-Shem Reuven, 'Around the City', in Leoni-Zopperfin Eliezer (editor), *Kowel: Testimony and Memorial Book of Our Destroyed Community*, Tel Aviv: Arazi Publishing, 1957, (Hebrew), pp. 63-72.

Ben-Shem Ruth (née Halberstatdt). *The Days of My Three Lives*, (private manuscript), (Hebrew).

Ben-Yerucham Chen (Merchavia Melech Hen), *Book of Bethar, Volume I (To The People)*, Tel Aviv: Jabotinsky Institute Publishing, 1969, (Hebrew).

Berman Adolf – Abraham, *Where Fate Destined Me to Be, with the Jews of Warsaw, 1939-1942*, Israel: Hakibbutz Hameuhad and Lohamei Haghetaot (Ghetto Fighters' House), 1977, (Hebrew).

Blumental Nachman and Kermish Josef, *Resistance and Revolt in the Warsaw Ghetto, A Documentary History*, Vol. 5, Jerusalem: Yad-Vashem, 1965.

Bryskier Henryk, *The Jews of Warsaw Under The Swastika, A Testimony from The Ghetto Days*, Jerusalem: Yad-Vashem, 2018, (Hebrew).

Bursztein Jean-Gerard, *La Psychanalyse des Nazis -Essai Sur la Destruction de la Civilisation*, Tel-Aviv: Resling Publishers, (Hebrew), 2004.

Chaba Efrat, *My Portion in the Land of the Living, Avraham Carmi's Story*, Tel Aviv: Miskal -Yedioth Ahronoth Books and Chemed Books, 2013, (Hebrew).

Dreifuss (Ben-Sasson) Havi, '*We Polish Jews'?*, *The Relations between Jews and Poles during the Holocaust – The Jewish Perspective*, Jerusalem: Yad-Vashem, 2009, (Hebrew).

Dreifuss (Ben-Sasson) Havi, *Warsaw Ghetto – The End, April 1942-June 1943*, Jerusalem: Yad-Vashem, 2017, (Hebrew).

Eck Dr. Nathan, 'Emanuel Ringelblum', in Cohen Israel (editor), *Buczacz Memorial Book*, Tel-Aviv: by The Committee to Commemorate Buczacz, Am Oved Publishers, 1956, (Hebrew & Yiddish), pp. 225-227.

Eisenberg Eliyahu (editor), *Płock Memorial Book, A History of an Ancient Jewish Community in Poland*, Tel Aviv: Hamenora Publishing House, 1967, (Hebrew & Yiddish), pp. 70-74.

Engel David, 'A Problematic Tradition? Comments on the Political Tendencies and Culture of the Jews of Poland Between the Two World Wars', in Bartal Israel and Gutman Israel (editors), *The Broken Chain, Polish Jewry Through the Ages, Vol. II, Society, Culture, Nationalism*, Jerusalem: The Zalman Shazar Center, 2001, (Hebrew), pp. 649-665.

Feldshuh (Ben-Shem) Reuven Dr. (editor), *Lexicon of Jewish Society, Poland I, Warsaw*, Warsaw: Yiddisher Leksigraphisher Verlag, (Yiddish), 1939.

Goldberg Amos, *Trauma in First Person, Diary Writing during the Holocaust*, Israel: Kinneret Zmora-Bitan Dvir, 2012, (Hebrew).

Gutman Israel, *Issues in Holocaust Scholarship, Research and Reassessment*, Jerusalem: The Zalman Shazar Center for Jewish History and Yad-Vashem, 2008, (Hebrew).

Gutman Israel, 'Emanuel Ringelblum: The Historian and His Era', in Gutman Israel, (editor), *Emanuel Ringelblum: The Historian and his Era*, Jerusalem: Yad-Vashem, 2006, (Hebrew).

Gutman Yisrael, *The Jews of Warsaw 1939-1943, Ghetto – Underground - Uprising*, Jerusalem: Yad-Vashem, 2011, (Hebrew).

Kaplan Chaim Aron, *Scroll of Agony: Hebrew Diary of Ch. A. Kaplan Written in the Warsaw Ghetto 1st September 1939 – 4th August 1942*, Tel-Aviv: Am Oved Publishers LTD, and Yad-Vashem, Davar Edition, 1966, (Hebrew).

Klinger Chajka, *I am Writing These Words to You, The Original Diaries, Będzin 1943*, Israel: Yad-Vashem and Moreshet, 2016, (Hebrew).

Kovner Aba, *Fareynegte Partizaner Organizatsye – FPO in the Camps, From Herman Kruk's Estate*, in Korchak Reizl (Ruz'ka), *Flames in Ash*, Israel: Moreshet and Sifriat Poalim Worker's Book-Guild (*Hashomer Hatzair*), 1965, (Hebrew).

Küchler (Küchler-Silberman) Lena, *My Children*, Paris: Editions Polyglottes, October 12, 1948 (Yiddish).

Kuchler-Zilberman Lena, *We Accuse, Children's Testimonies from the Holocaust*, Israel: Sifriat Poalim, 1969, (Hebrew).

Kulka Dov Otto, *Landscapes of the Metropolis of Death*), Tel-Aviv: Proza, Yediot Ahronot and Chemed Books, 2013, (Hebrew).

Leoni Eliezer, 'From Poor Education to the Hebrew Gymnasia, The History of the Hebrew Education in Kowel' in Leoni-Zopperfin Eliezer (editor), *Kowel: Testimony and Memorial Book of Our Destroyed Community*), pp. 127-160, Tel Aviv: Arazi Publishing, 1957, (Hebrew).

Levi Aharon and Blorai Mordechai, 'The Young Guard', in Leoni-Zopperfin Eliezer, *Kowel: Testimony and Memorial Book of Our Destroyed Community*, Tel Aviv: Arazi Publishing, 1957, (Hebrew), pp. 298-306 .

Levi Primo, *If This Is a Man*, Tel Aviv: Am-Oved Publishing, 2011, (Hebrew).

Levi Sarid Arye, *The Moreshet Journal*, The organization *Revenge* – its History, Image, Deeds – part A), no. 52, pp. 35-43, April 1992, (part A), (Hebrew).

Lewin Avraham, *From the Notebook of the Yehudiya Teacher: The Warsaw Ghetto, April 1942-January 1943*, Tel-Aviv: Ghetto Fighter's House and Hakibbutz Hameuchad Publishing, (Hebrew), 1969.

Lunski Khayk, *Characters and Images from the Vilna Ghetto Written in Turbulent Times*, Vilno: Farlag fun dem fareyn fun di yidishe literatn un zshurnolistn in Vilne, 1920, (Yiddish).

Mahler Raphael, 'Dubnow's Method and His Jewish Historiography Achievements', in *Historians and Historical Scholarship, Selected Lectures from the 7th Convention for the Study of History* (Hanukah 1962), Israel: The Israeli Historical Society, 1977, (Hebrew), pp. 93-116.

Meisel Nachman, 'Dr. Emanuel Ringelblum', in Kats Pinye (editor), *Warsaw Memorial Book*, Tomb I, Former Residents of Warsaw and surroundings in Argentina, Buenos Aires: Graficon Publishers, 1955 (Yiddish), columns 1173-1188.

Melamed Mordechai, 'Reflections about *Hashomer Hatzair*', in Leoni-Zopperfin Eliezer (editor), *Kowel: Testimony and Memorial Book of Our Destroyed Community*, Tel Aviv: Arazi Publishing, 1957, (Hebrew), pp. 307-311.

Miron Guy, *To Be a Jew in Nazi Germany, Space and Time*, Jerusalem, Israel, The Hebrew University Magnes Press and Yad-Vashem, (Hebrew), 2021

Rawitz Melech, 'Emanuel Ringelblum', in Cohen Israel (editor), *Buczacz Memorial Book*, Tel-Aviv: by The Committee to Commemorate Buczacz, Am Oved Publishers, 1956, (Hebrew & Yiddish), pp. 227- 228.

Michael Reuven, *Jewish Historiography from The Renaissance to the Modern Time*, Jerusalem: The Bialik Institute, 1993, (Hebrew).

Miron Guy, *From Memorial Community to Research Center, The Leo Baeck Institute*, Jerusalem, Israel: The Leo Baeck Institute, 2005 (Hebrew).

Neumann Boaz, *The Nazi Weltanschauung, Space, Body, Language*, Haifa: Haifa University Publishers, 2002, (Hebrew).

Opochinsky Perez, *Sketches from The Warsaw Ghetto*, Tel Aviv: Ghetto Fighters' House & Hakkibutz Hameuchad, 1970, (Hebrew).

Perehodnik Salek ,*The Sad Task of Documentation, A Diary in Hiding*, Jerusalem: Keter Publishing House, 1999, (Hebrew).

Seidman Hillel, Dr., *Diary of the Warsaw Ghetto*, New York: The Jewish Week, 1957, (Hebrew).

Szac-Wajnkranc Noemi, *Gone with The Fire, Notes about the Warsaw Ghetto written in Hiding by Noemi Szac Wajnkranc*, Jerusalem, Yad-Vashem, 2003, (Hebrew).

Talmon L. Jacob, *The Riddle of the Present and the Cunning of History*, Jerusalem: Bialik Institute, 2000, (Hebrew).

Temkin-Berman Batia, *City Within a City, Underground Warsaw Diary 1944-1945*, Tel-Aviv: Am Oved Publishing Ltd, Yad-Vashem, 2008, (Hebrew).

Benjamin Tenenbaum (compiler and editor), *One of a City and Two of a Family*, a selection from amongst one thousand autobiographies of Jewish children in Poland), Palestine: Sifriyat Poalim – Workers' Book-Guild (*Hashomer Hatzair*) 1947, (Hebrew).

Turkow Jonas, *There Once Was A Jewish Warsaw*, Tel Aviv: Mifaley Tarbut Vechinuch LTD., 1969, (Hebrew).

Wdowinski David, *And We Are Not Saved*, Jerusalem: Yad-Vashem, 1986, (Hebrew).

Books in Other Languages

Apfelbaum Emil, Dr. Med. (Chief editor), *Maladie de Famine: Recherches cliniques sur la famine exécutées dans le ghetto de Varsovie en 1942 (Clinical Research about Hunger Related Diseases in the Warsaw Ghetto in 1942),* Warsaw : American Joint Distribution Committee, 1946, (French).

Ben-Shem (Dr, Feldszuh) Reuven, *Czerwone dusze (Red Souls)*, Warsaw: Perły, 1932, (Polish).

Descartes Rene, *Discours de la méthode, Pour bien conduire sa raison, et chercher la vérité dans les sciences (Discourse on the method of rightly conducting the reason, and seeking the truth in the sciences),* (1637), La Gaya Scienza, June, 2012, (French).

English Internet Sites

Blösche Josef, Holocaust Historical Society. https://www.holocausthistorical society.org.uk/contents/germanbiographies/josefblosche.html 12.4.2019.

'Das Warschauer Ghetto. Ein Kulturdokument für Adolf Hitler' (The Warsaw Ghetto. A cultural document for Adolf Hitler). https://www.yadvashem. org/yv/he/exhibitions/warsaw_ghetto/introduction.asp. Accessed, 20.9.20202.

Dickstein Hanna, Internetowej Bazie danych getta warszawskiego (The Internet Database of the Warsaw Ghetto). https://new.getto.pl/en/People/D/Dickstein-Hanna-Unknown, accessed, 11.12.2020.

Dubnow Simon, YIVO Encyclopedia. http://www.yivoencyclopedia.org/article. aspx/Dubnow_Simon. Accessed 7.11.2017.

'The Zonabend Collection: Documentation From the Łódź Ghetto', EHRI, Holocaust Research Infrastructure, https://portal.ehri-project.eu/units/il-002798-4019640, accessed 19.5.2020.

Garbarini Alexandra, 'Holocaust Diaries', YIVO Encyclopedia https://yivo encyclopedia.org/article.aspx/Holocaust/Holocaust_Diaries. Accessed 1.1.2020

Genesis, chapter 3, verse 19. http://www.vatican.va/archive/bible/genesis/docu ments/bible_genesis_en.html accessed 24.5.2019.

Heydrich Reinhard, Yad-Vashem. https://www.yadvashem.org/odot_pdf/Microsoft%20Word%20-%206366.pdf, accessed 8.5.2019.

Justice Jackson H. Robert, Chief of Counsel for the United States, opening statement to the International Military Tribunal, Nuremberg Trials, November 21, 1945, the Palace of Justice at Nuremberg, Germany. The Robert H. Jackson Center. https://www.roberthjackson.org/speech-and-writing/opening-statement-before-the-international-military-tribunal/, accessed: 13.6.2021.

Kusociński Janusz Tadeusz, 1907 – 1940, Polskie radio. https://www.polskieradio.pl/39/156/Artykul/1023044,Janusz-Kusocinski-nieugiety-na-biezni-i-na-polu-walki, accessed: 24.3.2019.

Merriam-Webster Dictionary. https://www.merriam-webster.com/dictionary/monumentum%20aere%20perennius. Accessed: 26.3.2020.

Photographs from the Warsaw Ghetto, Yad-Vashem. https://www.yadvashem.org/yv/he/exhibitions/warsaw_ghetto/introduction.asp And: https://www.yadvashem.org/yv/en/exhibitions/warsaw_ghetto/introduction.asp, accessed: 20.9.2020.

Namysło Aleksandra, The story of the 'Krysia' Bunker, August 2017, Polin, Museum of the History of Polish Jews, https://sprawiedliwi.org.pl/pl/historie-pomocy/historia-bunkra-krysia. Accessed 20.3.2021.

Photographs of the Warsaw ghetto, The Jürgen Stroop collection, which he entitled: 'Es gibt keinen jüdischen Wohnbezirk in Warschau mehr'. https://www.yadvashem.org/yv/en/exhibitions/warsaw_ghetto/introduction.asp, accessed: 20.9.2020.

Polonsky Antony, 'Hirszfeld Ludwik', YIVO Encyclopedia. https://yivoencyclopedia.org/article.aspx/Hirszfeld_Ludwik, accessed 22.5.2021.

The house committees, EHRI, Holocaust Research Infrastructure. https://training.ehri-project.eu/jewish-administrations, accessed: 15.10.2020.

Timeline of Events, United States, Holocaust Memorial Museum. https://www.ushmm.org/learn/timeline-of-events/1933-1938/law-on-alteration-of-family-and-personal-names, accessed, 23.3.2019.

Volksdeutsche, Yad-Vashem. https://www.yadvashem.org/odot_pdf/Microsoft%20Word%20-%206345.pdf. Accessed, 9.2.2021.

Weichert Michael (Michał), YIVO Encyclopedia. https://yivoencyclopedia.org/article.aspx/Weichert_Micha%C5%82', accessed 19.9.2019.

United States of America, Plaintiff, v. John Demjanjuk, Defendant, No. C77-923., United States District Court, N. D. Ohio, E. D., June 23, 1981. https://law.justia.com/cases/federal/district-courts/FSupp/518/1362/2128864/ accessed: 28.7.2020.

Discovery of one section of the Łódź Ghetto Archive, November 1946', Yad-Vashem. https://www.yadvashem.org/holocaust/this-month/november/discovering-lodz-ghetto-archive.html, accessed 19.5.2020.

Hebrew and Yiddish Internet Sites

Hamashkif, 10.4.1945, 'Dr. Feldschuh wrote 11 notebooks about the Jews' situation in Poland During Nazi Occupation, (Hebrew). https://www.nli.org.il/he/newspapers/hmf/1945/04/10/01/?&e=————-he-20—1—img-txIN%7ctxTI————————1, Accessed 21.3.2021. The newspaper stated that Ben-Shem was head of a committee designated to help the survivors.

Hamashkif, Dr. Feldschuh in the Newspaper of Journalists: The Survivors Testimony – Unity to Redeem the People', 11.11.1945, (Hebrew), p. 4. https://www.nli.org.il/he/newspapers/hmf/1945/11/11/01/?&e=————-he-20—1—img-txIN%7ctxTI————————1,accessed 22.7.2020.

Hamashkif, 28.10.1945, A Branch Plucked out of the Burning [Zechariah, 3, 2], Fighters, Jews Arrived to the Shores of the Land of Israel, the Transylvania Immigrants in the Haifa Port', (Hebrew), p. 4. https://www.nli.org.il/he/newspapers/hmf/1945/10/28/01/?&e=————-he-20—1—img-txIN%7ctxTI————————1, accessed: 21.10.2020.

Hazfira 'A New Shomerit Organization in Poland', 20.01.1927, (Hebrew), p. 4. https://www.nli.org.il/he/newspapers/hzf/1927/01/20/01/?&e=————-he-20—1—img-txIN%7ctxTI————————1

Haskel Amir, 'Dr. Reuven Feldschuh [Ben-Shem] and The Archived Diary', 18.9.2011, (Hebrew), chrome-extension://efaidnbmnnnibpcajpcglclefindmkaj/https://meyda.education.gov.il/files/noar/yoman.pdf, accessed 13.03.2017.

Meisel Nahman, 'From week to Week', *Literary Journal,* 20.01.1939, (Yiddish). Historical Jewish Press, the National Library of Israel. Ahttps://www.nli.org.il/he/newspapers/ltb/1939/01/20/01/article/16.2/?e=————-he-20—1—img-txIN%7ctxTI————————1. Accessed, 20.6.2020.

Internet Site in Polish

Głos Gminy Żydowskiej. Organ Gminy Wyznaniowej Żydowskiej w Warszawie, maj 1938 r., nr 5, ('Voice of the Jewish Community. Organ of the Jewish Religious Community in Warsaw', May 1938, No. 5), 'Uroczystość przekazania pierwszego samolotu eskadry im. młodzieży żydowskiej Armii Polskiej' (The ceremony of delivering the first airplane named after The Jewish Youth of the Polish Army), (Polish), p. 121-122, accessed 18.10.2024. file:///C:/Users/User/Desktop/G%C5%82os%20Gminy%20%C5%BBydowskie j%20_%20organ%20Gminy%20Wyznaniowej%20%C5%BBydowskiej%20w%20Warszawie.%20R.%202,%201938,%20nr%205.pdf.

Online Conferences

Bartov Omer, *Genocide from Below: Rewriting the Holocaust as First-Person Local History,* Discussion with Jan Burzlaff, December 9, 2020, The Holocaust Studies Program at Western Galilee College.

Bibliography

Bartov Omer, *The Ringelblum Archive as the Earliest Historiography of the Holocaust and its Impact on Research*, November 5, 2020, hosted by European Network Remembrance and Solidarity, https://www.youtube.com/watch?v=_PEG 7QII2cw&t=2287s, accessed: 5.11.2020

Dreifuss Havi, Jewish Responses to the Holocaust, Lecture: *Warsaw Ghetto, the End, April 1942-June 1943*, The Emil A. and Jenny Fish Center for Holocaust & Genocide Studies, Yeshiva University, accessed, 18.4.2021.

Newspapers

Bettelheim Bruno, 'Eichmann; The System; The Victims', *The New Republic*, June 15, 1963, Vol 148, no, 24, pp. 23-33.

Daily News Bulletin, JTA News (Jewish Telegraphic Agency), New York: Volume IX, no. 146, Sunday, June 28, 1942.

Grupińska Anka, 'Ja myślałam, że wszyscy są razem, Z Emilką „Marylką" Rozencwajg (Szoszaną Kossower), łączniczką żydowskiego i polskiego podziemia, rozmawia Anka Grupińska' (I thought that They Were All Together, Anka Grupińska Talks with Emilka 'Marylka' Rozencwajg (Szoszana Kossower), a liaison officer of the Jewish and Polish underground), *Tygodnik Powszechny*, no 18, 6.5.2001. (Polish). https://www.academia.edu/11008478/ Shoszana_Kossower_Ja_my%C5%9Bla%C5%82am_%C5%BCe_wszyscy_s% C4%85_razem, accessed: 30.3.2021.

Podhoretz Norman, 'Hannah Arendt on Eichmann: A Study in the Perversity of Brilliance', *Commentary*, Vol. 36, No. 3, September 1963, pp. 201-208.

Rosen Claire and Schulman Robin, 'How an Astounding Holocaust Diary Surfaced in America', *Smithsinian Magazine*, editor's note: 30.10.2018. https://www. smithsonianmag.com/history/astonishing-Holocaust-diary-hidden-world-70-years-resurfaced-america-180970534/, accessed 15.1.2019.

Żbikowski Andrzej, Opaski z gwiazdą Dawida - wstęp do Holokaustu, *Najnowsze* 1.12.2016, (Polish). https://opinie.wp.pl/opaski-z-gwiazda-dawida-wstep-do-holokaustu-6126041529271937a, accessed, 3.6.2019.

Interview

Interview with Nekamia Ben-Shem, 17.6.2017.

www.ingramcontent.com/pod-product-compliance
Lightning Source LLC
LaVergne TN
LVHW090404170525
811180LV00001B/2